THE NEW AND REVISED CATALOG OF

AMERICAN ANTIQUES & AMERICAN COLLECTIBLES

THE NEW AND REVISED CATALOG OF

AMERICAN ANTIQUES & AMERICAN COLLECTIBLES

by William C. Ketchum, Jr. Photography by John Garetti

GALLERY BOOKS
An Imprint of W. H. Smith Publishers Inc.
112 Madison Avenue
New York City 10016

CONTENTS

INTRODUCTION TO THE COMBINED EDITION 6

Introduction to Catalog of American Antiques 10

Introduction to Catalog of American Collectibles 23

*Antique Furniture: Chairs and Tables	51
*Antique Furniture: Chests and Other Pieces	74
†Collectible Furniture	99
*Folk Painting and Sculpture	128
*Antique Glass	146
†Art Glass	159
†Collectible Glass	178
*Antique Pottery	192
†Art Pottery	214
†Collectible Pottery	230
*Antique Silver and Pewter	244
†Collectible Silver	258
*Copper and Brass	274
†Bronze	290
*Iron and Tin	302
*Textiles	322
*Woodenware	338
*Basketry	354
*Lighting Devices	368
*Tools	386
*Toys	402
†Games	422
†Sports Memorabilia	434
*Antique Decoys	442
*Weathervanes and Whirligigs	450
*Tramp Art	458
*Scrimshaw	474
*†Advertising Memorabilia	480
*Posters, Postcards, and Other Printed Material	514
*Photographic Memorabilia	528

Catalog of American Antiques © 1976 by Rutledge Books, Inc.
Catalog of American Collectibles © 1979 by Mayflower Books, Inc.
This edition published in 1990 by
Gallery Books, an imprint of W.H. Smith Publishers, Inc.
112 Madison Avenue, New York, New York 10016

Gallery Books are available for bulk
purchase for sales promotions and
premium use. For details write or telephone the
Manager of Special Sales, W.H. Smith Publishers, Inc.,
112 Madison Avenue, New York, New York 10016, (212) 532-6600.

Printed in the United States of America.

ISBN: 0-8317-6306-X

†Cameras   538
*Political Memorabilia   552
†Clocks and Watches   558
†Indian Crafts   568
†Vintage Clothing   582
†Jewelry   596
†Radios, Phonographs, and Jukeboxes   612
†Militaria   626
†Gambling Devices   632

Note: Chapters that were originally in *The Catalog of American Antiques* are marked with an asterisk; chapters that were originally in *The Catalog of American Collectibles* are marked with a dagger. The chapter on Advertising Memorabilia contains material from both books.

PAGE 1. **Rear:** Chest, pine, New England, ca. 1850; $250-400. **Center:** Bannister-back side chair; Connecticut, late 18th century; $300-500. **Right:** Candle stand, pine and maple; New England, ca. 1820; $600-1,200. **On floor:** Woven rag rug, New York. ca. 1860; $125-200. PAGES 2-3. Weathervane, copper and tin, old paint; New York, 1890-1910; $4,000-7,500. Horse and rider vanes are less common than those featuring the horse alone. **Left:** Fine Victorian bed, pine and oak; late 19th century; $500-750. Typical of the high-quality factory-made furniture from Grand Rapids, Mich. **On bed:** Diamond quilt in blue, tan, and white; New York, early 20th century; $250-400. **Bottom Left:** Six-board chest, pine; East, late 19th century; $250-450. PAGES 6-7. Footed blanket chest, grain painted; East, mid-19th century; $850-1,500. **On chest:** Horse and rider push-pull toy, East, late 19th century; 1,500-3,500. Arrow-back Windsor rocker, pine and hickory, yellow paint on black; East, mid-19th century; $1,200-1,800.

INTRODUCTION TO THE COMBINED EDITION

It has been well over a decade since the first publication of *The Catalog of American Antiques* (1977) and *The Catalog of American Collectibles* (1979). During that period a great deal has changed in the collecting world. The old distinctions between antiques, which technically are objects at least one hundred years old, and the newer collectibles have broken down. More and more enthusiasts collect in both areas and are interested less in the age of an object than in its appearance, nostalgia or potential investment value.

The new and revised combined edition of *The Catalog of American Antiques & Collectibles* responds to this new reality by providing the reader with a single volume in which he or she will find coverage of every important field of American collecting along with current prices and a brief introduction to each section bringing the reader up to date on what is happening with prices, popularity

and availability within the collecting category. Moreover, that increasing number of collectors who prefer to carry their reference books with them to shows or sales will find the combined volume easier to handle and just as complete.

Those familiar with the original books (which have themselves been revised and reprinted numerous times) will recognize that the chapters in this volume are arranged so as to reflect both the age of the objects and the growth of the collecting fields. Traditional categories common to both books such as furniture and silver begin with a chapter on the antique then follow that with one on the newer collectibles. In two cases, glass and pottery; there is also a separate chapter on Art Glass and Art Pottery reflecting the great popularity of these studio created objects.

A third and extensive area is that of items, ranging from basketry, lighting devices and Indian crafts to toys, sports memorabilia and cameras, where the things collected are considered more by history or use than by age and there is no significant distinction based on antiquity alone. Here the antique and the collectible merge; and as with the more tradi-tional antiques and collectibles, chapters from the two books have been combined so as to provide the reader with logical and easily accessed information covering most of the objects likely to be encountered at antiques shows and auctions and in dealers' shops.

Armed with this single complete, fully illustrated catalog, the wise collector may venture forth into a world of antiques and collectibles which continues to expand and to grow both more rewarding and more complex with every passing day.

William C. Ketchum, Jr.

Opposite: Victorian oil painting; $800-1,500. **Center:** Sugar bucket, pine and hickory; $110-170. Double drawer chest, pine, gray paint; $175-260. **Bottom:** Floral hooked rug; $75-130. All, East, 19th century. **Left:** Two-drawer Empire work table, fine grained paint; East, ca. 1840; $2,000-2,750. **On table at right:** Excellent gooseneck teapot toleware; New England, ca. 1830; $1,200-1,500. **Bottom:** Hooked rug, rag on burlap; East, late 19th-early 20th century; $200-275. **Below:** Tilt-top candlestand, pine and hardwood, with inlaid checkerboard and green legs made from tree roots; East, mid-19th century; $1,300-2,000.

Introduction to Catalog of American Antiques

It would be nice if there were no need for antiques price guides. There was such a time, but it was long ago. The memoirs of early collectors tell of snatching Shaker chairs from village dumps, rescuing decoys from woodboxes, and offering modern factory china to farmers who happily exchanged it for sgraffito-decorated pottery plates. While not all these stories are literally true, of course, they do reflect a time when collectors were few (and, generally, very wealthy) and antiques were abundant. Alas, such is no longer the case.

Today, the collector army is legion and the demand insatiable. This condition has had two results: prices for all kinds of antiques have risen steadily

Above: View of Niagara Falls in carved wood frame, one of a set of painted circus panels; 19th century; $1,500-2,500. **Right:** Federal grandfather clock, wood with handsome painting; Connecticut, ca. 1820; $12,000-18,000. **Opposite:** Extremely rare miniature pewter cupboard, oak, with doll-sized treen dishes; New England, 1780-90, $900-1,500.

over the past few decades; and the definition of what constitutes an antique has been expanded greatly. There was a time, for example, when the only American glass of interest to antiquarians was early pressed and free blown; bottles in general were ignored. Now, bottle collecting in all its facets is one of the most popular American pastimes.

It is likewise in all other fields of antiques. Although the legal definition still requires an object to be at least one hundred years old to qualify as an antique, the popular idea of an antique admits to the fold objects that are considerably younger—sometimes as young as twenty or thirty years. This expanded definition has come about partly because of the rise in prices: as certain kinds of antiques have become inaccessible to the collector of average means—for whom this book was written—he has turned his interests to new, and younger, fields.

These changes have presented serious problems, as well as opportunities, for the average collector. As has been indicated, certain areas—silver, pewter, and eighteenth-century furniture, for instance—are largely closed. Few examples exist outside museums and large private collections, and when examples do come on the market, their prices are prohibitive. Yet these are the very areas in which prices have over the years become relatively stabilized and predictable. The collector may not be able to pay for it, but at least he can figure out pretty much what it will cost! The "new" antiques or collector's items—objects less than a hundred years old—are something else again. Many of them, such as advertising materials or candy bottles, were not even considered worthy of collecting a decade ago. And their prices fluctuate widely from region to region, day to day, and show to show. Without some sort of guide to current prices, the antiques collector soon becomes confused and bewildered.

Much of the confusion about the prices of antiques exists because people tend to overlook the unique nature of the business. And business it is, although some dealers see it more as a holy pilgrimage. Antiques shop proprietors are business people—they buy and they sell. But their work differs in one very important respect from other retail operations. When an antiques dealer sells a piece of pottery or an oak rocker, he cannot just ring up the wholesaler and order another. It may be weeks or even years before a

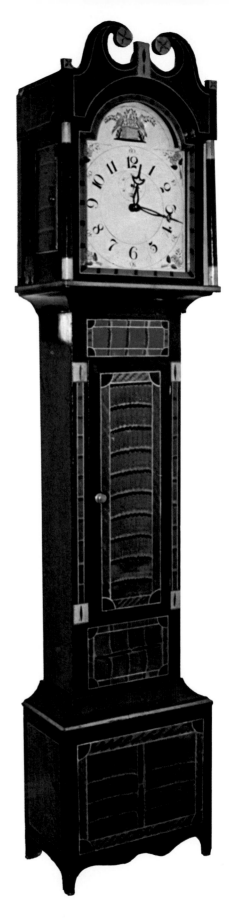

comparable piece comes his way, and he may pay more (or, possibly, less) for it than he paid for the first. There are no fixed wholesale prices in the field; and since the dealer's asking price to the public is to a great extent based on what

he himself has to pay, his price must inevitably vary from time to time. Similarly, unlike the usual retail situation, many antiques come to the seller in a damaged condition. If he must make repairs or pay someone else to do so, that too must be figured into the ultimate price.

Nevertheless, certain pricing standards have developed that make it possible to determine the range within which a given antique will be sold. At its simplest, this general rule prevails: a given antique object is worth whatever a person will pay for it. This standard is most evident at auctions. When a piece goes up at auction, it is usually unique—that is, another similar piece is not likely to be sold at that auction. All present have a chance to indicate what they will pay. In the usual course, several people will start to bid. As the price climbs, most will drop out, indicating that the object has now passed what they perceive as its value. One of the remaining bidders will eventually prevail, and the price that he pays will fix the value of the object at that place and time.

However, anyone who has spent much time around auction barns knows that the next time a similar (or identical) example comes up, it may sell for far more or far less than its predecessor. There are a variety of reasons for this. Sometimes it's a matter of personality. Two competing bidders gripped by "auction fever" may become so caught up in their personal duel that they push the price far beyond the value of the item. The presence of serious collectors can also create an unnatural situation. When dealers bid, they must keep in mind how much they themselves can ultimately sell the piece for. When the price is bid up too high, their margin of profit disappears and they drop out. This is not true of the collector who buys only for himself. He will go as high as is necessary (and as he can afford) for a desired addition to his collection. The size of the crowd present at an auction; the auctioneer's knowledge (if he isn't aware of an object's value, he won't push it); the absence or presence of insiders paid to bid up prices—all these can have a major effect on auction prices. So auction prices alone are a poor guide to value.

A somewhat better standard is set by dealers prices. Since the antiques dealer must sell to survive, his prices over the long run will have some

Opposite: Jelly cabinet, walnut and poplar. Pennsylvania, ca. 1840; $600-900.
On top of cabinet, left to right. Hand painted checkerboard painted pine; New York, late 19th century; $125-175. Goose decoy; New York. 19th century; $250-450. Pair of Indian clubs in black paint, New England, early 20th century; $50-75. Stoneware keg, Ohio, mid-19th century; $275-350. Splint fruit-drying basket, Maine, late 19th century; $150-200. Painted boxes, birch, and pine; East, second half 19th century; $75-250 each; second from bottom, Shaker, $450-750. **Below:** Empire secretary, grain-painted pine, East, mid-19th century; $2,500-4000. An interesting piece with highly detailed painting.

relationship to what the public is willing to pay, and hence, though roughly, he will approximate the market price. However, many factors may affect these prices. As previously mentioned, dealers' prices are greatly influenced by what the dealer has had to pay. Overhead, such as rent and electricity, are also figured into the price. Since these costs tend to be lower for country dealers than city, they tend to ask lower prices; thus, they become wholesale suppliers to city dealers, who can in turn ask more, since they deal with a much larger clientele.

Moreover, dealers—like collectors—vary greatly in their knowledge of the field. Some keep reference libraries and research any piece that is not within their area of immediate knowledge. Others, though in business for years, never seem to learn very much. These are the individuals through whose fingers slip the great buys of the decade.

A third and often very important source of accurate information on pricing is the sophisticated collector. In

Above: Center and right: Grained desk, pine and maple; 1830-45; $650-$1,000. Step-down Windsor side chair; 1820-40; $225-350. Birdcage Windsor side chair; 1820-40; $300-550; **Above desk:** Primitive oil of sailing ship; late 19th century; $1,500-$2,000. All, New England.

Above right: Portrait, oil on canvas; East mid-19th century; $900-$1,6000. Blanket chest, pine and maple, green and tan graining over red; Hudson Valley, N.Y.; ca. 1810; $1,500-2,500. Right: Map of Scholharie County, N.Y., paper; mid-19th century; $225-350. Eastlake-style sewing machine cabinet, oak; Midwest, early 20th century; $200-275.

PAGE 16:
Double-door cupboard, pine, old yellow paint; New York, ca. 1870; $250-350.
On floor, left to right: Cricket bench, painted pine; East mid-19th century; $50-85. Stoneware canning jar; Pennsylvania, ca. 1880; $95-130.

every area of antiques, there are collectors who have spent long years buying and studying their favorite pieces. They attend all the important auctions and visit shops on a regular basis. They are frequently far more aware of prevailing prices within their specialty than are most dealers.

In preparing this catalog, the services of all these authorities—auctioneers, dealers, and knowledgeable collectors—have been used, in an attempt to overcome the problems

terminology—"crock with blue decoration, $35"—into something meaningful in terms of his own piece of stoneware will immediately recognize the value of this approach.

As a further aid to identifying a prospective purchase, considerable extra information is given for each entry. For instance, the place in which an item was made, narrowed down as accurately as possible, is cited wherever this would help to identify a piece: an early nineteenth-century chair handmade in Maine will differ in

particular object was made and, by extension, how to spot reproductions and outright fakes; how to identify styles; how to tell whether a piece is really old; how to choose objects that the average person can afford—Art Deco silver, for instance—and what types are priced beyond his means; how to identify the outstanding items in any field; how to find areas that have attracted little attention as yet and so are worth exploring—children's board games, for example; how to form a collection of the objects that particularly

Clawfoot oak table; 1930–40; $250–280. Oak-framed wall clock; by Sessions Manufacturing Co.; 1945–55; $145–165.

inherent in existing price guides. Unlike the usual practice, the prices arrived at for this book are presented not as a single figure but as a range, since, as should be evident from the foregoing discussion, it is impossible—except at the moment of sale—to pinpoint a single price for a given object. Having a range of prices at his disposal will enable the collector to determine approximately what is a fair price for any individual antique. Moreover, since "a picture is worth a thousand words," every object whose price is given is also illustrated. Anyone who has ever tried to translate the standard price-guide

important details from one made in Pennsylvania at the same time, whereas the region in which factory-made goods of a later period were made—political campaign buttons, for example—is of little or no significance. Similarly, the name of the maker or manufacturer is cited wherever it is known. Every attempt has been made to determine the date of a piece, the reasons for this in an antiques catalog being all too obvious.

Furthermore, each antiques area covered in the book is discussed in its own introductory text. These chapters examine such vital concerns as how a

fascinate you; where to look for the best buys; and how to know whether a prospective purchase is a good investment. It is hoped that these chapters will give the collector a deeper understanding of his specialty and enable him to make future purchases with increased wisdom and confidence.

Adding a few words of caution is also in order here. The reader is advised to take the term price guide quite seriously. Keep in mind that the prices quoted, though they are the best approximations available, are still only guidelines. Prices are not fixed in the

antiques field (indeed, we hope they never will be), and many factors may cause the price of an object to vary somewhat from that set forth here. One of the major differentials is the condition of the piece. The prices given here are for pieces in good average condition sold at the retail level, which means, in effect, what one may expect to pay a dealer for an object that shows natural wear but is not damaged or missing essential parts. Damage, such as chips in glass or missing feet on a piece of furniture, generally reduces the value of a piece by 30 to 50 percent. The specific reduction will vary greatly, though, dependent not only upon the extent of the damage but on the buyer's attitude toward it. In certain categories—glass and paper goods are good examples—damage is difficult to repair and will dramatically lower the price. Many dealers will not even handle cracked or chipped glass, regarding it as worthless. Others will immediately devalue such objects by as much as 90 percent. Damaged stoneware pottery and furniture, on the other hand, usually fare better. Cracks and chips in a hundred-fifty-year-old stoneware jug are considered serious only if they affect decorated areas (a crack through the design on a bluebird jug, for instance) or structural integrity (a missing spout on a teapot). In furniture, early specimens often have replaced pulls or cracked tops. If the piece has been well repaired, its original value will be reduced by not more than 25 percent.

INTRODUCTION TO THE FOURTH EDITION

With some one hundred fifty thousand copies in print, *The Catalog of American Antiques* has become by far the most widely read hard cover fully illustrated price guide to antiques made in the United States. This success, of course, reflects the continuing popularity of those objects, from baskets to pottery to furniture, which Americans choose to collect. This enthusiasm for Americana has increased by leaps and bounds during the six years which have elapsed since the last revision.

A piece of American furniture has brought 12.1 million dollars at auction, five duck decoys have sold for over $100,000 each, a piece of stoneware has topped the $200,000 mark and a tiny Shaker box, less than three inches in diameter, has gone to a new owner for just over $12,000!

Yet, those comparing this edition with the previous one will soon see that, contrary to what some dealers and most Auctioneers would like you to believe, not all movement is in an upward direction. The prices of some things have changed little over the past few years. Some have not changed at all, and quite a few, such as hand made tools, post cards and medium range bottles, have actually declined. The prices of antiques go up and down, and any accurate price guide will reflect that fact.

Specific areas covered in this book seem, at present, to be taking the following directions:

High style furniture, Queen Anne, Chippendale and Federal periods, remains extremely strong with several pieces selling for prices in the millions; but Pilgrim Century items attract little attention. The hot items are Shaker, a tall chest just brought $99,000, a revolving chair, $88,000 and a candlestand, $92,000; rustic or "Adirondack" and good painted furniture. Empire, other than for early gilded and ormalu mounted pieces, remains dead; while the "rough" (read, crudely made) country furniture pop-

ularized by decorators has taken a dive. Collectors are getting wiser. They want quality, not just the false "look" promoted by the so-called country magazines.

Folk Art remains very hot. Paintings by major artists such as Ami Phillips and Edward Hicks can reach the million dollar mark. But, watch out for fakes and reproductions in a field fraught with fraud. Good buys can still be found in the underpriced areas of calligraphy, sandpaper paintings and reverse glass. Theorems, memorial paintings and anything in water color from Pennsylvania are out of sight!

Glass remains relatively quiet. Bottles at the top end are picking up after a long slow period, but anything below the $500 level stirs little enthusiasm among collectors. Pattern glass, long plagued by reproductions, continues flat; but anything in color brings some money. Areas to watch are early pontil marked proprietory medicines in colored glass and blown three mold pieces, especially decanters. Remember, condition is crucial here; and watch out for repairs with new epoxies which can't be detected by a Black Light.

Hottest in the ceramics field is blue sponge with factory made pitchers from the 1920s bringing $300-600. Yellowware, especially choice items like colanders and rolling pins, is very popular. Stoneware is strong at the top, but soft everywhere else; while the best redware, sgrafitto and slip decorated platters, commands its own price from a more sophisticated audience. Rockingham and white ironstone remain flat.

There is little movement in the early silver field, but Victorian examples from Tiffany (the father) and Gorham are sought after; and the real excitement is with elaborate electroplate. Fabulous presentation pieces, ice water containers and the like are suddenly bringing prices in the tens of thousands. Again, condition is the key. If you resilver a piece you kill it for this market!

Except for 18th century specimans by major American manufacturers, pewter remains extremely sluggish. It may be a

good time to invest in this field, but buy only marked examples in very good condition.

Copper and brass have their own, relatively tranquil, market. What movement there is is slowly upward. Top of the heap are marked 18th century brass or brass and iron andirons which may bring several thousand dollars per pair. Check every set of andirons for a maker's mark.

Early iron remains undervalued, though the movement is generally upwards. Don't be fooled by spectacular but later examples; like the Connecticut dealer who paid tens of thousands for a set of relatively common Bradley and Hubbard irons which now are selling in the $1,000-2,500 range!

Tole is hot! Any piece of well decorated period tin can bring several hundred dollars, and coffee pots now range above $2,000. On the other hand, undecorated tin pots, pans and so forth have little value.

Among the textiles, its still quilts and samplers. Examples of both have broken the $100,000 mark. Needlework pictures are also in the stratosphere, and pictorial hooked rugs are attracting increasing attention. Early 19th century woven coverlets may bring several thousand dollars each, if signed, dated and of appealing pictorial design, but there is still room for improvement in this undervalued area.

Woodenware continues to move up, particularly painted pieces and those, such as oval boxes, which can claim a Shaker provenance. Burl bowls maintain their climb, but watch for European examples. Ordinary wooden kitchen objects remain one of the most reasonably priced areas of American antiques.

There are legions of basket collectors. For those with money to burn there are Nantucket examples and the often hard to identify Shaker and Taconic vessels. For the rest of us there are thousands of wonderful late 19th and 20th century splint, willow, rye straw and sweet grass baskets. Look for form, condition and patina and don't pay a lot of money for someone else's questionable attribution of "Shaker" or "Taconic".

Page 2: Iron and brass bed; ca. 1890; $250–300. Bed spread and pillow case; $75–80. Side table; 1920–30; $125–140. Boudoir lamp; 1900–10; $300–350.

The category of lighting devices is highly specialized. Serious collectors continue to pay hundreds or even thousands for a rare old form, while for the less ambitious there are hundreds of different pressed glass kerosene lamps. All categories remain steady or are moving up.

Tools have suffered a major setback since our last edition. With the exception of elaborate pieces (brass and ivory inlay, for example) and those marked by important early makers, most 19th century hand made tools have stagnated or declined in value. The bright spots in the field are "patent tools", usually of cast iron, made from 1880 on into this century. These, especially products of the Stanley tool company, have attracted a loyal following. Still, not a field to invest in for retirement!

The toy field is a large one offering the collector a wide range of choice. Generally, prices are up, shockingly so in the area of mechanical banks where a few wealthy dealers seem to be manipulating the market. Condition is extremely important here, and collectors should be aware that there are now sources for reproductions of almost any part for almost any toy!

Decoys hit their top around 1986 with several examples flying over the $100,000 mark. Since then, things have cooled off a bit, particularly at the low end of the market. Remember, the maker's name is everything here. Hot numbers now are Mason's factory and old standby carvers like Cobb, Crowell and Lincoln. Watch for fakes and for European decoys now entering the market.

Weathervanes and whirligigs are among the most spectacular examples of folk art, and they continue to attract the dollars. A vane has exceeded the $100,000 mark, and great "gigs" regularly bring in the tens of thousands. Prices are climbing; but watch for fakes, especially among the carved and painted pieces.

Tramp art continues to plod along. Prices move up slowly with the best pieces, particularly if large or in paint, being seen as folk art rather than tramp. Buy big and buy color. The cigar box mahogany finish is out!

For many collectors scrimshaw is synonymous with fraud. The proliferation of fakes and reproductions over the past decade has scared away lots of collectors. Yet, the prices for "right" pieces continue to escalate. A range of $25,000-35,000 for such a hot item as a "Susan's Tooth" (carved on the bark Susan in the

Right: Turn-of-the-century wallpaper forms a charming background for a spindle hat rack and 1930s hats.

early 19th century) is commonplace. A field for the bold and knowledgable!

Advertising prices are moving up. The old favorites, Coca Cola and Moxie collectibles, remain strong while anything featuring Blacks is guaranteed to sell. Lithographed advertising signs and posters are particularly hot at the moment.

Photographic memorabilia is recovering from the doldrums of the late '70s and early '80s. Images are leading the way with daguerreotypes of outdoor scenes, early homes and tradesmen especially sought after. Since the photographer is often anonymous, subject matter is the key. Anything Indian, goldmining, disaster, war, etc., is a sure winner. Cameras, which were made in far greater numbers than early collectors ever imagined, are off except for the rarer forms.

Posters and other paper goods or ephemera present a mixed market. Lithographed advertising and patriotic posters, particularly those by well known artists or promoting such activities as circuses and magic shows, are in a rising market. On the other hand, post cards have tumbled, and magazines are dead. Watch for trade catalogs, especially those by fishing tackle, carriage and weathervane manufacturers.

Political memorabilia, another highly specialized field, continues strong. Collectors have the resources to buy what they want, and whenever anything important comes on the market it is snapped up. But, remember this is a highly selective market. No two posters, pins or ribbons are the same, though they may feature the same politician. You must know what you are doing.

Yes, when all is said and done, knowledge is the key to the successful buying, selling and collecting of American antiques. If you read, visit museum exhibitions, antiques shows and auctions you will establish a foundation of knowledge which will enable you to make your own decisions about what to collect and how much to invest. You will not need "fine arts advisors" or self-interested auction house personnel to tell you what to buy or how much to pay. And you will have a lot more fun!

Introduction to
Catalog of American Collectibles

In the early 1970s, some promoters of antiques shows began to advertise their extravaganzas as "antiques and collectibles" shows or even simply as "collectibles" shows. This was more than a change in language; it was a reflection of a fundamental alteration in the nature of both the collecting public and what it collected.

Before the Second World War, antiques buying was limited. An antique is legally defined by U.S. Customs as an object one hundred or more years old, so nothing later than 1850 was of much interest to most antiquarians. Furthermore, even among the older objects, much was left untouched. Collectors were for the most part rich, eccentric, or both, and they concentrated their efforts on a limited field: fine arts, furniture, silver, and certain glass and pottery. Those few who explored other areas of eighteenth- and nineteenth-century arts and crafts found low prices and little competition.

By 1950 all this had begun to change. A huge new class of collectors emerged during the postwar years—people who had never before had the time or the money to collect. Younger and more adventuresome than their predecessors, they

began to expand the concept of "antique." Scouring the country for old things, they discovered the "new" antiques: quilts, folk art, decorated stoneware pottery—even bottles. Much of what they acquired was truly antique in that it was a century or more old—so the older generation of collectors could quarrel with the younger collectors on aesthetic grounds but not on temporal ones. On the other hand, a lot was collected that everybody knew wasn't very old: hooked rugs from the turn of the century and country baskets from the 1930s. Still, these items were "folky," and everyone tacitly agreed to forget about age and call them antiques.

The source of this inspired reasoning was, to a great extent, the antiques dealer. Before the postwar boom, most antiques dealers had been people who sold to feed their own collecting habit. Few of them made much money, and few hoped to. Their rewards were of another kind. Suddenly, however, it became possible to make a living selling antiques. What had been a hobby became a business—a big business—and as more and more dealers entered the field, the demand for salable merchandise greatly increased. Dealers searched the countryside and even trav-

Fashion dolls; 1900-30; $150-325
each. Textile-boudoir lamp; 1920-30;
$65-115.

eled to Canada and England—where American antiques (or things that looked like American antiques) could be obtained. But there was still not enough pre-1850 merchandise to go around. The only way out was to call things antiques if they looked the part—regardless of age. Since many objects, such as baskets, woodenware, and pottery, are hard to date precisely, this solution pleased almost everyone.

As the 1960s dawned, a new situation developed. Victoriana became the rage, and because the Victorian era extended up to the time of the First World War, collectors who pursued this interest suddenly found themselves peering across the very narrow gap between Victoriana and the roaring twenties—and all that lay beyond. Tentatively, they began to collect Art Deco objects, adding them to their already acceptable accumulations of similar Victorian Art Nouveau accessories.

The forbidden wall was breached, and hordes of hungry collectors poured into the promised land of the 1920s and 1930s. For some it was a matter of nostalgia—they were collecting the very objects they had grown up with. For others it was more practical; Depression glass, Fiesta ware, and Jim Beam bottles were cheap and plentiful. It was possible to build a collection without mortgaging the homestead, a situation that even as early as the mid-1960s no longer existed in the world of classical antiques collecting.

The dealers responded to this new interest. A mass of Occupied Japan figurines, Orphan Annie premiums, and 1940s comic books began to appear on dealers' shelves and at shows. Some promoters responded negatively. Secure in the continuing boom for "true" antiques, they

Opposite: Wurlitzer jukebox; 1940-50; $3,500-4,500. **Left:** Whiskey and medicine bottles; late 19th-early 20th century; $5-20 each. **Below:** Antiques shop interior. The clutter is in the best Victorian traditon.

Below: Overstuffed sofa and two chairs in walnut veneer; 1935-40; $2,500-4,000 the set. Bar in walnut veneer; 1930-40; $650-1,000. **Below right:** Art Nouveau bronze table lamp with beaded-glass shade; 1910-20; $325-450. **Bottom:** Art Deco plaster and cardboard fireplace; 1930-40; $650-900. **Opposite:** Dressing table and mirror in walnut veneer; 1938-45; $600-850.

shut the doors on the new dealers and their merchandise. But other show managers embraced the new objects, and the public swarmed to buy. The collectibles boom was on!

Collectibles can be defined as objects less than a hundred years old, but as a matter of practice the term is almost always confined to pieces manufactured since 1920. Moreover, at most collectibles shows it is evident that most of the merchandise displayed dates from the 1930s, 1940s, and even the 1950s. It is also clear that although collectibles are very much American in the sense that they are collected here by Americans, many of them are of foreign origin. In the international world in which we live, national boundaries have less and less to do with collecting. Much art glass, for example, was made outside the United States—as, of course, were all Occupied Japan ceramics. Yet no book on American collectibles would be complete without these foreign-made items.

The present-day collector will observe that, unlike during those halcyon days of the 1960s and early 1970s, some collectibles are no longer inexpensive. Oak furniture made by Gustav Stickley in the early 1900s has sold for as much as $14,000 for a single desk and chair. Certain pieces of 1920s carnival glass command prices in the thousands, and the same is true for rare commemorative or special-issue Jim Beam whiskey bottles, though the latter date only to the 1960s. But it is still possible to purchase interesting things for reasonable sums—it just requires patience and knowledge. The patience is an acquired talent—it is our hope that the chapters of this book will provide the knowledge. However, one

Opposite top: Vase by Van Briggle Art Pottery; Boulder, Colorado; 1920-30; $100-150. **Opposite bottom:** 1900s-'style office with oak furniture. Flat-top desk; $400-550. Library table; $325-425. Swivel chair: $145-210. Combination chair and coat hanger; $75-100. **Left:** Oak dining table; 1905-15; $4,700-6,200. Set of four oak "V-back" side chairs; 1905-10; $2,800-3,600. Brass chandelier; 1900-10; $7,500-9,500. An extremely rare piece. Hammered-copper serving plate; 1910-12; $800-950. All pieces by Gustav Stickley.

should also be aware of some of the unusual factors that are affecting today's market.

In the first place, inflation and the steady decline in the purchasing power of the dollar have led to a situation in which many people feel that objects are worth more than money, particularly if the money can be put into objects that will increase in value over a period of time. Thus, for the first time, speculation has entered the collecting field. People with little knowledge of or real interest in either antiques or collectibles have decided to put their wealth into these objects rather than into stocks or bonds. This is unfortunate for the true collector and appreciator of these objects because it means that at best he will have to pay more for his acquisitions and at worst he will not be able to afford them at all. Longing for the "good old days" will not take the speculators out of the market. Moreover, some wise collectors who purchased things they loved in the 1950s and 1960s are discovering to their delight that these objects have increased in value tenfold or more. Only the most obtuse collector will ignore the investment potential in his acquisitions.

Another factor the collector must consider is the auction phenomenon. Before the Second World War, with the exception of a few auction houses in major cities, auctions served primarily to redistribute used household goods and farm equipment. With the antiques boom, dealers and collectors discovered that there was gold in those old houses and barns, leading to an unparalleled growth in the auction business.

In the 1970s, auctions have become a way of life for many collectors. Oper-

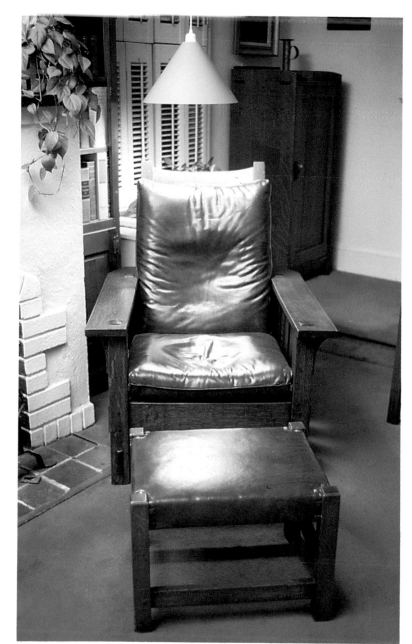

Opposite: Dressing table, stool and mirror in maple veneer; 1930-40; $700-900 the set. Clock; 1920-40; $65-90. Wall light sconces; 1935-45; $75-135 each. Feather hats; 1930-40; $40-65 each. Mannequin; 1925-35; $95-175. **Above:** Morris chair in oak and leather; 1901-16; $3,500-5,000. Footstool in oak and leather; ca. 1912; $850-975. Music cabinet in oak; 1910-12; $3,300-4,400. All pieces by Gustav Stickley.

ating on the sometimes erroneous theory that they can always buy cheaper at an auction, collectors have swarmed to the auction galleries. The auctioneer has the problem of providing merchandise. This competition for salable goods—be they early paintings or the art pottery of the 1900s—explains the recent change major auction galleries have made in the percentage fees that they charge for their services.

American auctioneers have traditionally charged a percentage of the amount realized at a sale to cover their services in promoting and selling the goods. This charge has generally ranged from 15 to 25 percent and is payable by the consign-or whose merchandise was sold. However, the recent trend is to charge the consignor less (usually 10 percent)—thus encouraging consignments—and to pass the cost on to the purchaser in the form of a 10 percent premium added to his purchase price. Collectors have been unhappy with this innovation, but it has had no appreciable effect on buying or attendance at auctions. Nevertheless, collectors attending auctions should keep in mind that they will often have to pay their bid price plus 10 percent.

Unfortunately, collectibles enthusiasts must now also contend with dishonesty. High prices and the possibility of making substantial profits bring out the

Above: Oak table; $6,500-8,500. Glass-fronted china cabinet in oak; $4,200-6,700. Oak bench; $3,500-5,500. Fall-Front desk in oak; $7,000-9,000. Hammered-copper chafing dish; $1,200-1,950. All pieces by Gustav Stickley; 1903-17.

Opposite: Extension table in oak; 1910-25; $400-550. Set of six press-back chairs in oak; 1890-1900; $350-450. Apothecary shelves in oak; 1880-1900; $2,500- 3,500.

Display of advertising items set up in
a simulated country store.

Top: Fiesta ware; 1935-45; $3-25 each. Round pedestal-style dining table in oak; 1920-25; $450-650. Set of six oak side chairs; $400-600.
Above: Utilitarian glass from various manufacturers; 1930-40; $3-40 each.
Right: Nippon Japanese porcelain tea set in American-made chrome frame; 1920-30; $175-265.

worst in some people. Reproductions of collectibles are becoming all too common. They range from increasing the value of an Austrian Lotz vase tenfold by inscribing on it a bogus Tiffany signature to the wholesale reproduction of various popular pressed-glass patterns. The best defense against this sort of chicanery is knowledge. The more you know about your chosen field, the less likely you are to be fooled. Lacking this knowledge, the would-be collector is advised to buy only from knowledgeable dealers who are willing to guarantee their merchandise. Anyone purchasing a piece that is worth a substantial sum is entitled to a written statement of authenticity signed by the dealer. If the dealer is unwilling to give such a statement, there may be a very good reason!

But disagreeable factors such as high prices and fakery are only a small part of the collectibles scene. For the most part, collectibles are alive and well, and this is due in no small part to their great variety. During the nineteenth century, the typical home was furnished with a surprisingly small amount of useful objects; and these were made from relatively few materials: glass, pottery, metal, wood, and textiles. By the end of the 1800s, however, the number of objects had begun to expand, and in this century expansion has become deluge. Not only did people become better off financially during the past seventy years (and therefore better able to afford the things that we now regard as collectibles)—there was also a great increase in the number of materials from which these objects could be made.

Early in the century celluloid appeared as a medium for the manufacture of everything from dolls to imitation

Top: Pomo Indian feather basket; California; early twentieth century; $500-$800. Baskets like these were often given as wedding presents. **Above:** Sterling silver coffee set; by Tiffany; 1890-1900; $2,750-3,750.

ivory. Celluloid was soon followed by Bakelite, which largely replaced wood in handles and tops, and finally came the plastics that today threaten to usurp the roles of all other materials. Plastics of the 1950s and 1960s are already becoming valued collector's items.

New metals have also entered the field. To the pewter, tin, and iron common in the 1880s have been added aluminum, stainless steel, and chrome. Chrome, in particular, is the metal of the 1920s and 1930s. Chrome's shining, readily cleaned surface was particularly suitable for use on the modernistic tables and in the sleek furnishings of the period.

Pottery and glass, of course, are not new to us, but the roles they have played in the past century are quite different from their traditional ones. The rise in the 1880s of the small potteries and glassworks devoted to making art glass and art pottery led to the development of a whole new area of collectibles. Names such as Galle, Rookwood, Tiffany, and Weller guarantee lovely objects, all of them collectible, but few of them now inexpensive. For bargains, the collector

Left: Pair of Art Deco tubular-steel sofas 1938-40; $6,000-9,500. These sofas are similar to prototypes by the designer Courvosier.

Above: This group of twentieth-century hat forms are extremely popular with collectors today. Depending on size and condition, they sell for $150-$400 each. The small beaded lamp on the right is a hot collectors' item at $75-$100.

Right: Mission-style sideboard in oak; 1910-20; $650-800. **Opposite:** Art Deco table and chairs; by Alvar Aalto; 1935-40; $6,500-9,500. Cabinet in blond maple and maghogany; 1935-40; $950-1,300. Mirrored glass panel; 1930-40; $3,000-5,000. Salt and pepper shakers; 1935-45; $15-25 each.

Below: Bedside table in painted pine; 1935-40; $175-255.
Right: Many collectors prefer to mix their antique periods. The circa 1900 Oriental rug ($1,000- $1,500) in this room is complemented by a 1930s/sofa ($700-$1,100) and an early nineteenth-century Grandfather clock ($2,000-$2,500).

must look elsewhere.

Well-made factory furniture in the sleek, blond style of the Art Deco period is still available at reasonable prices. Much the same may be said of wicker furniture. It is possible to furnish a whole house in 1920s wicker at prices far less than one would pay for comparable contemporary furniture.

There are also bargains in glass. Much 1930s glass is still underpriced, and with the exception of certain hard-to-find colors and patterns, the ever-popular Depression glass is still available and inexpensive. A similar situation exists in the field of pottery. Fiesta ware is still readily obtainable, and the less-well-known variants, such as Harlequin and Luray, represent real bargains.

For those who prefer textiles, clothing of the 1920s and 1930s is still showing up in thrift shops and at house sales at unbelievably low prices. Although the same may not be said for the extremely popular Victorian garments, Victorian jewelry, if not set with precious stones, can be a fine investment. Also available are later pieces, particularly costume jewelry.

Quite simply, the world of collectibles is full of real bargains—and not all of them have been discovered yet. A crafty collector, wanting to get a little jump on the competition, might just thumb through a couple of those reprints of early-twentieth-century Sears Roebuck and Montgomery Ward catalogs. They tell us what was available back then, and you will be surprised at just how much is still waiting to be discovered.

Opposite: Piano in tiger wood; 1929-31; $3,500-4,500. Pair of stools in laminated wood; 1930-40; $450-650. Glass wall plaque; by Lee Lowery; 1930-35; $3,500-5,000. Art Deco Scatter rug; 1930-40; $125-195. **Above:** China cabinet in oak; 1910-25; $400-650. Art pottery, by Artus Van Briggle; $50-900 each. **Right:** overstuffed chair; 1910-1920; $ 200-300

INTRODUCTION TO THE THIRD EDITION

In the decade since the first edition of this book appeared both the definition of a "collectible" and the popularity of such items have undergone substantial change. Ten years ago collectibles were recognized as those objects which were of interest to some pioneering collectors but which, not being one hundred years old, could not properly be termed antiques.

Today, at least if we accept the self aggrandizing definitions of some editors in the price guide field, a collectible is any inexpensive mass produced item no matter how recently it may have been made and regardless of its obvious lack of artistic or historical merit.

Moreover, definitions of collectibility invariably fail to take into consideration the fact that some items, such as Native American crafts and political memorabilia, commonly regarded as "collectibles" are often of sufficient age to be antiques. However, recognizing the essentially schizophrenic nature of the field, we continue to include these within the coverage of this work.

Popularity is another matter. It is safe to say that the field of collectibles, no matter how defined, is booming. With antiques escalating in value and with the maturation of a generation which regards the 1950s and even the '60s as ancient history; more and more people are turning to mass produced objects to satisfy their acquisitive cravings.

As a consequence, prices in general have risen, in some cases sharply. However, fluctuation rather than a steady acceleration is the general rule, and the sharp-eyed reader will note that some fields are slow and that in most there are areas of weakness.

Moreover, collectibles far more than antiques are subject to manipulation by the unscrupulous. So-called "limited editions" of collector plates (which may, in fact, run into the tens of thousands) and hyping of common items as rare or desirable by auction houses, dealers and writers may mislead the unwary. A classic example of the latter was the absurd prices realized for ordinary factory made cookie jars at the auction of the estate of the controversial artist and self-promoter Andy Warhol.

Trends are often hard to define in the world of collectibles, but at present we may make the following observations regarding categories covered in this book:

Maker marked or attributable Arts & Crafts or Mission oak furniture is way up with some items bringing

prices in the tens of thousands. Ordinary, factory oak, on the other hand, is flat as is Colonial Revival and the so-called Tudor style of the 1930s. Good period wicker is popular as is unusual horn and rustic or "Adirondack" furniture. Watch for recent reproductions in the former area.

Art pottery is generally strong, especially the "buzz-word" brands such as Teco, Grueby and Ohr which work so well with Mission furnishings. The more ordinary lines from Weller, Roseville and Van Briggle are going nowhere.

Utilitarian pottery remains just that. You can still set a table with Fiesta ware at modest prices unless you insist on cobalt blue or red. But, anything Deco is up, and Occupied Japan ceramics are on the move.

Art glass is slightly off with Tiffany hurt by a host of reproductions. On the other hand, interest in Lalique has been spurred by recent books and exhibitions, and Galle and Daum continue to command high prices. Watch for the '50s glass from Italy (particularly that of the designer Venini) and Scandanavia and for the increasingly collectible Heisey products.

Carnival glass remains dull and Depression Glass steady. Rare patterns and colors are still the hot items in both categories. Any Art Deco glass has potential, while the Twentieth Century collector bottles, (Beam, etc.) have fallen on hard times.

Sterling silver by good makers, especially Gorham, Tiffany the elder and Arts & Crafts, remains strong; and electroplate, (boosted by some auction results running to five figures!) is a success story for the '80s. Anything by Georg Jensen is good, and Deco forms are also popular.

Bronzes are in demand, though there are continuing problems with reproductions. Hot American makers are Tiffany and Bradley & Hubbard, while the work of the French "animaliers" remains popular.

Country store or advertising memorabilia, popularly termed "advertiques" is up, especially well done lithographs, dolls and unusual promotional items. Some of the latter have brought in excess of $5,000. Age is less important than "look" here!

Household accessories is a broad category with a great price range, generally on the modest size. Chrome by Chase and Manning-Bowman is strong, and copper by Gustav Stickley and other Arts & Crafts designers has gone through the roof. Many trays, candlesticks and the like routinely bring prices in the thousands. Aluminum is attracting growing attention, and anything within the category of Black memorabilia brings money.

Fine jewelry, as always, does well. Art Nouveau items remain strong, and wise collectors are stockpiling enamel on silver bracelets, pins and pendants in the Art Deco mode.

Photographic memorabilia has rebounded from the doldrums of the early '80s with images of Western scenes, tradesmen, accidents and the bizarre leading the way. Cameras, on the other hand, are somewhat off. Age is no guarantee of success here. Condition and rarity are critical. Keep an eye out for the red hot Art Deco design cameras of the 1930s.

Clocks and watches, collected by the few and knowledgable, continue to escalate in value. Pocket and wrist watches are the hot area with hunting cases, Art Deco and Nouveau and the famous Swiss makers leading the way.

American Indian crafts have taken off! A Navajo rug recently broke the hundred thousand mark at auction, and early baskets and pottery regularly trade in the low thousands. To be avoided are most post 1950 items and non traditional ceramic forms such as ash trays, tiles and toys.

Sports memorabilia is booming with fishing tackle (several tiny metal fish lures have sold for over $15,000 apiece) and decoys leading the way. With the latter maker is everything. If you can't attach a famous carver's name to your piece it probably won't be worth much. The new frontier is golfing memorabilia. Check the attic for old wooden handled clubs, some of which have sold for $5,000-7,000 each.

Clothing, except for Victorian ladies' whites is very quiet. Hats can be of interest, but shoes, ties and other vintage accessories of the 1890-1960 period are off.

Radios, phonographs and juke boxes are highly specialized but generally modestly up. The big news of the past decade is bakelite—brightly colored radios in this early plastic can bring good prices. Otherwise, its the rare form that rings the bell. Ordinary, though old, radios and photographs won't sell for much.

Militaria is solid with fine early Pennsylvania rifles and any weapons associated with the old West selling well. World War II weapons are also strong.

Gambling devices are popular enough now to have their own specialized auctions, and a small but well-heeled audience will pay in the thousands for choice rarities.

Board games may well be the big surprise of the 1980s. These modest though colorful sets have doubled, tripled and more in the past year spurred on by a couple of spectacular auctions. Top games will top a thousand dollars, though far more can be found in the $75-750 range.

And, finally, the fact that we can now price most of "Tomorrow's Collectibles" indicates clearly that if an item is available there is probably someone who will collect it!

Antique Furniture: Chairs and Tables

The form and variety of early American furniture are accurate reflections of the condition of its owners. The earliest immigrants to these shores brought few possessions with them other than some boxes, a cook pot, and the clothes on their backs. But among those early arrivers were counted some skilled cabinetmakers; and as the immigrants prospered, they built homes and stocked them with a multitude of furnishings. This tradition persists today, with Americans owning greater numbers and types of furniture than any other people.

The furniture field is one of the most active areas of antiques collecting. It is ironic that whereas the resale value of modern factory-made furniture is, for the most part, essentially nil, pieces made in earlier times continue to increase in value. The price range is extraordinary. One can easily pay as much as thirty-five thousand dollars for a Chippendale highboy or as little as five dollars for a late-Victorian press-back side chair. The two pieces are worlds apart, yet they have two things in common: they both can be used, and they both will become more valuable with time.

The seventeenth- and early eighteenth-century colonial home contained but a handful of furnishings—a table, some stools, a chair or two, and a few storage chests. People often slept on the floor, and what beds there were have vanished with the passage of time. By the 1750s, these few items had been augmented by a variety of useful objects: highboys and lowboys, chests of drawers, sofas, beds, and cupboards. The basic types of furniture did not disappear, however. In fact, they increased in both quantity and kind so that today there are literally thousands of early chairs, tables, and chests available on the market. Of these, the chair was produced in the greatest number of forms.

Stools and Benches

Stools and benches were certainly the first structures intended for sitting on. A few early examples—the "joint stools" put together of seasoned oak—have come down to us. They seem far too small to accommodate comfortably the ample twentieth-century posterior; but then our ancestors—working harder and eating less than we do—were smaller than we are. The joint stool was essentially a horizontal board joined to two or more verticals, and its form has persisted. Small stools for milking, footstools, and the backless benches of the Shaker meetinghouse all recall the former preeminence of this simple but sturdy object.

Chairs and Sofas

When we turn to the chair, we find a much greater variety of types. Few examples are available of the heavy oak Carver chair favored by the settlers at Plymouth Bay; but if one fancies ladder-backs, press-backs, kitchen chairs, or wicker, pieces can be collected by the dozen and at very reasonable prices. It is best to go about the business somewhat systematically; to do that, it is important to know something about the various types of chairs and how each was made.

The earliest American chairs—the so-called Pilgrim chairs—were built of oak, with bulbous sausage turnings made on a crude lathe. Since there are few authenticated native examples— many were imported from England and Europe—purchase of them is risky as well as expensive. By 1700, however, pine and hardwood ladder-back chairs had appeared in this country, and they have continued in production right down to the present day.

All ladder- or slat-backs—so-called for their several horizontal back splats—are put together in essentially the same way. Horizontal dowels—called "sticks," from which comes the term *stick furniture*—and slats of dried wood are inserted into holes and slots cut in vertical members, which are made of unseasoned wood. As the unseasoned, or "green," wood shrinks with age, it locks onto the unshrunken dry pieces, forming a tight bond. Until about 1860, this union was further assured by the use of hardwood pegs, which were driven into holes placed at points of stress—such as the juncture of the back posts with the top back slat. From 1860 to 1900, nails replaced pegs, and after the turn of the century, pinning disappeared completely.

While the ladder-back was seen in all homes in the early years, the well-to-do soon turned to chairs whose design was influenced by European taste. The dichotomy between native and European-influenced styles existed in all areas of furnishings; in fact, we may characterize all American antique furniture by dividing it into two general areas: fine furniture, whose style changed periodically with the infusion of new ideas from abroad; and country furniture, which continued substantially unchanged for generations.

There are seven recognized periods of so-called fine furniture, each with its distinctive elements of style. These are:

Pilgrim or Jacobean	1630–1690
William and Mary	1690–1725
Queen Anne	1725–1755
Chippendale	1755–1785
Federal (Sheraton and Hepplewhite)	1785–1810
Empire	1810–1840
Victorian	1840–1910

The basic characteristics of all these styles were developed on the Continent and found their way to these shores through the influence of English cabinetmakers. As a general rule, the American product was more restrained and less formal in concept than its European counterpart.

We have already discussed the Pilgrim chair, whose form had remained basically unchanged since the Middle Ages. In the late seventeenth century, it was replaced by several different styles, which shared the general characteristic of an elegance previously unknown in American chairs. The William and Mary style is distinguished by cane seats and backs, elaborate carving on legs, arms, and back, and shaped or ball feet, elements rarely seen in modern furniture. Like Pilgrim chairs, however, William and Mary examples are so rare as to be unavailable to all but a few museums and collectors.

Such is not the case with Queen Anne examples. These exist in large numbers as both side chairs and armchairs, and they are great favorites with collectors. The formal Queen Anne style is distinguished from its country cousin by its curved cabriole leg and pad foot; its rural counterpart is usually found with a vaselike back splat and elaborately turned lower legs and front stretcher. Both forms are expensive, though the country pieces may occasionally be found for very little at country auctions or house sales.

One type of Chippendale chair resembles the Queen Anne except for its cabriole leg, which is generally carved and has a ball-and-claw foot. The other form is distinguished by a straight, square, or rectangular front leg. Although walnut was a preferred wood in the William and Mary period, both Queen Anne and Chippendale chairs are made of several woods, including mahogany, maple, birch, and walnut.

Federal chairs are lighter in construction and more delicate in design than those of the preceding periods. Two types are noted: the Hepplewhite, with a shield or oval back, and the square-back Sheraton. Both have tapered legs, and ornamentation—by inlay, painting, or carving—is common. Until rather recently, Federal chairs were, like other furniture of the period, of no great interest to collectors, but enthusiasm and prices have increased greatly during the past decade.

In contrast, the heavy-handed design, broad veneered surfaces, and massive proportions of Empire furniture have not appealed to antiques lovers, with the exception of examples traceable to the shops of such famous cabinetmakers as Duncan Phyfe (whose work bridged this and the preceding style). Empire side chairs may still be bought at reasonable prices, and armchairs and wing chairs can still be found for a fraction of what one would pay for their equivalents from an earlier period.

Country examples of Empire continued the trend toward painted furniture that had begun in the Federal era. Best known and most desirable are the Hitchcock chairs: slat-back, rush- or cane-seated pieces with elaborate stencil decoration. Hitchcocks bearing the original maker's label are very desirable, but reproductions are common and faking of labels is not unknown.

Typifying the baroque taste of their era, Victorian chairs were made in a wide variety of styles, too numerous to categorize. The mid-nineteenth century saw the beginning of factory-made furniture, and Victorian manufacturers were eclectic, taking design elements from many different periods and blending them freely. All styles of Victorian furniture are popular today, particularly armchairs and sofas. The country, or "kitchen," versions are generally made of pine and oak, with decorative motifs that were stamped into flat surfaces by giant steam presses; these have appreciated steadily in value over the past decade but can still be purchased reasonably, particularly in rural areas. Matched sets of four or

more are an excellent investment.

While the Hitchcock and press-back chairs enjoyed great popularity in rural homes, the ladder-back was always preeminent. Some of the finest specimens were made in the nineteenth century by craftsmen of the Shaker sect, whose religious communities were scattered throughout the northeastern United States. Shaker-made chairs are characterized by textile tape rather than rush or splint seats and are often labeled. Today, Shaker side, arm, and rocking chairs command premium prices. Other ladder-back chairs are much more reasonable—particularly if they lack a seat or require stripping away many layers of old paint. Good examples can often be acquired for as little as five to ten dollars.

A second favorite chair style is the Windsor. Starting from a squat English prototype, characterized by a row of vertical dowels forming the back of the chair, American chairmakers developed an almost endless number of variations: the hoop back, continuous arm, birdcage, writing arm, arrow back, and rod back, to mention but a few. The finest Windsors were manufactured prior to 1850, but the form persisted well beyond that date. A good-looking specimen in old paint always runs well above a hundred dollars.

Far less expensive and more readily obtainable are wicker chairs and sofas They were factory-made in great numbers from 1870 on and are now very popular. All but the most elaborate can be acquired for less than fifty dollars. Watch out, though, for modern pieces just in from Hong Kong or Taiwan! These will lack the signs of wear—frayed ends or cracking paint—evident on the originals and are generally less complex in construction. Wicker fits in with most other furniture and offers an interesting field for exploration.

Tables

The earliest American tables were massive affairs—great oaken boards six feet or more long set on thick turned legs. As time passed, a variety of tables developed, but the Pilgrim style persisted in the harvest and the sawbuck table. The latter could be dismantled and placed out of the way, a practical development seen also in the chair table, whose top tilted back to reveal a handy bench. Both forms were well suited to the crowded conditions of the small colonial house. These early pieces generally lacked hinges and often nails

as well; they were pegged together like a chair, and the lift tops, where present, swung on carved wooden swivels.

As the eighteenth century progressed, with its increased standards of elegance and comfort, the number of tables in use greatly increased. The family harvest table was augmented by smaller candlestands and tea tables, whose tops often tilted aside to make more space in the room or to serve double duty as fire screens. Small rectangular work or side tables, often with drawers, were placed about the room; and in public places, tap or tavern tables resounded to the clang of pewter mugs. The drop-leaf and the gateleg tables largely replaced the chair table as a space saver.

While early tables were most often made of oak, later forms come in various woods—maple, walnut, cherry, mahogany, and poplar. They often had pine tops, which frequently wore out over the years or became lost, to be replaced by others. One of the most difficult matters in buying an old table is to determine whether you are getting the original top. To be sure, always look under the table. Nail or screw holes in odd places, signs of finish on what should be an unfinished surface, and uneven wearing are all indications that a change has been made.

The frames of these tables were occasionally nailed together; but more often they were either pegged or dovetailed, a technique in which triangular openings were cut in two pieces of wood to be joined at a right angle. When the pieces were properly matched, the joint fit perfectly and held securely without benefit of glue or nails. Tops were nailed or pinned on with wooden pegs. Like early chairs, these tables were customarily painted, since the use of several different woods in one piece of furniture created contrasts displeasing to the colonial eye. Today, much of this original paint has been lost. Since its presence always enhances the value of a piece, the temptation to replace it always exists. In recent years there have come on the market several excellent milk-base paints that accurately reproduce the early colors: "Shaker" red, for instance, or "Amish" blue. In the hands of an expert, these can be applied so as to be almost indistinguishable from the original finish.

Fine, or "high-style," tables show a progression similar to that seen in chairs. William and Mary examples are heavy, with turnip feet and applied decoration. Queen Anne pieces bear the cabriole leg and show a preference for mahogany or its American-grown substitutes, cherry and walnut. In the Chippendale period, either the knee is carved in leafy patterns or the entire leg is a plain, tapered shaft. The Federal leg is square if Hepplewhite, or, if Sheraton, round and reeded, tapering down from top to bottom. By the Empire period, the leg has become a thick block turned above and below. Carving and a variety of shapes reappear in the Victorian era.

Tops are rarely of pine in the better pieces. Usually they match the wood of the base, and they may be scalloped, rounded, cut at the corners, or, in the case of drop leaves, shaped in a half circle. Decoration is largely confined to the skirt, or valance, beneath the tabletop. This was usually just cut in a shape, such as a scroll, in the earlier periods, but it was often inlaid in the Federal era and veneered in the Empire.

Victorian tables were frequently topped with marble, a custom developed during the Empire period; Victorian pieces also employed such conceits of the preceding era as cast-iron or bronze feet and various metal fittings. Carving, which had not been prominent since the late eighteenth century, reemerged with a vengeance or was imitated in cheaper pieces by the use of pressed-wood designs. Cast-iron and wicker tables became popular, and the latter are seen in some variety, though rarely are they larger than a modern card table.

Tables are less common than chairs, and their prices do not vary as greatly. Good early examples, both high-style and fine country pieces are costly, especially when painted. Since few tables are bought for show alone, they tend to be sold for their functional as well as esthetic quality, and even plain country examples from the last century sell for over a hundred dollars. Until a few years ago, oak Victorian tables were a good buy, but their prices have now skyrocketed. Wicker is still an inexpensive substitute, and simple country dining and work tables, particularly those of the Empire period, can be found at appealing figures.

Three examples of painted country ladder-backs. **Left:** Ash, brown paint, Virginia, ca. 1900; $65-90. **Center:** Maple and hickory, blue paint; New York, ca. 1900; $80-140. **Right:** Ash and maple, old red paint; Connecticut, early 19th century; $200-275.

Tripod stool, pine, traces of red paint; East, late 18th-early 19th century; $75-125. The earliest form of household seating.

Small bench, pine, traces of old blue paint; Maine, mid-19th century; $75-135. Typical of small benches used as milking stools and footstools.

Windsor-style tripod stool, pine and maple; New England, first quarter 19th century; $225-300.

Bench, painted pine, New England, mid-19th century; $100-150. Possibly a school bench.

Wagon seat, pine, original gray paint with yellow striping; Maine, 19th century; $250-350.

Slat-back side chair, pine and maple, old black paint; New England, early 18th century; $300-425.

Early 19th century ladder-back chairs; New England. **Left:** Pine and maple, pine seat; $75-110. **Right:** Ash and maple, old black paint; $85-175. Original paint adds to the value of this piece.

Country Queen Anne Spanish-foot side chair, maple, old black paint; 18th century; $1,500-$2,500. A New England example of a popular chair.

Rare Queen Anne-Chippendale transitional side chair, mahogany; Pennsylvania, mid-18th century; $3,500-7.000.

Country Chippendale ribbon-back side chair, maple; Massachusetts, late 18th century; $1,800-2,500

Queen Anne side chair, balloon seat, mahogany; Massachusetts, ca. 1760; $2,500-4,000.

Lyre-back Chippendale side chair, mahogany; New York, late 18th century; $3,000-4,500.

Country Chippendale lyre-back side chair, ash and hickory, old black paint; Massachusetts, late 18th century; $900-1,500.

Country Chippendale side chair, cherry; Maine, late 18th century; $600-900.

Oval-back Hepplewhite side chair, mahogany; New England, ca. 1800; $800-1,400. One of several variations on the Federal-period side chair.

Empire side chairs with cane seats, child and adult size, walnut; New England, ca. 1820. **Left:** $150-225. **Right:** 125-160.

Hitchcock-style side chair, white with green striping; New England, 1820—40; $125-175. These chairs generally of maple, have been widely reproduced; only early examples are of interest.

Decorated late-Empire side chair; multicolored stencil on black; Connecticut, mid-19th century; $135-200.
Left: Rod-back Windsor side chair; $130-180.
Right: Step-down rod-back Windsor side chair; $225-350.
Both, Maine, early 19th century, pine and maple.

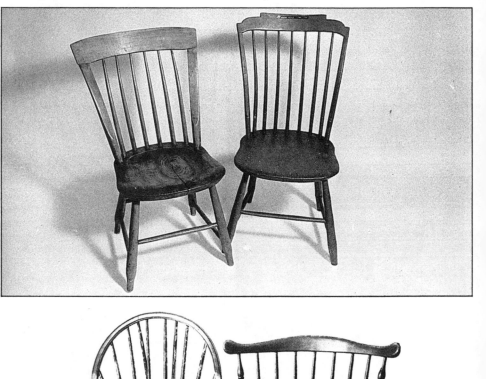

Bow-back Widsor side chair, pine and maple; New Hampshire, ca. 1830; $300-500.

Two New England, Windsors, both in ash and maple, early 19th century.
Left: Brace-back bow armchair; old black paint; late 18th century; $1,900-2,800. **Right:** Fan-back side chair, black paint; $1,000-1,500.

Left: Modified birdcage Windsor, bamboo turned, black and gold paint; New England, 19th century; $225-350.
Right: Late Windsor-style kitchen chair, pine and maple; Maine, ca. 1900; $25-40.

Carved Victorian side chair, rosewood, New York, ca. 1850; $175-350. A good example of an early Victorian chair.

One of a set of side chairs in the Victorian mode, oak; Boston, Mass., early 20th century; $70-90.

Left: Late Windsor-style rod-back kitchen chair; pine and hickory, white paint; $25-35. **Right:** Empire-style side chair, walnut, cane seat; $55-75. Both, New England, 19th century.

Two late Victorian factory-made side chairs, hickory and ash; New York, early 20th century. **Left:** $40-60.
Right: With stamped decoration, so-called press-back; $70-100.

Chippendale wing chair, mahogany;
Massachusetts, late 18th century;
$3,500-9,000.

Hand-carved armchair, oak; Maine, 19th
century; $275-450. An extremely crude
piece of the sort made from 1630 to
1930.

Hepplewhite wing chair, mahogany, New
England, ca. 1800; $2,500-6,000.

Lyre-back Sheraton armchair, paint and
inlay on maple, New England, ca. 1810;
$1,500-2,000.

Firehouse Windsor armchair, pine and
hickory, light blue over old dark blue
paint, New England, late 19th century;
$75-125.

Victorian wing chair, rosewood; New York, 1840--65; $500-750. The most sought-after examples in this genre are by Belter of New York City.

Wicker armchair; Midwest, late 19th century; $275-280.

Wicker armchair, white paint; Midwest, early 20th century; $175-250.

Folding chair, birch and hickory; New England, mid-19th century; $275-400. An unusual prototype of the modern folding chair.

Ladder-back rocker, maple; New England, early 19th century; $325-475. Good arms and four slats make this a desireable specimen.

Spanish-foot country Chippendale chair converted to rocker, pine and maple; Maine, 18th century; $200-275. Conversion to a rocker greatly reduces the value of any piece.

Ladder-back rocker, old black paint; Maine, mid-19th century; $175-225.

Left: Child's ladder-back rocker, ash and maple, old black paint; $150-225. **Right:** Full-size ladder-back rocker, hickory and maple; $100-135. Both Massachusetts, first quarter 19th century.

Rod-back Windsor rocker, pine and maple; New England, ca. 1840; $225-425.

Victorian overstuffed rocker, rosewood, New York, ca. 1860; $350-550.

Comb-back Windsor rocker, pine and maple; New Hampshire, ca. 1820; $450-575. A stylish example of a popular and hard-to-find rocker.

Boston rocker, pine and maple; New England, ca. 1860; $80-120. Lack of decoration accounts for the lower price.

Stencil-decorated Boston rocker, pine and maple; Massachusetts, ca. 1840; $280-350. A style that has been widely reproduced.

Thumb-back Windsor rocker with a potty hole, pine and birch, old black paint; New York, mid-19th century; $100-160.

63

Victorian caned rocker, birch; New Jersey, late 19th century; $165-210.

Two press-back rockers, pine and ash; New York, early 20th century. **Left:** $165-195. **Right:** $75-110. Good investments in the rocker field.

Firehouse Windsor rocker, pine and hickory, old green paint; New York, late 19th century; $110-150.

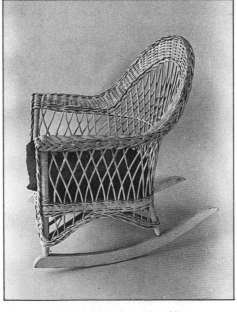

Wicker rocker, white paint; New York, early 20th century; $150-230.

Victorian swivel-base desk chair, cane and oak; East, early 20th century; $275-350.

Child's armchair, pine and maple, old red paint; Maine, 18th century; $165-245.

Early infant's potty chair, pine, green paint; Pennsylvania, 18th century; $225-350. Potty chairs always sell at prices well below comparable examples with solid seats.

Late Windsor-style child's armchair, pine and hickory, black paint with gold trim; New York, ca. 1850; $120-180.

Windsor-style potty chair, pine and maple, old green paint with gold striping; Maine, ca. 1860; $85-110.

Infant's high chair, pine and maple, old red paint, New England, late 18th century; $400-600.

Windsor-style infant's high chair, pine and hickory, old black paint; Pennsylvania, mid-19th century; $275-400.

Child's rocking chair, wicker, yellow paint, New England, late 19th century; $325-475.

Windsor-style settee, pine and birch, old yellow paint; Massachusetts, ca. 1870; $450-600. Benches of this sort were made throughout New England for use in churches and public halls.

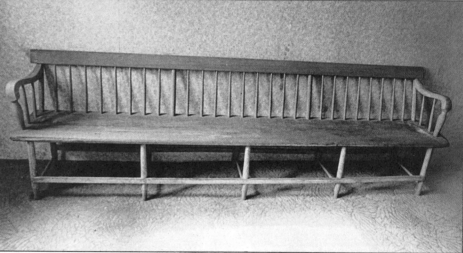

Hepplewhite sofa, mahogany; Connecticut, ca. 1800; $1,100-1,350.

Sheraton sofa, mahogany; New England, ca. 1810; $4,000-5,500.

Sheraton sofa, mahogany; New York, ca. 1800; $3,000-4,500.

Victorian fainting couch, rosewood and pine; Massachusetts, ca. 1880; $150-275.

Wicker fainting couch, white paint; Midwest, early 20th century; $350-550.

Empire sofa, the so-called Grecian couch, walnut; ca. 1820; $900-1,500. Much less common than the full-backed version.

Scallop-back wicker sofa, white paint; Midwest, early 20th century; $500-750.

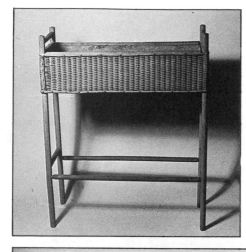

Wicker planter; Midwestern, ca. 1900;
$75-150.

Wicker settee; New York, ca. 1920;
$350-450.

Turnip-foot tavern table, walnut and
pine; Rhode Island, late 17th century;
$2,700-3,500.

Early tilt-top table, pine and ash; Maine,
18th century; $1,500-2,200.

Tavern table, pine, scalloped corners and
green paint; Maine, 18th century;
$1,200-1,600.

Tap or tavern table, pine; New York, early 19th century; $700-1,100.

Side table, breadboard top, pine, old red paint; New England, early 19th century; $600-850.

Side table, pine, grain-painted in brown; New England, mid-19th century; $300-450.

Swing-leg tavern or tea table, pine, traces of old red paint; New York, 18th century; $900-1,500.

Queen Anne tilt-top table, mahogany; New England, 18th century; $1,700-2,700.

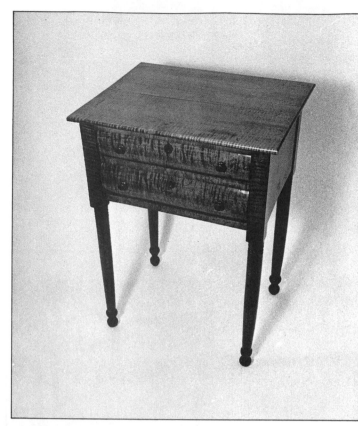

Shearton-style two-drawer side table,
tiger maple, New Hampshire, ca. 1810;
$800-1,200. Tiger-maple grain adds
value to any piece of furniture.

Sheraton-style single-drawer side table,
pine; Maine, ca. 1820; $350-475.

Empire-style two-drawer Pembroke
table, cherry and pine; New York, ca
1840; $150-225.

Victorian spool-turned side table, pine;
Massachusetts, late 19th century; $125-
175.

Harvest table, pine, old blue and white paint, light brown top; Maine, ca. 1860; $850-1,200.

Sawbuck table, pine, base in old blue paint; Maine, early 19th century; $900-1,500.

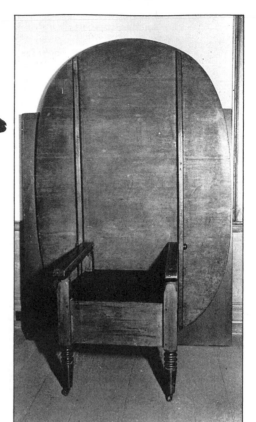

Sheraton-style chair table, walnut; Pennsylvania, ca. 1800; $2,000-3,500.

Queen Anne drop-leaf table, tirfid-foot, walnut, New England, mid-20th century; $3,500-4,500.

Queen Anne-style drop-leaf table, mahogany; Massachusetts, 18th century; $2,750-3,750.

Hepplewhite two-part dining table, mahogany; New England, ca. 1800; $5,000-7,500. An extremely fine example of a rare piece.

Country Hepplewhite Pembroke table, cherry with apple top, traces of old gray paint; Maine, ca. 1820; $270-500.

Country Hepplewhite drop-leaf dining table, cherry, New Hampshire, ca. 1810; $550-750.

Sheraton drop-leaf dining table, mahogany; Maine, ca. 1820; $900-1,500.

Square-base drop-leaf table, pine and pample; Vermont, early 19th century; $400-550.

Empire pedestal-base dining table, mahogany; Massachusetts, ca. 1820; $400-600. Empire tables continue to be undervalued.

Victorian pedestal-base dining table, oak; East, late 19th century; $500-700. A very popular type today.

Empire drop-leaf dining table, walnut, New Jersey, ca. 1840; $250-400.

73

Chippendale-Hepplewhite transitional candelstand, mahogany inlaid with white wood; Massachusetts, ca. 1790; $1,750-2,750.

Shaker lamp table, pine and maple, old red paint; New Hampshire, first half 19th century; $3,000-4,500. An otherwise prosaic piece of furniture turns to gold when identified as Shaker.

Spider-leg candlestand, mahogany; Maine, early 19th century; $650-900.

Spider-leg tilt-top candlestand, cherry; Massachusetts, late 18th century; $900-1,500.

Hepplewhite snake-foot candlestand, pine, base in black paint and rural scene in oils on top; Maine, ca. 1810; $2,200-3,000. A fine example of country decoration.

Large tilt-top tea table, maple; New Hampshire, late 18th century; $1,000-2,000.

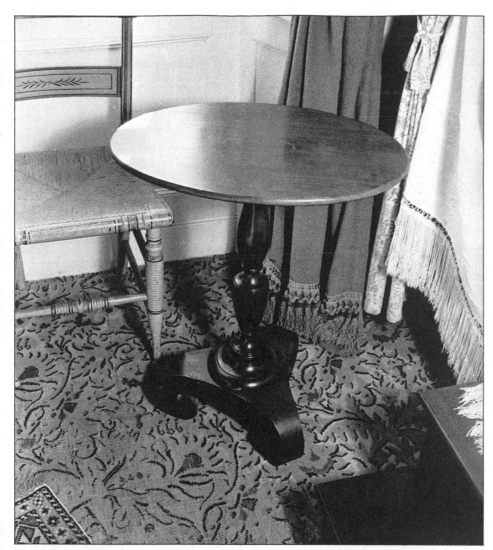

Empire candlestand, mahogany; New England, ca. 1830; $200-300.

Victorian candlestand, walnut; Midwest, ca. 1860; $150-200.

Ottoman or foot rest walnut; Grand Rapids, Mich., ca. 1880; $100-140. Pieces of this sort were very popular in the late Victorian period.

Hepplewhite spade-foot games table, maple with burl maple veneer; New England, ca. 1800; $3,500-6,000.

Antique Furniture: Chests and Other Pieces

Case Furniture

Case furniture refers to furniture that encloses a space, from an early meaning of the word *case,* a "chest." Included in the term are chests, bureaus, highboys and lowboys, desks, trunks, and cupboards. The term is used to distinguish these usually solid pieces from the group known as *stick furniture,* in which relatively slender vertical members—that is, legs—form an important part of the construction. Tables, chairs, and all other seating pieces may be called stick furniture.

The earliest American case pieces are chests that date well back into the seventeenth century. Stout of proportion and sturdy of build, they are made of oak as the base wood, with carving and applied decorative devices worked in a contrasting wood such as maple. Like the earliest American chairs, they resemble their more numerous European cousins, so if you are going to spend the money on a representative example, the transaction should be carried out with a dealer who can guarantee the local origin of his pieces.

Also like the early Pilgrim chairs, seventeenth-century case pieces rarely come on the market anymore. It's much easier—and cheaper—to buy a fine old six-board chest, a simple form that takes its name from the number of pieces of wood that compose it: one board for each of the four sides, and one each for the top and bottom. Such chests were made from 1700 on and may be found in plain pine or walnut or decorated in a variety of ways, including painted-on graining, often in red and black or yellow and brown. The choicest decoration is seen on the so-called dower chests from Pennsylvania, Virginia, and New Jersey, which often show hand-painted names, dates, and decorative motifs such as flowers and human figures. These may sell for thousands of dollars. Note that repainted or newly painted dower chests are appearing on the market. Most are so poorly done as to fool no one, but watch for those telltale signs that indicate the authenticity of an old piece: spidered or chipped paint, worn spots at points of contact, and early hardware.

Chests were usually nailed or dovetailed together, and hardware and construction methods give important clues to age. The earliest specimens —those made before 1800—will often have snipe hinges (interlocking hairpin-shaped pieces of wrought iron) and will be constructed with crude hand-shaped nails. Most pieces made after 1830 will contain square-headed cut nails and wrought-iron butt hinges. Screws will be hand-finished, with off-center slots and flat points. The presence of wire nails or modern screws and steel hinges indicates that the chest either has been repaired or is of an extremely late date.

Traveling chests—the predecessors of the steamer trunk—are found in many different forms. Some were covered with cowhide and studded with brass nails. They may be as large as a full-sized chest or as tiny as a cashbox. Smaller examples are sometimes extremely attractive, and all but the painted Pennsylvania and New England examples are greatly undervalued. Nineteenth-century travelers, particularly in the years after the Civil War, also carried pressed-tin and wood trunks, and these have recently become desirable. They may have flat or domed tops, frequently with attractive lithographs pasted inside their lids. Tin trunks may still be found for as little as ten dollars at country sales and auctions.

Cupboards, both standing and wall varieties, evolved from chests. They are popular functional pieces of antique furniture and command a good price. Originally, they were usually built into the walls of a house, so that many were destroyed or drastically altered after removal. Their most common woods were pine, poplar, or cherry, and they were almost always painted; but since that paint has often disappeared—either through wear or by some well-intentioned but ill-informed owner—those pieces that still possess a good original finish command premium prices. As with chests, the age of a cupboard can be determined by nails, construction, and hinges. Backboards were left unfinished, so that the original saw marks can be seen. These saw marks are another clue to age; straight saw cuts indicate a date before 1840, since the circular mill saw was not widely introduced before that time. Drawers should have a few big dovetails rather than the numerous uniform small ones evident in factory furniture, made after 1880.

Highboys are really an early and sophisticated type of cupboard. There are few of them available; indeed, few of them were made, for most colonists could not afford such an expensive luxury. Country-style examples are even less common than those made by city cabinetmakers. Lowboys too are costly and hard to come by, but in their later form as the bureau or chest of drawers, they are more familiar. Empire and Victorian bureaus with their lavish oak and walnut decoration and fine beveled mirrors are an excellent buy. They are still plentiful and reasonably priced and will appreciate in value, something one can't expect from their modern counterparts. A particularly good buy at present is Victorian cottage furniture—inexpensive, factory-made pieces with hand-painted decoration; they were originally used in middle- and working-class homes (hence the name *cottage*) and have a "folk" quality that goes well with modern furnishings.

The earliest desk was a mere box with a slant top, often intended simply to hold the family Bible. The form survived well into the nineteenth century, but long before that, someone had thought to put a frame or set of legs on the box and thus create the desk as we know it. A few William and Mary specimens may be found, but the earliest common types date to the Queen Anne and Chippendale eras. Any halfway decent desk of this age commands a price above a thousand dollars, but country examples such as the schoolmaster's desk are much more reasonable. These were generally made in pine and may be decorated by graining. High-style Empire and Victorian desks were much more lavish as well as considerably larger; and one type, the Wooton desk, which was custom-made for offices and countinghouses, contains literally dozens of drawers. The few Wootons on the market today sell for as much as a pre-1800 desk.

Beds

Beds did not appear to any extent before the Queen Anne period and were rare until the Federal era. Empire beds are big and cumbersome and most Victorian examples are extremely lavish except for two types, the brass and the spool-turned. Brass and brass-trimmed iron beds are extremely popular today and command a high price. They look well in the modern bedroom, but one should be aware that a large number of similar examples is being manufactured today. At present, though, these are themselves so expensive as to make it highly unlikely that they would be represented as antique.

Spool-turned furniture appeared after the Civil War and lingered on past 1900. Beds in this style may be found in pine, walnut, or maple. They are inexpensive and attractive, particularly the single beds, which may be used as couches. They may often be obtained at country sales and auctions for no more than twenty dollars.

Mirrors, Frames, Shelves, and Racks

Mirrors were rare in early American homes. Aside from the puritanical injunction against vanity, glass was expensive and was reserved for a more crucial use in windows. Until the 1750s, most people who wanted to look at themselves had to be content with a peek into the water bucket. Queen Anne, Chippendale, and Federal mirrors were reserved for the rich and

hence are elaborate and costly. More accessible to the average pocketbook is the extremely attractive walnut-veneer ogee mirror of the Empire period. Its simple lines blend well with twentieth-century decor, and its low cost causes this mirror to appear often in shops and homes. Victorian mirrors, on the other hand, are factory-made and rather plain, and the demand for all things Victorian makes them carry higher prices than they would otherwise merit.

Anyone who has purchased a modern picture frame knows how exorbitant the price of glass has become. If you have pictures to frame, look for old frames. Antiques dealers stock large quantities, usually with the original glass, for a fraction of what one would pay for a cheaply designed modern counterpart. Nineteenth-century frames, particularly from the Victorian period, were made in an enchanting array of styles; many are absolutely unique, being the handmade product of the well-bred lady's idle moments. They are fun to own and are all reasonably priced. Look especially for

the folk art frames, those constructed of the unusual materials the Victorians so delighted in—shells, pinecones, birch bark, or (from a later period) even popsicle sticks.

Wall shelves and racks are also a good buy. Shelves in various forms appeared early, and some, such as the eighteenth-century pipe racks of New England and Pennsylvania, are extremely expensive. Watch out for later reproductions of these treasures. The fakes are usually put together with modern wire nails or brads and show neither the right patina nor signs of wear an old piece should have.

Victorian wall shelves come in various forms and woods. Walnut is popular, and pine may be stained to imitate it or may be painted in a variety of fanciful colors. Some of these racks are expandable. Others may be cut with a jigsaw to produce decorative patterns, such as Masonic symbols or patriotic motifs. Hall racks for coats and hats are also common, and some may be massive, multipurpose pieces frequently incorporating a marble-topped table and brass or bronze fittings.

Chippendale chest of drawers, mahogany and flame mahogany veneer. Massachusetts, ca. 1780; $6,500-9,500.

Framed low chest, pine and oak, old red paint; New England, early 18th century; $850-1,000.

Pilgrim chest, oak and maple; New England, late 17th century; $10,000-12,000. An example of the earliest American chests.

Footed six-board chest, pine, red, and yellow graining. Pennsylvania, mid-19th century; $550-800.

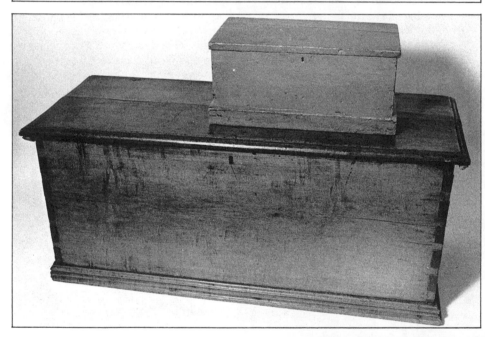

Top: Small chest, pine, old mustard paint; Connecticut, mid-19th century; $75-125. **Bottom:** Six-board chest, maple, snipe hinges and traces of old red paint; New York, late 18-early 19th century; $450-600. Six board chests in maple are rare.

Blanket chest, pine, old red paint; Vermont, early 19th century; $650-900.

Hepplewhite swell-front chest of drawers, mahogany; New Hampshire, ca. 1800; $4,000-6,500.

Empire chest of drawers, mahogany; New England, ca. 1830; $600-800. A fine chest subject to the general prejudice against Empire; hence the relatively lower price.

Sheraton bow-front chest of drawers, mahogany; Massachusetts, ca. 1810; $3,00-4,500.

Well-decorated Victorian chest of drawers, grain-painted pine; Rhode Island, ca. 1890; $300-400.

Victorian cottage burean, pine, blue, white, and red, hand decorated on blue and gray ground; Midwest, late 19th century; $350-425.

Queen Anne chest on chest, maple, old black paint; New Hampshire, ca. 1760; $10,000-15,000.

Victorian-style bureau, oak and pine, old brown paint; New England, late 19th century; $350-450.

Hepplewhite high chest of drawers, flame mahogany; Connecticut, ca. 1800; $4,500-6,000.

Above: Single-door paneled cupboard, pine and maple; New York, early 19th century; $2,200-2,800. **On cupboard :** Small painted dome-top chest; Pennsylvania, ca. 1860; $325-450.

Right: Unusual fish sizer, wood; Great Lakes area, early 20th century; $750-1,200.
Double-drawer blanket chest, red and yellow grain painting; Pennsylvania, mid-19th century; $3,500-5,000. A fine example of painted furniture. **Pages 130-131 :** Rod-back kitchen chair, old green and red paint; East, early 20th century; $35-65. Coal and wood stove, "porcelain" over iron; East, early 20th century; $600-900. **On stove:** Banded yellowware bowl; Ohio, early 20th century; $45-75.

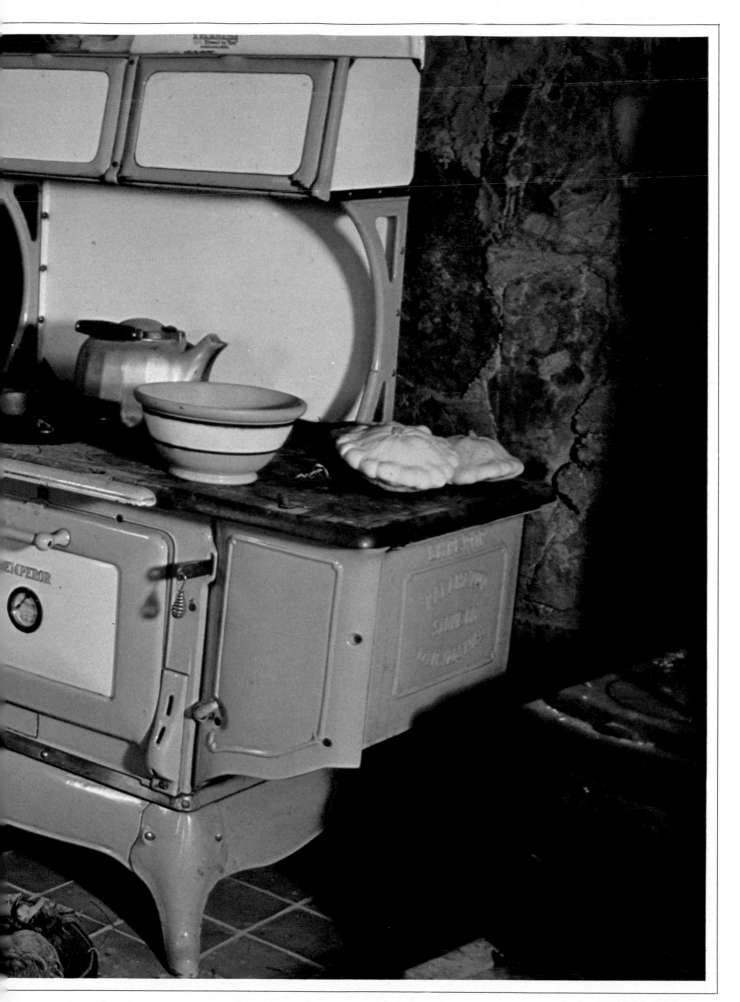

Opposite top: Victorian rocker, hickory and oak; Midwest, late 19th century; $165-225. Bed, brass and iron; East, late 19th century; $350-525. Sheraton-style candle table, pine and ash; New York, ca. 1835; $235-300. **Opposite Bottom:** Four-slat ladder-back armchair, maple and pine; Pennsylvania; $225-300. Four-door pine cupboard; New England; $1,500-2,750. Both mid-19th century; good country pieces. **Above :** [UF6]On wall: [UF4]High-quality hooked rug, wool on burlap; 19th century; $2.200-3,000. Table, walnut; New England, 18th century; $1,600-2,300. **On table:** Two pieces of Connecticut toleware, mid-19th century. Coffeepot; $1,100-1,450. Deed box; $900-1.400. **Above right:** Corner cupboard, pine and poplar; Pennsylvania, ca. 1840; $1,000-1,800.

Opposite: Left to right: Model of Amish buggy; Pennsylvania, 1910-20; $650-950.
Weathervane; 1900-10; $600-750. Queen Anne corner chair; New England, 1760-70; $3,500-5,000.

Left: Decoy, early 20th century; $250-400. Federal Bench in original paint; New England, 1810-25; $2,000-2,600. **Above, on wall:** Geometric quilt; Pennsylvania, 1900-10; $800-1,200. **Below:** Harvest table, pine and maple, 12' long, Pennsylvania, mid-19th century; $900-1,200. A variety of country chairs, pine and hardwood, some with splint seats; $75-225 each, depending on condition.

Page 136: Tin-paneled pie safe, old salmon paint, New Jersey-Pennsylvania, mid-19th century; $750-1,000. **Above it:** A variety of wood and earthenware bowls; second half 19th century; $75-175.

William and Mary highboy, walnut and walnut veneer; Rhode Island, late 17th-early 18th century; $35,000-50,000.

Hepplewhite sideboard, mahogany; Massachusetts, ca. 1800; $9,500-14,000. All sideboards are rare enough to command a good price.

Queen Anne highboy, maple; New Hampshire, late 18th century; $12,000-19,000.

William and Mary chest on frame, oak, original red and black paint; Massachusetts, late 17th century; $25,000-35,000.

Early Empiree sideboard, mahogany; New York, ca. 1820; $1,500-1,750. A well-done transitional piece with traces of Sheraton.

Hepplewhite washstand, pine;
Massachusetts, ca. 1800, $900-1,200

Queen Anne bonnet-top highboy, maple,
New England, ca. 1770;
$25,000-35,000.

Sheraton washstand, pine and maple;
New Hampshire, early 19th century;
$900-1,200.

Queen Anne Dutch-foot lowboy, maple;
Connecticut, ca. 1760; $15,000-25,000.

Empire washstand, walnut and walnut
veneer; New England, ca. 1840;
$250-450.

Hanging cupboard, oak; New England, late 17th century; $4,500-6,000.

Victorian commode, oak and oak veneer; Midwest, late 19th century; $275-375. Factory made but increasing in popularity.

Victorian cottage commode, pine, blue, red, and white design on blue and gray ground; Midwest, late 19th century; $300-450.

Small corner cupboard, pine; New England, ca. 1870; $275-350.

Hanging cupboard, pine, grained finish; Maine, mid-19th century; $450-550.

Victorian commode, oak; late 19th century; $150-225. Another good buy in early midwestern factory furniture.

Standing cupboard, pine; New York, early 19th century; $400-600.

Cupboard, pine; New England, early 19th century; $550-700. Probably originally built-in piece.

Large cupboard (7' tall), pine; Midwest, mid-19th century; $700-900.

Open-top cupboard, poplar and pine; Pennsylvania, ca. 1850; $1,200-1,600.

Cupboard, blue and white paint; New York, ca. 1860; $3,000-3,500.

Small painted chest, pine; Pennsylvania, ca. 1820; $650-900. A dome-top lady's chest with excellent decoration.

Circular traveling case, cowhide, with brass studs; New England, ca. 1840; $150-250.

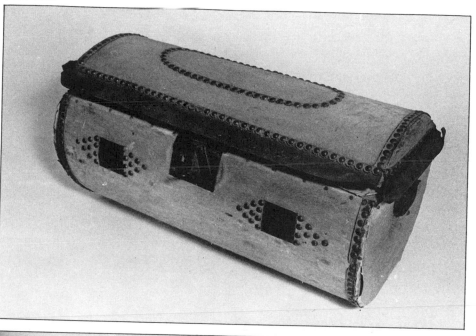

Document box, cowhide with brass studs; New York, mid-19th century; $135-185.

Victorian dome-top traveling chest, painted tin and wood; Maine, late 19th century; $100-150.

Child's chest, wood and lithographed paper; New England, late 19th century; $110-140.

Empire spice chest, walnut and walnut veneer; Massachusetts, ca. 1840; $400-600.

Federal cellarette, mahogany; New England, early 19th century; $1,000-1,500.

Tabletop or lap desk, pine; Maine,
mid-19th century; $125-175.

Schoolmaster's desk, pine with black on
brown graining, New England, mid-19th
century; $550-750.

Schoolmaster's desk, pine and maple
with traces of old red paint; New York,
ca. 1870; $350-475.

Chippendale fall-front desk, mahogany;
New Hampshire, ca. 1790; $6,500-9,000.

Sheraton lady's desk, mahogany; New England, ca. 1810; $2,500-3,500.

Federal fall-front desk, mahogany; New England, ca. 1800; $3,500-5,000. A transitional piece with a simple interior.

Spool-turned desk, pine; Vermont, late 19th century; $150-200.

Victorian roll-top office desk, golden oak; Boston, Mass.; early 20th century; $1,500-2,100.

Sheraton canopy bed, mahogany;
Massachusetts, ca. 1800; $6,000-8,500.

Early Empire carved bed, walnut; Maine,
dated 1818; $2,500-3,500.

Left: Late Federal-early-Empire
transitional bed, mahogany and pine;
Maine, ca. 1820; $3,000-5,750.
On bed is a wooden bed key used to
tighten ropes that support the mattress;
ca. 1820; $20-35. **Right:** Trundle bed,
pine; Maine, ca. 1820; $375-500.

Victorian spool bed, old red paint;
Massachusetts, ca. 1870; $350-400.

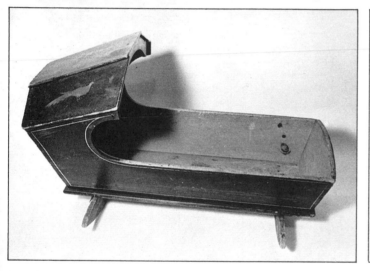

Hooded cradle, pine, stencil decoration
on blue, pale blue interior; New England,
ca. 1840; $650-900.

Hooded cradle, pine; Maine, mid-19th
century; $150-275.

Queen Anne child's playpen with split
spindle siding, pine; Maine, late 18th
century; $550-850. A rare piece.

Chippendale mirror, walnut; New England, late 18th century; $300-950.

Sheraton girandole mirror, gilded pine; New England, ca. 1800; $1,500-2,500.

Sheraton-Empire transitional mirror, pine, black paint and gilding with reverse glass painting; New York, ca. 1830; $250-450.

Empire ogee-frame mirror, walnut veneer on pine; Connecticut, mid-19th century; $85-125. An example of an inexpensive and attractive mirror that is readily available.

Victorian decorative frame, pine cones on pine; South, late 19th century; $35-75.

Ogee-frame mirror, walnut; New England, mid-19th century; $75-100.

Victorian wall mirror in Sheraton style with oil painting of lighthouse possibly replacing an earlier reverse-glass painting; $300-400.

Factory-made wall mirror, pine with silver paint and decorative lithographs; Midwest, early 20th century; $35-60.

Victorian saw-cut wall shelves, walnut; Midwest; late 19th century; $75-150.

Hanging shelves, oak; New York, late 19th century; $100-150.

Wall magazine rack; pine; Midwest, early 20th century; $45-75.

Victorian coat rack, bronze and walnut; New England, late 19th century; $75-140.

Collectible Furniture

People who collect American furniture manufactured during the past century are presented with a bewildering variety from which to choose. They are confronted with furniture styles that range from the myriad styles of the Victorian period to the "Danish modern" that is still popular in many contemporary homes. They encounter a great deal of factory-made furniture as well as a great deal of furniture that was made—wholly or in considerable part—by hand. They are overwhelmed with golden oak, but soon discover that there is abundant furniture available made from other woods, such as pine, mahogany, rosewood, and walnut. They also find furniture made from other materials, such as plywood and tubular steel. It is a field of infinite variety and opportunity.

To start at the beginning, we must turn to the furnishings of the late nineteenth century. By the time of the 1876 centennial, American furniture was so different—in both design and method of construction—from the furniture that had preceded it that the public could easily accept the earlier pieces, which included Federal- and Chippendale-style furniture, as mementos of an almost forgotten past. And this was the furniture that their grandparents had used—and in some cases were still using! To understand how so great a change could come about in so short a period of time, one needs to know something of the factory system and its development in the United States.

Until about 1840, most American furniture was made by hand: it was put together by craftsmen who through long apprenticeship had learned how to make a piece from start to finish, from planing down the rough wood to applying the final paint or varnish. During the late Empire period—a period of massive and somewhat overdone furniture—small furniture-making factories began to appear, and the men who worked in these small factories had rather specialized duties. One would turn legs on a lathe, another would carve moldings, yet another would paint. Pieces would thus be put together not by a single cabinetmaker but through the joint efforts of several workers.

The exigencies of the Civil War greatly accelerated the process of job diversification. In support of the war effort, great factories sprang up throughout the northern United States, and the first production lines made their appearance, with each employee performing only a small part of the total task. After the war, as the territories were opened to settlement, the pioneers moving west needed large quantities of furniture. In the past, such needs had been filled by small shops located in the developing areas, but the new methods of construction had changed all that. Huge furniture factories were built in Grand Rapids, Michigan, and other midwestern cities, and thousands of pieces of inexpensive, machine-cut and production-line-assembled furniture poured out to fill the need. Quickly made and inexpensively sold, much of this furniture was not well constructed, and "Grand Rapids" became a synonym for cheap and shoddy.

However, it is possible that those early critics—many of whom were still accustomed to hand-crafted furnishings—judged too harshly. Today's collectors have discovered that late-nineteenth-century furniture was, for the most part, better made than the furniture that we have available today. Moreover, the nineteenth-century householder was offered a remarkable variety of furnishings. The Victorian era was eclectic: rather than adhering to a single clearly defined style, such as Queen Anne or Empire, designers used elements of many different styles in combination. Names such as Renaissance Revival, Gothic, and Egyptian Revival were used in an effort to create the illusion of unifying styles, but such really did not exist. Most pieces of Victorian furniture show the influence of several earlier styles. Sometimes, though not always, the result is pleasing.

Inevitably, there was a reaction to such over-elaboration. By the end of the century, one form and one wood came to predominate. In England,

Art Deco dining room table and set
of six chairs in laminated walnut;
1930-40; $4,000-6,500 the set.

as early as the 1860s, the poet and designer William Morris (1834 to 1896) preached the virtues of simple oak furniture designed on the order of ancient Gothic pieces—with the joinings and construction clearly exposed (something the Victorian cabinetmakers had always tried to avoid). But Morris was before his time, and it was not until the 1880s that the public came to accept his ideas. The result was a type of plain, rectilinear furniture that is often called Mission Oak because of a fancied resemblance to the furnishings made in the early Spanish missions of the American West.

From the 1880s on into the 1920s and even 1930s, vast quantities of oak household and office furniture were manufactured throughout the United States. Some of this was in the Mission style, and some was in the so-called Eastlake style, a slightly more decorative and curvilinear mode patterned on the designs of Charles Lock Eastlake (1836 to 1906), whose book *Hints on Household Taste* had a great influence on many American homemakers.

However, the greatest American exponent of oak furniture was Gustav Stickley (1857 to 1942). Born on a midwestern farm, Stickley was trained as a chairmaker and later established a furniture factory in Syracuse, New York. The lines of his furniture, which was almost totally without decoration, were extremely severe. Moreover, his furniture violated Victorian tenets in an even more fundamental way—it was almost entirely hand-made!

Though they displayed some elements of the Mission style as well as certain features found in American colonial furniture, Stickley's pieces were distinctly his own. Angular and solid, made from oak, beech, or elm, they, in Stickley's words, had "strong, straight lines and plain surfaces to . . . emphasize the natural character that belonged to the growing tree."

From 1901 until 1916 Stickley produced chairs, tables, and case furniture, such as desks and chests of drawers, intended for sale to families of modest means. Most of these pieces were originally marked or labeled. He also designed simple, functional homes in which his furnishings might be used to greatest advantage. Unfortunately, Gustav Stickley's furniture was both too plain and too popular. It was easy to copy, and as soon as it began to sell well, a slew of cabinetmakers, including the Roycrofters of East Aurora, New York, and Stickley's own brothers, began to turn out very similar furnishings. As a conse-

quence, the collector will frequently encounter pieces that look like Stickley but are unmarked or bear some variation of marks such as Cottage, Quaint, Art Craft, Mission, or Craft. None were made by Stickley's shop, but all are now quite collectible.

This competition combined with his own somewhat grandiose schemes (including a magazine-publishing venture and a gargantuan showroom in New York City) led to Stickley's downfall. He went bankrupt in 1915 and died alone and unheralded.

Nor did death put an end to the cruel tricks played by fate on Gustav Stickley. For, today, after being neglected for decades, Stickley furniture is once more the rage. But it is doubtful that the artisans and factory workers for whom it was designed will be able to afford it, for even the smallest and most ordinary examples sell for many hundreds of dollars.

Not all late-nineteenth- and early-twentieth-century furniture makers were as practical and aesthetic as the producers of Mission-style furnishings. The Victorian fondness for the gaudy died hard, and, in some ways, the last years of its existence were its most extreme.

Horn furniture is a good example. The 1880s and 1890s were great years for the sportsman. Buffalo hunters scoured the western plains. Elk, deer, and moose hunters decimated the herds. All these beasts had horns, and in the last decades of the century, furniture makers such as Charles Fletcher decided to make use of them. They made horn chairs (often with woven rawhide seats), desks, tables, hat and coat racks, even horn chandeliers. The horn of the longhorn cow was the one most frequently employed, though it was often combined with other types.

Originally used primarily in hunting lodges, country homes, and men's clubs, today horn furniture is considered a suitable embellishment to the dining or living room. It is not too common, however, and prices for the larger pieces have been growing steadily.

Horn was not the only unusual material used. Hunting lodges were also frequently furnished with rustic furniture made from branches and twigs of trees nailed or bound together without removing the bark. These rather crude pieces were known in upper New York State as Adirondack furniture, but similar examples (some with painted decoration) were made from 1890 until well into the 1930s throughout the forested areas of the northern United States. Though tables and chairs are most common, large wardrobes, chests of drawers, and even desks are known.

Rustic furniture, too, has undergone a revival. Not only are older specimens being collected and refurbished, but new pieces are being made. Newer examples can be distinguished from the originals by the lack of wear and aging in the wood.

Another form of rustic furniture was made of iron, cast and bolted together. Appropriately enough, the iron was often cast to resemble the rough surface of tree bark. Such furnishings were primarily a product of the late nineteenth century, and most were intended for use in the garden or on the sun porch. Chairs and settees are most common, though a few small tables can be found. Weight greatly limited the size and variety of this furniture.

On a more sophisticated level is the work of Michael Thonet (1796 to 1871) and his successors. Thonet, an Austrian, designed a variety of furnishings made from hardwood rods shaped under pressure. His pieces, which have a distinctly modern look, have long been called bentwood. Though other pieces were made, the technique lends itself particularly well to the forming of tables and chairs, including rockers. The flowing lines of these pieces owe much to the Art Nouveau style prevalent when Thonet was active.

Thonet's business prospered to such an extent that he opened overseas offices and shipped his furniture (which could be disassembled for transportation) throughout the world. Following expiration of the original design patent, bentwood was made by many different manufacturers, but for collectors the most desired examples are those bearing the mark of Michael Thonet.

Wicker is another furniture type that has persisted into the modern era. Made of wicker or rattan cane woven over a framework of wood or, later, bamboo, such furnishings were originally intended for use on the lawn or porch, but by the 1920s they had become popular living room and dining room furniture as well. Chairs, small tables, and sofas are the most frequently found examples, but cradles, planters, bookshelves, bedsteads, and desks are also available.

Although it looks fragile, wicker is strong, pliable, and quite weather resistant. Victorian examples can be distinguished by the narrower wicker employed as well as by the elaborate, curvilinear patterns in which they were woven. Post-1900 pieces tend to be loosely woven, of larger-diameter cane, and square or rectangular in form.

Wicker was at first made entirely by hand, but by the 1890s a certain amount of machine production had been introduced and today wicker furniture is handcrafted only in Asia and Africa. With the introduction of machinery came a simplification in style, so most collectors tend to favor the more elaborate Victorian examples. Recently, though, there has been an increase in interest in 1920s and 1930s wicker as collectors and homemakers discover that it provides a relatively inexpensive and extremely attractive form of furniture.

The early decades of this century brought no fundamental changes in furniture design. The Victorian mode prevailed, and Mission made its modifications, but nothing really new happened until the First World War. When the soldiers returned home after that cataclysmic engagement, they found a truly industrial society awaiting them. Just as after the Civil War, great technological advances had taken place during the war. And for this new society, only industrial design would suffice.

What that meant in the world of furniture soon became evident. Because machine production requires simple forms, furnishings in the 1920s became abstract in design rather than being based on natural forms. Decoration, too—where it existed—was simplified. The major sources of inspiration became the arts, where cubism prevailed, and the crafts, where the German Bauhaus school was preaching the doctrine of less is more.

Steel, the symbol of the new industrial age, played a major role. The Frenchman Marcel Bruer, inspired by the shape of bicycle handlebars, designed the first tubular steel chair, in 1925, and other designers, including the Finn Alvar Aalto, went on to combine the steel with shaped plywood and eventually to use the wood alone, creating flowing, curvilinear furniture.

Art Deco furnishings, whether of wood or metal, are characterized by rounded, industrial shapes and tooled steel accessories. But at the same time that forms were being simplified, modern technology made possible the use of extremely thin veneers, and a great deal of the furniture made during the 1920s and 1930s is finished in such veneers, particularly in the light blond woods so favored at the time.

Interestingly enough there was a countervailing movement. Many people were simply too conservative to accept the new mode. For them, American cabinetmakers offered a continuation of the mass-produced furniture of the early 1900s. This furniture was in the so-called Jacobean manner, with great knobby turnings, elaborate machine-cut moldings, and darkly stained woods. Such furnishings were sturdy—if boring—and like so much early-twentieth-century furniture, they have now been discovered by collectors.

Furniture of the past century offers an increasingly interesting field for the collector. Both in variety and availability it generally surpasses the furniture of earlier American periods. However, certain areas, such as Gustav Stickley furniture, are already overpriced, and the wise investor will buy now.

Oak occasional table with cabriole legs; 1920-25; $130-175.

Child's side chair in turned oak with laminated wood crest rail; 1915-25; $45-65.

Oak collapsible rocker-stroller combination; 1900-10; $225-285. This chair reflects the victorian fondness for furniture that served more than one purpose.

Oak rocker with cane seat and spindle back; 1890-1900; $90-135. The design on the crest of this chair · was created by use of giant pressing machines—hence the name "press back."

Mission-style oak armchair; 1905-10; $850-1,250. The plain lines and exposed construction of this piece are in the best Mission style.

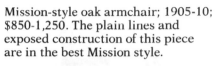

Oak press-back rocker with well-turned spindles; 1900-10; $135-175.

Oak occasional table with curved cabriole legs and paw feet; 1890-1905; $165-235. An example of quality in a common form of table.

Oak commode; ca. 1910; $145-185.
Commodes of this sort were very
common the early 1900s.

Oak library table with pedestal
shortened to serve as a coffee table;
1915-25; $200-275. Collectors are
showing reluctance to buy such
altered pieces.

Oak chest of drawers with marble
top and ceramic inlay; 1910—20;
$375-500. This much decoration is
unusual with oak of this period.

Oak ladies' dressing table; 1910-20;
$300-375. An unusually small size.

Art Nouveau oak shaving stand;
1890-1910; $450-600. Oak in the Art
Nouveau mode is relatively hard to
come by.

Oak file cabinet with writing surface top; 1920-30; $350-420. From 1890 until well into the 1930s, most office furniture was made of oak.

Interior of eleaborate oak armoire; 1920-30; $800-1,200. Shows well-made drawers and shelves. This piece is nearly eight feet tall and seven feet wide.

Oak hanging wall cabinet; 1915-25; $120-160.

Oak double file box; 1930-40; $60-90.

Oak dental cabinet; by Harvard Co.;
Canton, Ohio; 1915-25; $1,200-1,500.
Elaborate pieces of this sort are in
great demand.

Oak desk and bookcase, 1890-1910;
$650-850.

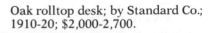

Oak rolltop desk; by Standard Co.;
1910-20; $2,000-2,700.

Oak rolltop desk; 1910-20;
$2,000-2,700. Oak office swivel chair;
1910-20; $85-115. Rolltop desks still
bring good prices.

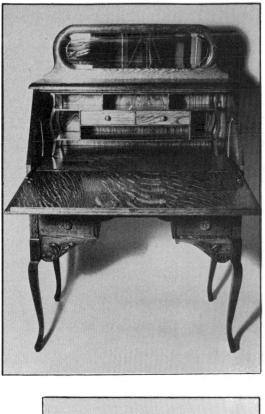

Oak fall-front desk with mirror;
1925-35; $375-500.

Kerosene oil lamp with ceramic
fount and glass shade; 1890-1900;
$300-375.

Art Nouveau table lamp; 1890-1900;
$650-800. This silver figure is an
electrical work of art.

Copper and mica desk lamp; by Dirk
Van Erp; San Francisco. Calif.;
1910-15; $3,500-5,000. Work of a
major arts & crafts designer.

Bronzed pot-metal desk lamp with
slag-glass shade; 1920-30; $225-350.

Cast-iron floor lamp with green-glass inserts and textile shade; 1910-20; $185- 245.

Turned wooden floor lamp with elaborate textile shade; 1925-35; $300-375. These were popular parlor and bedroom lamps.

Pot-metal floor lamp in bronze finish with gold trim; 1920-25; $160-190.

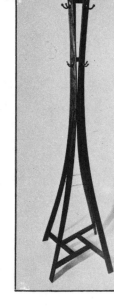

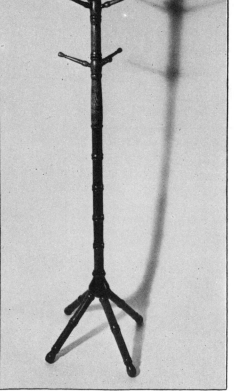

Turned oak coat rack; 1925-35; $55-80.

Mission-style oak coat rack; 1910-20; $85-125.

Oak pedestal-style plant stands; 1890-1910; **Left:** $145-185. **Right:** Mission style; $165-200.

Victorian Gothic oak umbrella stand; 1880-90; $90-130.

Oak revolving bookshelves; 1920-30; $165-225. These Mission-style shelves are relatively uncommon.

Mission-style oak mirror; 1920-30; $115-145.

Oak and cast-iron combination mirror and coat rack; 1890-1900; $165-195.

Left; Miniature oak extension table; 1910-20; $55-75. **Right:** Miniature oak bureau; 1890-1900; $65-95. Both pieces were intended to serve as toys or, possibly, as salesman's samples.

Oak player piano; by Gulbransen-Dickinson Co.; New York, N.Y.; 1900-10; $3,000-4,500.

Minature Empire style pine fainting couch, 1880-1910; $65-95

Eastlake-style oak table; 1900-15; $200-275.

Miniature oak morris chair; 1920-30; $135-195. A salesman's sample in the Mission style.

Eastlake-style child's collapsible walnut rocker; 1880-90; $135-175.

Eastlake-style oak dining table; 1920-30; $650–800. Dining tables remain the most popular of oak furniture.

Oak and leather footstool; by Gustav Stickley; 1905-12; $900-1,200. There are many oak footstools, but few bear the Stickley signature.

Oak and wicker desk lamp; by Gustav Stickley; ca. 1912; $2,750-3,250. The craze for signed Stickley pieces has inflated the price of this uncommon lamp.

Oak plant stand with tile insert top by Grueby Faience Co.; 1901-02; $4,500-6,500. Signed by Gustav Stickley.

Miniature steerhorn armchair with felt upholstery; 1880-1900; $650-850. This rare example is possibly a salesman's sample.

Steerhorn platform rocker with upholstery; 1880-90; $1,000-1,500. Horn furniture is in great demand today among certain collectors.

Elk-horn and leather side chair; 1880-90; $950-1,200.

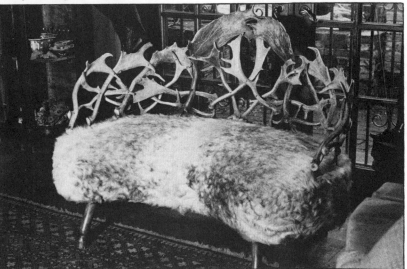

Moose-horn sofa; 1880-1900; $2,800-3,700. Sofas in horn are rare and desriable.

Elk-horn and wood desk; 1885-1900; $2,200-2,700.

114

Deer-horn and carved-wood
magazine rack; 1900-10; $300-450.

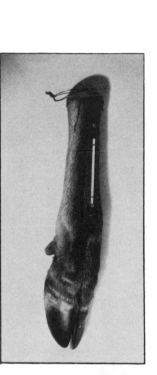

Thermometer mounted on the foot of
an elk; 1915-25; $75-125. Grisly
trophies of this sort were popular
with early-20th century sportsmen.

Wine cooler constructed from an
elephant's foot mounted in wood and
brass; 1900-10; $550-750.

Wooden hat rack or hall tree with
two carved bears; 1900-10;
$2,000-2,600.

Wooden umbrella rack; 1890-1900;
$1,200-1,600.

Library steps, c. 1920; $25-40.

Front: Wooden storage or trinket box decorated with small carved bear; 1910-20; $90-140. **Rear:** Wooden lamp decorated with small carved bears; 1910-20; $175-235.

Cast-iron fish tank; 1890-1900; $550-675. Cast-iron furnishings were extremely popular during the late Victorian period.

Stoneware garden armchair; 1880-85; $500-700. Made in the rustic form so favored by Victorians, cement and pottery garden chairs are relatively uncommon.

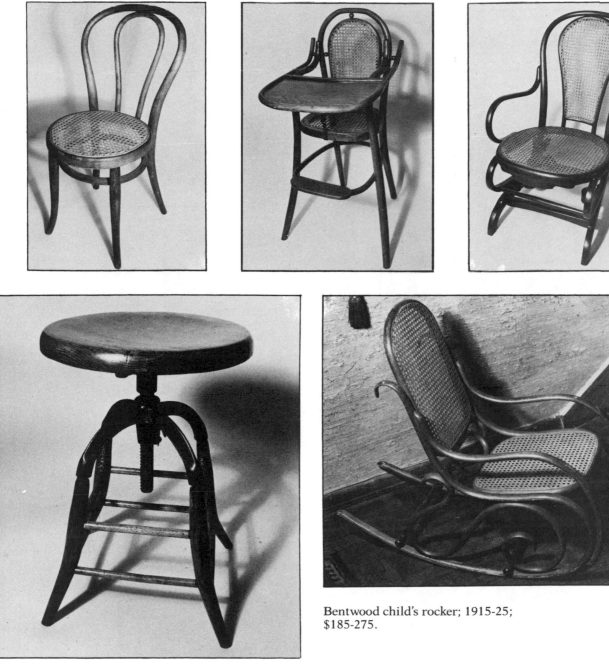

Brentwood chair for a child; 1920-30; $65-95. Developed by Michael Thonet, bentwood has proved so stylish and so practical that it is still in fashion.

Oak bentwood high chair with cane back and seat; 1910-20; $255-325.

Oak and ash bentwood platform rocker with cane seat and back; 1910-25; $275-350. A fine example of the bentwood form.

Oak bentwood piano stool with cast-iron fittings; 1915-25; $55-80.

Bentwood child's rocker; 1915-25; $185-275.

Natural finish wicker armchair with floral pillows; 1930-40; $200-300. This interesting piece has sockets in the arms for glasses and magazines.

White wicker rocker with floral material covering seat; 1920-30; $145-185.

White wicker pedestal table; 1930-40; $135-165

White wicker jardiniere, or planter, on stand; 1910-20; $75-135.

Rattan and wood jardiniere; 1890-1900; $70-110.

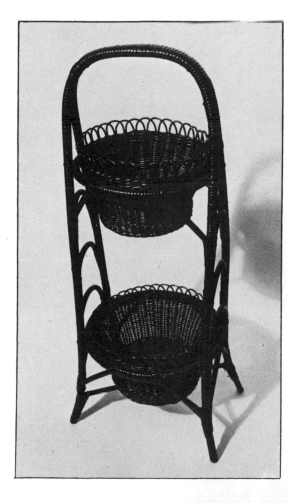

Natural finish wicker double jardiniere; 1890-1900; $120-165.

Rattan and sea grass occasional table; 1920; $70-110. The Art Deco form of this piece contrasts sharply with the material of which it is made.

Rattan and copper wastebasket; by Dirk Van Erp; San Francisco, Calif.; 1910-15; $800-1,200. Very few people can boast of a waste-basket made by a major American designer of the Arts and Crafts school.

Art Deco oak china cabinet; 1930-40; $265-395.

Overstuffed armchair in green baize;
1937-45; $300-450.

Art Deco overstuffed armchair in
blue velour; 1930-40; 250-325

Metal and Naugahyde armchair;
1930-40; $150-225.

Walnut and Naughahyde side chair;
1930-40; $550-700.

Art Deco mahogany side table;
1930-40; $90-120.

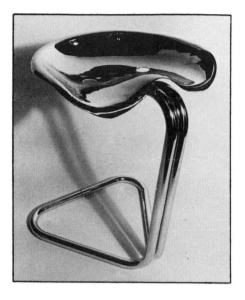

Stainless-steel stool; 1950-60;
$75-115.

Black lacquered end table; 1930-40;
$95-175. **On table at left:** Glass and
black enamel humidor and tray;
1930-40; $65-100. **On table at right:**
Bronzed pot-metal desk lamp;
1930-40; $75-115.

Art Deco walnut veneer end table;
1930-40; $60-90.

Art Deco maple and walnut veneer
dining table; 1925-35; $2,500-3,000.

White table with inset blue-glass top; 1935-45; $75-125. Blue-glass tabletops were very popular during the late Art Deco period.

Art Deco maple veneer sewing table; 1935-45; $65-95.

Bleached mahogany veneer dressing table 1935-45; $445-635.The "waterfall" style popular during the late Art Deco period.

Oak and oak veneer dressing table; 1935-45; $335-420.

Maple veneer kitchen cupboard; 1930-40; $350-475. These so-called Hoosier cupboards are popular in small city kitchens.

Walnut veneer, glass, and chrome bar; 1930-35; $1,200-1,700. Though in great demand, portable bars are rarely found intact.

Art Deco inlaid maple set of drawers; 1925-35; $60-95.

Bird's-eye maple veneer bedside cupboard or nightstand; 1930-40; $100-170.

Art Deco miniature maple veneer chest of drawers; 1930-40; $70-125.

Solid walnut desk; by Morris Adams, Ltd., 1930-40; $900-1,400.

Oak and pine library shelves; 1925-35; $125-165.

Bamboo bar counter; 1940-50; $300-500. Naugahyde and tubular steel bar stools; 1940-50; $90-125 each. **On bar:** Set of cocktail shaker and glasses; 1940-500; $55-80.

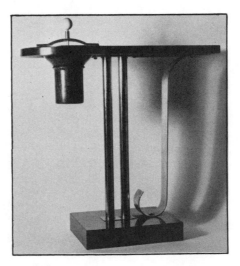

Art Deco wood and metal standing floor ashtray; 1935-40; $75-100.

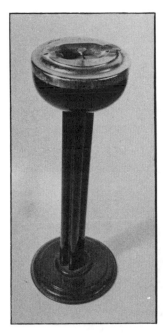

Sheet tin and steel ashtray, painted black; 1940-45; $35-65.

Painted pine standing floor ashtray; 1930-40; $ 55-85.Ashtray stands in the form of popular comic figures such as Jiggs were fixtures of many 1930s living rooms.

Sheet brass and black wood piano lamp; 1930-40; $150-225.

Glazed pottery and frosted glass table lamp; 1945-55; $35-55

Emeralite desk lamp with green-glass shade and bronzed pot-metal base; 1910-20; $270-375. Mass produced for decades, Emeralite lamps are now once again in great demand.

Bronzed pot-metal desk lamp; 1935-45; $75-125.

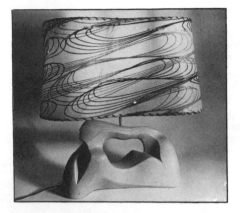

Wooden figural table lamp; by Rima; 1930-40; $230-300.

Tudor-style oak secretary desk with leaded glass doors; 1910-30; $550-650. A style popular with furniture factories.

Queen Anne-style oak dropleaf table; 1920-35; $200-325. Furniture factories often revived past styles during the 1920s and 1930s.

Queen Anne-style oak and pine tilt-top candlestand; 1920-30; $75-125.

Tudor-style oak plant pedestal; 1930-40; $65-90.

Whatnot stand made of thread spools painted white; 1890-1900; $265-335. Making folk furniture from discarded spools was a popular Victoran pastime.

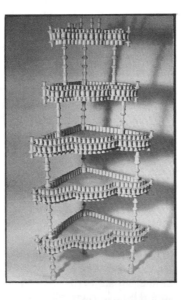

Sheet tin and steel radio speaker; 1925-30; $185-275. An unusual piece.

Jacobean-style oak ladies' dressing table with turned legs and brass fittings; 1930-35; $275-375.

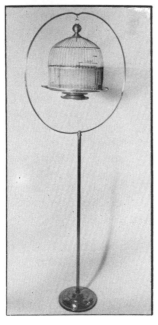

Brass birdcage; 1900-10; $250-375.

Folk Painting and Sculpture

Many attempts have been made to formulate a precise definition of American folk art, and the boundaries of the definition have varied considerably from time to time. The pioneer collectors of folk art, in the early decades of the present century, confined their interest largely to paintings—oils at first, followed by various types of watercolors. However, under the pressure of decreasing supply and increasing demand, as well as the recognition that folk art is to be found in other mediums, the term has been broadened to include drawings, silhouettes, cut paper, and especially sculpture of various kinds.

Painting

The line between academic and folk painting is, superficially at least, rather easy to draw. The academic painter has been trained; he is aware of and employs perspective and color and size relationships in an attempt to create a faithful likeness of an object, person, or scene. The folk artist, on the other hand, is not skilled in these techniques and is not really interested in them. He does not paint what he sees so much as what he remembers, using what has been called non-optical vision; he puts down what he perceives to be the essence of his subject—the very thing sought by the modern abstract painter. Primitive or folk paintings are, therefore, likely to be flat, lacking in depth. Color is put on in blocks without much shading, and figures vary in size depending upon the artist's feeling about their importance.

With the exception of work done at women's academies, there was little of what we call folk painting prior to the very late eighteenth century. Until then, only the rich could afford paintings, and those that they owned were created by European academic painters or by Americans trained in the same discipline. With the general increase in prosperity after the Revolution, it became possible for farmers and small merchants to afford paintings. They initially sought portraits in oil, the very things that the wealthy had been commissioning previously. Since academic painters were not available to the country folk, these people turned instead to local artists, men and women who might have been sign painters, furniture decorators, or writing masters. From 1800 until the invention of the

128

camera destroyed their craft at the middle of the century, itinerant folk artists roamed the hinterlands of New England and the Middle West, stopping here and there and painting for all who would pay. What they created forms the core of what we now call folk art.

Buying folk art is tricky business. Portraits, the most desirable of folk paintings, are simple works, for which the artist was paid anywhere from three dollars to twenty-five apiece; today they may sell for as much as five thousand dollars or more. Some bear the signature of a known artist, such as Prior or Hamblen, and these bring a fancy price indeed. Most folk portraits are unsigned, however, and with them one plays the game of attribution. Even the faintest similarity of a given work to one signed by a known folk artist brings forth exclamations of delight and a big jump in price. But paying a lot of money for an oil of somebody's great-grandmother just because it happens to look faintly like a Prior is risky at best.

While not as popular as portraits, oil paintings of animals, ships, and landscapes all have their devotees and are far from inexpensive. There are, however, primitive oils that can still be purchased reasonably. First, there is a large group of Victorian landscapes that were done in this country, probably by copying European paintings or artist's manuals. Many are rather ordinary (but in truth, so is much high-priced folk painting), while others may contain "foreign-looking" elements such as Swiss roofs or non-American peasant costumes. Much of this work is now classified loosely under the term *Hudson River School* in an attempt to relate it to the bucolic and very expensive American landscapes done by such outstanding native painters as Church and Cole. Certainly, some of these largely unsigned paintings are of American scenes; but, more important, they all offer an area of native painting that has been largely ignored.

Oil painting was done primarily on canvas, artist's board, or wood, but specimens on other mediums are found. Victorian women often painted on velvet, and toward the end of the nineteenth century there was an interest in painting on glass and pottery. Potteries sold "blanks"—undecorated pieces of pottery—that could be painted at home. There are quite a few such

examples around, and they are often both charming and inexpensive.

Reverse glass painting—wherein the image is painted on the back of a piece of glass—was a popular technique for many years. The earliest were done with the aid of standardized designs previously engraved on the glass; but throughout the nineteenth century, freehand examples were also executed, primarily for use in clock panels and mirror tops. Reverse glass portraits are most desirable, while the late Victorian patriotic paintings of Mount Vernon, the White House, and the Statue of Liberty represent excellent buys at present.

Watercolor has been employed for many years in this country, and most early examples are by women. Portraits are relatively uncommon, and most appear to have been done by amateurs. Apparently, most professional painters and their customers preferred oils. Young women were trained, often at school, to execute two types of watercolor. The first was the theorem, which was a picture—usually of a basket of fruit or a vase of flowers—created by use of various stencils. Theorems flourished until about 1870; they have a "hard line" quality very attractive to many collectors, and they are quite expensive. Almost equally desirable are mourning pictures, which were executed in watercolor, charcoal, or a combination of either with embroidery on cloth. These memorials to dead loved ones incorporate such universal—and stereotyped—symbols as a tomb, an urn, a weeping willow or two, and the mourning survivors; they were popular from about 1790 to 1840. With such stereotyped material, it is hardly surprising that the results often seem stiff and uninspired. Nevertheless, these works were generally composed freehand and have a certain archaic charm; they are in demand, particularly if they contain identifiable elements such as a specific house or recognizable locality.

An extremely important area of watercolor is fraktur painting, the decoration of birth or marriage records, created by people of German descent in Pennsylvania and New Jersey. Examples known from the very early 1700s consist of a text lettered completely by hand (in a style similar to the sixteenth-century typeface called Fraktur; hence the name); this is surrounded by an elaborate tinted border containing angels, birds, and flowers. These first fraktur are expensive, extremely so. By 1820, however, printers were issuing preprinted frakturs to which only the decoration was added by hand; and by 1900, when the art was dying out, even the decoration was being printed. Some of the printed fraktur with freehand decoration are very well done, and they are, on the whole, a good buy. Genealogical records in watercolor also appear, as do a wide variety of landscapes and folk scenes. All are highly collectible.

Drawing and Paper Cutting

Drawing in charcoal was especially popular during the Victorian period. While most such work is on paper, some interesting examples were done on sandpaper, or "marble," as it was known, a medium that imparts an eerie quality to the picture. Charcoals on sandpaper are generally landscapes, often copies of earlier European prints or oils. As they are beginning to attract enthusiasts, now is the time to buy them.

Pencil drawings are generally small and late. A few portraits exist, mostly from the 1870s and 1880s, but much of the work consists of sketches done as preparation for oils or watercolors. Such is not the case with ink drawing. Fancy, or "flourished," work in ink, commonly known as calligraphy, was popular in Europe in the seventeenth and eighteenth centuries. Many of the motifs seen in American calligraphic drawings of the nineteenth century, presently much sought after, are derived from the earlier foreign examples. Calligraphy is closely associated with handwriting of the so-called Spencerian school, so that many pieces incorporate writing as well as pictorial elements. Larger calligraphic pieces are priced quite high at present, but smaller work, such as that found in autograph books, can be had for less. Never pass up an old autograph book without thumbing through to see whether it contains some drawings; good calligraphy comes to light regularly in this way.

Silhouettes, called in their day "shades," are simply black paper cutout representations, in which the sharp contrast of the black and white and the precision of the cutting combine to produce a very dramatic effect. While a few scenes were done, the vast majority are portraits, generally either of a bust or the full figure, usually seen in profile. Since they could be cut quickly by an expert, silhouettes were inexpensive. Until the camera preempted the field, they served as the most accessible form of family portrait. A substantial number of silhouette cutters earned a living in the first half of the nineteenth century by cutting likenesses of their customers, often adding embellishments such as tinted facial color and hair. Many silhouettes are signed by their creators. They are being made today, though, and are easily faked, so it is best to buy from a reputable and knowledgeable dealer.

Another rather unusual art form, also practiced by women, was paper cutting. Entire compositions might be created from various carefully prepared paper elements. Watercolor was often also employed in this work, and in some cases tinsel rather than paper was cut and pasted to achieve a spectacular shimmering effect. Tinsel drawings are clearly related to theorems and seem to represent a later development of that style, being generally attributable to the second half of the nineteenth century.

Sculpture

Folk sculpture, like painting, does not lend itself to ready definition. At one end of the spectrum are highly professional pieces such as the popular plaster groupings by the academically trained John Rogers, whose work is folk only in the choice of subject matter. At the other end are many different wooden figures, some crude, some not, some charming, some not, but all sharing in common the fact that they were created by nonprofessional—untrained—sculptors. Professional wood-carvers there were, of course, and in abundance. Every shipbuilding town had at least one man who could be counted on to shape figureheads and do the fancy work for the bow and captain's cabin. There were artisans who carved wooden weathervanes and others who manufactured cigar-store Indians, smaller shop figures, and a variety of ornate signs. These were all professionals, but none appears actually to have been trained as a sculptor. As a result, their work has the flat, primitive look so appealing to today's collector.

There were also legions of whittlers who formed small statues, toys, and useful objects for others or just for their own amusement. Some, like Wilhelm Schimmel of Pennsylvania, have become famous for their work. Most have vanished; only their objects remain. These vary greatly in quality. For the collector, there is also the problem of fakes. Whimsical carved pieces are very popular today, and their very crudeness makes it easy for them to be duplicated or for new pieces on an old theme to be designed. Everything from ship models to cigar-store Indians is subject to reproduction, so one must proceed here with caution.

Metal sculpture is much less common than that in wood. It is by and large the work of smiths, something they turned out in their spare time as gifts or for limited sale. Tin, iron, and copper were all used. With the exception of weathervanes, which are treated later in this book (Chapter 16), metal sculpture is not much in vogue today. Prices are on the low side, and some good buys can be made.

Though not really folk art since it was cast in factory molds, chalkware is treated as such by most collectors. During the period 1850 to 1900, a vast quantity of these plaster-of-Paris figurines were turned out in New England and Pennsylvania. Birds, animals, human figures, fruits, and vegetables may be found. They were designed to imitate fine porcelain and earthenware mantel pieces, such as those made at Staffordshire, England, and they were colored (in strong primary colors) and gilded. Originally, they must have appeared extremely garish; today, with their hues muted by time, they are interesting and attractive. Whether they are attractive enough to justify the prices asked for them is another matter. Chalkware is generally one of the more over-priced areas of antiques, these mass-produced items being offered at prices in the hundreds of dollars.

Shellwork is of interest to some collectors. Outstanding in this category are the ornately designed shell pieces known as sailors' valentines. Few were made in this country; they were, rather, souvenirs purchased by American sailing men in such places as the West Indies and brought home for display. Later, at the end of the nineteenth and in the early twentieth centuries, shellwork was made in this country for sale to tourists. It was usually mounted on a cardboard frame or box and bore a slogan such as "Remember Me" or "Souvenir of Fort Lauderdale, Florida." Such pieces are not terribly old but are low-priced and should begin to attract considerable attention.

Oil on board, **Grinning Cat:** mid-19th century; $1,000-3000. A fine example of the sort of animal painting now attracting attention. Unsigned, as are most such paintings.

Oil on board in daguerreotype case, miniature portrait; 19th century; $450-900.

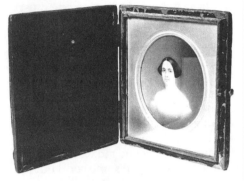

Oil on wooden bowl, **Tabby Cat;** late 19th century; $750-950. Painting on wooden plates and bowls was frequent during the 1880s and 1890s.

Oil on canvas, **Sailing Ships;** second half 19th century; $2,500-4,500. Typical of the strong, well-painted marine scenes now so popular.

Oil on canvas, **Winter Scene;** signed "Clara Beers, Nov. 20, 1880, Jonesville, N.Y."; $3,500-6,000. An outstanding signed primitive painting.

131

Oil on velvet, **Waterlilies;** Victorian still life of a sort frequently found in New England; $165-215/

Oil on velvet, **Still Life;** New York, mid-19th century; $750-1,700.

Oil on stoneware preserve jar, **Cloverleaves and Flowers;** Maine, late 19th century; $125-175. Paintings on pottery appear frequently in the coastal Maine area. They are real bargains in the folk art field.

Reverse-glass theorem painting, oil on glass; New England, first half 19th century; $2,000-3,500. Theorems are hardly common, and they are rarely seen in reverse-glass technique.

Oil on stoneware urn, **Landscape;** another example of pottery painting from late-19th century Maine; $150-250.

Reverse-glass painting, **Statue of Liberty;** oil on glass; ca. 1890; $125-170. Victorian reverse-glass paintings remain underpriced.

Reverse-glass painting, **Landscape;** oil on glass, late 19th century; $75-100.

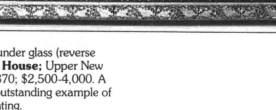

Oil on glass and under glass (reverse glass), **Victorian House;** Upper New York State, ca. 1870; $2,500-4,000. A remarkable and outstanding example of reverse-glass painting.

Reverse-glass paintings, oil on glass; found in Maine, attributed to Prior-Hamblen school, first half 19th century; $600-850 each. **Top: George Washington, Bottom: Martha Washington.**

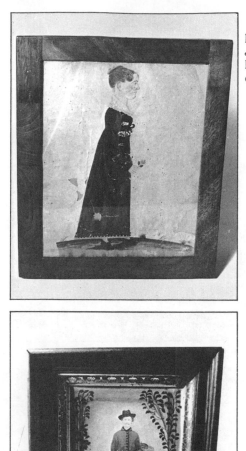

Fraktur-type watercolor, attributed to Jacob Maentel, **Woman Holding a Flower;** Pennsylvania, first half 19th century; $2,500-4,500.

Watercolor, miniature portrait, late 18th-early 19th century; probably European; $750-1,000.

Watercolor, **Civil War Soldier;** ca. 1865; $750-1,200.

Watercolor, house; Maine, first half 19th century; $2,000-4,500.

Rare watercolor, **Dancing for Eels, Catherine Market;** New York City, 1820; $4,500-7,000. An important documentary painting of old New York.

Trompe-l'oeil watercolor, *Feathers,* brilliant colors; signed "J.F. Bell," 19th century; $350-500

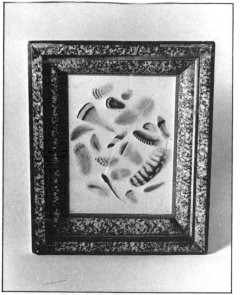

Fraktur painting, birth record; Pennsylvania, dated 18116; $1,700-3,200. The chip-carved original frame is a forerunner of 20th century tramp art.

Watercolor, family record; signed "William Murray, 1799"; 3,500-6,500. A fine example of a hand-lettered genealogical chart.

Watercolor and printed family record; Maine, first quarter 19th century; $450-650.

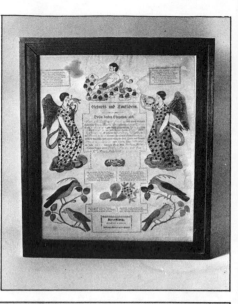

Watercolor and printed marriage record; Lebanon County, Pa., 1831; $150-250. Hand-lettered fraktur are much more valuable than later printing-press editions such as this.

Theorem, oil on velvet; ca. 1820; $1,500 2,500. Theorems were essentially stencil pictures put together according to definite rules. Many were made in the 19th century, but current demand exceeds the supply.

Watercolor memorial painting of the Smith family; ca. 1830; $1,000-3,000. Memorials of this sort were often done in needlework.

Theorem, oil on velvet; first half 19th century; $1,200-1,900.

Theorem, oil on paper; first half 19th century; $1,300-2,300.

Theorem, watercolor on paper; mid-19th century; $900-1,300. A fine bird enhances this piece, which shows the beginnings of Victorian influence.

Theorem, watercolor on paper; Maine, mid-19th century; $700-950. A very simple combination of white roses and green hummingbird.

Theorem, watercolor on paper; mid-19th century; $750-1,000. The hummingbird again, done with great charm.

Pencil sketch, **Young Child,** Maine, ca. 1880; $150-200.

Theorem, oil on velvet; ca. 1870; $75-125. A very late version.

Calligraphy and watercolor, **The Rescue;** second half 19th century; $3,500-5,000. An unusual and excellent example of calligraphy.

Calligraphy, **Spread-winged Eagle;** by Hosmer Godfrey, second half 19th century; $1,000-1,700. "Flourished" handwriting of this sort was very popular during the last century. Today, such pieces are becoming increasingly popular with collectors.

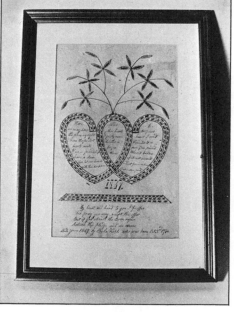

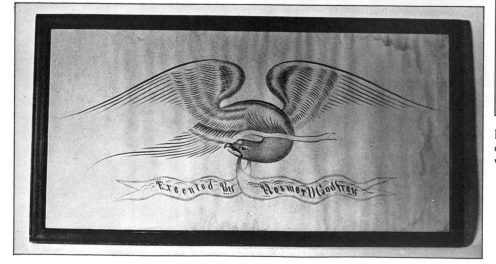

Ink on paper; 1849; $900-1,000. A colorful forerunner of the modern valentine.

Charcoal on sandpaper, **Landscape with Ruins;** Maine, ca. 1870; $150-300. The scene is highly suitable to the medium.

Tinsel painting, **Bird on Branch;** with well-decorated frame; East, late 19th century; $250-400. Tinsel paintings have been neglected and are still underpriced.

Charcoal on sandpaper, **River Landscape;** second half 19th century; $750-1,250. An unusual version featuring an Indian tepee.

Tinsel painting in the manner of a theorem; mid-19th century; $350-550.

Charcoal on sandpaper, **Monument with View of West Point, N.Y.;** mid-19th century; $900-1,700. An extremely important piece.

Silhouette of a man; mid-19th century; $175-200.
Since silhouettes are easy to duplicate, collecting them requires careful study and expertise.

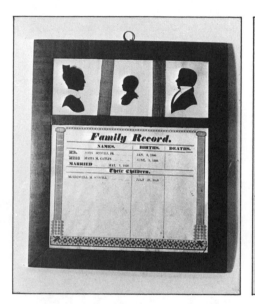

A most unusual family record with silhouettes of family members; New York, ca. 1830; $750-1,250.

Cut-paper picture; Pennsylvania, ca. 1885; $275-450. Decorative paper cutting is related to silhouette work but, unlike it, was usually done by women.

Elaborate cut-paper picture; Pennsylvania, mid-19th century; $650-1,000.

Left: Bird figures, pine; Pennsylvania, 19th century; $400-500. **Right:** Eagle, pine; 19th century; $175-350.

Eagle in flight, polychromed pine, carved on one side only; 1830—60; $1,500-2,000.

Free-standing eagle, pine, mid-19th century; 3,200-4,000. Probably intended as a rooftop adornment.

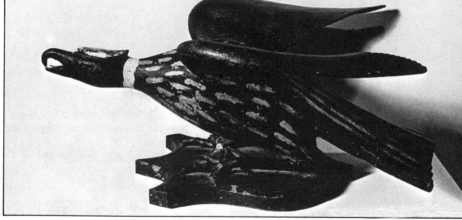

Eagle on shield, polychromed pine; 1840—65; $3,599-5,500. A particularly strong examle of primitive folk carving.

Wooden cigar-store Indian, detail; Michigan, ca. 1865; $14,000-22,000. Few tobacconist's figures were as sensitively portrayed as this one, which could almost be a portrait.

Eagle gatepost carved in the round, pine, 19th century; $2,300-3,400.

Ship's figurehead, polychromed pine; New England, ca. 1875; $20,000-35,500. Figurehead carving was an important craft during the 19th century.

Clothespin figure in pornographic pose, pine, 19th century; $250-300. Pornographic figurines of this nature were far more common in the supposedly austere Victorian era than one might at first suspect.

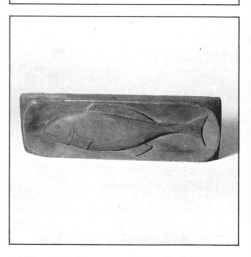

Half-modeled representation of a fish, pine; 19th century; $300-450.

Jigsaw-cut wall shelf, polychromed pine; $225-400. This was made as a souvenir of the Philadelphia Centennial.

Doll figure, hand carved, black paint; South, early 19th century; $900-1,500. This was probably intended as a toy.

Figure of Columbia, polychromed pine; Midwest, mid-19th century; $30,000-50,000. A rare large pilothouse figure.

Wall plaque with various patriotic and fraternal symbols, late 19th-early 20th century; $500-750.

Tradesman's symbols, polychromed pine; late 19th-early 20th century. **Top:** $75-100. **Bottom:** $225-375.

Whimsey, maple, inlaid with white wood; late 19th century; $300-475. Skilled carvers delighted in such tests of their skill. The decoration here is unusually lavish.

Half-modeled representation of a sailing vessel, wood; Maine, late 19th century; $350-650. Coastal communities produced many such shadow-box models.

Carved canes; New England, late 19th-early 20th century. **Top:** $175-300. **Bottom:** $210-320. Cane carving was a male pastime.

143

Giant carved pine shoes, probably an advertising device; Maine, 20th century; $100-125.

First Love, by John Rogers, plaster of Paris; 19th century; $425-575. While Rogers was an academic sculptor, his work was folk-oriented and was bought primarily by middle-class Victorians not far removed from the home farm.

Figure of a girl, plaster of Paris, or chalkware; Pennsylvania, 19th century; $250-375.

Plaque, polychrome plaster of Paris, or chalkware; 19th century; $750-1,000. An unusually large and detailed example of chalkware.

Figure of a bird, wrought-steel hollowware; early 20th century; $80-120.

Elaborate sailor's valentine, inlaid shells, 19th century; $750-1,200. Shellwork was a profitable tourist activity in many ports frequented by American sailors.

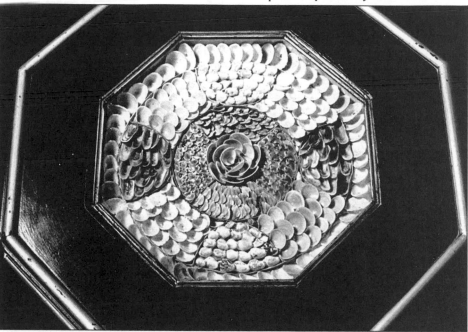

Scratch carving on fungus; late 19th-early 20th century; $40-60. This unusual art seems to have been practiced rather extensively in the Hudson Valley area of New York. So far it has had little appeal for collectors.

Sailor's valentine, box with inlaid shells, other materials, and motto "Remember Me"; $100-150. These pieces are just beginning to attract the attention of collectors.

Animal figures, wrought iron, probably produced as "end of day" pieces by a blacksmith. **Top:** $175-235. **Bottom:** $100-160.

Antique Glass

The collecting of early American glass, particularly glass bottles, ranks as one of our nation's major pastimes. Certainly, the present abundance of glass objects is one of the reasons for this phenomenon; yet, ironically, it was a great many years before the first settlers began to enjoy anything like an abundance of glass. The manufacture of glass is a difficult process that requires special materials and highly skilled workmen. The materials—sand for silica, potash as an alkali—could be found readily enough in the new land, but to mix and heat them properly required skills beyond those of most settlers. Several shops employing European glassblowers were opened in the seventeenth century, however—at Jamestown, New York, and Philadelphia. All failed. It was not until a German immigrant, Caspar Wistar, established a factory in Salem County, New Jersey, that a viable native industry could be said to have existed. That was in 1739! For a full century before, the colonists had had to depend on imported glass or go without.

Once the glass industry got started, however, it spread through the Northeast, along the Atlantic coast, and, after 1800, into the newly opened western states. The first products were bottles and window glass, and for decades these remained the major output of nearly every glass shop. Early bottles were crudely formed greenish-black ovals with long necks. They were blown by hand: the workman dipped a hollow iron pipe into a batch of hot glass, extracted a glob, and expanded it with his breath, much as a child blows a bubble through a straw. Black glass bottles are of interest to many collectors, but the native product is hard to distinguish from similar receptacles made in Europe and brought here in the eighteenth century or later.

The first bottles of distinctly American style were historical flasks, first produced around 1800. They are small vessels, usually no more than a pint or quart in capacity, that were blown in a mold. The mold, made of metal, wood, or pottery, was formed on the interior in the shape of the intended bottle. A glob of hot glass was inserted in the mold and expanded. The result was faster production of a group of vessels of more or less uniform appearance.

Historical flasks are embossed with a variety of motifs: important personages, such as Washington or Adams; patriotic slogans; flowers; trees; birds; and animals. There are hundreds of variations on these themes, and new ones are still being discovered. The flasks were filled with liquor, to be sold or given away at political rallies; but from the number that have survived, it is evident that many who drained the contents were equally interested in the container. Historical flasks have always been collected; and today they represent the highest priced and most active area of bottle collecting. The most common pieces go for thirty-five dollars, but a rare form was recently sold at auction for twenty-six thousand dollars. Many people keep their collections in vaults.

Fortunately for the collector, there are other less expensive types of bottles. Take medicine bottles. Until they were replaced by antibiotics in the second half of this century, proprietary medicines were the most common resort in time of illness. Many contained alcohol, and not a few relied for their healing qualities on such comforting agents as opium and morphine. Thus, whether for cure or comfort, it is not surprising that there are literally thousands of different types of medicine bottles. Many are plain blue or green vessels with nothing more than a manufacturer's name and address. A large minority, though, are embossed with interesting motifs or have unusual shapes. Bitters bottles, which contained a bitter but healing herb mixture (80 proof), may appear in the guise of cannons, human figures, log cabins, or even fish.

All figural medicine bottles and most bearing the word *bitters* are of value. But the great majority of common proprietaries sell for a dollar or two each. It's not that people don't collect them—thousands do—it's just that there are too many for them to command a higher price.

Much the same is true of canning jars. Prior to the invention of the Mason jar, in 1858, most food was preserved in salt or sugar and put by in wax-covered pottery crocks. The widespread acceptance of the vacuum jar around 1870 led to a proliferation of canning vessels. Most of these date from the period 1870 to 1930. Collectors became interested in them about a decade ago, and for a while prices soared; even the most ordinary examples went for five dollars. But the jars kept coming out of the woodwork. It seemed as if there were millions! Back down went the market. Today, the rare forms, such as experimental types and bottles produced prior to 1860, command a fair price. Everything else has gone back to the dollar-a-bottle flea market.

Interest has now shifted to less common types of bottle, such as embossed beer and mineral-water bottles. Perfume and cologne bottles are of great interest for the figural shapes they frequently assume. Many of them were made in Europe, but they were sold here and collectors often are happy to overlook their foreign origin. Much the same is true of the colorful poison containers. Odd shapes and bright reds, greens, blues, and yellows predominate in this group, and their usually small size makes it possible to amass a sizable number without squeezing oneself out of the living room. Prices in all these areas are holding well and moving up.

As a general rule in bottles, one should look for the colorful and the unusual. In early methods of manufacture, the bottle was held with a rod called a pontil while the neck was being finished; the removal of this rod left a jagged scar on the base of the bottle. The introduction of the holding device known as the snap case, around 1850, put an end to this practice, so that at present, the so-called pontil-marked bottles command a premium. Watch for these. Color is another indication of age. The impurities in bottle glass result in an aqua or green color; decolorizing agents produce a white. Other colors are the result of the introduction into the batch of coloring agents. Since these were expensive in the early period, red, yellow, or blue glass was rare prior to 1850. A pontil-marked bottle in color has to be a good find—unless, of course, it comes from Mexico or Italy. Factories in both these countries have been manufacturing reproductions of American bottles since the end of the Second World War. Unlike the excellent facsimiles of historical flasks that were made in Europe in the 1930s, however, these bottles are not intended to deceive. They look new, are machine-made (except for the necks, which are frequently hand finished), and appear in strange artificial colors, the likes of which were unknown in the nineteenth century.

Even before 1800, a certain amount of household glass—plates, bowls, goblets, and the like—was being hand-blown and shaped. The process, though, was slow, and the product was expensive. A better means of manufacture was required. It appeared in 1825, when John P. Bakewell, of the Pittsburgh glasshouse of Bakewell and Page, patented a machine for making pressed-glass doorknobs. The process was quite simple. A glob of hot glass was introduced into a pressing device that incorporated a mold of the desired shape. Down came the press and out came the glassware. The patenting of various modifications during the next decade resulted in a complete revolution in the glassmaking industry. Within a few years, cheap pressed-glass bowls, goblets, pitchers, dishes, platters, cups, and other objects flooded the American market.

In the last hundred years, literally thousands of different pressed-glass patterns have been patented, many of them in complete table settings. Collectors have shown great interest in this field, and prices here are high, though stable. The early Victorian glass is considered most desirable, and colored pieces, in amber, blue, yellow, or red, are choice. Anyone entering the field is advised to obtain one of the many available pattern books and to collect by the pattern rather than the piece.

The importance of color in pattern glass reached its zenith just after 1900 with the emergence of what is now commonly called carnival glass, then known as taffeta lustre. In 1906, Frank Fenton established the Fenton Art Glass Company for the manufacture of colored pressed-glass with a fired-on iridescence. The gleaming metallic quality of this iridescence was what set the ware apart from all previous pressed glass. Several other glass manufacturers, including Northwood, Westmorland, Millerburg, and Imperial, soon entered the field, producing a wide variety of patterns and, especially, colors. Through use of various metallic salts, they were able to create previously unknown color variations, to which they gave equally unusual names, such as Helois green and clam broth. By 1910, hundreds of thousands of pieces were being marketed annually, with much of the product being exported to England and Australia.

By 1930, the interest in taffeta lustre was waning, and substantial quantities were sold wholesale to stores and carnival proprietors to be given away as premiums (from which the material obtained the name carnival glass). Interest revived again in the 1960s, and carnival is now one of the most popular glasswares among antiques collectors. Prices for rare specimens frequently run into hundreds of dollars. Moreover, several companies are once again manufacturing new carnival glass, including two of the original firms still in existence, Fenton and Imperial. For the most part the collector should have little trouble distinguishing between the new and the old: the new ware is in new patterns not previously used and is clearly marked with the manufacturer's name, something the original ware usually was not. The risk of confusion does exist, though, particularly since it is not difficult to grind off the new makers' marks. Collectors should become familiar with the early patterns and be suspicious of "rare" or unworn pieces.

All bottles and bottle prices listed in this chapter are courtesy of Jim Whetzel, Jim's Bottle Shop, Ardsley, New York.

Barrel-shaped amber whiskey bottle; Binniger and Co., New York, mid-19th century; $150-220.

147

Left: green glass demijohn; early 19th century; $35-60. **Right:** Dark green porter bottle; 19th century; $60-85. Both, New England.

Pontil-marked dark green case gin bottle; East, 18th century; $80-135. Bottles of this sort were used for a variety of alcoholic beverages.

Very large yellow glass demijohn; New England, early 19th century; $150-225.

Rare deep-green bottle with seal; late 18th-early 19th century; $200-550. Bottles of this sort were made up with the initials of a particular customer.

Amber whiskey bottle with handle; Macy and Jenkins, New York, 19th century; $30-60.

Square-bodied amber whiskeys; Louisville, Ky.; 19th century. **Left:** Harris Distilling Co.; $20-30. **Center** Harris and Raleigh; $15-20. **Right** N. Muri and Co.; $10-15.

Tall amber whiskey bottles; 19th century. **Left:** Hayner Distilling Co., Ohio; $20-25. **Center:** Jones and Banks, New York, with rare inside stopper thread; $60-75. **Right:** Charles and Co., New York; $12-15.

Paneled whiskeys; Goldberg Distilling Co., New York, late 19th century. **Left:** Amber; $25-35. **Right:** Less-common aqua; $40-55.

149

Left: Clear glass strap flask; Charles Rosso Co.; $5-10. **Center:** Amber whiskey flask with embossed eagle; $15-25. **Right** Aqua whittled coffin flask; $5 10. All, New England, late 19th century.

Clear glass back bar bottles; 19th century. **Left:** Sunny Glen; $50- 70. **Center:** Whiskey; $35-70. **Right:** Linquist; $45-65. Bottles of this sort were filled from barrels of whiskey for use in taverns and hotels.

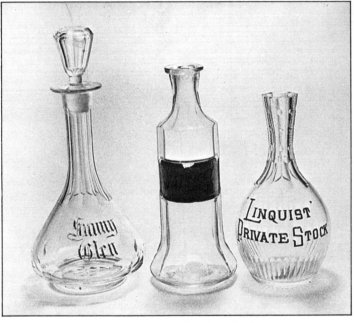

Washington flasks; New England, first half 19th century. **Left:** G I-59,* aqua, Washington bust, sheaf of wheat on reverse; $140-175. **Right:** G I-34, Washington, bust of Jackson on reverse; $300-400.

Sunburst flasks; New England, 19th century. **Left:** G VIII-8, dark green; New Hampshire, $ 500-650. **Center:** G VIII-16, light green; $450-550. **Right:** G VIII-18, amber; $475-575.

* This number, and the similar ones on these pages, are from the McKeann system of numbers for historical glass. A complete explanation and listing of the numbers will be found in **American Glass,** by George S. and Helen McKeann (Crown Publishers, 1941).

Left: Railroad flask, G V-5, green; New England, before 1850; $275-375.
Right: Comucopia, G III-13; Lancaster, N.Y., glassworks; $425-550.

Lafayette flasks; Coventry, Conn., before 1850.
Left: Green amber, G I-80, Lafayette, bust of DeWitt Clinton on reverse; $1,00-1,500. **Right:** Amber, Lafayette, Liberty Cap on reverse; $850-1,100.

Masonic flasks; New England, early 19th century. **Left:** G IV-1, blue green Justus Perry Masonic; $525-650. **Right:** G IV-24, amber half pint; $250-325.

Aqua pictorial flasks; ca. 1850.
Left: Deer, G X-1, embossed "Good Game"; $325-400. **Right:** Sailing ship, G X-9; $175-225.

Left: Aqua flask; Louisville, Ky., glassworks; $175-250. **Right:** Ship flask, reverse bust of Franklin, aqua; Dyottville, Penn.; $325-450. Both, first half 19th century.

Aqua Benjamin Franklin Masonic flask, G IV-36; New England, early 19th century; $1,300-1,700.

Left: Aqua flask with embossed anchor; Baltimore, Md., glassworks, Van Rensselaer,* Gp. 6#11; $110-170.
Right: Aqua flask with embossed figure marked "To Pikes Peak"; $60-100.

Clabashes. **Left:** Aqua, with figure of Jenny Lind, GI-103; $120-150. **Right:** Aqua, with figures of hunter and fisherman; $135-175. Both Midwest.

Eagle flasks; New England, mid-19th century. **Left:** Amber Van Rensselaer, Gp. 2, Div. 7; $80-110. **Right:** Amber double eagle, Van Rensselaer, Gp. 2 Div. 2, #4; $100-130.

Figural bitters bottles. **Left:** Dark amber Old Homestead; $200-250. **Center:** Aqua, barrel-shaped Hall's; $150-185. **Right:** Amber barrel-shaped Old Sachem; $200-235. All, Midwest.

* The Van Rensselaer numbering system, developed by Stephen Van Rensselaer in his book **Early American Bottles and Flasks** (1926), is supplementary to the McKeann numbering system.

Aqua bitters; East, late 19th century.
Left: Mandrake bitters; $10-15.
Center: Lash's; $4-8. **Right:** Atwood's;
$10-15.

Rare amber bitters; late 19th century.
Left: Congress; $450-650. **Center:**
Gordon's; $220-280.
Right: Koehler Red Star Stomach
bitters; $400-550. All unlisted in texts on
this type.

Labeled aqua propietary medicines;
East, late 19th century. **Left:** Dr.
Fenner's Cough Honey; $12-18.
Center: Dr. Bull's Cough Syrup; $16-24
Right: Hale's Honey; $20-30. Presence
of an original label adds to value of a
bottle.

Aqua sarsaparillas; East. late 19th
century. **Left:** Hood's; $3-5. **Center:**
Bell's; $15-20. **Right:** Dana's; $3-6.

Left: Amber Father John's Medicine;
$2-4.
Center: Willet's Bone Oil; $4-7. **Right:**
Amber Paine's Celery Compound; $5-8.
All, East, 19th century.

153

Pontil-marked aqua proprietary medicines; before 1850. **Left:** Hunt's Liniment; New York; $75-125. **Center:** Peter T. Wright and Co.; $40-65. **Right:** Jayne's Alterative; $55-85. Last two, Philadelphia.

Pontil-marked aqua bottles; before 1850. **Left:** Dr. McLaine's American Worm Specific; $35-55. **Center:** Golden Treasure ointment; $110-140. **Right:** Bottles #1 and #2 of Bachelor's Hair Dye; $35-50 each.

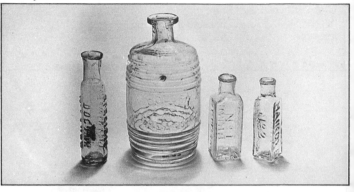

Left: Early tin-bound milk bottle, clear; $15-25. **Center:** Aqua floral pickle jar; $35-60.
Right: C lear glass pickle jar; $25-40. All, East, late 19th century.

Pontiled household bottles; before 1850.
Top Left: True Cephalic snuff; $35-55.
Top right: London snuff; $40-65.
Bottom: Dark green glass eagle blacking with original label; $150-225.

File-top aqua canning jar, embossed name and bust of Lafayette; New Jersey, 19th century; $125-165.

Open-pontiled inkwells and ink bottles; New England, 1830—50. **Left:** Amber cone; $75-100. **Left center:** Dark green three-piece mold; $150-200. **Right center:** Amber umbrella; $90-120. **Right:** Dark green three-piece mold; $120-160.

Open-pontiled aqua cologne bottles; mid-19th century. **Left:** Dancing Indian; $100-170. **Center:** Lion of St. Marks; 125-185 . **Right:** Monument; $90-130. It is doubtful that such colognes were made in the United States, but like barber bottles they have been adopted as "native."

Left: Light green pint master ink; $45-55. **Center:** Cardinal colored turtle-back ink; $60-90. **Right:** Amber half-pint master ink; $35-45. All, New England, 19th century.

Cologne bottles; 19th century.
Left: Green glass lantern with pewter top; $45-70.
Center: Open-pontiled aqua shoe; $35-55. **Right:** Open-pontiled floral; $55-85.

Clear glass colognes; 19th century. **Left:** Stove; $35-40. **Center:** Streetlamp; $35-55. **Right:** Shoe; $35-45.

Frosted glass figural bottles, probably used for liquors; 19th century. **Left:** Black waiter; $200-300. **Right:** President Cleveland; $110-170.

Rare clear glass figural bottle, President
Garfield; late 19th century; $400-600.
Probably a cologne.

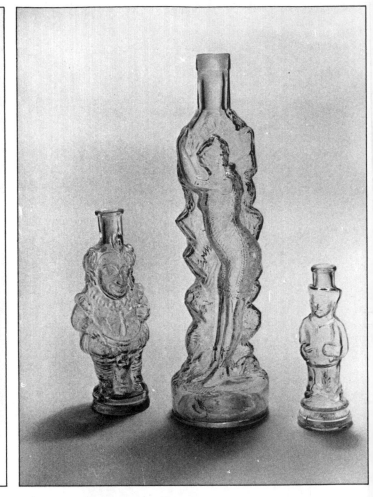

Clear glass figural bottles; 19th century.
Left: Jester, cologne; $65-110. **Center:**
Bather on rocks, whiskey; $150-185.
Right: Chinaman, cologne; $55-75.

Barber bottles; 19th century. **Left:**
Green, decorated in white; $110-140.
Center: Amethyst, multicolored
decoration includes the words "Bay
rum"; $100-125. **Right:** blue, with
flowers and oak leaves in blue; $85-110.

Barber bottles with hand-painted floral
decoration in the Bohemian style; 19th
century. **Left:** Light green; $70-95.
Center: Amethyst; $85-120. **Right:**
Green; $70-85.

Barber bottles; late 19th-early 20th
century.
Left: Reeded green and clear; $65-75.
Center: Cranberry; $85-110. **Right:**
Blue with hazel; $55-80.

156

Poison bottles; late 18th-early 19th century. **Left:** Sapphire diamond-pattern flask; $250-325. **Center:** Hobnail pattern, straw-colored flask; $230-290. **Right:** Quarter pint aqua diamond-pattern flask; $180-220. Early poisons of this period are rare and very expensive.

Cobalt poison bottles in shape of skull; 19th century. **Left to right :** $275-350; $325-400; $400-500. The smaller, the rarer.

Ribbed six-sided poison bottles; 19th century. **Left:** Peacock blue; $40-60. **Center:** Deep green; $45-65. **Right:** Cobalt blue; $45-65.

Coffin-shaped hobnail-embossed poison bottles; East, 19th century. **Left:** Amber; $65-95. **Center:** Amber; $40-65. **Right:** Cobalt; $90-175.

Candy container, ruby glass, gold trim; New Jersey, early 20th century; $45-70.

Mineral water bottles; East, last half 19th century. **Left:** Kissinger Water, green; $35-55. **Center:** Hathorn Spring light amber; $35-55. **Right:** Hotchkiss, Congress and Empire Co.; $50-75.

Mineral water bottles; East, last half 19th century. **Left:** Sek bottle green, Clark and White, $55-70. **Center:** Hathorn Springs. green, $45-60; **Right:** Hotchkiss, Congress and Empire "E"; $40-50.

Candy Containers; East, last half 19th century. **Left:** Wheelbarrow, wood and tin accessories; $40-55. **Center:** Windmill, tin blades and original candy; $55-85 **Right:** House; $85-115.

Machine-made candy containers; East, early 20th century. **Left:** Long hooded coupe; $60-85. **Center:** World War I tank; $55-85. **Right:** Locomotive; $50-70.

Candy containers, East, early 20th century. Left: Long hooded coupe $60-85. Center: World War I tank; $50-70; Right: Locomotive; $55-85.

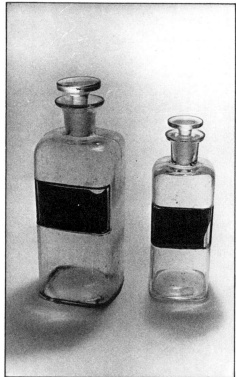

Cobalt blue druggist's bottles, with glass-covered labels; East, late 19th century.
Left: $65-90. **Right:** $55-75.

Clear glass druggist's bottles; Midwest, late 19th century. **Left:** $ 25-35. **Right:** $15-25.

Clear glass whiskey samplers; 19th century. **Left:** Oyster shell; $45-65.
Center: Dagger; $55-80.
Right: Powder horn; $40-65.

Milk glass bottles. **Left:** Mustard jar in form of owl; $90-125. **Center:** Cologne in form of Napoleon statue; $650-850.
Right: Reed's Apothecary; $40- 60.

Clear glass nursing bottles; East, late 19th-early 20th century. **Left:** The Eagle; $ 50-70. **Center:** Bostonia; $10-15. **Right:** Baby's Delight; $45-65.

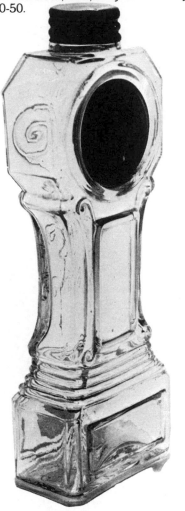

Unusual screw-top whiskey sampler in form of a clock; East, early 20th century; $30-50.

Blown three-mold decanters, New England, first half 19th century. **Left:** G III-5 quart; $200-285.
Center: G II-18, pint decanter; $185-245. **Right:** G III-24, quart decanter; $160-220.

Three blown wine goblets, Midwest, 19th century; $45-65 each.

Pressed glass; Midwest, late 19th-early 20th century. **Left:** Covered candy jar; $30-45. **Center:** Diamond-pattern flask; $25-40. **Right:** Yellow glass butter dish in form of iron; $45-65.

Pressed glass; Midwest, 19th century. **Left:** Celery jar; $35-55. **Center:** covered candy jar; $40-65. **Right:** Celery jar; $60-90.

Clear pressed glass, moon and star pattern; Midwest, late 19th century. **Left:** Fruit bowl; $30-55. **Right:** Celery jar; $40-60.

Very large opressed glass punch bowl, daisy and button pattern; New England, mid-19th century; $300-375.

Clear pressed glass; Midwest, late 19th century. **Left:** Bowl; $15-25. **Top center:** Pitcher; $45-75. **Bottom center:** Sauce dish; $15-20. **Right:** Compote; $35-65.

Clear pressed glass; New England, late 19th century. **Left:** Eggcup in scroll with flowers pattern; $15-25. **Center:** Spoon jar in New England Pineapple pattern; $45-60. **Right:** Open sugar in scroll with flowers pattern; $45-55.

Pressed glass; Midwest, late 19th century. **Left:** Goblet in Norman Key pattern; $20-30. **Center:** Blue glass celery in Vernon Honey Comb pattern; $50-65. **Right:** Celery in Tandem Bicycle pattern; $30-45.

Clear pressed glass pitcher in the double spear pattern; Midwest, late 19th century; $55-85.

Green pressed-glass pitcher, tray, and two tumblers in feather-duster pattern; New England, late 19th century. Pitcher; $125-160. Tray; $70-95. Tumblers; $20-35 each.

Castor set in daisy and button pattern with pewter tops, blue, yellow, and amber bottles; New England, mid-19th century; $175-235 the set.

Green pressed-glass footed bowl, with gold flashing, Colorado pattern; Midwest, late 19th century; $85-125.

Flashed ruby glass decanters, block pattern; New England, late 19th century; $80-130.

Ruby pressed glass; New England, late 19th-early 20th century.
Left: Flashed red low bowl in thumb-print pattern; $40-60. **Center:** Open sugar in ruby block; $35-45.
Right: Spoon jar in button arches pattern, inscribed "Lucy B."; 1902; $25-45. Piece at right is typical of flashed glass sold or given away as souvenirs.

Gold flashed pitcher and two tumblers in moon and star pattern; Midwest, late 19th century. Pitcher; $145-185. Tumblers; $30-55 each.

Carnival glass, pitcher and three tumblers in the orange-tree pattern; Midwest, early 20th century. Pitcher; $150-190. Tumblers; $40-55 each.

Art Glass

Art glass can be distinguished from its popular, or utilitarian, counterpart in much the same way that art pottery can be distinguished from common earthenware. In both cases the finer ware was made in limited quantities by sophisticated techniques and was sold for high prices to a discriminating and limited public. Unlike common glass, for which decoration was secondary to function, the main purpose of art glass was decoration, and each piece was viewed as a work of art.

Art glass has a long history—it was known in ancient Persia and in early Venice—but the flowering of the medium occurred in America and Europe during the late nineteenth and early twentieth centuries. Beginning about 1880, manufacturers such as Tiffany in the United States and Galle and Daum in France took advantage of technological innovations largely unknown to the ancients to create new colors and new methods of decoration that revolutionized the glassmaking industry.

The role that American manufacturers played in the development of art glass cannot be overestimated, and the greatest of the Yankee creators was Lewis Comfort Tiffany, son of the famous silver manufacturer. Tiffany trained as an artist and began working with glass in the 1880s. At first his interest lay mainly with stained glass, but by 1893, when he opened his own glassworks at Corona, New York, he had turned to art glass. In the following year he registered the mark *favrile* to cover his blown, iridescent glass, the weathered, multicolored surface of which reminded people of ancient glass. The brilliant shades of blue, green, brown, and yellow found in favrile, and the stylized motifs—likened to peacock feathers, seaweed, and fern fronds—were an instant sensation. Widely copied here and abroad, favrile was manufactured until Tiffany Studios shut down in 1920.

Favrile was not the extent of the Tiffany genius. Over the course of its existence the shop produced no less than five thousand different glass patterns, including many different types of vases and tablewares as well as the famous naturalistic lamps with leaded glass or blown shades, the latter frequently in the popular bell flower or lily patterns. The almost incredible prices now obtainable for some Tiffany pieces are proof of the skills of their creator. One should expect to pay substantial sums for much signed Tiffany. However, it is still possible to obtain smaller examples, such as stickpins and bowls, for prices in the low hundreds or even less. In fact, not all those stories about Tiffany shades purchased for pennies at flea markets are false. Unknowing people still let good pieces slip through.

One should not assume that Tiffany dominated the American art-glass market. He had worthy competitors. As early as 1874, the Mount Washington Glass Company of New Bedford, Massachusetts, was turning out large quantities of colored ware, including such specialties as amberina, a glass that was shaded from red to yellow, and the bluish white and pink ware called peach blow. Both types are very popular with today's collectors.

Another important New England firm was the Sandwich Glass Company, active at Sandwich, Massachusetts (1825 to 1888). The Sandwich works produced a substantial amount of art glass, including the lumpy, frosted ware known as overshot or craquele and the famous Mary Gregory enameled wares. Mary Gregory was a decorator who worked at Sandwich in the 1880s and specialized in quaint children's groups painted in white enamel on red, green, or blue glass. Her work is highly collectible today, though, unfortunately, its popularity has led to reproduction, both here and abroad.

The list of American manufacturers of art glass could go on and on, but it must include the brilliant cut and overlay glass made at the Pairpont Glass Company — a successor to Mount Washington — and the fine jadelike glass produced by the Steuben Glass Works of Corning, New York, during the directorship of the glassmaking genius Frederick Carder.

No true art-glass collector can confine himself to American products—not when the work of such greats as Galle and Daum is available. Emile Galle (1846 to 1894) was the outstanding French glassmaker of the nineteenth century. His experiments led to the creation of many unusual colors, including a vivid blue, but his basic interest lay not in color but in decoration. His shop, which remained active under other management until 1935, specialized in enameled glass as well as cameo. The latter was a form produced by cutting or etching through one layer of opaque glass to expose another contrasting layer that lay below it. Much Galle glass was made and signed, and much is available today, though prices for individual pieces are generally in the hundreds or even thousands of dollars.

Rivals of Galle were the Daum brothers, August and Antonin, also residents of the town of Nancy in France. Their acid-etched cameo glass, made after 1893, closely resembles that of Galle although it bears distinctive decorative motifs, such as bouquets of flowers, fruit, and pastoral landscapes. Daum ware is characteristically marked DAUM: NANCY.

A later glassmaker in the same community was Amalric Walter, who began working there in 1906, first using the Daum works, then, after the end of the First World War, acquiring his own shop. Walter specialized in pâte de verre glass, which is created by allowing a mixture of crushed glass and metallic oxide colorants to harden in a mold.

In Austria the leading exponent of art glass was Max Ritter von Spaun, who took over the Lotz glassworks at Klostermühle in 1879. Obtaining the services of a disgruntled former Tiffany employee, Von Spaun was able, by the 1890s, to produce a good imitation of favrile ware. In fact, since much Lotz glass is unsigned, collectors have recently been plagued by Lotz pieces with bogus Tiffany signatures. However, Lotz ware, which was sometimes marked LOETZ-AUSTRIA for export, is a high-quality collectible in its own right.

Much art glass—as can be imagined from the dates of its manufacture—is in the Art Nouveau manner. However, after 1900 the flowing forms were gradually replaced by straight lines and geometric patterns ornamented only by black enamel on a clear or opalescent white glass. Cutting and etching became more pronounced in the 1920s, and those factories, such as Daum and Steuben, that continued into the Art Deco period modified their designs to appeal to the new taste.

While Art Deco glass cannot yet be said to rival in popularity the art glass made in the earlier era, there is little doubt that its day is coming. In fact, good-quality American and European art glass of the period from 1920 to 1945 represents an excellent investment, marked or not.

Stained-glass hot plate; by Louis Comfort Tiffany; Corona, N.Y.; 1885-90; $600-700. Tiffany experimented with stained glass before producing his famed iridescent glass.

Favrile; by Louis Comfort Tiffany; Corona, N.Y.; 1900-10. **Left:** Goblet; $275-350. **Right:** Pitcher; $350-450. Tiffany is best known for his iridescent favrile, which resembles ancient glass in color and texture.

Pair of favrile candlesticks; by Louis Comfort Tiffany; Corona, N.Y.; 1900-05; $475-575.

Favrile vase; by Louis Comfort Tiffany; Corona, N.Y.; 1898-1910; $550-650.

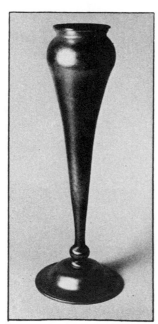

Favrile; by Louis Comfort Tiffany; Corona, N.Y.; 1900-15. **Left:** Plate; $350-400. **Right:** Bowl; $375-450.

Favrile scalloped bowl; by Louis
Comfort Tiffany; Corona, N.Y.;
1895-1905; $450 600.

Favrile bud bowl; by Louis Comfort
Tiffany; Corona, N.Y.; 1900 15;
$700-900.

Iridescent glass lamp with bronze
base; attributed to Louis Comfort
Tiffany; Corona, N.Y.; 1895-1910;
$2,000-3,000.

Seashell vase; by Steuben Glass
Works; Corning, N.Y.; 1905-15;
$375-475. Under the direction of the
master glassmaker Frederick Carder,
Steuben became one of America's
great art-glass manufacturers.

Tiny aurene bud vase; by Steuben
Glass Works; Corning, N.Y.; 1910-25;
$200-275. This white and gold vase is
typical of the pearlike finish known
as aurene.

167

Multicolored vase; by Quezal Art Glass and Decorating Co.,; Brooklyn, N.Y.; 1905-10; $250-350.

Violet vase encased in silver; by Quezal Art Glass and Decorating Co.; Brooklyn, N.Y.; 1901-12; $350-450. One of the smaller art-glass manufacturers, Quezal specialized in pieces encased in engraved silver.

Mercury glass; 1890-1900. **Left:** Goblet; $50-75. **Right:** Vase with multicolored enamel decoration; $75-125. Mercury glass, popular in the United States during the late 19th century, was made by injecting mercury between an inner and an outer wall of blown glass.

Blown glass footed compote edged in green; by Greystan Glass Co.; 1920-30; $150-250. An American company, Greystan was in business only a short time.

Agata glass miniature footed bowl; 1915-25; $60-75. Manufactured from a mixture of multicolored ground glass, agata was made at various American and European factories.

Mother-of-pearl pitcher; 1890-1900; $350-475. Also known as quilted satin glass, mother-of-pearl derives its distinctive pattern from air trapped between two layers of glass.

Mother-of-pearl vase in blue and white; 1890-1900; $250-325.

Mother-of-pearl oil lamps in pink; attributed to Sandwich Glass Co.; Sandwich, Mass.; 1881-85; $275-350.

Cranberry glass vase; 1890-1900; $75-95. Also known as ruby glass, cranberry's reddish color reflects the addition of gold oxide to the glass.

Mother-of-pearl glass; ca. 1890; **left** and **right:** Pink salt and pepper shakers; $165-215 the pair. **Center:** Pink and white pitcher; $325-400.

Cranberry glass bowl with clear glass handles; attributed to **Sandwich Glass Co.;** Sandwich, Mass.; 1880-90; $125-175.

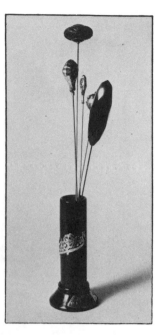

Cranberry glass hatpin holder mounted in sterling silver; 1890-1900; $55-75.

Pair of cranberry glass decanters with etched designs in the Bohemian manner; 1900-10; $150-200. Because so much colored glass was etched and cut with floral and pastoral scenes at the glass factories in central European Bohemia, glass of this sort is called Bohemian even though much of it was made in the United States.

Cranberry glass decorated in the Bohemian manner; 1890-1910. **Left:** Bowl; $80-110. **Right:** Chalice; $55-85.

Stretch glass compote; by Mount Washington Glass Works; New Bedford, Mass.; 1885-95; $125-175. The crackled surface of stretch glass appeals to many collectors.

Amberina glass pitcher; attributed to New England Glass Co.; 1885-1900; $325-400. Amberina glass shades from red to amber. It was developed in 1883 by Joseph Locke, a designer at New England Glass.

Amethyst glass perfume bottle; by Sandwich Glass Co.; Sandwich, Mass.; 1880-90; $75-100.

Iridescent green and yellow vase mounted in pewter; by Lotz (Loetz); Austria; 1890-1900; $350-450. The Lotz firm was Europe's answer to Tiffany, producing much fine favrile-like glass.

Overshot glass vase; attributed to Sandwich Glass Co.; Sandwich, Mass.; 1890-1900; $65-85. Overshot glass has an unusual frosted surface.

Left: Iridescent green bowl; $195-235. **Right:** Unusual aquamarine and brown vase; $600-700. Both by Lotz; Austria; 1890-1905.

171

Iridescent red vase mounted in pot metal; by Lotz; Austria; 1900-10; $250-310.

Green cameo glass bowl; by Emile Galle; Nancy, France; 1890-1904; $650-800. Cameo glass is produced by covering a piece of clear glass with a shell of colored glass and then cutting or etching away the colored glass to produce a contrasting composition.

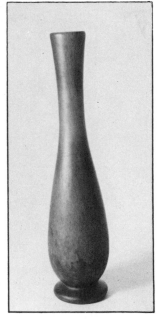

Green and gray cameo glass vase; by Emile Galle; Nancy, France; 1885-90; $1,500-2,000. The creator of modern cameo glass, Emile Galle is revered by art-glass enthusiasts, and his pieces are in great demand. This is an early example.

Cameo glass; 1895-1905. **Left:** Vase; by Emile Galle; Nancy, France; $750-900. **Right:** Vase; by August and Antonin Daum; Nancy, France; $600-800. Cameo glass by the Daum Brothers is similar to that of Galle.

Cameo glass vase; by Daum; Nancy, France; 1900-20; $400-500.

Purple cameo glass table lamp; by Daum; Nancy, France; 1910-20; $1,700-2,200. Cameo lamps are hard to come by.

lticolored cameo glass vase; by ller Brothers; 1900-10; 0-1,200. Great detail makes this mportant piece.

Cameo glass cologne bottle with sterling silver top; attributed to Stevens & Williams; England; 1890-1910; $450-550. In white and yellow, this piece is typical of the more classical English cameo.

English cameo glass; 1890-1900. **Left:** Tall vase; $375-450. **Right:** Squat vase; $325-375.

Tan and red cameo glass footed compote; by Charles Schnieder; 1890-1910; $675-800. This piece is in the Art Nouveau style.

Tan and green pate de verre bowl; by Amalric Walter; Nancy, France; 1910-15; $1,700-2,200. Walter specialized in pate de verre.

Small, green footed goblet; by Amalric Walter; Nancy, France; 1906-14; $975-1,250. In pate de verre technique, a mixture of crushed glass and colored oxides.

Enameled glass pitcher; by Emile Galle; Nancy, France; 1880-90; $1,100-1,400. Enameled glass has been known for centuries.

Enameled glass covered bowl; by Emile Galle; Nancy, France; 1900-10; $650-775.

Pair of vases in green glass decorated with purple and gold enamel; by Mont Joye Glass Co.; France; 1900-10; $650-750.

Enameled glass; 1890-1910. **Left:** Sherbet bowl in blue and black; $110-130. **Right:** Cordial glass in red, green, and blue; $140-165.

Enameled glass vase in shades of blue; by Daum; Nancy, France; 1910-15; $800-1,100.

Enameled glass vase in blue, red, yellow, and white; by Leune; France; 1925-35; $250-350. A good example of Art Deco art glass.

Enameled glass sugar bowl and creamer in red and clear glass with gold trim; by Heisey Glass Co.; 1930-40; $85-110 the set.

Venetian glass vases in threaded white on orange and green glass; 1910-20; $150-200. Though first employed in Venice, the techniques of combining or "threading" contrasting colors of glass have been employed in many countries.

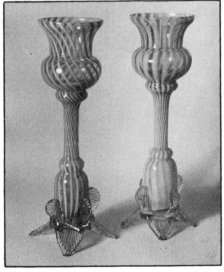

English Nailsea-type pink and white ribbed footed bowl; 1900-10; $85-125. Nailsea was a major English center for Venetian-type glass.

Frosted glass bowl decorated in black and yellow; by DeLatte; Nancy, France; 1915-30; $600-750.

Clear and frosted glass perfume decanter; by Rene Lalique; 1920-30; $600-750. Though best known for his perfume bottles, Lalique was a major producer of many types of frosted and cut art glass.

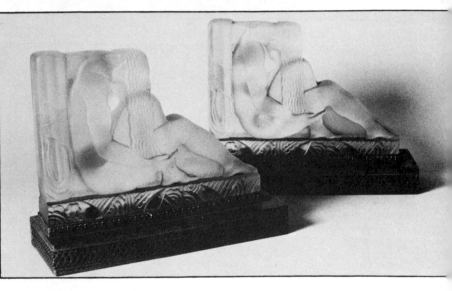

Pair of Art Deco frosted glass bookends; by Etling; France; 1930-40; $450-550.

Pair of clear and frosted glass bud vases mounted in sterling silver; 1910-20; $325-400.

Art Deco cut-crystal tumbler in clear and cobalt blue glass; 1925-35; $165-200.

Art Deco cut glass decorated in black enamel; 1930-40. **Left:** Ashtray; $60-95. **Right:** Decanter; $135-185.

Cut-glass goblet engraved with a forest scene in the Bohemian manner; 1910-20; $115-155.

Spatter glass vase in shades of red, blue, and green; by Charles Schnieder; 1900-10; $550-675. Multicolored spatter glass has been produced in both Europe and the United States.

Spatter glass vase in pink, yellow, and white; 1920-30; $175-250.

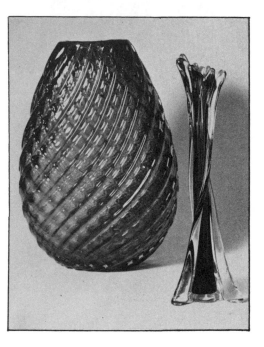

Art Deco glass; 1935-45. **Left:** Vase in pink and purple; $85-115. **Right:** Bud vase in clear glass and green; $50-75.

Spatter glass footed compote on pot-metal mounting; 1890-1900; $400-485. This piece, in shades of brown and yellow, is in the Art Nouveau style.

Vase with elaborate pastoral scene painted in enamels; 1880-1900; $450-500. Paintings of this sort were popular with the Victorians.

Clear glass figural liqueur bottles; 1925-35; $65-85 each. Made in molds, figural glass pieces are a popular form of art glass.

Clear glass figural candy bowl; 1930-40; $65-85.

Clear pressed-glass sherbet bowl;
dated 1876; $75-95. Issued in
commemoration of the 1876
Centennial.

Art Deco lampshade in green and
tan molded glass; 1920-30; $75-125.

Art Deco milk glass lampshade
decorated in black enamel; 1930-40;
$95-145. Lampshades were so
popular after the advent of
electricity that even Tiffany made
them.

Art Deco milk glass table lamp
decorated in black enamel with a
sheet tin base; 1925-35; $175-225.

Collectible Glass

It is difficult for the modern collector, confronted with a blinding array of collectible glass, to realize that during most of the nineteenth century glass was a choice and expensive item.

The majority of this early glass was tediously hand formed, piece by piece. A glassblower would dip his hollow blowpipe into a vat of molten glass and remove a glob (called a gather) of glass. He would then expand and shape the gather by blowing through the pipe—in much the same way as a child blows a bubble. Because of the skill and time required, such glassware was always rather costly.

There had to be a better way—and there was. For hundreds of years glassmakers had employed molds, hollow wood or metal forms with designs carved into their interiors. A gather of glass made to expand within a form of this sort would retain the shape of the mold. It remained for American ingenuity to take the mold and make it the foundation of modern glass manufacture.

In 1825, John P. Bakewell of Pittsburgh patented an automatic pressing machine. No longer did the glassblower have to expand each gather of glass in a mold. The glass was fed automatically from the vat into a stamping machine where individual items were pressed out like cookies.

Spurred on by this innovation, American glassmakers began to produce a great quantity of housewares—cups, dishes, decanters, bowls, and the like—collectively known as pressed or pattern (from the decorative patterns embossed on their surfaces) glass.

The period of popularity of this pressed glass coincided in its later stages with the development of art glass, a fine, hand-formed and elaborately decorated ware (discussed in the preceding chapter). Unlike pressed glass, which was usually clear, art glass was brightly colored and of great appeal to the late Victorians.

It was only a matter of time before someone combined the best characteristics of pressed glass (inexpensiveness and mass production) with those of art glass (color and iridescence). When this was done (around 1905), the resulting ware was called iridescent art glass or opalescent glass. We know it better as carnival glass.

Carnival glass, like so many good ideas, was simple in concept. A piece of clear or colored pressed glass was sprayed with a liquid mixture of metallic salts and then refired. The finished ware would be covered with an exceptionally tough, multicolored coating of remarkable luster. In some cases this ware was so attractive that it was favorably compared to Tiffany favrile, leading to use of the name poor man's Tiffany when referring to carnival.

At present no less than one thousand different patterns exist in carnival, many of them recycled pressed-glass designs. The colors fall into two categories: strong hues, such as the very common orange or marigold, the cobalt blue, and the green; and pastels, such as pearly white, clambroth, gray, and pink.

The makers of carnival glass, attempting to satisfy every taste, employed numerous patterns. There are naturalistic designs, many of which echo the sinuous curves of Art Nouveau; geometric patterns employing variations of the straight line; stylized abstractions; and designs that imitate popular cut-glass patterns.

It should be noted that the name carnival glass was coined by collectors and refers to the ware's period of decline in the late 1920s, when unused stock was often given away as prizes at fairs and carnivals. But carnival glass was not inexpensive. In fact, contemporary price lists show that it was more expensive than pressed glass and that it was sold in the best shops.

Practically all carnival glass was made by one of four factories: the Fenton Art Glass Company, the Imperial Glass Company, the Millersburg Glass Company, and the Northwood Glass Company. Of these companies only Northwood marked its wares (with variations of the letter *N*), so most carnival glass must be identified by pattern alone.

The majority of carnival-glass collectors concentrate on the period from 1905 to 1925, but quite a bit of ware, almost all of it marigold hue, was made during the 1930s. This glass is known as late carnival. Also, within the past decade carnival has been reproduced by the Fenton Art Glass Company and the St. Clair Glassworks as well as by Imperial.

Popular as it was in its heyday, carnival never approached the universality of the pressed glass of the 1930s and 1940s. This ware, advertised as "sparkling dinnerware," is now known as Depression glass because of both its association with that era and the fact that, unlike carnival, it was inexpensive: it sold for as little as three cents apiece and was given away as a premium with cereal or at movie house "dish nights."

Unlike the iridescent carnival glass, Depression glass came in only some twenty-five different colors. These were both clear and opaque and ranged from the extremely common clear pink and pale green to such rarities as ruby red, smoke gray, and opaque blue.

There are also fewer Depression-glass patterns than carnival patterns. At present only some ninety-five are known, and these can be divided into three distinguishable types. The first is mold etched, in which the piece is lightly stippled in semihigh-relief patterns, usually floral. Examples illustrated here are in the Adam and Florentine patterns. Less commonly seen are traditional molded patterns in which the design is formed by the shape and contour of the glass. The third type is chip molded, in which the overall pattern appears to be cut or chipped as it is in cut glass. Examples shown here are in the Sharon pattern.

All three pattern types are attractive, but the mold-etched variety is particularly popular with collectors, many of whom do not realize that it was often employed because the stippling helped to disguise the numerous bubbles and flaws found in cheap glass.

As with carnival, Depression glass is chiefly collected by pattern, though the ultimate goal is to obtain a complete set in a desirable color, such as cobalt blue or deep green. Such an ambition is complicated by the fact that within a given pattern and hue certain pieces are usually much harder to find than others. Saucers, plates, and creamers, for example, are relatively easy to come by; but such things as covered butter dishes, cookie jars, and handled sandwich servers may require a long hunt and substantial expense.

The great bulk of all Depression glass was made by eight companies: the Anchor Hocking Glass Company, the Jeannette Glass Company, the Indiana Glass Company, the Hazel Atlas Glass Company, the MacBeth-Evans Glass Company, the U.S. Glass Company, the Imperial Glass Company, and the Federal Glass Company. Researchers have been able to trace most Depression glass patterns to one or more of these plants.

It is also important to know that pieces may be generally dated by color. For example, pinks and greens were made from 1926 to 1940, yellows were produced between 1930 and 1934, and cobalts were produced only in 1936 and 1937. Amethysts were made in a single year, 1935, teal only in 1937, and ruby in 1940.

Though prices have risen during the last decade, Depression glass remains one of the most accessible and inexpensive of all twentieth-century collectibles. Vast quantities were produced, and even today it is possible to obtain a sizable collection with a minimum expense.

Throughout the first half of this century, many other types of collectible glass were manufactured in the United States. Much of this ware was of a higher quality than is generally associated with Depression glass. The A. H. Heisey Glass Company, in business from 1896 until 1957, produced a wide variety of fine pressed glass, and its products are now considered extremely desirable. Another company whose wares are much sought after is the Cambridge Glass Company, active from 1901 through 1954.

The Imperial Glass Company and several other manufacturers created an unusual and popular form—called stretch glass—during the 1930s. This frosted and richly curvilinear glass is found in several colors, including red, green, blue, and yellow. Because its lines go well with modern furnishings stretch glass is rapidly becoming a collector's favorite.

Extremely fine blown and etched tablewares have been made since 1887 by the Fostoria Glass Company. Fostoria wineglasses and tumblers are particularly prized for their fine designs and delicate forms. In recent years there has been growing interest in the products of the New Martinsville Glass Company, Libby, Steuben, and many others. Indeed, there are few twentieth-century factories whose wares have passed unnoticed by collectors.

Another growing field is that of modern, machine-made bottles. The invention of the automatic bottle-making machine in 1906 sounded the death knell for the traditional craft of glassblowing, and for many collectors 1906 marks the termination point of their bottle-collecting interests. However, rising prices for earlier bottles have forced collectors to look more favorably on later vessels. These can be distinguished from nineteenth-century examples by the fact that the mold marks on their necks run completely over the lip of the bottle rather than terminating somewhere along the neck.

Many unusual and interesting bottles, in both clear and colored glass, have been made since 1906, and prices for the most part remain relatively low. Popular types at present are beer and milk bottles, fruit jars and whiskies, but almost any twentieth-century vessel is potentially collectible.

Iridescent green carnival glass foooted bowl in Louwesa pattern; $65-85. A popular pattern and color.

Carnival glass. **Left:** Orange vase in panel and loop pattern; $30-40. **Center:** Green vase in ripple pattern; $40-55. **Right:** Orange vase in diampndpoint pattern; $30-40. Vases are among the most comomon pieces of carnival glass.

Pair of smoky yellow carnival glass candleholders in vertical panel pattern; $50-65. From 1905 to 1925 carnival glass provided an inexpensive substitute for art glass.

Left and **right:** Purple carnival glass punch cups in acorn pattern; $30-45 each. **Center:** Purple whiskey tumbler in grape and cable pattern; $175-220. The whiskey tumbler is a rare piece.

Peach opalescent carnival glass fruit bowl; $65-95.

Blue Phoenix glass vase with white floral design in relief; $65-75. Though not true art glass, Phoenix, like carnival, offered an inexpensive substitute for the one-of-a-kind pieces.

Phoenix glass. **Left:** Large pale blue flattened vase with white floral design in relief; $70-90. **Center:** Small yellow bowl; $15-25. **Right:** flat purple vase; $45-65

Adam pattern Depression glass. **Left:** Pink divided relish dish; $5-9. **Center left:** Pink pitcher; $15-25. **Center right:** Green dessert bowl; $4-7. **Right:** Green tumbler; $5-9. Made in many different colors and patterns, Depression glass was widely manufactured during the 1930s and 1940s. ▼

Cameo pattern Depression glass; by Anchor Hocking Glass Co. **Left:** Pale yellow grill plate; $6-9. **Right:** Pale green platter; $7-10. A delicate lacy pattern, cameo is popular with collectors. ▼

Bubble pattern Depression glass; by Anchor Hocking Glass Co. **Rear left:** Salad dish; $3-5. **Rear right:** Candleholder; $4-7. **Front left:** Soup bowl; $4-8. **Front right:** Cereal bowl; $3-6. All pieces pale blue. One of the more common patterns, bubble represents a good investment for the beginning collector.

Colonial pattern Depression glass.
Left: Pink pitcher; $25-35. **Center:** Pink shot glass; $4-8. **Right:** Clear covered butter dish; $32-40. Colonial is similar in style to 19th-century American pressed glass.

Cubist pattern Depression glass.
Left: Candy jar; $15-25. **Center:** Serving bowl; $7-10. **Right:** Powder jar; $15-20. All pieces pink. Its modern look has endeared cubist to many enthusiasts.

Florentine pattern Depression glass.
Left: Green tumbler; $5-9. **Left rear:** Topaz salad dish; $3-5. **Center rear;** Pink ruffled footed compote; $7-12. **Right rear:** Green cream soup bowl; $9-13. **Front:** Pink vegetale bowl; $9-15.

Floral pattern Depression glass; by Jeannette Glass Co. **Left:** Green divided relish dish; $7-11. **Center:** Pink covered vegetable dish; $12-18. **Right:** Green sherbet dish; $5-9. Floral is a common and popular pattern.

Forest green pattern Depression glass. **Left:** Tubular vase; $5-9. **Center:** Large, patterned vase; $10-18. **Right:** Bud vase; $5-8. All pieces deep green. Forest green is a lovely and underpriced pattern.

Iris pattern Depression glass; by Jeanette Glass Co. **Left:** Double candlestick; $10-20. **Center left:** Large vase; $13-19. **Center right:** Wine goblet; $11-16. **Right:** Footed tumbler; $9-15. All pieces clear. Another very attractive and moderately priced pattern.

Floragold pattern Depression glass. **Left:** Pink and gold salad bowl; $11-16. **Center:** Pink dogwood creamer; $6-9. **Right:** Dusky pink lace-edged serving bowl; $7-12.

Madrid pattern Depression glass; by Federal Glass Co. **Left:** Covered sugar bowl; $12-17. **Center:** Handled cream soup bowl; $5-8. **Right:** Pitcher; $20-30. **Rear:** Console bowl; $14-23. All pieces amber.

Mayfair pattern Depression glass. **Left:** Clear pitcher; $12-23. **Center:** Pink cake plate; $16-22. **Right:** Pink decanter; $40-55. Decanters are extremely rare in Depression glass. The price for this one would double in a more popular pattern.

Moderntone pattern Depression glass; by Hazel Atlas Glass Co. **Left:** Amethyst cup and saucer; $8-15. **Center:** Cobalt blue salt and pepper shakers; $25-35. **Right:** Cobalt blue Jell-O bowl; $10-17. This pattern is especially favored by fanciers of Art Deco.

Moonstone pattern Depression glass. **Rear left:** Clear and opalescent cologne bottle; $16-26. **Center rear:** Handled serving bowl; $9-17. **Right rear:** Vase; $8-13. **Front:** Pair of candlesticks; $18-27.

Mount Pleasant pattern Depression glass. **Left:** Footed sherbet bowl; $9-17. **Center:** Double candlestick; $21-33. **Right:** Three-footed bowl; $18-28. All pieces cobalt blue with gold banding. Cobalt is one of the most popular glass colors.

Patrician pattern Depression glass. **Left:** Green handled cream soup bowl; $5-9. **Center:** Amber covered cookie jar; $30-45. **Right:** Amber covered butter dish; $45-65. Patrician is one of the most favored Depression glass patterns.

Princess pattern Depression glass; by Anchor Hocking Glass Co. **Left:** Heart-shaped bowl; $12-17. **Center:** Footed tumbler; $10-15. **Right:** Oval vegetable dish; $9-14. All pieces pink

Sandwich pattern Depression glass. **Left:** Clear open sugar bowl; by Duncan Mills; $8-15. **Center:** Clear cookie jar; by Anchor Hocking Glass Co.; $18-28. **Right:** Dark green tumbler; by Anchor Hocking Glass Co.; $7-13. **Front:** Green bowl; by Anchor Hocking Glass Co.; $6-9.

Royal lace pattern Depression glass. **Left:** Pink tumbler; $6-9. **Center:** Blue plate; $10-18. **Right:** Pink covered cookie jar; $22-30. This is another popular pattern with good investment potential.

Sharon pattern Depression glass; by Indiana Glass Co. **Left:** Amber candy dish; $13-18. **Center:** Fruit bowl; $9-15. **Right:** Handled cream soup bowl; $8-14. Though not uncommon, amber is one of the more popular Depression glass hues.

Shell pink pattern Depression glass. **Left:** Snack set; $9-16. **Center:** Footed fruit bowl; $14-19. **Right:** Covered box; $10-17. All pieces opaque pink. Though generally less popular than clear glass, opaque Depression ware is attracting increasing attention.

Miss America pattern Depression glass; by Anchor Hocking Glass Co. **Left** and **right:** Clear glass cream and sugar bowls; $20-25 the pair. **Center:** Pink platter; $9-17.

English hobnail pattern Depression glass; by Westmorland Glass Co. Milk glass lamp base; $55-70. Depression glass lamp bases are not common.

Cherry delfite pattern Depression glass; by Jeanette Glass Co. **Left:** Tumbler; $15-25. **Center** and **right:** Cream and sugar bowls; $30-45 the pair. **Front:** Platter; $30-40. All pieces in opaque pale blue glass.

Laurel pattern Depression glass; by McKee Glass Co. **Left** and **right:** pair of candlesticks; $23-36. **Center:** Covered cheese plate; $35-50. All pieces in French ivory.

Jane Ray's jadite pattern Depression glass; by McKee Glass Co.; Plate; $2-4. Cup and saucer; $4-7. All pieces in opaque sea green glass. This pattern is substantially undervalued.

Doric and pansy pattern Depression glass. **Left** and **right:** Sherbet bowls; $5-9 each. **Center:** Bonbon dish; $14-19. All pieces in delphi blue. This lovely pattern should increase rapidly in value.

AKRO agate Depression glass. **Left:** Miniature white creamer; $5-9; green concentric ring dish; $2-5. **Center rear:** Blue and white planter; $10-17. **Center front:** Green octagonal plate; $7-9. **Right:** White octagonal plate; $3-6. Children's toy dish sets in AKRO agate are particularly in demand.

Sportsmen's Series glass. **Left:** Sailboat tumbler; $5-8. **Center left:** Fish decorated juice glass; $2-5. **Center right:** Fox hunter cocktail shaker; $12-20. **Right:** Skier ice bowl; $12-17. All pieces with transfer decoration on dark blue glass. This 1930s-era ware was intended for the game room or cocktail lounge.

Red glass cocktail set flashed in silver, $135-175. Well-designed sets of this sort date to the 1930s and reflect the modernistic designs of Art Deco.

Left: Vase; $7-12. Center left: Cocktail shaker; $15-22. **Center right:** Bud vase; $4-8. **Right:** Clear-top covered storage container; $9-16. All pieces are ruby glass, a popular and inexpensive 1930s glass.

Clear glass punch bowl set; by Heisey Glass Co. Bowl and stand; 1930-40; $235-315. Punch cups; 1930-40; $8-16 each. During its sixty-one years of existence the Heisey plant turned out a great quantity of collectible glass.

Left: Pink glass pickle dish; $15-25. **Right:** Clear pressed-glass hair receiver with electroplated silver top; $35-50. Both by Heisey Glass Co.; 1930-40.

Left: Frosted glass bonbon tray; $13-18. **Right:** Clear and frosted glass cocktail pitcher with stainless steel mountings; 1930-40; $60-80. Two examples of better-quality depression-era glass.

Stanhope pattern glass; Heisey Glass Co. **Left** and **center:** Cream and sugar bowls; $40-55 the pair. **Right:** Cup and saucer; $15-25. All are examples of Art Deco design. The fittings are in hard plastic.

Left and **right:** Pair of amber and clear glass cruets; $15-25. **Center:** Amber footed compote in chrome mounting; $30-40. All by Cambridge Glass Co. Though of fairly recent vintage, Cambridge is popular among collectors.

Purple footed compote in the Art Nouveau manner; by Cambridge Glass Co.; $75-125. The chrome mountings are by Farber Brothers.

Clear crystal glass candleholder in the form of a flying sea gull; by Cambridge Glass Co.; $55-70.

Purple and clear glass pitcher; by Cambridge Glass Co.; $55-75. An extremely fine example of stylish 20th-century utilitarian glass.

Pink and clear glass wineglases and goblets; by Fostoria Glass Co.; $15-25 each. All are in the pink Versailles pattern.

Left: Small purple bowl; $4-7.
Center: Dark purple fan vase; $25-35.
Right: Dark purple serving bowl; $20-30. All by New Martinsville Glass Co.

Stretch glass. Pair of matte green candleholders with white ribbing; $75-95. The rich colors of stretch glass made it one of the most popular mass-produced answers to art glass.

Stretch glass. **Left:** Bowl; $85-120. **Center:** Tall vase; $160-210. **Right:** Vase; $150-185. All pieces in various shades of red. Red is one of the less common colors in this glass.

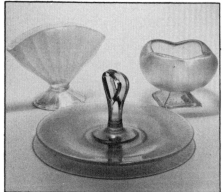

Stretch glass in vaseline finish. **Left:** Fan vase; $25-32. **Center:** Cake plate with clear handle; $35-45. **Right:** Footed rose bowl; $40-55.

Antique Pottery

Redware

Redware, the oldest native-made American pottery, is a relatively low-fired, fragile ware that can be decorated in a variety of ways. Because of this decoration, it was the first American pottery to attract the interest of collectors. Even before 1900, they were acquiring examples of redware plates and bowls bearing marvelous designs painted or incised on their surfaces. Today, such pieces sell for thousands of dollars.

Fortunately, not all redware is so expensive. Pottery as a whole, in fact, is subject to an enormous diversity of pricing, greater than that in any other area of American antiques. A category such as redware, for instance, may be priced far above another, such as white earthenware. And within a given category some items may be extremely expensive—sgraffito-decorated redware—while others are quite cheap—unglazed redware. On the whole, however, redware prices have climbed steadily over the past half century and show no signs of softening. If you are looking for a bargain or a new and unexploited field, you won't find it here!

Nevertheless, some types of redware are still available to the average collector. All redware, since it is porous, must have at least one glazed surface. One may find a variety of simple pieces—jugs, bean pots, and jars, undecorated and glazed only on the interior—at moderate prices. These humble vessels reflect the potter's unwillingness to use more than a minimum of lead-based glaze, which was expensive. Equally common and not much more expensive are pots glazed with a clear lead on both inside and outside. Quite often, particularly in New England, the potter would add manganese to his glaze to produce a shiny black finish, which can be exceedingly attractive. Black-glaze redware has never really caught on with collectors and at present offers one of the better buys in the field.

Of course, many people cannot be satisfied with such simple ware and seek more elaborate examples. Because it is fired at such a low temperature, redware may be glazed in a variety of colors; reds, greens, yellows, browns, blacks, oranges, and whites—which would disintegrate at a higher heat—may be combined to produce dazzling compositions. In Pennsylvania, slip decoration was combined with sgraffito, in which a design was cut through one layer of clay into another of contrasting color. Elaborate pieces of this sort were never standard items but were specially made as gifts or for the potter's own use. They are, accordingly, quite uncommon and in great demand.

Beginning redware collectors are well advised to decide early on whether they wish to collect the choice pieces, in which case they must think in terms of hundreds or even thousands of dollars, or whether they will buy modestly but selectively. If the latter is the choice, then form should be a prime consideration. A wide variety of objects were made in brick red clay, including inkwells, sugar bowls, soap dishes, toys, platters, and dishware of all sorts. Seek out the less common examples. In color, too, it is still possible to find pots glazed in more than a single hue—the black-on-red pieces from the Connecticut River valley for example. It is better to pay a hundred dollars for a well-formed or unusual example than spend the same amount on a half dozen common bean and preserve pots.

Stoneware

In contrast to redware, stoneware has only recently come into its own. This pottery is fired from a dense white clay found in only a few areas of the country. The difficulty of obtaining raw material severely limited the development of stoneware production; and though there were eighteenth-century stoneware kilns in New York, New Jersey, and along the mid-Atlantic coast, the craft did not prosper until after 1825, when the opening of the canals allowed for the relatively inexpensive shipment of both clay and finished product.

Nevertheless, vast amounts of stoneware were produced all throughout the nineteenth century, and largely because of its great strength (stoneware is of the same hardness as steel), much has survived. However, with the exception of a limited number of astute collectors, this ware found little acceptance among antiques buffs up until the last decade. There are two reasons for this. First, because of the temperature at which it is fired, stoneware can be decorated only with cobalt (blue) and manganese (shades of brown or black). Second, partly because of its relatively late arrival on the ceramic scene and partly because it does not take kindly to molding, stoneware has been produced in only a limited number of forms. A few inkwells, flasks, and the like may be encountered, but for the most part one is faced with a broad array of crocks and jugs.

The tide turned for stoneware in the early 1970s. Spurred on by several informative books and the soaring of prices for redware, collectors started buying the heavier pottery. But today, the boom has passed. Prices for middle-line pieces have declined sharply, and far too many collectors are now sitting with acquisitions worth half what they were five years ago. On the other hand, good decorated examples are still commanding high prices, and there is no reason to believe this will change. As in all areas of antiques, fine quality pieces remain a good investment.

What characteristics should one look for in collecting stoneware? Just the same things that are found in all good folk art: appealing form and decoration. The earliest pots in this medium were sparsely decorated, but even in the eighteenth century, designs—such as ships, flowers, faces, and so on—were scratched into the wet clay, and these were often then filled with blue. Such primitive but charming folk forms are eagerly sought and highly priced. As the nineteenth century advanced, incised or stamped decoration gave way to freehand painted designs in blue, which made use of a wide panorama of figures greatly influenced by the then-popular Spencerian school of handwriting. While such design can and often does become trite and mechanical, the overall effect is pleasing and can be spectacular. Birds, flowers, houses, ships, even animals such as dogs, elephants, and tigers, parade across these pieces, which are an endless source of pleasure to their owners.

As mechanization overtook the stoneware industry during the late years of the nineteenth century, molded stoneware began to appear on the market. Potteries, particularly in Ohio and New Jersey, produced vast quantities of mixing bowls, pitchers, covered butter crocks, and chamber pots. These were usually glazed in white and blue, green, or yellow. A variation appears in solid chocolate brown. All pieces have various figures, floral and animal, molded into their surfaces. Though hardly old, such stoneware is in demand and prices have climbed steadily.

Yellowware

Certain clays, found primarily in New Jersey and Ohio, fire to an attractive yellow. As early as the 1820s, American potters were employing such earth in casting pitchers and bowls. In the late nineteenth century, yellowware mixing bowls became popular, and they are still being made. The most simple are undecorated, though they may be cast in a mold that provides a figured exterior. More popular are those examples that are banded, usually in some combination of brown or white; many collectors strive to obtain a matching set ranging in size from as little as three to as large as twenty-four inches in diameter.

Other forms in yellowware are less common. Rolling pins, molds, custard cups, spittoons, and pitchers are found, as are pie plates and serving dishes. None, however, may be said to be common.

Common yellowware represents one of the best buys for the collector with modest means. It is not hard to find and is exceedingly attractive and inexpensive. It remains one of the few "new horizons" in American ceramics.

But, of course, there are exceptions to all rules, and Rockingham—a form of yellowware glazed in mottled brown—is one. It is not and for many years has not been inexpensive. Partly because of the magic name of the Bennington Pottery at which so much Rockingham was made (and to which so much has been falsely attributed), it has long been a prime collector's item. There are few

sleepers here, and buyers should recognize that they will have to pay top dollar for any piece, even spittoons and bedpans.

White Earthenware

White earthenware is an exciting and relatively untouched area of American pottery. Collectors have for years concentrated on English and European earthenwares, most notably ironstone, and neglected the domestic product. This was a problem in the nineteenth century as well, so that American manufacturers sometimes resorted to faking English marks in order to market their ware among a populace unreasonably prejudiced in favor of the European product. There is a wide variety of American whiteware: some entirely plain, some bearing molded decoration, some decorated by transfer printing or hand painting. It is possible through diligent effort to acquire a complete and matching dinner service bearing the mark of one of our nineteenth-century potteries.

It may take time to acquire such pottery, but it will not take much money. American white earthenware remains greatly undervalued in nearly all parts of the country. Plates go for a dollar or two, covered serving dishes for as little as five dollars; less common types such as coffeepots, sugar bowls, and molds cost little more.

Spongeware

Some whiteware and stoneware was decorated by the application of blue, green, or brown, usually with a sponge or brush—hence the name spongeware. Such pottery tends to be heavy and monotonous in form, but these characteristics are largely overcome by the spectacular results achieved through the application of color. Spongeware is, today, extremely popular indeed; as a

result, prices for it are still on the rise.

Fakes and reproductions exist in the pottery field, though they are generally a problem only in the area of redware. In this century, several potters have established reputations by making copies of nineteenth-century sgraffito ware. They have never intended to deceive and have, indeed, often marked their pieces. Unfortunately, unknowledgeable dealers sometimes represent unmarked specimens as being older than they really are. Similarly, Mexican and southern European glazed redware appears from time to time on dealers' shelves, being offered, often in good faith, as native American pottery. It takes experience to distinguish such imports; generally, they tend to be lighter in both weight and clay color than American pieces and to have slightly "foreign" shapes—pitchers, for example, have an hourglass shape.

There have been rumors of stoneware fakes during the last decade, and some crude examples are known, generally involving the painting of a blue design onto an old but previously undecorated pot. Such work is so bad as to be capable of fooling only the most inexperienced amateur. In addition, a considerable amount of nineteenth-century decorated German stoneware has been imported. It often exceeds in quality our own output; but as long as it is offered as imported ware, it presents no problem for the collector.

Yellowware is not a sufficiently lucrative field to attract the faker, with the exception of Rockingham; and there the major occupation is attributing all unmarked specimens to Bennington, a chore that could take a lifetime! The same may be said for white earthenware, where it is most likely that faking would run the other way; that is, labeling as English pieces that were made right here in the United States.

Redware glazed only on the interior; Pennsylvania, 19th century. **Left:** Bean pot; $20-35. **Center:** Miniature jug; $25-45. **Right:** Sugar bowl; $25-40. These pieces are typical of inexpensive earthenware still available to collectors.

Redware finished in clear lead glaze; New York-New Jersey area, mid-19th century.
Left: Preserve jar; $40-60. **Center:** Preserve or apple butter jar; $35-50. **Right:** Storage crock; $110-150. Matching top and fine shape put a premium on crock.

Redware; first half 19th century. **Left:** Water keg in clear glaze; Connecticut; $300-400. **Center:** Miniature keg, or rundlet, in mustard glaze; $450-600. **Right:** Water keg in clear glaze; Ohio; $275-350. Fine glaze and condition of center piece and incised date "1846" on keg at right are highly desirable.

Redware in lead-base black glaze; New England, 19th century. **Left rear:** Preserve jar; $35-55. **Left front:** Rundlet; $185-245. **Right rear:** Preserve jar; $65-90. **Right front:** Spittoon; $35-50. Black-glaze redware is an excellent buy at present; small size of rundlet enhances its value.

Redware. **Left:** Cake mold in clear glaze, black edging; New York, late 19th century; $75-95. **Center:** Ovoid jug in black glaze, fine early form; Vermont, ca. 1820; $65-110. **Right:** Bowl in clear glaze, black touches; Connecticut, ca. 1850; $150-225.

Left rear: Redware plate with white slip decoration on clear glaze; New England, mid-19th century; $300-450.
Left front: Redware mold in brown glaze; New York, ca. 1860; $90-130. **Right:** Redware preserve jar decorated in brown with green streaks on olive glaze body, New York, ca. 1840; $300-400.

Three pieces of redware, clear glaze splashed with black; Connecticut, mid-19th century. **Left:** Crock; $175-225. **Center:** Dish; $235-295. **Right:** Milk pot; $180-240.

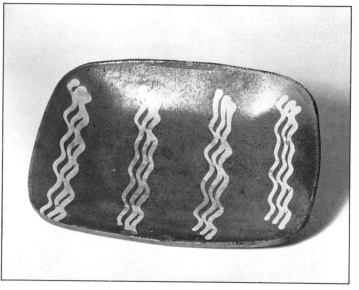

Connecticut redware. **Left:** Pie plate with yellow decoration; ca. 1850; $300-425. **Center:** Early creamer, clear glaze splashed with black; ca. 1830; $175-235.
Right: Saucer with yellow slip decoration; ca. 1850; $175-285.

Redware laof dish, yellow slip decoration on clear glaze; Connecticut, mid-19th century; $700-1,000.

Platter, yellow slip decoration; Maine, mid-19th century; $550-800. Fine form and good decoration.

Early stoneware jugs, ca. 1800 . **Left:** With mark of Clarkson Crolius, New York City; $800-950. Its open handles are characteristic of the period before 1815. **Right:** With blue-filled incised decoration; New York-New Jersey area; $750-900.

Left: Redware jug in white glaze; mark of Lorenzo Johnson, Newstead, N.Y., ca, 1870; $500-650.
Right: Clear glaze redware jug; mark of Alvin Wilcox, West Bloomfield, N.Y, ca. 1840; $450-600. Marked redware is extremely rare; Johnson piece is one of less than a half dozen examples known.

Fine examples of early and high-priced stoneware jugs; East. **Left:** In tan and umber salt glaze; Boston, Mass., ca. 1810; $450-550. **Center:** In dark brown glaze; New Jersey, ca. 1800; $300-375. **Right:** With blue decoration; by Clarkson Crolius, New York City, ca. 1840; $450-600.

Examples of early ovoid stoneware still available to collectors. **Left:** Cream jar; N. and A. Seymour, Rome, N.Y., ca. 1830; $100-150. **Center:** Jug; S.S. Perry, Troy, N.Y., ca. 1830; $85-135. **Right:** Cream jar; Warner and Humiston, South Amboy, N.J. ca. 1825; $70-95.

196

Mid-19th century stoneware from New England. **Left:** Salt-glazed flask; $75-110. **Center:** Inkwell; $60-90. **Right:** Mug with blue banding; $80-120.

Small stoneware. **Left:** Sander in brown glaze; New York, ca. 1830; $150-210. **Center:** Child's cup in salt glaze with blue banding; New Jersey, ca. 1800; $65 95. **Right:** Bank in brown glaze; Pennsylvania, ca. 1870; $40-55. Smaller pieces of stoneware are becoming hard to locate.

Stoneware milk pan in brown glaze; New Jersey, ca. 1860; $55-75. Brown glaze on this piece is called Albany slip and is frequently seen on pieces from second half of 19th century.

Left: Stoneware rundlet, blue lines; by Clarkson Crolius, New York City, ca. 1800; $1,200-1,800.
Center: Stoneware water cooler, cobalt and umber decoration; J.A. & C.W. Underwood, Fort Edward, N.Y., 1865-67; $350-450. **Right:** Gray-glazed stoneware water keg; Ohio, mid-19th century; $350-450. Age and rarity put a premium on rundlet; presence of both blue and brown on water cooler is unusual.

Ash-glazed jug; Goergia, ca. 1880; $150-250. This glaze, sometimes called "tabacco spit," was favored by Southern potters.

Metalic-finish stoneware. **Left:** Preserve jar in rich tan and black; Israel Seymour and Son, Troy, N.Y., 1850-52; $55-85. **Center:** Soap dish in orange brown; Ohio, mid-19th century; $75-110. **Right:** Jug in olive orange; Israel Seymour and Son, Troy, N.Y., ca. 1845; $55-85. Shiny and colorful metallic finishes can rival redware glaze in beauty. They are rare but unappreciated and undervalued.

Three stoneware preserve jars, salt glaze, blue decoration; Pennsylvania, ca. 1870. **Left to right:** $90-115; $125-155; $75-100. Jars of this sort were the forerunners of the Mason jar and the tin can.

Salt-glazed blue-decorated preserve jars; New York City. **Left:** By Francis Laufersweller, 1878-79; $145-190. **Center:** By Hudson River Pottery, 1850-55; $190-250. **Right:** By Louis Lehman, 1858-63; $225-285. An excellent demonstration of how regional preferences affect prices; to a New York collector these rather ordinary pieces of stoneware would be worth three times the quoted price.

Three dated cream jars in salt-glaze stoneware. **Left:** By Hudson, N.Y. Pottery; 1868 marks date the pottery opened; $200-250. **Center:** By N. Clark, Jr., Athens, N.Y.; $170-210. **Right:** By Clark and Fox, Athens, N.Y.; $225-285.

Blue-decorated stoneware. **Left:**
Salt-glaze pitcher; by Bosworth,
Hartford, Conn.; ca. 1880; $190-275.
Center and right: Two pieces by
Farrington, Elmira, N.Y., ca. 1890. Batter
jug; $375-460. Preserve jar; $125-185,

Salt-glazed storage crock with blue slip
decoration; by Lamsen and Swasey,
Portland, Maine, 1876; $285-335. The
inscribed date marks this as a Centennial
piece, one of a relatively small number
known. Dated examples are not
common, particularly those related to
recognizable periods or events; this
decoration greatly enhances value of an
otherwise mundane pot.

Unusual patented stoneware water
cooler, marked "The Gate City"; Ohio,
ca. 1886; $165-245.

Stoneware crock, fine slip and brush blue floral decoration; by Burger Brothers, Rochester, N.Y., ca. 1870; $325-475. Rochester produced some of the finest decorated stoneware.

Salt-glazed stoneware crock; by J. and E. Norton, Bennington, Vt., ca. 1855; $650-900. Decorated in sophisticated style for which Bennington is famous.

Two stoneware jugs with blue floral decoration; typical of J. and E. Norton, Bennington, Vt., ca. 1885.
Left: $125-175. **Right:** $90-135.

Stoneware jug with very fine parrot decoration in blue; by Whites, Utica, N.Y., ca. 1870; $450-625.

Blue-decorated stoneware churn; by W.J. Seymour, Troy, N.Y., 1870-80; $3275-400. Stoneware churns are not common, and this one is enhanced by a fine bird.

Salt-glazed stoneware crock, with unusual bird in blue; by Whites, Utica, N.Y., ca. 1870; $400-575.

Stoneware crock with blue slip rabbit; by David Weston, Ellenville, N.Y., ca. 1870; $475-585. Stoneware was occasionally decorated with fanciful objects such as lions, elephants, fish, and even houses. Such pieces are uncommon but frequently overpriced in relation to their artistic merit.

Molded stoneware pitchers with blue decoration; late 19th-early 20th century. **Left:** $75-110. **Center:** With stencil decoration; $45-50. **Right:** $155-185. Typical factory ware from the period.

Stoneware crock decorated with stamped, blue-filled cow; by Gardiner, Maine, Stoneware Company, ca. 1880; $185-285.
Impressed as opposed to incised or freehand decoration is rare in stoneware.

Molded stoneware poodle, glazed in brown Albany slip; Ohio, ca. 1870; $260-330. This was probably cast in a mold intended for the making of Rockingham doorstops.

Molded stoneware in green and yellow, with white-glazed interiors; early 20th century. **Left:** Straight-sided pitcher; $45-65.
Left center: Bulbous creamer; $35-45.
Right center: Mixing bowl; $25-35.
Right: straight-sided pitcher; $60-85.

Mass-produced molded stoneware in blue and white; early 20th century. **Left:** Storage crock; $60-85 (with cover). **Right:** Straight-sided pitcher; $65-95.

Identical molded stoneware pitchers slipped in brown, yellow, red, and green; early 20th century; $45-65 each. Pieces of this sort exist in rather large numbers, but a steady demand keeps prices relatively high.

Left: Molded stoneware casserole in brown slip; $15-25. **Right:** Molded stoneware creamer, brown-glaze; $15-25. Both, ca. 1920. Common commercial ware that has attacted attention in recent years.

Blue spongeware; late 19th century.
Left: Straight-sided pitcher; $325- 385.
Center: Low baking dish; $200-275.
Right: Pitcher with blue bands; $285-345. A stylish and unusual piece.

Left: Blue spongeware spittoon; $135-165.
Right: Banded blue spongeware mixing bowl; $190-245.
Both, late 19th-early 20th century. Excellent examples of factory-molded pottery consisting of a stoneware or white earthenware body decorated in blue or other colors by use of sponges and brushes.

Blue spongeware water cooler; late 19th century; $475-600. A rare piece; hence the high price.

Banded blue spongware bowl and pitcher set, late 19th century; $550-750.

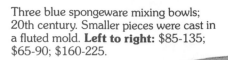

Three blue spongeware mixing bowls; 20th century. Smaller pieces were cast in a fluted mold. **Left to right:** $85-135; $65-90; $160-225.

Green and yellow spongeware; early 20th century. **Left:** Unusual small straight-sided pitcher; $55-75. **Center:** Deep bowl; $60-90. **Right:** Straight-sided pitcher with embossed flowers; $75-110.

Green and yellow spongeware; early 20th century.
Left: Crock marked "Sugar"; $65-90.
Center: Custard cup; $10-15. **Right:** Straight-sided pitcher; $75-100.

Three attractive banded green spongeware mixing bowls; late 19th-early 20th century. **Left to right:** $70-90; $95-120; $85-115.

Multicolored spongeware, green and orange on yellow; early 20th century.
Left: Covered sugar bowl; $70-100;
Right: Deep dish; $75-110.

Multicolored spongeware; late 19th-early 20th century.
Left: Bulbous pale blue pitcher; $85-125. **Center:** Very fine rust, green, and white serving bowl; $75-100.
Right: Pitcher (damaged) in rust, green, and yellow; $100-165 if in good condition.

Yellow earthenware; Ohio, late 19th century. **Rear:** Pie plate; $65-95. Unusual in that it was pressed out in manner of early redware plates rather than being molded like other pieces. **Left front:** Pitcher; $50-75. **Center front:** Serving bowl; $60-85. **Right front:** Custard cup in Victorian Gothic pattern; $30-45.

Yellowware mixing bowls; Midwest, early 20th century.
Left: $35-45. **Center:** White and dripped mocha banding; $75-95. **Right:** $25-35. Small or unusually decorated yellowware is a good investment.

Unusual Victorian Gothic molded spitton, yellowware; New Jersey, late 19th century; $125-175. A stylish, rare piece.

Yellowware from New Jersey, late 19th-early 20th century. **Left:** Crock with matching lid; $85-135. Rolling pin; $225-295. **Right:** Banded mixing bowl; $55-75. Brown and white banding distinguishes the hollware.
Rolling pins are uncommon and sought after in pottery; yellowware examples are most frequent.

Yellowware from New Jersey and Ohio, late 19th-early 20th century. **Rear:** Corn mold; $35-65. **Left center:** Miniature jug; $20-30.
Right center: Blue-banded custard cup; $20-25. **Right:** Molded mug; $25-35. For commercial pottery, yellowware comes in a rather wide varity of forms.

Rare yellowware bowl with sponged blue "seaweed" decoration between brown bands; Pennsylvania, late 19th century; $235-285. Unusually lavish decoration for yellowware.

Late 19th century yellowware; Midwest. **Left:** White-banded mug; $75-100. **Center:** Pitcher with embossed drapery; $85-110. **Right:** Small swirl mold; $40-65.

Embossed yellowware mixing bowl with pouring spout; New England, early 20th century; $45-75.

Banded yellowware; Midwest, early 20th century. **Left:** Mug; $110-145. **Center:** Miniature potty; $55-75. **Right:** Mug; $90-115.

Rare banded yellowware colander; Midwest, late 19th century; $175-250.

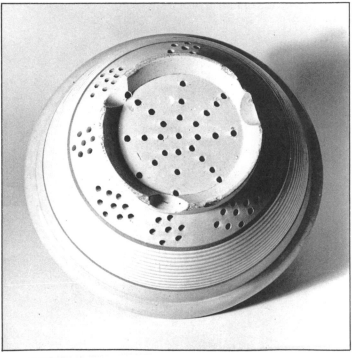

Rockingham serving dish; New England, mid-19th century; $85-115. Good strong color and fine shape distiguish this bowl.

Rockingham ware; New England, second half 19th century. **Left:** Deep dish; $75-100. **Center:** Custard cup; $20-35. **Right:** Large deep dish; $124-160.

Rockingham ware; East, second half 19th century. **Left:** small deep dish; $65-90. **Center:** Paneled mixing bowl; $90-125. **Right:** Creamer; $50-75. The white interior glaze of the creamer is a devaluing factor.

Rockingham ware; mid-19th century.
Left: Pitcher; Ohio; $150-210.
Center: Paneled custard cup; $40-50.
Right: Pie plate; $85-135. Both, New England.

Small objects in Rockingham ware; Midwest, second half 19th century. **Top:** Mug; $65-95. **Bottom, left and right:** Two soap dishes; $55-85; $45-65.

Three late Rockingham custard cups; Midwest, ca. 1890. **Left to right:** $15-20; $20-25; $20-25.

White ironstone; Midwest, 19th century. **Left:** Covered serving dish; $35-55. **Center:** Handleless cup and saucer; $20-30. **Right:** Covered butter dish; $45-65.

White ironstone plates lightly embossed; late 19th century. **Left to right:** 3-5; $6-10; $6-8. Such embossing generally doubles the value of an ordinary plate.

White ironstone serving dishes; late 19th century.
Left to right: $10-15; $20-30; $20-30. Like all ironstone they have been mechanically molded and given a clear glaze.

Three examples of the common white ironstone pitcher; Midwest, late 19th century. **Left to right:** $20-25; $30-40; $30-45.

White ironstone platters, late 19th century.
Left to right: $10-15; $12-15; $10-15. Light embossing on piece at left increases its value.

White ironstone platters; Midwest, late 19th century. **Rear:** $15-20.
Front: 14″ × 10″; $45-65. Larger pieces such as these are among more popular examples of American ironstone.

Pottery miniatures, 3″ high or less. **Left:** Bean pot; New England, ca. 1910; $20-35. **Top center:** Stoneware jug; Midwest, early 19th century; $35-55. **Bottom center:** Yellow glazed stoneware jug; Vermont, late 19th century; $15-25. **Right:** Redware porringer in clear glaze; Massachusetts, mid-19th century; $85-120. Miniatures are attracting attention and increasing in value.

Pottery miniatures. **Left rear:** Salt-glazed stoneware jug; New York, ca. 1870; $20-30. **Center rear:** Brown-glazed stoneware pitcher; $75-125. **Right rear:** Albany slip glazed stoneware jug; Vermont, late 19th century; $75-100.
Front left: Stoneware jug glazed in brown Albany slip; Norton and Co., Bennington, Vt., dated 1893; $250-350. Commemorative miniatures such as this, which marked the centennial of the old Norton Pottery at Bennington, are exceedingly rare. **Right front:** Redware jug; dated 1902; $45-70.

Art Pottery

Collector interest in art pottery has grown steadily during the past decade, encompassing everything from the limited output of individual potters, such as George Ohr, to the essentially mass-produced wares of great factories, such as Roseville and McCoy. The spreading enthusiasm has brought not only sharp price increases but also a redefinition of art pottery itself.

The term *art pottery* originally referred to pieces produced in limited numbers by a relatively small group of studio potters. Most of their ware was wheel turned and hand decorated, and many pieces were signed—or at least initialed—by the artist. Typical of this period is the work of such renowned kilns as the Grueby Faience, the Cincinnati Art Pottery, and the Lonhuda Pottery.

Unlike the common household pottery of the period—which was generally produced in the most rapid way possible and had a minimum of decoration—art pottery was frequently quite elaborate. It was made from various clays, ranging from the common red variety used for bricks to fine white earthenwares and even porcelain. It was usually dipped in a glaze consisting of a mixture of ground glass or lead to produce a surface that, depending on the potter's intent, could be either shiny or dull, the latter being the so-called matte glaze.

Decoration could consist of the glaze alone—the color of which could be varied by the addition of different metallic compounds—or of designs either painted over the glaze (overglaze decoration) or on the piece prior to the final glazing (underglaze decoration). A good example of underglaze decoration is the brightly decorated white glazed ware known as majolica.

Other decorative devices include designs incised or impressed in the soft pottery prior to firing. Or the pot could have sections cut out of it to create an attractive design (reticulation). And, finally, smaller molded or hand-shaped pieces might be applied to the pottery to give it form and surface texture.

Unfortunately, even when managed by practical potters, early art potteries were frequently in financial trouble. Their wares were costly to produce, and only a limited number of consumers could appreciate or afford them. Only a relatively small amount of ware was produced, and much of it is now gone. Consequently, the small, pre-1900 potteries offer a limited opportunity for the average collector.

However, businessmen, such as Samuel Weller of Ohio, soon recognized the economic potential of art pottery and set about standardizing forms and creating "lines" characterized by a similar glaze and decoration. At first such pieces were individually shaped and decorated and were often artist signed, but it was not long before this approach was, in most cases, abandoned. Weller was the forerunner of such modern production potteries as Stangl, Hull, and Roseville (whose kilns turned out thousands of pieces in a single year).

As the number of art pottery enthusiasts has increased, new collectors have gravitated toward the less expensive and more readily available wares of these larger and often later potteries. The term *art pottery* has therefore come to include attractive tablewares and mass-produced vases and planters as well as the limited-edition studio work.

The range in style and decoration found in art pottery is truly remarkable. Some of the earliest artists, such as Thomas J. Wheatley and Matt Morgan, both of Cincinnati, adhered to the eclectic styles of the Victorian period, producing vases cluttered with applied flowers and Moorish ornamentation. Others working at the same time were strongly influenced by new artistic currents. Maria Longworth Nichols's famed Rookwood Pottery reflected its founder's appreciation of the oriental ceramics she had seen at the Philadelphia Centennial of 1876 both in its production of wares decorated in the Japanese manner and in the hiring of a Japanese designer, Kataro Shirayamadani, in 1886.

Other studio potters, such as Teco Gates, were greatly affected by the teachings of the English artist and poet William Morris. Following Morris's admonition to avoid the often grotesque elaboration characteristic of Victorian decorative arts, they produced simple forms, often naturalistic in design.

The leaf, tree, and branch forms that Morris was so fond of were the hallmark of the Art Nouveau style, and few nineteenth- and early-twentieth-century art potteries were not affected by this mode. Perhaps the best application of Art Nouveau in American pottery was achieved by Artus Van Briggle, a young Colorado potter whose life was tragically cut short by tuberculosis. Recognizing that with Art Nouveau forms the least surface decoration is best, he developed a series of soft matte glazes that beautifully complemented the sinuous lines of his pottery. Other important kilns, such as Rookwood, Weller, and Roseville, produced art pottery in the Art Nouveau style.

As the twentieth century advanced, tastes changed. Increasing interest in the new forms of visual art, cubism, and the Italian futurist school began to have an effect on the plastic arts, too. The style known as Art Deco gradually came to dominate the output of many art potteries. One of the best-known producers of Art Deco ware is the Cowan Pottery of Liverpool, Ohio, but other shops, such as Coors of Colorado and Weller, also manufactured Art Deco ceramics.

The Great Depression signaled the end for most of the smaller and less efficient art potteries. With the buying public sharply diminished, only those factories that could produce a wide variety of inexpensive wares could hope to survive. The field of art pottery for the period 1930 to 1940 is therefore confined to the output of such factories as Weller and Roseville, the latter with one hundred and fifty different lines.

Following World War II, there was a revival of interest in art pottery, both in the collecting of older forms and the making of new. Influenced by Japanese and Scandanavian forms and methods, a new generation of potteries has taken to the field. Some of these potters have attained the status of factories, but most operate modestly, producing a few hundred or thousand pieces a year, most of which are offered for sale at craft fairs or through shops. It is this ware that is the true art pottery of today, and among these often struggling artists will be found the Van Briggles and the Ohrs of the second half of the twentieth century. Wise collectors are scouring the shops and fairs for the finer examples, and money is probably better spent on such ware than on the mass-produced commercial "art pottery."

If one wants to collect earlier examples, it is best to stick to marked examples from the more prestigious potteries. A collection of artist-signed pieces is always preferable, and these are almost certain to increase in value. As a practical matter, many collectors cannot afford such examples when available, but one should avoid those specimens that are neither marked nor identifiable from catalogs. Since so much art pottery was marked, unmarked pieces are less desirable.

Portrait tile in rich brown glaze; by Low Art Tile Works; Chelsea, Mass.; 1880-81; $700-850.

Left: White vase with multicolored landscape set in electroplated silver base; ca. 1880; $825-950. **Center:** Green vase with yellow and white applied floral decoration; 1878-80; $600-800. **Right:** White vase with multicolored landscape; ca. 1800; $750-925. All by Odell & Booth Brothers Pottery; Tarrytown, N.Y. Odell & Booth operated less than five years, and its ware is extremely scarce.

Portrait tile in green glaze; by Low Art Tile Works, Chelsea, Mass.; ca. 1881; $750-900. This tile bears the initials of Arthur Osborne, who designed tiles for Low from 1877 until at least 1893.

Blue vase with pink and green applied floral decoration; by Wheatley Pottery; Cincinnati, Ohio; 1880-83; $1,500-1,900. An early pottery, Wheatley's wares are rare and expensive.

Wall plaque in olive green glaze; by Chelsea Keramic Art Works; Chelsea, Mass.; ca. 1872; $3,000-4,000. This extremely rare stoneware wall piece was probably molded by Hugh Robertson, a member of the Chelsea firm.

Double-handled bowl in blue glaze with gold overglaze; by Matt Morgan Pottery; Cincinnati, Ohio; 1883-84; $425-575. Morgan pottery was in operation only a year, and examples of its Moorish ceramics are rare.

Left: Handled vase in brown glaze; $800-890. **Center:** "Lollypop: vase in green glaze; $450-550. **Right:** Pilgrim flask in blue glaze with incised representation of a dog; $775-900. All by Chelsea Keramic Art Works; Chelsea, Mass.; 1875-89.

Left: Vase in white stucco-like material with red and green applied floral decoration; ca. 1890; $700-850. **Right:** Cast mug in gray green glaze; 1887-90; $215-275. Both by Cincinnati Art Pottery; Cincinnati, Ohio.

Left: Blue porcelain box with pink and white applied floral decoration; $350-475. **Right:** Vase shaded light to dark blue with pink and white floral decoration; $850-1,100. Both by Faience Manufacturing Co.; Greenpoint, N.Y.; 1880-82.

Kerosene lamp base in pale tan glaze with gold highlights; By Avalon Faience Co.; Baltimore, Md.; ca. 1890; $750-1,000. Avalon was a division of Baltimore's Bennett Pottery.

217

Portrait of Gen. Ulysses S. Grant in green glaze; by American Encaustic Tiling Co.; Zanesville, Ohio; ca. 1885; $150-225. Portrait tiles were among the most popular of all art tiles.

Double inkwell in blue and tan crystalline glaze; by American Encaustic Tiling Co.; Zanesville, Ohio; 1880-90; $225-285. Though far better known for its tile, AETCO also produced a good line of pottery.

Left: Bowl; $200-275. **Right:** vase; $300-385. Both by Lonhuda Pottery; Stuebenville, Ohio; 1892-95. Both pieces are light brown with green and white floral decoration. This popular brown ground and underglaze decoration was deveolped by William Long, who later worked for both the Weller and Owens factories.

Left: Puzzle mug in rich brown glaze; 1888-1906 $325-450. **Right:** Drinking mug in clear glaze on red clay body made as a presentation piece; dated 1896; $415-485. Both by George Ohr; Biloxi, Miss.

Left: Vase in green glaze. **Right:** vase in tan glaze. Both by George Ohr; Biloxi, Miss.; ca. 1890; $475-650 each. Ohr pottery is characterized by extremely thin walls and distinctive glazes.

Left: Inkwell in the form of a ship's bell in yellow glaze on a brown base; ca. 1890; $600-750. **Right:** Miniature hat in blue glaze, ca. 1900; $375-475. Both by George Ohr; Biloxi, Miss.

Left: Rare unglazed white earthenware bowl banded in blue and pink; 1890-1900; $135-180. **Center:** Vase with crimped top in mustard and brown glaze; ca. 1900; $365-485. **Right:** Gourd-shaped bud vase in blue and green; ca. 1890; $335-415. All by George Ohr, Biloxi, Miss. Like much Ohr ware, these pieces are signed by the potter.

Left: Footed bowl or planter in black glaze with blue and white Cyrano pattern; ca. 1898; $200-250. **Right:** Utopian- ware jug in glossy brown glaze with green and white underglaze floral decoration; ca. 1897; $300-375. Both by J. B. Owens Pottery; Zanesville, Ohio.

Plate depicting General Washington's headquarters at Newburg (sic) N.Y., blue on white; by Volkmar Pottery; Brooklyn, N.Y.; ca. 1895; $450-575.

Candlesticks in blue green glaze with gold highlights and bases by Durant Pottery; Westchester County, New York, early 20th century; $350-450 the pair.

Left: Small bud vase in green matte glaze; $275-365. **Right:** Vase in blue matte glaze; $500-750. Both by Grueby Faience Co.; Boston, Mass.; 1897-1910. During its relatively brief existence, this pottery produced high-quality matte-glazed ware in classic forms.

Left: Footed bowl in pink glaze with blue interior. **Right:** Round vase in shades of pink. Both by Volkmar Pottery; Brooklyn, N.Y.; ca. 1905; $225-315 each.

Portrait tiles of George and Martha Washington; by Beaver Falls Art Tile Co.; Beaver Falls, Pa.; 1899-1927; $775-975 for both. These pink and tan examples are among the more sought after art tiles.

White porcelain bisque mug; by Clewell Ware; Canton, Ohio; ca. 1908; $145-195. Though Charles W. Clewell worked from 1902 to 1955, he made only a limited amount of pottery. His pieces were usually given a metallic bronze coating. This example, of the sort called a Holland Stein, was never glazed.

Mug in green matte glaze in the Arts and Craft mode; by Teco Pottery, Terra Cotta, Ill.; ca. 1909; $325-475. Leaves, flowers and similar naturalistic motifs are common on ware from this pottery.

Left: Aurelian glaze pitcher in chocolate and white on light brown ground; ca. 1900; $250-325. **Center;** Indian style bowl in tan and white matte glaze; ca. 1920; $90-140. **Right:** Chengtu pattern vase in orange red matte glaze; 1920-25; $100-165. All by Weller Pottery; Zanesville, Ohio.

LaSa Ware vases with metallic overglaze decoration in iridescent gold; by Weller Pottery, Zanesville, Ohio; 1920-25. **Left to right:** $275-345; $400-550; $325-435. This spectacular line of pottery was developed by John Lassell.

Dickinsware vase with incised figures of Mr. Dombey and his son filled in black and white on a tan ground; by Weller Pottery; Zanesville, Ohio; 1900-04; $650-850. Pieces bearing the likenesses of characters from the works of Charles Dickens are among the most popular of Weller creations.

Left: Creamer; $65-115. **Right:** Vase; $90-145. Both by Cowan Pottery; Lakewood, Rocky River, and Cleveland, Ohio; ca. 1917. Both pieces are in iridescent shades of pink, blue, and green.

Art tile. **Left:** Head of a warrior in green glaze; by Cambridge Art Tile Works; Cambridge, Mass.; 1887-1927; $90-120. **Center:** Head of Lincoln in blue and white; by Mosaic Tile Co.; Zanesville, Ohio; 1920-300; $65-95. **Right:** Angel in olive green; by Trent Tile Co.; Trenton, N.J.; ca. 1930; $85-135.

Left: Compote in red and green crystalline glaze with reticulated (cut out) base; $350-465. **Right:** Blue vase with green and white applied floral decoration; $145-215. Both by Fulper Pottery; Flemington, N.J.; ca. 1920. A former stoneware pottery, Fulper produced much art pottery between 1910 and 1935.

Handled ewer in the so-called standard glaze, yellow on tan ground; by Rookwood Pottery; Cincinnati, Ohio; ca. 1889; $550-675.

Velum pattern vase decorated by the painter Leonore Asbury, tan and blue on white; by Rookwood Pottery, Cincinnati, Ohio; ca. 1905; $535-665.

Three-handled chalice in green matte glaze decorated with raised abstract representation of a crab; by Rookwood Pottery; Cincinnati, Ohio; early 20th century; $335-450.

Bowl in tan and green matte glaze; by Roodwood Pottery; Cincinnati, Ohio; dated 1910; $85-100. This bowl, though fourteen inches in diameter, was a standard production piece.

Bookend in the form of a reclining leopard, light brown; by Rookwood Pottery; Cincinnati, Ohio; ca. 1925; $115-165. Animal forms and decorative devises were popular at Rookwood.

Rook or crow, mottled brown glaze, by Rookwood Pottery; Cincinnati, Ohio; ca. 1926; $275-385. The rook was adopted as a symbol of the Rookwood Pottery because of the kiln's founder, Maria Longworth Nichols, had grown up near rook-filled woods in England.

Console set consisting of center bowl and pair of candlesticks all on elephant bases, pink and pale green, by Rookwood Pottery; Cincinnati, Ohio; ca. 1929; $175-275.

Figure of a woman on a horse in the style of DiChirico, white glazed earthenware; by Rookwood Pottery, Cincinnati, Ohio; ca. 1930; $350-450.

Left: Large deep blue vase; ca. 1919; $175-250. Center: Green flower frog; 20th century; $15-25. Right: Pale blue commemorative vase; 1934; $95-145. Made for Cincinnati meeting of the National Conference of Catholic Charities. All by Rookwood Pottery; Cincinnati, Ohio.

Left: Ewer in butter-fat glaze; ca. 1946; $185-255. Center rear: Vase, green on cream butter-fat glaze; ca. 1944; $225-285. Center front: Bowl in green matte glaze; ca. 1914; $75-135. Right: Bud vase, blue on gray drip glaze; ca. 1916; $90-130. All by Rookwood Pottery; Cincinnati, Ohio.

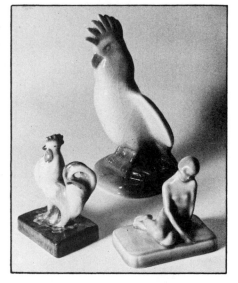

Left: Cock, jewel glaze on white ground; ca. 1946; $120-155. Center: Cockatoo in white butter-fat glaze; ca. 1943; $155-245. Right: Female figure in green butter-fat glaze; ca. 1945; $135-185. All by Rookwood Pottery; Cincinnati, Ohio.

Statuette in blue green matte glaze; by Artus Van Briggle; Colorado Springs, Colo.; ca. 1930; $95-145. This piece, made to fit into a matching bud bowl, was pictured in 1930-40 catalogs, where it was called "The Lady of the Lake" and described as a masterpiece of design.

Left: Squat blue green vase; ca. 1930; $35-55. Center: Tall purple vase; ca. 1922; $45-85. Right: Blue green vase; 1922-29; $35-65. All by Artus Van Briggle; Colorado Springs, Colo. Van Briggle was particularly fond of flowing Art Nouveau forms.

Turquoise bowl; by Artus Van Briggle; Colorado Springs, Colo.; ca 1950; $65-95. The glaze employed was described in catalogs as "velvet embroidery" in clay.

Pair of double candleholders in blue matte glaze with violet highlights; by Artus Van Briggle; Colorado Springs, Colo.; 1945; $35-55. When new the pair sold for $6.75.

Indian-head wall plaques marked "Big Buffalo" and "Little Star," pink and peach, by Artus Van Briggle; Colorado Springs, Colo.; 1930-45; $175-245 the pair.

Left: Tan and green vase; ca. 1910; $500-675. **Center:** Vase in black matte glaze; dated 1907; $700-900. **Right:** Squat vase in mustard glaze; dated 1903; $675-850. All by Artus Van Briggle; Colorado Springs, Colo. These are rare colors.

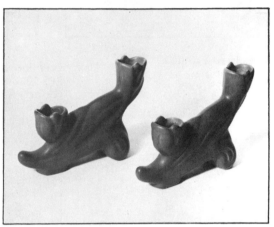

Vase, green and purple glaze in rich tones; by Artus Van Briggle; Colorado Springs, Colo.; ca. 1930; $85-135. Simple flowing forms and rich glazes characterize this ware.

Bud vase in rose and green matte glaze; by Muncie Pottery; Muncie, Ind.; 1925-30; $35-65. Flowing glazes like this were typical of Muncie ware.

Pair of tall bud vases in rose and green matte glaze; by Muncie Pottery; Muncie, Ind.; 1925-300; $60-85. The Muncie Pottery was in operation from 1922 to 1939.

Left: Vase; $20-35. **Right:** Planter; $15-30. Both by Red Wing Art Pottery; Red Wing, Minn.; 1925-30. Both pieces are in green matte glaze on tan background with glossy green interiors.

Art Deco vase in pink glaze with green interior; by Coors Porcelain Works; Golden, Colo.; ca. 1930; $45-75. Though essentially utilitarian in nature, Coors pottery is often quite well formed.

Left: Teapot in the form of a chicken in yellow glaze; $25-45. **Right:** Pitcher in white glaze with brown highlights; $20-35. Both by Red Wing Art Pottery; Red Wing, Minn.; 1940s. These are the products of a stoneware factory turned to art pottery.

Left: Windsor pattern handled vase in blue glaze with green highlights; ca. 1931; $75-95. **Center:** Inkwell in Rozane Egypto pattern in green matte glaze; ca. 1906; $175-220. **Right:** Egypto pattern footed bowl in green matte glaze; ca. 1906; $185-245. All by Roseville Pottery; Zanesville, Ohio.

Teapot in tan and green with yellow zephyr lily pattern; by Roseville Pottery; Zanesville, Ohio; ca. 1947; $65-95. During its long life, Roseville produced dozens of different pattern lines.

Left: Apple blossom pattern wall pocket in blue with white floral decoration; ca. 1948; $45-60. **Center:** Snowberry pattern wall pocket with green and white floral decoration; ca. 1947; $55-75. **Right:** Zephyr lily pattern wall pocket in dark blue with yellow floral decroation; ca. 1947; $50-65. All by Roseville Pottery; Zanesville, Ohio.

Left: Blue magnolia pattern basket-handled vase with pink and white floral decoration; 1943-44; $50-75. **Center:** Peony pattern tray in pink and green with yellow floral decoration; ca. 1942; $55-70. **Right:** Water lily pattern conch shell vase in green with white floral decoration; ca. 1943; $40-55. All by Roseville Pottery; Zanesville, Ohio.

Left: Pitcher in pink glaze with eagle motif; $25-35. **Center:** Pink bud vase; $15-25. Right: Blue vase $20-30. All by Niloak Pottery; Benton, Ark.; 1935-40. All are in matte glazes.

Pair of vases in tan matte glaze; by Niloak Pottery; Benton, Ark.; ca. 1940; $30-50. Though better known for its marbleized wares, Niloak made much cast art pottery in solid colors.

Left: Two-handled bowl in red and green splotch glaze; ca. 1930; $25-45. **Center:** Three-handled sea green vase; ca. 1950; $15-25. **Right:** Olive green coffee warmer; ca. 1950; $10-15. All by Stangl Pottery; Flemington, N.J.

Ovenproof baking pot in the form of a nesting hen, brown glaze; by Hull Pottery Co.; Crooksville, Ohio; 1960-65; $25-45. Though some don't consider later Hull ware art pottery many collect it as such.

Multicolored plate in style of majolica; by Stangl Pottery; Flemington, N.J.; 1940-50; $20-35. Stangl is the successor to the old Fulper Pottery of New Jersey.

Left: One of a pair of saltshakers, green and yellow design on white; $10-15 the pair. **Center:** Pink teapot with green and white floral decoration: $25-35. **Right:** Planter in the form of a pig, pink and white; $15-20. All by Hull Pottery Co.; Crooksville, Ohio; ca. 1940.

Cookie jar in the form of Little Red Riding Hood, multicolored glaze on white ground; by Hull Pottery Co.; Crooksville, Ohio; ca. 1950; $50-75. Despite the Warhol sale, cookie jars still aren't much of an investment.

Cookie jar in the form of a bear, brown and red on white; by McCoy Pottery, Clarksburgh, W.Va.; 1943-45; $60-85. Like Hull, McCoy is a producer of the "new" art pottery.

Savings bank in the form of an eagle, brown and white; by McCoy Pottery; Clarksburgh, W. Va.; 1960-65; $10-20. Made for the Emigrant Industrial Savings Bank.

Wall plaque or Easter plate in white glaze; by Frankoma Pottery; 1972; $25-45. A modern art pottery, Frankoma's wares are attracting substantial collector attention.

Left: Sugar bowl; $15-20. Center: Wall pocket; 15-25. Right: Creamer; $20-30. All by Frankoma Pottery;1960-70. All are in metallic green glaze.

229

Collectible Pottery

At the end of the nineteenth century, the American pottery industry—until then a relatively coherent entity—split apart. The traditional craft potteries, unable to compete with the more efficient mass producers, failed and were replaced by the art potteries (discussed in the preceding chapter). These art potteries catered to a select few; their wares were expensive to produce and therefore cost more than the average buyer could afford. The rest of the industry, of course, was composed of the mass producers, the great factories of Ohio and New Jersey, which provided the bulk of the nation's essential ceramics.

This so-called popular pottery has recently drawn the attention of a growing number of collectors. It remains inexpensive, and it makes an excellent field for the beginning collector. Produced between 1900 and 1970—by such manufacturers as Homer Laughlin and Regal China—the field is comprised of ornamental figures, storage vessels, vases, and tablewares. Tablewares are probably the most open area today, and preeminent among tablewares is Fiesta.

In January 1936, the Homer Laughlin pottery company of Newell, West Virginia, introduced a spectacular line of dinnerware at the annual Pittsburgh Pottery and Glass Manufacturers' Show. Named Fiesta and designed by the English potter Frederick Rhead, the new ware combined modern design with strong color. Rejecting the traditional "busyness" of most prior tablewares, in which a great deal of floral decoration had usually been superimposed on a neutral background, the creators of the style opted for simple lines and bold, solid colors. The most sought-after colors are red and ivory, though cobalt blue remains a favorite of many collectors.

Fiesta, which once sold for a few pennies per piece, has been increasing in price, and collectors have begun to turn to other, similar ware. Chief among these is Harlequin, which was introduced by Homer Laughlin in 1938 and manufactured until 1964. Though made in many of the same colors as Fiesta, Harlequin was quite different in design. The bold lines and cone shapes of Harlequin were distinctly Art Deco in concept. The new line, moreover, was not marked, as Fiesta had been. Also, it was sold primarily through the Woolworth chain of dime stores.

Another popular tableware line of the 1930s and 1940s was Luray, which was produced by several manufacturers and came in a variety of pastel shades. Both Harlequin and Luray sell for substantially less than Fiesta, and it is possible to assemble complete dinner sets for modest sums.

Not all tableware of the period from 1930 to 1960 was inexpensive. Many potteries, both American and European, produced high-quality lines that were made in limited quantities and sold for substantial sums. Particularly where blessed with strong Art Deco design or decoration, European pottery by such makers as Carlton and Fraunfelter is fully as collectible as the homegrown product. In fact, with popular pottery—as with many areas of twentieth-century collectibles—the sophisticated enthusiast looks for the best, no matter where it may have been made.

Foreign-made pottery includes Occupied Japan collectibles. Japan has long been a major ceramics manufacturer. From the end of the Second World War until 1952, American military administrators controlled the Japanese potteries, and the ware was marked "Occupied Japan." These pieces, which range from fine china dinnerware to a multitude of pottery and porcelain figures in every imaginable style, were imported into this country in great quantity. Today, they rank as one of the major areas of American collectibles.

Perhaps the most appealing aspect of Occupied Japan ceramics is their variety. Some companies, such as Noritake and Satsuma, produced thin-walled, hand-painted porcelain in a tradition going back to the seventeenth century. Other factories turned out imitations of everything from Meissen china to contemporary Hummel figurines. The figural pieces are the most common.

There are hundreds of different examples, many of which can still be purchased for a few dollars each.

The United States was not devoid of figural pottery. Very little was made during the 1800s (the rare primitive examples in redware and the sophisticated china pieces from New York and Philadelphia are now both expensive), but by 1900 figurines in the Art Nouveau style had begun to appear. By the 1920s, these forms were abundant and had begun to assume the hard lines and sleek look of the Art Deco style.

During this period figural pottery was perceived primarily as a decorative accessory, something to go on a shelf or a table. It was never really collected for itself until the advent of the pictorial whiskey bottle in the early 1950s.

Throughout most of the nineteenth century, glassmakers produced figural whiskey bottles in various shapes and sizes. Their appearance was clearly intended to promote the sale of their contents, and it is doubtful that the manufacturers foresaw that the receptacles would be collected. Collected they were—to the extent that "historical flasks," as they are now known, may sell today for thousands of dollars each. For both technical and aesthetic reasons, though, very few similar ceramic vessels were produced.

In 1953, Kentucky's James B. Beam Distilling Company put on the market a pottery Christmas decanter (filled with bourbon whiskey, of course). This, the first of the so-called Beam bottles, was such a success that since then literally hundreds of similar containers have been manufactured by Beam and by such competitors as Ezra Brooks and Ballantine. Beam bottles were among the first of the "controlled collectibles"—the value of the item is directly related to the number issued and the decision as to quantity lies in the hands of the manufacturer.

While the collecting of figural whiskey bottles has expanded greatly over the past two decades, many collectors have completely overlooked the many interesting figurines of the 1920s and 1930s. One may find everything from saltcellars to bookends and powder jars. Both the mass-produced dime-store pieces and the sophisticated examples by fine potteries, such as Fulper of New Jersey, are available. Most pieces can be obtained inexpensively—it is just a matter of seeking them out.

Fiesta ware in cobalt blue glaze;
1936-39. **Left:** Covered casserole;
$40-55. **Center top:** Coffeepot;
$55-75. **Center bottom:** Sugar bowl
with cover; $20-30. **Right:** Teapot;
$35-45. Cobalt blue is one of the most
popular Fiesta ware colors.

Fiesta ware in green glaze. **Left
bottom:** Cream soup bowl; 1936-59;
$15-20. **Left top:** Sugar bowl with
cover; 1936-69; $15-25.
Right top: Creamer; 1936-69; $10-15.
Right bottom: Nappy; 1936-69;
$5-10.

Fiesta ware in sky blue glaze. **Left:**
Marmalade bowl; 1936-46; $40-55
(with cover). **Center:** Sauce boat;
1939-73; $15-25. **Right:** Salt and
pepper shakers; 1936-73; $20-30 the
pair. **Underneath:** Chop plate;
1936-59; $15-25.

Fiesta ware in red glaze; 1936-43 and
after 1959. **Left bottom:**
Three-section plate; $20-30. **Left top:**
Teacup and saucer; $20-35. **Right:**
Demitasse cup and saucer; $35-50.
Red is one of the least common and
most sought after Fiesta colors.

Fiesta ware in ivory glaze. **Left top:**
Deep dish; 1936-69; $10-15. **Left
bottom:** Dinner plate; 1936-73;
$5-10. **Right top:** Eggcup; 1936-58;
$15-20. **Right bottom:** Ashtray;
1936-73; $15-20.

Fiesta ware tidbit tray in yellow and
sky blue glaze with stainless steel
rod; 1939-69; $45-65.

Fiesta ware. **Left:** Mixing bowl in cobalt blue glaze; 1936-44; $20-30. **Center:** Bread and butter plate in rose glaze; 1936-73; $2-5. **Right:** Plater in turquoise glaze; 1939-69; $5-10.

Left top: Fiesta ware ice-water pitcher in yellow glaze; 1939-73; $20-30. **Left bottom:** Fiesta ware utility dish in yellow glaze; 1936-46 ; $15-20. **Right top:** Fiesta ware carafe in yellow glaze; 1936-46; $35-50. **Right bottom:** Harlequin ware sugar bowl with cover in yellow glaze; 1938-64; $10-15.

Harlequin ware in turquoise glaze; 1938-64. **Left:** Pitcher; $15-20. **Center:** Salt and pepper shaker; $10-15 the pair. **Right:** Teapot; $20-30. Somewhat softer colors and a distinctly Art Deco style set Harlequin off from the usually more expensive Fiesta.

Harlequin ware; 1938-64. **Left:** Platter in dusky rose glaze; $5-10. **Right:** Serving bowl in sky blue glaze; $8-12.

Harlequin ware; 1938-64. **Left:** Sauce boat in red glaze; $12-18. **Center:** Sugar bowl with cover in blue glaze; $15-20. **Right:** Nappy in red glaze; $7-13.

Harlequin ware in green glaze;
1938-64. **Left:** Water jug; $20-30.
Right: Cup and saucer; $8-14.

Harlequin ware; 1938-64. **Left:**
Bread and butter plate in green
glaze; $2-4. **Right:** Dinner plate in
turquoise glaze; $4-8.

Luray Pastels ware in pale green
glaze; 1940-50. **Left:** Creamer; $3-6.
Center: Sugar bowl with cover;
$7-13. **Right:** Miniature pitcher;
$6-12. Though not particularly
popular in its day, Luray is fast
becoming a new collector's favorite.

Luray Pastels ware in pale pink
glaze; 1940-50. **Left:** Cup and saucer;
$3-5. **Center:** Soup bowl; $2-4. **Right:**
Creamer; $5-8.

Luray Pastels ware in pale blue
glaze; 1940-50. **Left:** Platter; $5-9.
Center: Vegetable bowl; $4-8. **Right:**
Sugar bowl with cover; $8-12.

Luray Pastels ware in pale yellow glaze; 1940-50. **Left:** Dessert bowl; $2-4. **Center:** Large platter; $7-11. **Right:** Cup and saucer; $5-9.

Green ironstone teapot; by Hall China Co.; 1938-50; $25-40. This attractive ware was designed for restaurant use.

Left: Red pottery storage vessel; $35-50. **Right:** Blue water cooler; $55-70. Both by Hall China Co.; 1935-45. These pieces were made for use in Westinghouse refrigerators.

Ovenproof syrup pitcher with metal and plastic top, in white glaze with red and green floral decoration; 1945-55; $15-25.

Ovenproof water pitcher in cream glaze with red, yellow, and green floral decoration; 1945-55; $20-30.

Porcelain powder box with chrome wash; 1935-40; $30-45. Designed for use with Estee Lauder cometics.

Hand-painted procelain plate; by Roycrafters; East Aurora, N.Y.; 1920-30; $150-235. This plate is typical of the fine designer-styled ceramics produced by Arts & Crafts groups.

Blue-on-white majolica serving plate; by Rambord; Pasadena, Calif.; 1930-40; $35-50. Ware of this sort was always sold in limited quantity.

Rayalite Electric China Ware coffee urn, creamer, and sugar with cover in cream glaze with green and orange decoration; by Fraunfelter China Co.; 1930-40; $400-600 the set. An extremely rare set.

Demitasse set in orange and black porcelain; by Carlton China Co.; 1930-40; $250-350.

Art Deco vase in cream glaze with pink and green decoration; 1925-32; $165-245.

236

Porcelain tobacco jar in pink and gold glaze; 1880-90; $275-350. The inscription indicates this piece was made as a gift.

Occupied Japan porcelain tea set in white with blue and pink flowers; 1945-52; $85-135. Made under the auspices of the American occupation forces, this ware has long been regarded as an American collectible.

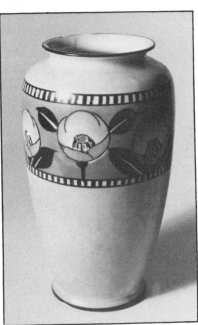

Occupied Japan porcelain vase in pink and black; 1945-52; $55-75.

Occupied Japan chocolate set in cream and dark red; 1945-52; $95-145. Tea, coffee, and chocolate sets are among the most common Occupied Japan pottery.

Occupied Japan porcelain gravy boat in cream with green and yellow decoration; by Noritake China Co.; 1945-52; $55-75.

Occupied Japan majolica covered box in blue, green, and cream; 1945-52; $20-35.

Occupied Japan majolica toby pitchers in pink, blue, green, and tan; 1945-52; **Left:** $20-35. **Center:** $65-95. **Right:** $35-60.

Occupied Japan bisque Hummel-type figures; 1945-52. **Left:** Girl in yellow and green; $25-40. **Right:** Boy in green and blue; $30-55.

Occupied Japan bisque frogs;
1945-52. **Left:** Green and blue;
$10-15. **Center:** Green and yellow;
$20-30. **Right:** Yellow, orange, and
green; $10-15.

Pair of Occupied Japan bisque lamp
bases in shades of pink, gray, and
white; 1945-52; $60-85.

Jim Beam china figural whiskey
bottles. **Left:** Donkey clown; ca. 1968
; $ 25-45. **Right:** Donkey boxer; ca.
1964; $35-55. A phenomenon of the
1950s and 1960s, Jim Beam
collecting continues unabated.

Jim Beam china figural whiskey
bottle, Ponderosa Ranch; ca 1969;
$25-35.

Jim Beam china figural whiskey
bottle, Harolds Club; ca. 1968;
$25-40.

Jim Beam china figural whiskey
bottle, Beam's Trophy; ca. 1962;
$25-35.

Jim Beam china figural whiskey
bottle, Armanetti Liquors Award
Winner; 1969; $10-20.

Jim Beam china figural whiskey
bottle, New York World's Fair; 1965;
$35-45.

Jim Beam china figural whiskey
bottle, Bing Crosby National Pro-Am;
1970-73; $20-30.

Jim Beam china figural whiskey
bottles. **Left:** The Wonderful World of
Ohio; ca. 1966; $15-25. **Right:** New
Hampshire; ca. 1966; $15-25.

Jim Beam china figural whiskey
bottles. **Left:** New Jersey; 1964;
$70-95. **Right:** Alaska Purchase
Centennial; 1967; $25-35.

Jim Beam china figural whiskey
bottle, 200th anniversary of the
California missions; 1967; $35-55.

Jim Beam china figural bottles. **Left:**
Grecian flagon; 1965-70; $15-25.
Right: Florida seashell; 1968-69;
$10-20.

White earthenware penny bank hand
painted in red and blue; 1910-20;
$70-95. An example of the country
pottery still being made in the
United States during the early 20th
century.

Pottery head with mask in pink,
yellow, green, and blue; 1930-35;
$75-100.

Art Deco covered bowl in orange,
green, blue, and black glaze; by
Crown Devon Pottery; 1928-34;
$90-135. A good example of the more
spectacular commercial pottery of
the 1920s and 1930s.

Art Deco pottery vase in black and
white glaze; 1930-40; $65-85.

Three-piece set of bath salts
containers in black and yellow glaze;
1932-38; $60-95.

Art Deco Phoenix ware vase in blue, tan, pink, and yellow glaze; 1925-35; $150-240.

Art Deco powder box in pink and blue glaze; by Fulper Pottery; 1930-37; $200-325.

Art Deco covered box in gray glaze with black speckles; 1930-40; $350-450. A rare and unusual example.

Pair of planters in crackled white glaze; 1935-40; $65-95.

Antique Silver and Pewter

Silver

The collecting of American silver poses both problems and opportunities for the enthusiast. The chief problem is that most eighteenth-century examples that are marked or otherwise clearly identifiable, with the exception of spoons and tablespoons, are unavailable to the collector of average means. The great bulk of them were long ago acquired by museums or wealthy individuals, and few are ever offered for public sale. On the other hand, eighteenth-century hand-wrought silver is only a small portion of the total produced in America in the past two hundred years. There is a vast quantity of fine sterling and plated ware still available. Most of it was manufactured between 1840 and 1930, in quantities sufficient to assure a reasonable opportunity for every silver lover to obtain a fair share.

The problems that exist in the collecting of silver are related to the nature of the metal itself. Silver is a precious and rare substance. Though much effort and wealth were invested in attempts to uncover local silver deposits, there were no major strikes in the continental United States until the great Nevada claims of the 1850s, by which time American silversmiths could well afford to import silver ingots. This was not the case in the eighteenth and early nineteenth centuries, though; experts believe that most early American silver was made by melting down coins or by recasting other silver objects that were either damaged or outdated. This alone may explain the dearth of eighteenth-century pieces today. Certainly, the shortage of silver was acute, so much so that some smiths even preserved, for later reuse, the tiniest silver filings produced in the course of finishing an object.

In discussing silver, it is perhaps best to begin by defining the terms. Silver in its pure state is too soft to utilize; it cannot hold a shape and would serve no purpose. The addition of a small quantity of copper, however, produces a lustrous, workable, and strong alloy, which has come to be known as sterling. It is .925 pure silver, or .925 "fine" in the parlance of the silversmith. The term *coin*, which was frequently stamped on silver from the period 1830 to 1860, refers to silver that is less than .900 pure silver. In England and other European countries, there were guilds of silversmiths that rigorously enforced adherence to proper weights, as well as assay offices run by the government that mandated the quantity of silver permissible in silver alloy. In the colonies, with the exception of a brief and unsuccessful venture in Baltimore, assay offices were never established; as a result, the use of the term *sterling* for an American piece does not always assure that it is of standard weight.

Despite the lack of legal safeguards, chemical analysis has shown that most early American sterling silver compares favorably in silver content with that produced at the same time in England and on the Continent. There are good reasons for this. Most silversmiths were the product of a five- to seven-year apprenticeship (either in America or abroad), during which one of the basic teachings was honesty. A worker who for years had dealt honestly with his master's wealth of silver was not likely to offer low-weight goods to his own customers. Moreover, if he did so, other smiths would be quick to call the public's attention to this fact. Also, the mechanics' societies that sprang up throughout the colonies following the War for Independence resembled the guilds in their enforcement of standards of honesty and workmanship.

The earliest American silver articles were made either by casting in molds or by raising—shaping by hand and tool from sheets of silver. Casting was for the most part confined to smaller articles such as porringers and to decorative elements that would later be soldered to the wrought vessel. Raising was a tedious process involving a variety of tools in order to transform the sheet of silver into a fully rounded piece—a coffeepot, say, or a bowl. A more rapid method was devised in the 1820s when the "spinning" of silver became popular. This procedure involved pressing a sheet of metal against a wooden form while the material was turned on a lathe. Under pressure, the metal assumed the shape of the form.

Spinning was greatly facilitated by the development of Sheffield plate. This was literally a metal sandwich, consisting of a sheet of copper pressed between two thinner sheets of silver. The resulting composition was harder than sterling and easier to work on a lathe. Since it was in large part copper, it was also much cheaper than sterling. Sheffield had been developed in the eighteenth century, but it did not reach full acceptance until the advent of more powerful rolling machines and the spinning process in the early nineteenth century.

In the 1840s, technology went a step farther with the discovery of electroplated silver, our modern silver plate; it was created by immersing a base metal, usually Britannia metal, in an electrolytic solution containing silver, which produced a chemical bond between the base metal and the silver. Both Sheffield and silver plate suffered from various defects, including the annoying fact that with time and use the silver would wear off. Nevertheless, both were relatively inexpensive, and they opened the silver market to a whole group of middle-class buyers, who up to that time had been unable to afford objects worked in such a precious medium. From 1840 on, vast quantities of silver plate were manufactured in American factories, and much of it is now readily available to the collector. Particularly desirable at present is sterling and plate in the Art Nouveau style so popular at the end of the last century. The rich, flowing lines of Nouveau pieces have a universal appeal, and they offer an excellent field for investment. Silver in the Art Deco style, a fad of the 1920s and 1930s, is just beginning to attract interest, and it too should find an eager public.

A maker's mark is an important element in the identification of American silver. In the colonies, the customs surrounding silver manufacture were greatly affected by the policies of the British government related to the making of objects in precious metals. In order to assure quality and uniformity, the British government required that all English silver bear a hallmark indicating the maker, the town in which the maker worked, and the year in which the object was made. These rules were never implemented in the colonies, and American smiths customarily marked their wares only with their initials, full name, or full name and city of origin. Some, particularly in the eighteenth century, did use false hallmarks in an attempt to create the impression that their goods were imported, but hallmarks were never required. Every serious student of American silver should own and use one of the standard books of American silvermakers' marks.

As one might suspect, silver, being valuable and in demand, has been faked. One of the most common techniques of deception is to remove the hallmark, and hence the proof of foreign origin, from a piece of English silver and pass it as an unmarked American piece. More sophisticated forgers actually impress a popular American mark in the altered piece; such famous manufacturers as Paul Revere, Myer Myers, and John Burt have thus had their ciphers placed on silver that never came within thousands of miles of their shops. Often, one can spot an altered mark by the fact that the wear normally covering the surface does not extend into the area of the mark. This too can be tampered with, though, so if in doubt, buy only from a reliable dealer who guarantees his wares.

Collectors of American silver can count on having a variety of forms from which to choose. In the 1600s, when few but the churches and the wealthy owned it, the metal was used primarily for shaping chalices, flagons, beakers, tankards, and the ever-popular porringer. In the eighteenth century, though, many other forms appeared, including coffee and tea sets, castor sets, trays, plates, bowls, pitchers, salts, boxes, candlesticks, and, of course, spoons in various sizes. As the nineteenth century progressed, these forms multiplied to provide the vast number available today.

Pewter

Though its popularity has declined considerably, pewter was for nearly two hundred years of major importance to the American household. Despite its softness and fragility, it was always preferred to wood and often to pottery. Accordingly, pewtersmiths were among the first metalworkers to appear in the colonies. Richard Graves is listed as working at Salem, Massachusetts, as early as 1635, and the oldest piece of marked American pewter bears the stamp of Joseph Copeland, active from 1675 to 1691 at Jamestown, Virginia.

These pioneer artisans worked under a major handicap. Pewter consists primarily of tin, to which a percentage of copper is added. But in those times, no tin deposits had been discovered in North America; all raw tin had to be imported from the vast mines at Cornwall, in England. The English at an early date put high duties on block tin while placing no duty at all on finished pewter. As a result, British pewter poured into the colonies, and for many decades local pewtersmiths were limited to repairing and reworking old pieces rather than making new ones.

What pewter local craftsmen did make was strongly influenced by European, particularly British, examples. Areas such as New York and Delaware, which had been settled by other national groups, showed traces of Continental styles, though these gradually disappeared as the English extended their control over these territories. In all cases, the colonial product differed from the Continental: it was of simpler construction, with clean and unpretentious lines—a direct consequence of the lack of material and the inability to afford costly bronze molds.

If the first American pewtermakers had problems, they also had advantages. The control of the European craft guilds did not extend to these shores, and our pewtersmiths were free to create and to develop without the rigid limitations that the guildhalls placed on workers. The "touch," or mark, of the colonial artisan was not controlled by law, and many of these people were highly individualistic. True, American workers tended to use variations of makers' marks found in their country of origin—for example, the rose and crown, the golden fleece, the lion, lamb, and dove of England—but in all cases they added unique elements of their own. The worker's initials, his hometown, or even some motto might appear on a piece. These early examples of marked American pewter are highly prized and expensive today.

After the Revolution, marks gradually became more standardized. At first there were patriotic motifs, particularly the eagle, which might be encircled with dots or stars representing the states, the number being increased with each new admission. Even these vanished, soon after 1812, to be replaced with simply the initials, full name, or name and locality of the pewtersmith. The vast majority of old pewter either is marked in this fashion or bears no mark at all. The absence of a mark, however, is no assurance that a given specimen was made in this country. While European pewter by law was required to be marked, not all of it was, and a substantial quantity of unmarked ware has entered this country over the years.

The fragile nature of pewter and the time required to manufacture ware that, although it sold for far less, had to be constructed basically in the same manner as silver—by casting or by handwork—put it at a disadvantage in competition with glass, tin, and pottery. Accordingly, manufacturers long sought a more practical medium. In the early years of the nineteenth century, the English found this in Britannia ware, first known as "hard metal," which consisted of an exceptionally durable and workable alloy of tin, antimony, and copper. Britannia could be cast or rolled into thin sheets without cracking and thus was accessible to metal spinning, an industrial process already used with brass and silver. Britannia was introduced on this continent in 1825, and within a few years pewter shops became small factories producing large quantities of standardized Britannia ware.

While perhaps less interesting to many collectors, Victorian factory-made pewter is a good investment. It is in general a good deal cheaper than earlier ware, and it comes in a wide variety of interesting forms.

Pewter forms tend to follow those of silver—it was not without reason that the former was known as "poor man's silver." The porringer, a small, handled, all-purpose vessel looking something like a cup, was the most common early type. It displays most of the decoration possible with pewter, primarily piercing or openwork, for the metal was simply too soft to bear the elaborate embossing and punching common on silver. Other early shapes are tankards; plates with a simple, smooth rim; bowls; large, round platters; and various teapots and coffeepots. At a later date, castor sets, pitchers, and a variety of lighting devices appeared on the market. In all cases, the forms, while clearly influenced by silver, show a much greater simplicity of design and decoration.

Coin silver spoons; first half 19th century. **Top:** Teaspoon marked "A.G. Stone," Massachusetts; $5-10. **Bottom:** Small serving spoon marked "Coin Silver"; $10-20.

Set of four large coin silver serving or tablespoons, East, ca. 1800; $180-240 for set of six matching spoons.

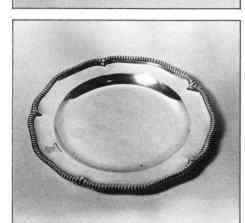

Coin silver serving dish with reeded rim; East, late 18th century; $200-300.

Left: Sterling silver and ivory tea strainer; $175-245. **Right:** Sterling silver grape scissors; $50-75. Both East, mid-19th century.

Left: Sterling silver cup; East, ca. 1800; $90-135. **Right:** Sterling silver baby cup, East, ca. 1860; $60-85.

Sterling silver bud vase with a variety of decoration, including embossing, punchwork (hammered decoration), and incised work; East, ca. 1890; $115-155.

A group of sterling silver Victorian buttonhooks; East, mid-to late 19th century. **Top to bottom:** $35-45; $20-30; $20-25; $15-20.

Sterling silver Art Nouveau pin dishes; late 19th century. **Left:** $60-90. **Right:** $50-75. Nouveau silver is still plentiful and inexpensive.

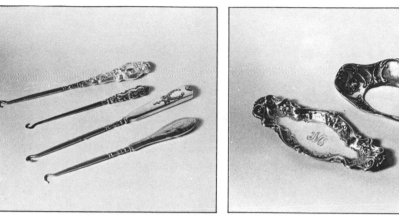

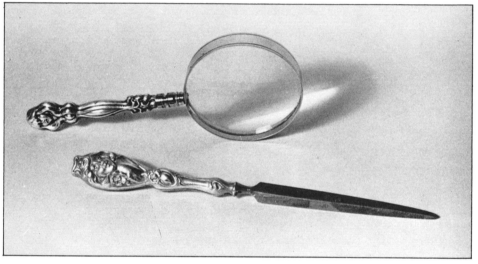

Art Nouveau Sterling silver; ca. 1900. **Top:** Magnifying glass; $75-100. **Bottom:** Letter knife; $55-85.

Sterling silver Art Nouveau match safe; East, late 19th century; $90-130.

Unusual sterling silver Art Nouveau lorgnette; East, late 19th century; $135-200.

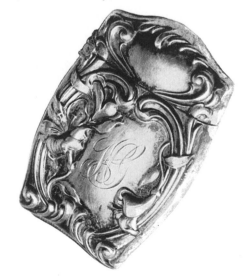

Silver-plate Art Nouveau brush and mirror; East, late 19th-early 20th century; $135-215. These sets are a good silver investment.

Strawbery spoon, sterling silver with gold wash; Tiffany and Company, New York City, early 20th century; $85-125. Any piece with the Tiffany mark is a wise purchase.

Top: Unusual sterling silver thermometer case; $60-85. **Bottom:** Two sterling silver pencils; $55-85 each. All East, ca. 1910.

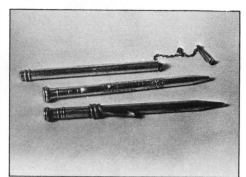

Napkin rings, early 20th century. Example at left is sterling; others are silver plate. **Left to right** $35-50; $10-15; $10-15; $15-20.

Sterling silver mesh evening purse; early 20th century; $85-145.

Two sterling silver purses; East, early 20th century. **Left:** $75-115. **Right:** $110-155.

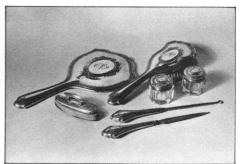

Sterling silver dressing table set; by
Webster, ca. 1905; $250-325.

Art Deco dressing table set, sterling silver
and cut crystal, East, early 20th century;
$300-400.

Left: Sterling silver hair locket; late 19th
century; $125-175. **Right:** Sterling silver
compact; early 20th century; $110-160.

Silver plate creamer, sugar bowl, and
tray; F.B. Rogers, early 20th century;
$65-95.

Pewter porringer; New York, 18th century; $275-375. Porringers with openwork handles like this one were widely made in the New York area.

Pewter teapot, marked Boardman, Connecticut, early 19th century; $275-350.

Pennsylvania, pewter coffeepot; by Whitlock, Troy, N.Y. first half 19th century; $250-315. Marked pewter is always more valuable than unmarked.

Pewter coffeepot; New England, mid-19th century; $150-185.

Pewter coffeepots, mid-19th century.
Left: Maine; $70-135. **Right:** Massachusetts; $90-150.

Pewter service pieces; 19th century.
Left: Teapot; $125-155. **Center:**
Coffeepot; $200-275.
Right: Sugar bowl; $60-95. Handles of
teapot and coffeepot are made of
ebonized wood.

Fine pewter syrup pitcher, marked
"Simpson and Benjamin," New York, ca.
1845; $350-500. Pieces of this shape
were modeled on the famous Liverpool
pottery jugs.

Left: Britannia metal teapot; marked
"Dixon and Smith"; $175-225. **Center:**
Pewter salt and pepper set; $75-115.
Right: Pewter and glass castor set;
$125-165. All, East, 19th century.

New England, pewter, 19th century.
Left: Porringer; $175-225. **Top center:**
Cann, or mug; $120-165. **Bottom
center** Warming dish; $75-135. **Right:**
Covered tankard; $250-350.

Pewter measuring cups; East, 19th century.
Left: $60-85. **Right:** $75-100.

19th century New England, mugs. **Left:** Pewter; $120-160. **Right:** Britannia metal; $85-115.

Bulbous pewter measuring cups; East, mid-19th century.
Left: $75-95. **Right:** $60-80

19th century New England pewter. **Left:** Deep bowl; $135-185. **Center:** Tall cann, or flagon; $160-220. **Right:** Mug; $65-80.

Two pewter bowls, New York area, mid-19th century; $105-155 each.

Very large (16" diameter) pewter charger, or serving plate; New York, first quarter 19th century; $275-345.

Pewter bowls; New England, mid-19th century. **Left:** $135-185. **Right:** $105-135.

Pewter deep dish, 12" in diameter; New York, mid-19th century; $135-160.

Pewter plates, 6" and 8" diameters; East, first half 19th century. **Left to right:** $75-110; $50-65; $65-85. Plate at left has simple rim characteristic of early American pewter.

Pewter plates ranging in size from 6" to 10" in diameter; East, 19th century. **Left to right:** $70-100; $55-75; $60-90.

Mid-19th century New England, pewter. **Left:** Camphene lamp; $175-235. **Center:** Large (14" diameter) charger; $210-255. **Right:** Handled cup; $75-90.

Pewter pieces from New York, 19th century. **Left:** Marrow knife; $85-125. **Center:** Porringer-shaped baby feeder; $135-185. **Right:** Matchbox; $60-95.

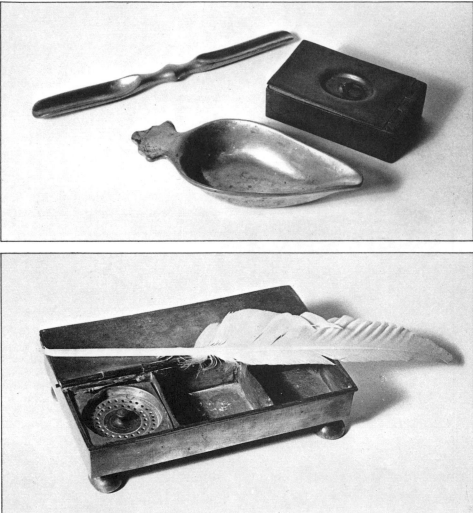

Left: Double-burner pewter camphene lamp; $175-250. **Right:** Pewter inkwell; $90-140. Both, New York, mid-19th century.

Footed pewter desk set; New York, early 19th century; $275-350.

Small pewter salt; New England, mid-19th century; $65-85.

Left: Pewter egg cup; $75-105. **Right:**
Large pewter ladle; $125-160. Both,
East, first half 19th century.

Child's pewter tea set; Massachusetts,
late 19th century; $85-135.

Pewter foot or bed warmer;
Pennsylvania, mid-19th century;
$90-135.
Pair of fine early pewter candlesticks;
East, first quarter 19th century;
$300-425 the pair.

Pair of pewter candlesticks, first half 19th
century; $160-230 the pair.

Tall pewter candlestick; New England, first half 19th century; $165-210.

Mid-19th century pewter candlesticks, East. **Left:** $70-90. **Right:** $100-140.

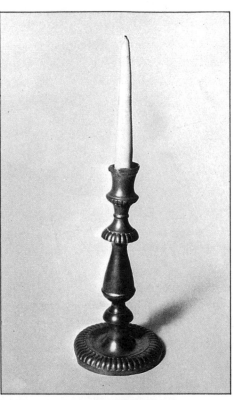

Tall pewter candlestick; New York first quarter 19th century; $150-190.

Single-burner pewter camphene lamp; New England, mid-19th century; $150-220.

Double-burner pewter camphene lamp; with mark of Sellow, active in Cincinnati, Ohio, mid-19th century; $275-350. Marked camphene lamps are uncommon.

Pewter whale-oil lamp; New England, first half 19th century; $145-185.

Pewter fat lamp on pedestal, a so-called rabbi's lamp; East, first quarter 19th century; $225-275.

Pewter kerosene lamp with reflector; Pennsylvania, second half 19th century; $240-290.

Pressed or pattern glass whale-oil lamp, with pewter top, New England, first half 19th century; $175-235.

Pewter kerosene lamp on stand, a so-called student lamp; 1880-90; $350-500.

Double-burner camphene lamp, glass and pewter on marble base; East, mid-19th century; $225-275.

Collectible Silver

Although there were American silversmiths active as early as the seventeenth century, only a relatively small amount of pre-1860 silver is available, and what can be found is invariably high priced. This is because until the discovery of Nevada's Comstock Lode in 1858 there was practically no native silver bullion available.

Following the Civil War, major silver manufacturers in Massachusetts, Connecticut, and New York began to turn out a bewildering variety of forms, all designed to cater to the tastes of an expanding and opulent middle class.

One of the first in the field was Charles Lewis Tiffany (1812 to 1902), father of the famous glassmaker. The elder Tiffany was in business by 1860, won a prize at the Paris Exposition of 1867, and by 1890 headed the largest silver factory in the world. In 1893, at the height of its prominence, the Tiffany firm held appointments to twenty-three crowned heads of state, including Queen Victoria and the Czar of Russia.

Tiffany is by far the most popular silverware of the late nineteenth and early twentieth centuries. In style it varies from early Victorian eclectic to Art Nouveau, with pieces in the latter mode regarded as most typical. The Tiffany output was enormous and varied—everything from hatpins to gigantic commemorative centerpieces is available. There is a great deal of flatware, including such oddities as baby feeders and napkin holders as well as objects of adornment ranging from brooches to belt buckles.

Tiffany concentrated on sterling silver, which is 92.5 percent pure ore, and the combination of weight and reputation assures that Tiffany's products are expensive collector's items. There are many other makers, however, such as the Meriden Silver Company of Meriden, Connecticut, which manufactured less-expensive electroplated silver. Electroplate is produced by passing an electric current through a silver solution, which causes the silver to adhere to bars of copper or pewter submerged in the liquid. The result is a thin coating of silver over the base metal—a much less expensive product. Late-nineteenth- and early-twentieth-century electroplate is often elaborate to the point of tastelessness, but well-designed examples can be found, and they represent a good investment. One should choose only specimens that show minimal wear—otherwise one must be prepared to undergo the expense of resilvering. Electroplate with the dull red glow of copper showing through the plating is not a particularly attractive acquisition.

Another major American maker of both sterling and electroplate was the Gorham Manufacturing Company of Providence, Rhode Island. Established in 1831, Gorham began producing silver in 1871, when it brought over the famous English designer William T. Codman, who developed the distinctive line of hammered silver known as martele and the sophisticated Art Nouveau style called athenic. During its long existence, Gorham has turned out much fine silver, including a variety of flatware, serving pieces, trinket boxes, vases, whiskey flasks, cigarette cases, inkwells, and complete tea and coffee sets.

Unger Brothers was a manufacturer with a more limited output than Tiffany or Gorham, but its ware is in great demand today. Unger was active in New Jersey from 1881 to 1910 — the period of his greatest productivity coincided with the height of the Art Nouveau movement—and the company is famous for teaspoons, dresser sets (matching mirror, brush, and comb), belt buckles, and doorknobs decorated with the profiles of young women with long, flowing hair. Marked U.B., Unger Brothers ware is highly collectible and still somewhat underpriced.

As the twentieth century advanced, major producers such as Reed and Barton and the International Silver Company dominated the field, and much of their ware made during the period from 1910 to 1940 lacks creativity. However, there were a number of individual silversmiths and small firms active in large cities, and sophisticated collectors are now seeking out their products. Sterling by such makers as Pier Smed (active in New York City, from circa 1830 to circa 1835) and Dominick and Haff (active in New York City, from circa 1888 to circa 1890) is well made and attractively styled. It is also just the sort of thing that may be overlooked by dealers and collectors bent on acquiring a piece of marked Tiffany or Gorham. In this, as in every area, knowledge pays!

Nor should one overlook the fine Art Nouveau and Art Deco silver manufactured abroad and imported into this country. Such makers as W. H. Haseler of Birmingham, England—manufacturer of the famous cymric pattern sold by Liberty from 1899 until well into the 1920s—produced quality ware that has been used and collected in this country for decades. There is also the famous Danish silversmith Georg Jensen. The ware he made while in his native land is among the finest produced in this century; but some collectors are not aware that during the Second World War he established himself in this country, and it is possible to obtain American-made Jensen silver.

The styles of collectible silver are many and varied. Before the turn of the century, Art Nouveau was dominant, but Tiffany, Gorham, and the electroplate manufacturers turned out pieces in many other highly eclectic Victorian modes, such as Egyptian Revival, Renaissance, and Gothic. After 1900, certain manufacturers returned temporarily to the slim lines and simple shapes of the neoclassic, but by the 1920s, Art Deco had taken hold. The geometric forms and strong, definite shapes characteristic of this mode prevailed until well into the 1940s.

Because silver is a valuable metal, collectors must anticipate paying for weight as well as form. Therefore, larger pieces in any style are always expensive. Beginning collectors or those of modest means should look for small pieces with interesting form and decoration. Such things as comb and pencil cases, belt buckles, spoons, perfume flasks, table bells, match safes, and sewing paraphernalia can often be purchased inexpensively. Moreover, because most silver manufacturers marked their ware, it is possible to find items bearing the coveted ciphers of Tiffany, Gorham, or Unger.

When seeking out silver, bear in mind that experts agree that compared to European examples, American-made silver remains underpriced in today's inflated antiques market. As such it offers the rare combination of both a beautiful acquisition and a practical investment.

Footed serving tray with enamel decoration; by Tiffany Studios; 1920-25; $550-650.

Covered serving dish; by Charles Lewis Tiffany; 1880-90; $950-1,200. Tiffany was the dean of late 19th-century silver makers.

Covered box; by Tiffany Studios; 1920-25; $225-275.

Powder boxes; 1900-10. **Left:** by Tiffany Studios; $190-240. **Right:** $140-190.

Left: Powder box, by Tiffany Studios; 1900-10; $125-175. **Center:** Belt buckle; by Tiffany Studios; ca. 1900; $65-95. **Right:** Art Nouveau whiskey flask; 1890-1900; $225-285.

Sewing tools; 1880-1920. **Top left:** Pincushion; $20-35. **Center left: Bobbin; $ 40-50. Bottom left:** Thimble; $20-30. **Center:** Thread holder; $115-125. **Top right:** Bobbin sheath; $70-85. **Bottom right:** Darning egg; signed by Charles Lewis Tiffany; $225-275.

Set of teaspoons; by Baker Silver Co.;
1890-1900; $30-45 each. **Center:**
Bonbon spoon; by Tiffany Studios;
1885-95; $95-135.

Napkin holders;1885-1930. **Left:** By
Tiffany Studios; $90-125. **Center left:**
$40-60. **Center right:** $105-145.

Hot-water reservoir; by Gorham
Silver Co.; ca. 1892; $1,200-1,450.

Tea set; by Gorham Silver Co.;
1900-05; $5,500-6,500. This choice
set is in the hammered martele style
developed by Gorham's William
Codman.

Tea set; by Gorham Silver Co.;
1895-1905; $1,200-1,600.

Pierced bonbon bowl; by Gorham
Silver Co.; 1910-20; $125-165.

Utensils; 1890-1910. **Top:** Fish fork;
by Sheibler Silver Co.; $35-45. **Top
center:** Teaspoon; by Shiebler Silver
Co.; $25-35. **Bottom center:** Seafood
spoon; by Gorham Silver Co.; $40-55.
Bottom: Seafood fork; by Wallace
Silver Co; $35-50.

Athenic pattern vase; by Gorham
Silver Co.; 1900-15; $750-965.
Designed by William Codman.

Art Nouveau trinket box; by Gorham
Silver Co.; 1900-05; $175-255.

Heart-shaped trinket box; by
Gorham Silver Co.; 1900-05; $85-110.

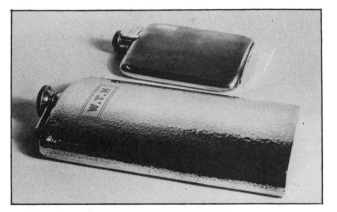

Left: Whiskey flask: 1900-10; $190-240. Center: Perfume flask; dated 1909; $125-155. Right: Perfume flask; by Gorham Silver Co.; 1900-10; $185-235.

Top: Art Deco whiskey flask by Gorham Silver Co.; 1930-40; $135-175. Bottom: Whiskey flask; by International Silver Co.; 1940-50; $120-150.

Inkwell; by Gorham Silver Co.; 1920-25; $250-350. The glass fount is by Pairpont Glass Co.

Ashtray and match holder; by Gorham Silver Co.; 1900-05; $120-145. This piece, which was probably used in a yacht club, is inlaid with enamel in blue and green.

263

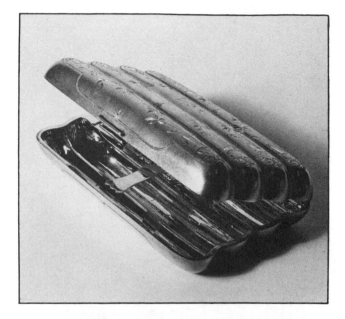

Unusual cigar case; by Gorham Silver Co.; 1880-85; $145-180.

Art Nouveau spoons; by Unger Brothers Silver Co.; 1905-10; $25-45 each.

Left: Cigarette case and matching comb case; $335-385 the pair. **Bottom:** Brooch; $30-45. **Right:** Bracelet; $300-355. All by Unger Brothers Silver Co.; 1890-1915.

Baby cup; by Reed and Barton; 1920-25; $65-85.

Flagon or tall cup; signed and dated by Pier Smed; 1934; $3,500-4,750. Smed's work is relatively uncommon.

Pitcher; by Dominick and Haff; ca. 1881; $700-850.

Cigar lighter in the shape of a candlestick; by Dominick and Haff; 1880-90; $165-215. The surface of this piece is hammered in a manner similar to that employed by Gorham during the same period.

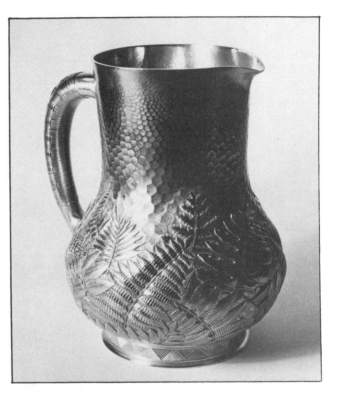

Bamboo pattern tea set; by Bisanda; 1900-20; $1,400-1,800. This set weighs forty-two ounces.

Mug; by Ball, Black & Co., ca. 1880; $170-215.

Cymric pattern flagon; by Liberty
Manufacturing Co.; ca. 1905;
$9,500-12,500. An extremely rare
piece.

Art Deco tea set; 1925-35;
$1,700-2,300.

Child's dinner set; 1890-1900;
$375-475.

Beaker; 1910-15; $75-95. Beakers of
this sort were usually made in sets.

Silver and copper drinking mug in
the Arts and Crafts mode; dated
1903; $475-575. Inscribed " 'My only
books were women's looks and folly
all they taught me.' From a girl in
Paris."

Baby spoons; 1890-1920; $45-85 each.

Dinner-table bells; 1880-1930; $75-135. Servants' bells were customary in some homes until the late 1930s.

Art Deco box; by Alphonse LaPaglia; ca. 1925; $215-265.

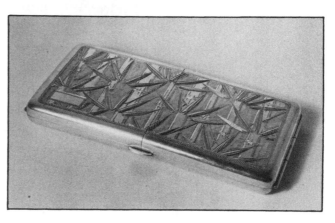

Cigarette case; 1930-35; $250-300.

Art Nouveau visiting-card case; 1890-1900; $240-320.

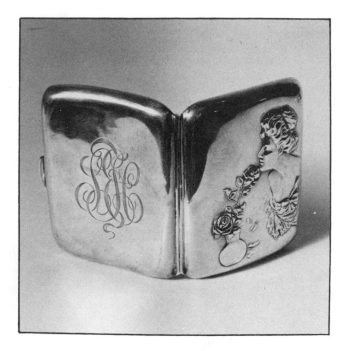

Pressed-glass dresser bottles with sterling silver tops; 1890-1910. **Left to right:** $70-90; $40-60; $55-70; $35-50; $85-125.

Cut-glass dresser or vanity bottles with sterling silver tops; 1890-1910. **Left:** 50-80. **Right:** $80-130.

Nut dish with goat's head finial on the handle; 1880-90; $170-245.

Left: Paneled perfume flask; 1890-1920; $125-155. **Center top:** Silver overlay whiskey flask; 1890-1920; $200-300. **Center bottom:** Art Nouveau flask; 1890-1920; $190-260. **Right:** Silver and crystal flask; dated 1902; $90-120.

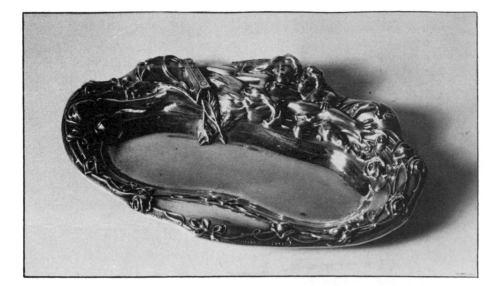

Art Nouveau card tray; 1890-1905; $185-245.

Match safes; 1890-1920. **Left:** Art Nouveau; $70-95. **Center:** $45-65. **Right:** $50-70.

Cigarette case decorated with golfer in black enamel; 1920-25; $155-185. Golfing memorabilia is increasing in value.

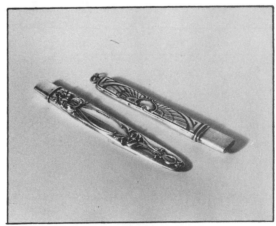

Left: Art Nouveau sealing-wax seal; 1900-05; $90-110. **Right:** Sealing-wax seal; 1910-15; $85-100. Even as late as the 1920s many people sealed their letters with wax, using initialed seals.

Pencil holders; 1910-20. **Left:** $55-70. **Right:** $50-65. These holders protected small, flat pencils of a sort rarely seen today.

Left: Silver chatelaine with gold insert; 1890-1900; $155-195. **Right:** Belt buckle; 1890-1900; $105-145. Chatelaines were worn on the belt to hold keys and similar items.

Sterling silver accessories; 1890-1930. **Left bottom:** Baby rattle; $135-175. **Left top:** Rouge box; $55-70. **Center top:** Bottle corker; $75-95. **Right:** Dance pad; $70-90.

Left: Brooch; 1910-20; $110-145. **Top:** Unusual snake brooch; 1900-05; $200-265. **Right:** Letter opener; 1890-1900; $70-90.

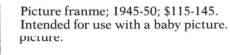

Picture franme; 1945-50; $115-145. Intended for use with a baby picture. picture.

270

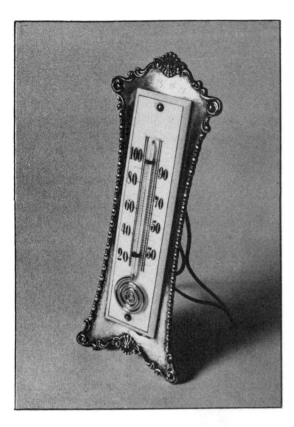

Porcelain thermometer with stand;
1910-15; $125-155.

Bowl; by Georg Jensen; New York,
N.Y.; 1940-45; $450-550.

Pair of electroplated vases;
1890-1900; $175-245. Less expensive
than sterling, silver plate swept the
United States in the second half of
the 19th century. Now it's making a
comeback with collectors!

Electroplated tea set; 1930-35;
$300-450. This stylish set is in the
Art Deco mode.

Electroplated nut dish; 1910-20;
$65-85.

Electroplated Art Nouveau lift-top
box; 1890-1900; $85-125.

Electroplated bud-vase stand with
cut-and engraved-glass insert;
1890-1900; $95-125.

Electroplated Art Nouveau card tray;
1880-1900; $750-950. A high quality
of craftsmanship is displayed in this
fine piece.

Electroplated card tray; 1890-1900;
$125-165.

Electroplated card try; 1880-1900;
$95-125.

Electroplated ashtray with
pressed-glass bowl; 1925-35;
$145-185.

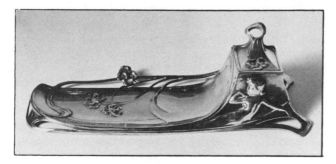

Electroplated inkwell; 1890-1905;
$155-190. The elongated form and
swirling surface decoration are
typical of Art Nouveau design.

Electroplated
paperweight;
1890-1900; $195-265.

Electroplated sailing trophy; dated
1925; $95-155. Pieces of this sort
usually have more historical than
aesthetic interst.

Copper and Brass

Copper

No areas of American antiques present so many problems for the collector as do copper and brass. These metals have been known since prebiblical times, and advertisements make it clear that from the early eighteenth century American craftsmen were working in both mediums. But unlike silversmiths, these workers seldom chose to mark their products. Moreover, most native ware closely resembles its European counterpart. When one adds to this the enormous number of brass and copper objects that were imported into this country from southern Europe in the years after World War II, one can recognize the great potential for confusion that exists in assigning a date and place of manufacture to individual items. Nevertheless, the color and general attractiveness of both metals make them favorites among collectors.

Copper was used for weapons and utensils before the dawn of recorded history. It is a rather soft, malleable ore with an attractive reddish cast, and it takes a good polish. It does not form well in molds but can be wrought into many forms. Since it is a good conductor of heat, it was formed into warming pans, for instance, to warm the beds in the days before adequate heating of houses; in colonial times, a round or oblong copper pan, rather shallow in depth, would be filled with hot coals and passed between the bedclothes to take the chill off before the inhabitants climbed in. Warming pan covers were often decorated with punched or pierced designs; hung on a wall when not in use, the utensils provided a bit of beauty in the often somber colonial home.

Teakettles of copper are another favorite with collectors. Smiths in New York and Pennsylvania developed a flaring gooosenecked form that is unique to these shores and though rarely marked can be recognized as distinctly native. Since raw copper imparts an unpleasant taste to food and may be harmful to health as well, copper cooking ware was lined with tin. A variety of such lined utensils is found, including open-hearth cooking kettles, oblong fish kettles and pans, saucepans, giant apple butter kettles, and a few field plates—copper dishes with an iron belt loop that were designed to be carried by workers for use at the mid-day meal.

Other and generally unlined copper ware includes measures of various sizes for both grain and liquids, funnels, components for liquor stills (always handy in those days before government control of distilling), lamp bases and filling vessels, skimmers, and flatirons.

The rust-resistant characteristic of copper also made it particularly suitable for the construction of objects that would be exposed to the weather. Weathervanes and trade signs come immediately to mind. Various garden accoutrements such as vases and gutters were also fashioned of the metal. Fishermen employed it both in ship's hardware and in the manufacture of various fishing lures.

Brass

Brass is an alloy, a combination of two parts copper and one part zinc. It too is of great antiquity, for the secret of smelting brass ingots by heating raw copper along with zinc-bearing compounds was discovered at the dawn of recorded history. The traditional process was a slow one, though, and a much better method for directly fusing copper and zinc was discovered, in 1781, by one James Emerson. Thereafter, more brass became available, though American producers suffered for many years from a lack of native zinc; the importation of the material forced them to price their goods higher than comparable foreign examples, which may be the reason that there has always been an abundance of non-American brass in this country.

Unlike copper, brass can be cast as well as stamped or wrought. As a result, there is a somewhat greater variety of brass objects available to the collector. The metal is also harder than copper, ductile, and highly malleable. It is easily joined and takes a high polish, resembling gold, for which it was often substituted.

The casting of brass household objects by founders skilled in the trade was an important area of early American metalcraft. First, a form or pattern in the shape of the desired object was carved of wood. It was then pressed into wet sand and enclosed within a boxlike container known as a flask. When the impression was satisfactory, the pattern was withdrawn and molten brass poured into the cavity. Once hardened, the final product was

polished and trimmed for use. Many objects were cast in brass, among the most important of which in the eighteenth and nineteenth centuries were furniture fittings: hinges, handles or pulls, and escutcheons to cover keyholes; all were collectively known as ormolu. Some are found with makers' marks, but none of these has so far been proved to be American.

Andirons were equally important products since fireplaces were the sole means of heating until the mid-nineteenth century. The many andirons produced were usually made either entirely of brass or of iron and brass combined. Styles varied, and andirons may be found with ball, urn, steeple, or lemon finials, and with ball, snake, or ball-and-claw feet. The leg was generally curved in the shape known to furniture experts as the cabriole. A good pair of andirons was expensive, even in the 1700s, and more than one brass master recognized this value by placing his name on his work, a thing he would not do with lesser objects made in the metal. Among the craftsmen who thus signed their work is Paul Revere. Prices for signed andirons start in the hundreds of dollars.

Numerous other items were cast in brass—the best buttons, for example, particularly those for military uniforms. Caspar Wistar, the famous Philadelphia glass manufacturer, was also one of our nation's first button makers. His button factory in Pennsylvania advertised for years in the Philadelphia newspapers, and the business was carried on for many decades by Wistar and his son. Important national figures such as George Washington wore initialed buttons, specimens of which bring high prices today. Other brass items commonly seen are doorknobs and knockers, candlesticks, irons, trivets, and heavy jelly kettles.

Cast brass is so heavy, though, that it is unsuitable for many purposes. Since the metal also can be wrought, hammered brass cooking utensils were standard ware in eighteenth- and nineteenth-century kitchens. In the 1850s, a more efficient method was developed when H. W. Hayden invented the process of spinning brass. In this method, a brass disk was rotated on a lathe between a die on the headstock and a rotating device on the tailstock. The worker pressed a tool against the turning disk, forcing the disk against the die until it conformed to the shape of the die. Spun-brass kettles and other similarly made vessels may be recognized by the multitude of concentric circles scarring their bottoms. Most spun ware was made in Connecticut, and much was marked with the name of its manufacturer—a rare occurrence with brass objects, as has been mentioned. Spun-brass kettles were light of weight and quite durable. They became an instant success and were sold throughout the East and Midwest by peddlers who piled great stacks of them upon their wagons or even carried them on their backs from town to town. Basins, measures, funnels, warming pans, dippers, and chocolate pots were also constructed in this manner.

As previously mentioned, the recent influx of European copper and brass (much of which is itself quite old) has presented serious problems for collectors. The chief objects that are imported seem to be dippers, warming pans, and kettles from Portugal and Spain and andirons and fireplace equipment, such as tongs and shovels, from England. Much more brass than copper is arriving. Among the former is a great deal of modern ware, but the careful collector should be able to recognize this since it is much lighter in weight than earlier pieces, shows no wear, and just doesn't look old. But the older pieces do present a serious threat to the market. Some collectors are already reluctant to buy anything other than marked pieces, such as spun kettles, or clearly identifiable American types, such as gooseneck copper teakettles. As in other areas, the most satisfactory solution is to buy from a reputable dealer.

Prices for both brass and copper are high and have been so for some years. Both are attractive accessories, and the pieces in greatest demand—marked andirons, kettles, and early buttons—command large sums. Warming pans and trivets are also expensive. For the collector of modest means, the accessible objects in these metals are the smaller utensils and the later spun-brass kettles.

Copper saucepans with brass handles; East or West, 19th century. **Top:** $85-115.
Bottom: $65-95.

Copper cooking pot with wrought-iron
bail handles; New England, 19th
century; $60-80.

Crude cooper saucepan; New York,
mid-19th century; $35-45. This was
probably used by a craftsman rather than
in the home.

Vey large, shallow-lipped copper cooking
or baking pan; Pennsylvania, 19th
century; $85-135.

Left: Copper skillet, second half 19th century; $110-150. Right: Rare copper spinner's skein holder; early 19th century; $150-200.

Copper funnels, East, late 19-early 20th century; $25-35. Right: $35-45.

19th century copper; East. Left: Funnel; $55-75. Center: Mug; $35-45. Right: Ovoid mug; $45-60.

Jelly press, hickory, pine, and copper; Pennsylvania, 19th century; $95-145.

Left: Copper field dish with iron belt loop; South, early 19th century; $75-125. Center: Copper kerosene lamp with brass fittings; New York, late 19th century; $65-95. Right: Unusual copper fishing lure; Maine, mid-19th century; $125-165.

Top: Copper tobacco box, New England, ca. 1840; $60-75.
Bottom: Unusual rose-brass pie crimper; East, 19th century; $90-125, Rose brass contains more than two parts copper to one of the zinc common to brass.

Copper oilcan, Maine, late 19th century; $30-45.

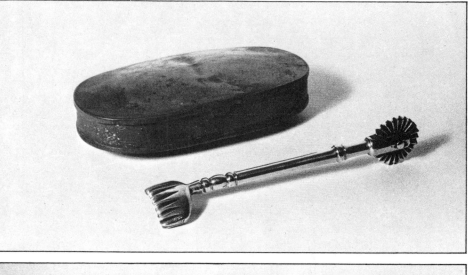

Fine engraved copper matchbox; New York, late 19th-early 20th century; $95-145.

Copper double-bottom pot, probably used to heat wax or oil; New England, late 19th century; $35-65.

Copper foot warmer; Pennsylvania, 19th century; $75-125.

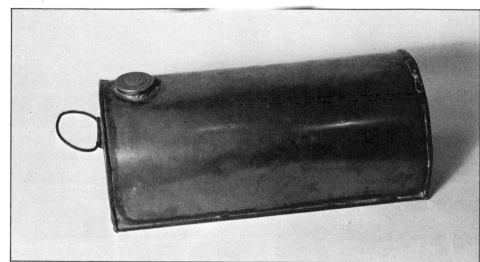

Copper rooftop ornament, Pennsylvania, ca. 1890; $160-240.

Copper spittoon; late 19th-early 20th century; $25-40.
Hardly a common item, but of little interest to collectors.

Copper barber's hot-water reservoir; East, late 19th century; $130-180. This vessel was placed over a fire to maintain a supply of hot water.

Left: Glass whale-oil lamp with brass base, lacking burner, early 19th century; $75-110.
Right: Rare early copper-plated push-up candlestick, late 18th century; $175-275. Both, New England.

Copper pipe for roof drainage system; East, late 19th century; $130-185.

Left: Copper funnel; $35-50.
Right: Rare five-spout copper oil lamp; $140-185. Both, mid-19th century.

Copper and glass kerosene lantern; East, late 19th century; $80-125.

Left: Very rare copper three-burner fat lamp with reservoir; New York, early 19th century; $175-245. **Right:** Pewter camphene lamp; mid-19th century; $170-230.

Unusual copper standing or hanging fat lamp; East, late 18th-early 19th century; $175-245.

Large copper whale-oil lamp; New England, first half 19th century; $145-195.

Brass kettles with wrought-iron bail handles; New England, 19th century.
Left: $100-140.
Right: $75-115. Piece at left is older and shows good hammer work.

Brass gooseneck teakettle, New York, 19th century; $225-275,

Brass jelly kettle with wrought-iron bail handle; Connecticut, mid-19th century; $80-130. A good example of a spun-brass kettle.

Punch-decorated brass bed warmers; Pennsylvania, 19th century. **Left:** $150-180. **Right:** $250-350.

Top left: Brass cattle bell; $20-35.
Top right: Brass chamber stick; $75-105. **Below:** Brass warming pan; $80-110. All, New England, mid-19th century.

Unusual brass hand-held skimmer, first half 19th century; $75-125.

Left: Brass spoon; $35-55. **Center:** Rare brass candle reflector in shape of miniature Queen-Anne-style tilt-top table; $240-300. **Right:** Brass spoon; $30-50. All, East, 19th century.

Brass skimmer with wrought-iron handle; Pennsylvania, mid-19th century; $80-125. Pieces similar to this are being imported from Europe.

Top: Hammered brass dipper or ladle with wrought-iron handle; New Jersey, ca. 1850; $75-115. **Bottom:** Small stirring spoon, cast brass with cutout handle; Pennsylvania, mid-19th century; $60-90.

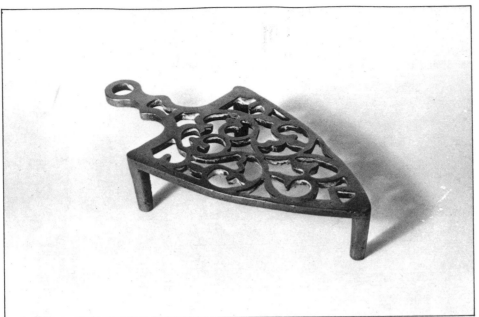

Cast-brass trivet, late 19th-early 20th century; $75-115.

Set of brass animal bells, late 19th-early 20th century; $75-125.

Pair of brass and iron penny-foot andirons; New York, ca. 1800; $450-650.

Pair of brass and iron andirons, East, first half 19th century; $275-375.

Brass folding telescope; New England, mid-19th century; $175-250.

Brass and iron fireplace tongs; New York, ca. 1800; $125-225.

Brass and iron goffering iron for use in pressing clothing; East, first half 19th century; $220-290.

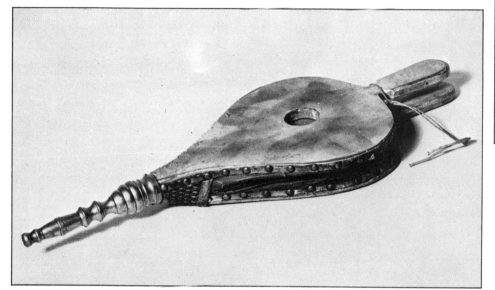

Brass, leather, and wood fireplace bellows; New England, mid-19th century; $75-150.

Fine-quality brass merchant's scale; Delaware, mid-19th century; $190-260.

Small brass scale of the sort often used by jewelers; Connecticut, 19th century; $65-110.

Craftsman's brass door marker or advertising sign; 19th century; $225-275. A quite uncommon piece.

Left: Brass and bone snuffbox; $65-95. **Center:** Brass and horn powder horn; $75-125. **Right:** Brass pie crimper; $65-90. All, New England, 19th century.

Upper left: Brass and glass candleholder; $110-160. **Upper right:** Rare brass carpenter's scribe; $60-90. **Bottom:** Brass snuffer tray; $30-45. All, 19th century.

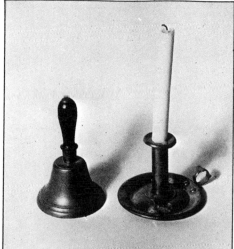

Left: Brass school bell; New England, late 19th-early 20th century; $30-45. **Right:** Sheet brass candlestick; New York, 19th century; $40-65.

Extremely tall brass wedding ring push-up candlestick of hog scraper variety; Connecticut, mid-19th century; $350-475.

Left: Brass candleholder designed to be fitted with wooden handle; East, early 19th century; $185-255. **Right:** Miniature cast-brass candleholder with snuffer, late 19th century; $100-145.

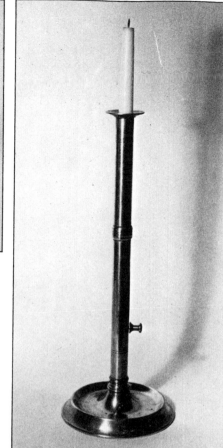

Tall spun-brass candleholder; East, late 19th century; $200-270.

Possibly an altarpiece.

Grouping of cast-brass candlesticks; Maine and Massachusetts, first half 19th century. **Left to right:** $60-90; $165-225; $90-1500; $210-260.

Rare miniature brass candle lantern; New York, early 19th century; $165-225, Brass lantern with slide door and isinglass shield; New York, mid-19th century; $185-255.

Left: Brass scoop; $25-35. Right: Very rare brass pump lamp; $240-310. Both, East, mid-19th century.

Brass and pressed-glass lamps; mid-19th century.
Left: Camphene lamp; $150-200.
Right: Whale-oil lamp; New England; $135-185.

Left: Brass whale-oil lamp; New England, first quarter 19th century; $110-140.
Right: Brass fat lamp; early 19th century; $145-210.

Brass kerosene hand lamp, East, late 19th century; $165-225. An interesting early kerosene lamp.

Small brass kerosene lamp; East, late 19th century; $85-125.

Triangular kerosene lantern with brass fount and tin top; New England, ca. 1880; $85-115.

Two brass kerosene lamps; New England, early 20th century. **Left:** $95-125. **Right:** $45-65.

Left: Brass kerosene lamp designed for wall bracket; $70-100. **Right:** Brass kerosene hand lamp; $60-75. Both, New England, early 20th century.

Bronze

Collectible bronze can be divided into two general categories: the purely decorative sculptural pieces, including figures or busts of humans and animals; and the utilitarian items that, though they too may incorporate figural elements, are intended primarily to serve a function. These latter range from floor lamps and ash stands to tiny seals used in correspondence.

Traditionally, only the sculptural pieces were regarded as worthy of collection, and because they were generally one of a kind—were, in fact, works of art—they were expensive even when new. However, late in the nineteenth century advanced technology made possible the issuance of hundreds—even thousands—of duplicate pieces based on a single master figure. *Bronzes d'edition* as they were known in France, enabled the sculptor to reach an audience that had previously been unable to afford his work.

These multiple editions have proved a mixed blessing to the collector, for the work of many late-nineteenth- and early-twentieth-century sculptors has been reissued so many times that the later editions are no better than reproductions. Figural bronzes by major artists are expensive, and it behooves the collector to know his field or to buy from a reputable dealer. The presence of an artist's signature in no way guarantees that a piece is not a recent casting.

Bronze is an alloy containing approximately eighty-eight parts copper and twelve parts tin, though zinc or lead may be added to vary color or strength. In an untarnished state the metal appears reddish brown, and with age it acquires a blue green, gray, or black patina. Because bronze is easily cast, most collectible objects are made in that manner.

Since the 1880s, most casting has been done in large foundries, such as the Barbedienne in Paris and New York's Roman Bronze Works. The techniques developed in these shops are largely responsible for the proliferation of bronze art in the past century.

Today's collector can choose from literally hundreds of different figural bronzes ranging from reproductions of Renaissance works to Art Deco pieces produced in the 1920s and 1930s. Quality varies greatly. Even the most recent versions of masterworks are preferable to some of the Victorian-period pieces, which were created solely to capitalize on a fashion or to mimic the style of a well-known sculptor. One must make careful choices, and personal taste or professional advice will prove the key to wise investment.

There are certain artists whose work is always a desirable acquisition. American collectors are constantly seeking examples by the great painter and sculptor of the West, Frederic Remington. Remington executed his first bronze in 1895, and before his death in 1910 he produced several dozen excellent renditions of cowboys, Indians, and western animals. Remington bronzes have been widely reproduced.

European bronzes popular among American collectors include the work of Les Animaliers as well as the works of those sculptors who specialized in representations of contemporary actresses and dancers. Les Animaliers was a group of sculptors, headed by the renowned Antoine Louis Barye (1795 to 1875), who prided themselves on anatomically correct renderings of animal forms. Their work, which was at its height during the period between 1890 and 1915, was generally of small scale and was naturalistic and highly detailed. Bronzes by Barye and his successors Georges Gardet and François Pompon now bring high prices.

Quite a different group were those sculptors, such as the Frenchman Raoul Larche, who cast likenesses of the great entertainers of the day—women like the dancer Looi Fuller and the actress Sarah Bernhardt. The work of these artists was much more traditional in mood than that of Les Animaliers, and it exploited fully the Art Nouveau preoccupation with female nudes. Though out of style since early in the century, these pieces are

making a comeback

Figural pieces represent only a small portion of the bronze available to present-day collectors. There are also the utilitarian objects. Everything from mirror and picture frames to doorstops and lamp bases has been cast in bronze, and it's all collectible. Moreover, much of the best is American made.

As in the fields of glass and silver, the name Tiffany is important. Louis Comfort Tiffany began experimenting with metalwares in the 1890s and soon developed a fondness for bronze. By 1901 his bronze lamp bases were winning awards at the Buffalo Exposition.

Before 1900, Tiffany bronze was stamped T. G. & D. CO. (Tiffany Glass and Decorating Company). After that year, the Tiffany Studios mark was used. Like most of his other products, Tiffany metal is usually marked.

Bronze can be colored through the application of chemicals, and Tiffany Studios employed four such basic patinas: dark green, golden bronze, brown, and pure gold. The ware, which numbered dozens of different objects—from candlesticks and figurines to inkwells and letter openers—was made in several characteristic patterns, the most popular of which were those known as pine bough, grape vine, and zodiac. Though hardly in-expensive, Tiffany bronze is within the reach of most collectors and offers an interesting field—if only because of the large variety of objects produced. It is possible, for example, to assemble a substantial collection of different Tiffany candlesticks or desk sets.

Tiffany Studios was not the only manufacturer of bronze accessories during the early twentieth century. The Revere Studios, another major producer, made ware in a pattern so similar to grape vine that, though properly marked, it is frequently confused with the more desirable Tiffany.

The Roycrafters, of East Aurora, New York, made bronze candlesticks, bookends, and inkwells in the Arts and Crafts manner. These pieces, which are sometimes marked BRADLEY & HUBBARD, are eagerly sought as complements to Mission-style furniture. Many other companies, not all of which marked their products, made bronze ware, particularly writing implements. The abundance of these, particularly inkwells and writing boxes, is explained by the fact that the expansion of literacy at the close of the nineteenth century combined with the institution of universal penny postage in 1898 led to a great increase in letter writing. Much of the equipment that was manufactured to fill the need for writing materials remains today to fill the need for collectibles.

Small bronze incense holder;
1940-50; $15-25.

Figure of a youth; by Raoul Larche; 1890-1905; $900-1,300. A sculptor in the classic tradition, Larche made castings of actresses and dancers that are in great demand.

Figure of the goddess Astarte; 1890-95; $500-750.

Figure of a woman; by Tiffany Studios; 1910-20; $185-255, set. One of a set of bookends, this piece is typical of the whimsical figures produced by the Tiffany shop.

Figure of a discus thrower; by R. Tate McKenzie; ca. 1929; $1,500-2,100.

Figure of Diana the huntress and deer, set in marble; 1930-35; $185-225. A typical example of unsigned factory-produced bronze.

Bust of Shakespeare; by A. Carriere; 1895-1905; $700-850.

Art Nouveau bust of a young woman; 1890-1900; $350-425.

Bust of George Washington; 1910-20; $175-275. As in the 19th century, 20th-century sculptors produced many figures of early patriots such as Washington, Adams, and Lincoln.

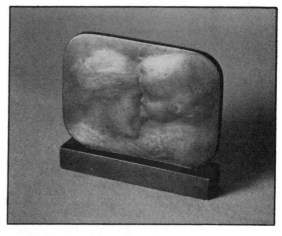

Tiny relief sculpture of mother and child; 1900-10; $135-175.

Relief sculpture of a young woman and man; by Ruth Milles; 1910-20; $1,000-1,500.

Bust, possibly of U.S. Grant;
1890-1900; $160-180.

Relief sculpture of a young woman;
by Theodad; 1920-30; $225-275.

Trophy plaque for Spalding Olympic;
dated 1925; $125-155.

Miniature head; 1890-1910; $35-55.

Sculpture of a lion and python; by
Antoine Louis Barye; ca. 1890;
$900-1,300. Barye's work is in great
demand.

Sculpture of two deer; by P.
Camolero; 1910-20; $1,500-1,900.

Sculpture of a dog; by Louise Allen;
dated 1914; $500-750.

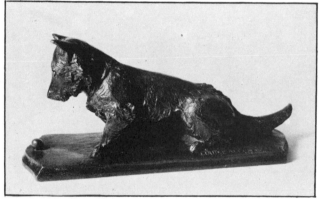

ylized miniature figure of a dog;
Haganauer; 1930-40; $90-145.
ry popular with collectors of Art
co.

Sculpture of a dog; 1905-15;
$135-175.

Miniature animals; 1900-20. **Left:**
Bear; $25-40. **Center:** Duck; $20-25.
Right: Penguin; $25-40.

Art Nouveau card tray; 1930-35;
$135-195. Stamped on the back is
"Diamond Jim Brady Room,
Luchow's New York." Memorabilia
from a famous New York City
restaurant.

Art Nouveau handled platter;
1905-15; $125-175

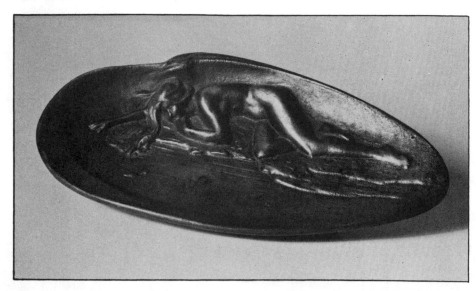

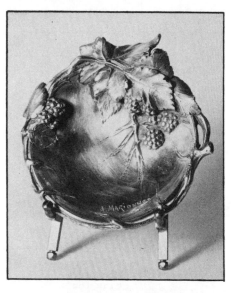

Art Nouveau card tray; by A.
Marionnet; 1890-1900; $330-480.

Candleholder; 1920-30; $75-95.
Simple but attractive pieces such as
this are still underpriced.

Art Nouveau candleholder;
1890-1910; $250-350. Wonderful
detail greatly enhances the value of
this fine piece.

Art Nouveau candleholder with gold
wash; 1890-1900; $650-850.
Gold-washed bronze has the weight
and appearance of solid gold.

Candelabra; by Tiffany Studios;
1910-15; $900-1,250 the pair.

Candlestick; by Tiffany Studios;
1900-10; $450-600.

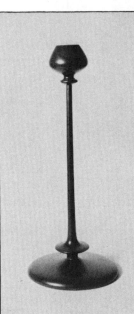

Desk set; 1890-1900; $600-750. Desk
sets were among the most popular of
Art Nouveau bronze ware.

Desk fixtures; 1920-35. **Left:** Double
inkwell; $90-120. **Center:** Stamp box;
$60-90. **Right:** Inkwell; $125-175.

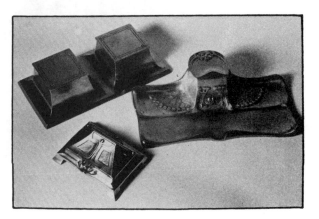

Inkwell in the shape of a gondola;
1900-10; $90-125.

Inkwell decorated with beetles in
relief; by Tiffany Studios; 1900-02;
$2,600-3,300. So-called scarab
inkwells are rare and valuable.

Art Nouveau inkstand; 1890-1900;
$120-170. A common factory form.

Inkwell in the form of chicken;
1900-10; $215-255.

Top: Inkwell; by Tiffany Studios; 1905-15; $375-450. **Bottom:** Letter opener with handle in the form of a buffalo; 1905-15; $170-210.

Set of blotter ends; 1880-1900; $200-275.

Sealing-wax seals. **Left:** Art Nouveau head; 1890-1900; $125-155. **Center:** Abstract form; 1890-1900; $65-95. **Right:** Art Deco head; 1920-25; $135-185.

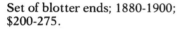

Paperweight in the form of a hand; 1910-15; $135-165.

Paperweight in the form of an African woman with a brass necklace; 1935-40; $35-55 The racist and colonialist quality of such pieces has limited their appeal to most collectors.

Pair of Art Deco bookends; 1920-30; $100-175

Pair of bookends, Dante and Beatrice; cast by Pompeian Bronze Works; 1920-30; $235-295.

Pair of Arts and Crafts bookends; by Bradley & Hubbard; 1925-30; $110-175

Art Nouveau match holder; 1880-1900; $135-185. Usually, the earlier the Art Nouveau figure, the more modestly she is dressed.

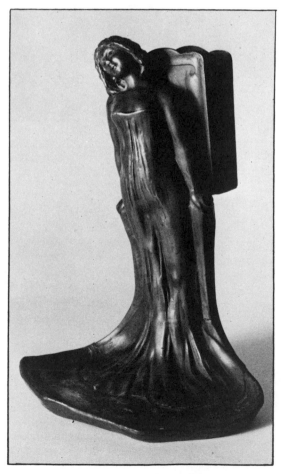

Match holder; 1920-30; $65-95.

Match holder for wooden matches;
by William Bernard; New York, N.Y.;
1890-1900; $40-55.

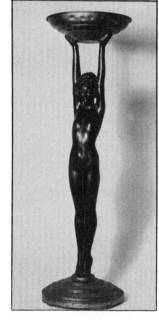

Standing ashtray; 1920-30;
$265-340.

Standing ashtray; 1930-40;
$175-245.

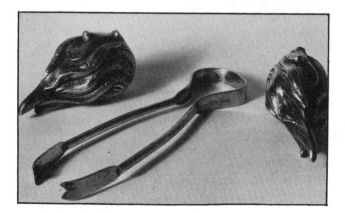

Left and **right:** Pair of finials;
1890-95; $75-115. **Center:** Ice tongs;
1940-50; $25-45.

Iron and Tin

Ironware

Objects of iron and tin are closely related, and both have been on the American scene for many years. Wrought iron, which is hammered into shape at a forge, was being made at Jamestown, Virginia, in 1607, and by 1685 there was an iron furnace at Saugus, Massachusetts, where the rich supplies of native iron ore were converted into bar iron for domestic use as well as for export to England.

The few pieces of identifiable seventeenth-century American iron are practically indistinguishable from their European cousins, but by the early eighteenth century, a distinct native style began to emerge. It was characterized by simplicity, lack of noticeable ornamentation, and a direct relationship between form and function. These qualities have remained the hallmarks of good American ironware.

Some of our earliest wrought iron was intended for the kitchen hearth, and such cooking utensils as pots, grills, roasting skewers, and trivets are among the most popular objects sought by collectors. Wrought door hinges, tools, and weapons are also of great interest.

Most iron cooking pots were not wrought but rather cast, by pouring molten metal into sand forms. Cast iron contains a substantial amount of carbon and is consequently hard and brittle; it cannot be worked at a forge. Since it does not withstand shock well, it saw limited use in the earliest period; but by the early 1800s, it was used to fashion many types of objects—stoves, flatirons, machinery, and household utensils. Today, much of our collectible iron is cast iron.

Wrought iron may be distinguished from cast iron by its grainy appearance in the rusted state, whereas cast and milled iron (a mid-nineteenth-century form of industrial iron) rust to an even, orange-peel-like surface showing no discernible grain. In addition, a series of coarse ridges may often be seen running through wrought pieces in the direction in which they were "drawn," or shaped by the smith.

There are several varieties of collectible wrought- and cast-iron objects, including fireplace and kitchen equipment; builders' hardware, such as nails, door hinges, and latches; cabinet hardware; locks; and iron used on horse-drawn vehicles.

Most examples are plain and undecorated. Only rarely do names or dates appear, and when they do, they greatly increase the value of a specimen. A few metalsmiths, such as the well-known Peter Derr of Pennsylvania, signed their work, and such items bring a premium. Except for such rare examples, however, prices in this field are quite reasonable. Old iron comes up often at yard sales, flea markets, and country auctions, and a nice collection can be made without any great expenditure.

For many years, collectors could buy native iron without concern for reproductions or importations. Alas, such is no longer the case. Since the Second World War, a substantial quantity of wrought and cast iron has been imported, primarily from southern Europe. Many of these forks, spatulas, and spoons are practically indistinguishable from American-made products. True, some are more elaborate; and any ornamental piece must be regarded with suspicion, for with the exception of some Pennsylvania hardware, little American iron was highly decorated. But much of the imported ware is plain—and old. For a few dollars, a chance may be taken on a doubtful piece, but better-quality iron should be purchased only from a reputable dealer who guarantees the authenticity of his wares.

Tinware

Tinware is made predominantly of iron. A lighter-weight metal, it is formed by running sheet iron through rollers to produce an extremely thin body; this is then dipped in molten tin, which covers the sheet iron with a shiny and rust-resistant surface. Many items that could be manufactured in iron—pots, kettles, and so forth—could also be made in tin; and the lighter weight of the tin made it particularly attractive to itinerant peddlers who traveled the back roads of this country in the nineteenth century bringing much-needed utensils to isolated families and communities.

Perhaps 90 percent of all old tinware found today is undecorated. For some tinsmiths, such as those of the Shaker communities, this was a matter of principle. They were producing an honest, functional product, and decoration would have been contrary to both their religious principles and their

esthetic judgment. Among the bulk of the tin manufacturers, more practical considerations governed. Decoration took time, and time was money. New tin had an appealing gleam; in fact, along with pewter it was often referred to as "poor man's silver." But since it was fragile and aged quickly, neither producer nor consumer was much interested in fancy frills.

Certain pieces, on the other hand, customarily were decorated. Teapots and coffeepots, bread trays, and various storage containers were normally seen in the dining room as well as the scullery, and for these there had to be some adornment. In many instances, the metal alone might be worked. Elaborate designs could be produced by punching, scalloping, crimping, or piercing the surface of the tin, by hand or machine.

Pennsylvania-made tinware, in particular, is often decorated by piercing or punching. The former technique, which created a pattern by cutting holes completely through the metal, was employed on foot warmers, cheese molds, colanders, and the tin panels of pie safes. Punching, on the other hand, resulted in a raised design of individual dots. It was favored for teapots and coffeepots. A variation was wriggling, in which a pattern was incised on the vessel by striking it with a sharp implement that was moved slightly at each stroke. Neither punching nor wriggling broke the surface of the metal. Both techniques might be combined in the same piece, such as a candle shade or barn lantern.

Painting on tin, or japanning, was also extremely popular. As early as the eighteenth century, tin was gilded with gold leaf; in the nineteenth century, a major industry concerned itself with "flowering," or painting, tin. The decorators—who were often women—first coated the metal with japan, a soft, lustrous, tar-base black paint. They then decorated it in oils, freehand or with the aid of stencils. Though few such pieces were ever signed, experts can frequently determine their place of origin through the decorator's use of distinctive motifs and patterns.

In Pennsylvania and New Jersey, painted decoration was often combined with crystallization, generally on the bottom of a bread or bundt tray, produced by applying acid to the surface of the tin. The sparkling texture gave added charm to showpieces, which were frequently displayed to visitors and carefully preserved for generations.

Painted tin, or toleware, has long been collected. It is extremely popular and also expensive. Most pieces show wear and may have lost a portion of their decoration, yet all but the meanest examples sell for sums in excess of a hundred dollars. Such a seller's market has, naturally enough, led to reproduction, some innocent, some not quite so. Painting on tin, often old tin, is a recognized craft, and some of the modern compositions are taken directly from old examples. They may be very well done, and if artificially aged, they can present a problem for the unwary. In seeking to determine the age of a given specimen, first check to see whether there are scratches and signs of wear in the japanning. It is softer than the oil decoration and on old pieces will have abraded. The oil paint itself will be "alligatored," or covered with a pattern of hairline age cracks, and there will also be wear on the unpainted bottom. Finally, the piece should not be "too perfect." Old-time decorators worked fast and made mistakes—they smudged the surface, painted off center, and didn't balance their compositions. Modern imitators are likely to be more exacting.

Graniteware

In the late nineteenth century, factories began to produce large quantities of granite- or agateware—sheet iron coated with a porcelainlike substance. Graniteware was largely intended for the kitchen and the bath; thus, cups, bowls, dippers, soap dishes, coffeepots, platters, pans, and pie plates are the most common objects in this medium. Unlike the older ironware and tinware, graniteware forms are rather prosaic; but the charming and fanciful surface is most appealing. The background color is generally white, with which any number of other hues—gray, blue, green, red, yellow, or brown—may be mixed in a swirled design.

The making of tinware was centered in the Northeast, generally along waterways, where there was ready access to raw material, which was mostly imported. Such centers as Berlin, Connecticut; Stevens Plains, Maine; and Dedham, Massachusetts, became famous for their production. There were in addition extensive manufactories elsewhere. New England tinsmiths often spent the winter working in the South; Pennsylvania, Ohio, and Virginia were major sources; and there were even floating tin shops on the Mississippi River! As a result, tin, particularly of the undecorated variety, may be found almost anywhere in the United States.

With the exception of tole, tinware is moderately priced and offers an interesting field for collectors. It has much variety, and attractive examples are common, particularly in the area of graniteware, where whole sets of a particular color combination may be acquired.

A variety of tin scoops, New England, late 19th-early 20th century; $10-25, depending on size and form. Scoops were used in both home and shop and are quite common.

Teakettle, cast iron; Hutton Foundry, Troy, N.Y., ca. 1860; $185-245. A fine example of the gooseneck teakettle.

Footed drip pan, cast iron; New England, late 19th century; $35-55.

Left: Unusual griddle, cast and wrought iron; New England, early 19th century; $135-160.
Combination of feet and hanging loop on a griddle is rare. . .
Center: Wafer iron, wrought iron; Maine, ca. 1860; $100-150. **Right:** Fireplace toaster, wrought iron; Maine, mid-19th century; $175-250.

Left: Warming pan, sheet metal and brass; 20th century; $14-21. **Center:** Pot with handle, cast iron; ca. 1850; $45-60. **Right:** Small pot with handle and hook, cast iron; ca. 1850; $35-40. All from Maine.

Left: Gooseneck teakettle, cast iron, with unique hanging fixture; ca. 1830; $175-245. **Center:** Fine grill, wrought iron; $85-165. **Right:** Footed frying pan, cast iron; $70-100. Both grill and frying pan are mid-19th century. All pieces, New England.

Three wrought iron oven peels for use in baking; Maine, mid-19th century. **Top to bottom:** $100-135; $60-85; $135-175.

Left: Hanging griddle, cast iron, New Hampshire, ca. 1860; $90-150. **Right:** Oven peel, wrought iron; Massachusetts, ca. 1870; $60-90.

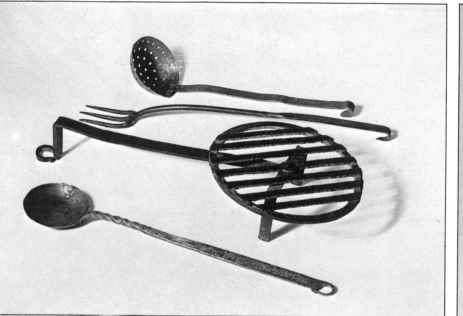

New England wrought iron, mid-19th century. **Top to bottom:** Strainer; $25-40. Fork; $45-60. Rotating footed grill; $90-155. Spoon; $85-140.

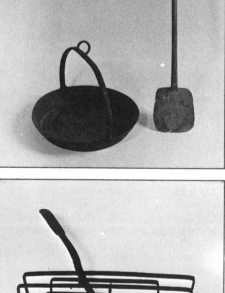

Top: Well-decorated fork, wrought iron; Pennsylvania, ca. 1830; $145-190. **Bottom:** Punch-decorated spatula, wrought iron; New Jersey, ca. 1850; $90-130.

Swivel-base toaster, wrought iron; Maine, ca. 1850; $225-275.

Skewer rack and skewers, wrought iron;
New England, mid-19th century;
$175-255.

Three New England trivets; 19th century.
Left: Sheet iron and wood; $55-75.
Center: Triangular wrought iron;
$50-65. **Right:** Wrought iron with good
finial; $85-135.

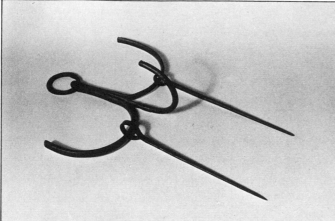

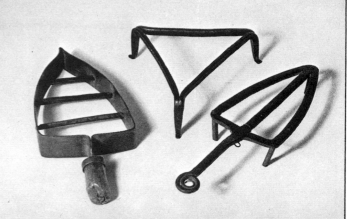

Left: Eggbeater, steel and cast iron;
Midwest, ca. 1900; $20-30.
Center: Long-handled chopper, wood
and wrought iron; New York, ca. 1860;
$35-65. **Right:** Bread knife, steel and
cast iron; Ohio, early 20th century;
$10-20.

Muffin pan, cast iron; Midwest, early
20th century; $75-125.

Three elaborate choppers, hardwood and
steel; Pennsylvania, mid-19th century;
$65-95; $55-80; $50-75.

Candy mold in shape of a lamb, cast iron; East, early 20th century; $75-125.

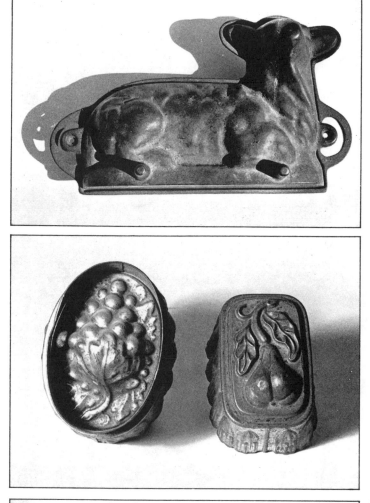

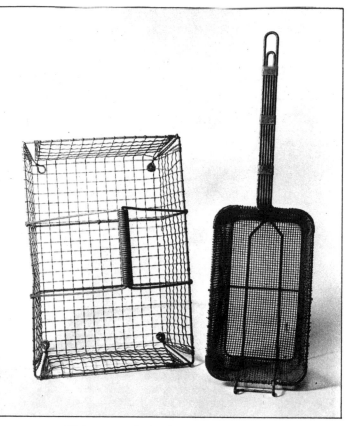

Iron wireware; 20th century **Left:** Fruit or vegetable carrier; $20-30. **Right:** Deep fryer; $15-20.

Fruit-shaped molds, cast iron; Midwest, early 20th century. **Left:** $50-75. **Right:** $40-55.

Rattrap, iron wire and sheet steel; New England, late 19th century; $55-85.

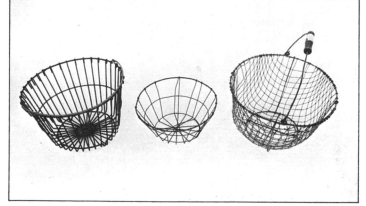

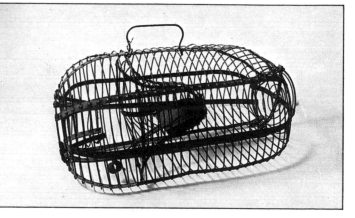

Egg and produce baskets, iron wire; 20th century. **Left to right:** $ 30- 55; $10-15; $25-40.

Charcoal-heated cast flatiron; New England, 19th century; $55-60.

Clockwise from left: Sadiron, cast; $20-25. Flatiron, sheet and cast iron; Midwest, mid-19th century; $50-75. Sadiron, cast with wrought handle; $25-50.

Front to rear: Elaborate bootjack, cast iron, New England, late 19th century; $55-85. Bootjack, wrought iron New York, ca. 1850; $40-65. Sadiron, cast, with wrought handle; late 19th century; $35-60.

Tobacco cutter, cast iron; Connecticut, late 19th century; $25-35.

Sewing bird, cast iron; New England, 19th century; $125-175. An extremely attractive specimen of a popular collector's item.

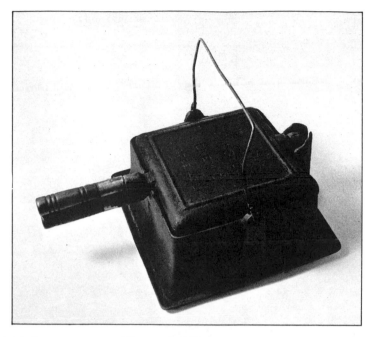

Waffle iron, cast iron; Ohio, early 20th century; $50-85.

Coffee mill, cast iron and wood, red and gold paint; manufactured by Charles Parker, Meriden, Conn., late 19th century; $450-600.

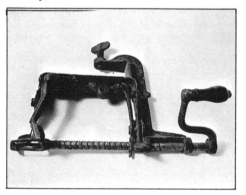

Patented cherry pitter; New Hampshire, 19th century; $45-70.

Bread-dough mixer, sheet and cast iron; Midwest, late 19th century; $25-40.

Scale, cast iron and steel; 19th century; $75-125.

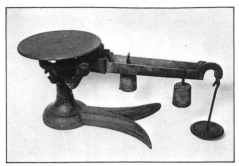

Tole-decorated scale, iron and tin; East, 20th century; $55-85.

Parlor stove, cast iron; Atlanta Stove Works, Georgia, late 19th century; $275-400.

Teapot, tin and wood; Maine, early 19th century; $65-95. A remarkable example of the reproduction in tin of a silver form. Pot is modeled on a silver teapot of the late 18th century.

Coffeepot, tin and brass; New England, mid-19th century; $55-85. Fine style, interesting construction.

Field coffeepot, tin and iron; New England, late 19th century; $45-70. A good piece typical of those widely used in shops and factories.

New England tinware, 19th century. **Left:** Scalloped candleholder; $40-65. **Center:** Small covered roasting pan; $25-40. **Right:** Small tea caddy, black paint; $15-25.

Connecticut tinware; 19th century. **Left:** Dipper; $15-25. **Center:** Shallow bowl; $15-2-.
Right: Funnel; $10-15. Good specimens of readily available tin.

Large roasting pan, sheet tin; New York, late 19th-early 20th century; $25-40.

Brown-bread molds, tin; New England, late 19th century. **Left to right:** $15-25; $15-20; $20-35; $10-15. Reeded pieces are more desirable.

Hinged bread-baking mold, tin; Maine, late 19th century; $25-40. An attractive form.

Massachusetts tinware; 19th century.
Top left: Brown-bread mold; $20-30.
Top right: Barrel, old green paint; $40-65.
Bottom left: Storage box; $10-15.
Bottom right: Storage box, old black paint; $15-20. Unusually small pieces.

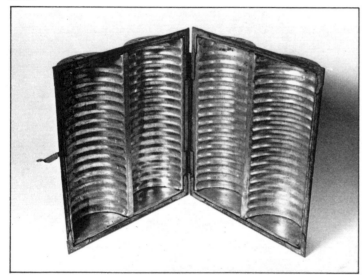

Candy molds, tin; New England, early 20th century. **Left to right:** $5-10; $5-10; $15-20. The more ornate the form, the higher the price.

312

Shaker dipper, tin and iron wire; New York, mid-19th century; $175-265. Good workmanship and simplicity of design typical of Shaker pieces.

Left: Funnel, tin; $20-35. Center: Crimped mold, tin; $25-45. Right: Food grater, tin and wood; $65-90. All, New England, 19th century.

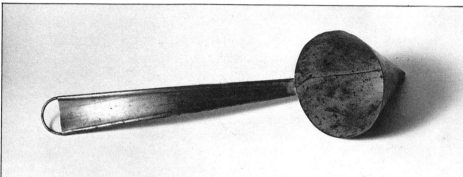

Group of tin plates, New England, late 19th-early 20th century; $10-20, depending on size and condition.

Tinware.
Left: Scoop; $5-15. Center left: Drinking cup; $5-10. Center right: Canning funnel; $10-15. Right: Open-handled drinking cup; $10-15. All, early 20th century.

Left: Child's cup, stamped tin; Pennsylvania, late 19th century; $45-75. Right: ABC plate, stamped tin; Massachusetts, late 19th-early 20th century; $65-95.

Top left: Eggbeater, tin; $20-30.
Top right: Flour sifter, tin; $5-15.
Bottom: Potato ricer, tin; $15-25. All, 20th century.

Egg poacher, tin, marked "Kreamer," 20th century; $20-35.

Group of tin measures, New England, 20th century. **Left to right:** $3-5; $5-10; $10-15.

Group of sifters, tin and iron wire; late 19th-early 20th century. **Left to right:** $20-30; $25-40; $20-35; $15-25. Handle and small size add value to example in right foreground.

Tin lunch boxes; Connecticut, early 20th century. **Left:** With inner compartments for hot foods; $25-40. **Right:** In old black paint; $20-30.

Left to right: Tin sander, oil pot, and gum pot; Maine, 19th century.
Left to right: $25-35; $25-40; $5-8.

Double-lid lunch box, tin wih pierced decoration; Connecticut, mid-19th century; $100-160.

Tinware, New York, late 19th century.
Left: Scraper; $3-6. **Center:** Shaker; $10-15.
Right: Covered canister; $12-25.

Map case, tin, old green paint; New York, late 19th century; $85-115.

Extremely elaborate pieced colander; Pennsylvania, mid-19th century; $250-350. An example of fine decoration on tin.

Left: Coffeepot with offset spout, tole; Connecticut, ca. 1860; $350-500. Rather sparse decoration in red and yellow on black somewhat limits the value of this piece. **Center:** Coffeepot, undecorated tin; $40-65.
Right: Syrup pot, undecorated tin; $10-20. Both, New England.

Left: Tin matchbox, black and gold stencil; $15-25. **Center:** Set of tin spice cans in holder, black paint; $50-75. **Right:** Unpainted tin milk can; $15-25. All, Connecticut, late 19th century.

Painted tinware; Maine, 19th century. **Left:** Hanging matchbox, old blue paint; $25-40. **Center:** Deep dish, tole, red and yellow on black; $200-300. **Right:** Hand-painted drinking cup; $15-25.

Box with lift top and brass handle, tin, decorated with stencil designs in red, yellow, and gold; Pennsylvania, mid-19th century; $225-300,

Tole-decorated boxes with lift tops, tin, red, green, and yellow on black, **Left:** Maine, mid-19th century; $275-375.
Right: Extremely well-decorated example with brass handle; New York, ca. 1840; $750-1,200.

Left: Oval serving tray decorated in green and silver stencil; $75-135. **Right:** Stenciled, red on black scalloped serving tray; $90-145. Both, Connecticut, late 19th century.

Serving tray, tin, stencil decorated; New England, mid-19th century; $175-265. Stencil-decorated oblong serving trays; New York, late 19th century. **Left:** Gold and silver stencil on black ground; $110-160.
Right: Red and silver stencil on black ground; $145-195.

Stencil-decorated covered roasting pans, gold and silver on black; Pennsylvania, 19th century. **Left:** $200-275. **Right:** $175-225. Covered pans of this sort are quite uncommon.

Covered pitcher, tin, white with hand-painted green and yellow decoration; New York, late 19th century; $100-115.
Vessels of this sort are often mistaken for watering cans, but this piece is part of a set that includes a similarly decorated washbowl. The set was used with Victorian cottage furniture.

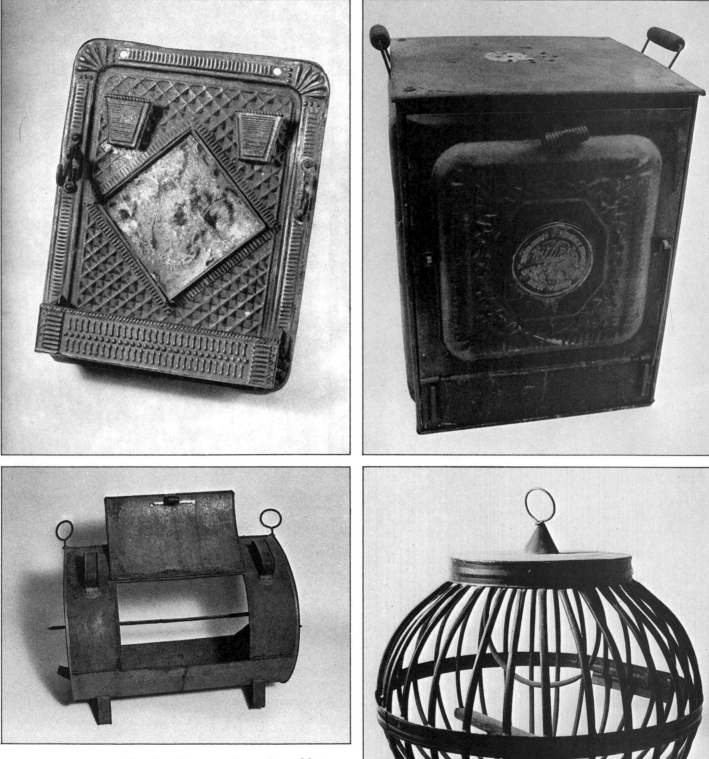

Wall mirror and accessory box, stamped tin and glass; Massachusetts, late 19th century; $25-45. Stamped mirrors and boxes of this sort were particularly common in the late Victorian period.

Stove-top bake oven, tin and iron; marked "The Ideal—New York," early 20th century; $45-85.

Fireplace bake oven, tin and iron; Maine, ca. 1825; $250-400. An extremely early and fine tin accessory.

Birdcage, tin, recent black paint; Maine, late 19th century; $175-325. A spectacular form.

Baby bath, tin and iron wire, old white paint; Maine, late 19th century; $50-70. Interesting form and color, but something that hasn't caught on.

Sterno stove, tin and iron; Ohio, 20th century; $10-20.
New England tinware, late 19th century.
Left: Gardener's insect sprayer; $10-20.
Right: Maple syrup vat whistle; $25-45. When the sugar reached a boil the whistle would alert the workers; a rare piece.

Watering can, tin; East, early 20th century; $20-35.

Foot warmer, pierced tin and pine; Rhode Island, ca. 1850; $125-175.

Rare wriggle-decorated dustpan;
Pennsylvania, ca. 1870; $230-290. A
most unusual piece.

Churn, undecorated tin; New York, late
19th century; $50-85. A rather
uncommon use for tin.

20th-century granitware; New England.
Left: Coffeepot, violet on white;
$65-100. **Right:** Colander, white on
blue; $25-40.

Washbowl, graniteware, blue on white;
New York, early 20th century; $35-65.

Blue on white graniteware; Midwest, 20th century. **Left:** Pie plate; $15-20. **Right.** Cooking pot with spout and bail handle; $35-60.

Green and white graniteware; New York, 20th century.
Left: Washbowl; $5-10. **Right:** Pie plate; $15-25. While the overall green of the bowl is common, the flowed green on white, as seen in the pie plate, is not frequently encountered.

Graniteware, New York, 20th century. **Left:** bowl, mottled red and orange; $15-25. **Center:** Pie plate, speckled white on blue; $10-15. **Right:** Serving bowl, white with blue banding; $5-10.

Common gray graniteware; Midwest, 20th century. **Left and right:** Pie plates; $10-15. **Center:** Very large (14″ diameter) tray; $25-40.

Gray graniteware; Midwest, 20th century. **Left:** funnel; $15-25. **Right:** Slop jar; $25-40.

Textiles

Before the era of factory-made goods, most textiles for the home were made at home: blankets, sheets, clothing, and even in some cases carpets. In the rugged early years of colonial life, these articles were primarily utilitarian. With the enormous burden of chores, and few resources, women had all they could do to keep the family warmly clothed; they had little time to think about decoration. But by the early eighteenth century, especially in the cities and on southern plantations, wealth had created leisure and a taste for luxury. Beyond merely providing for the family, women could now turn their attention to embellishing their homes and the clothing they wore.

Embroidery

The chief decorative technique at their disposal was needlework, specifically, embroidery. Even in the seventeenth century, personal inventories had frequently mentioned "wrought" or "needleworked" cushions, carpets, and cloths. About the same time, the sampler came into existence, both as an educational device—to train a girl in the various embroidery stitches—and as a showpiece—to display her talents. The earliest samplers, such as the one created in 1653 by Lora Standish, daughter of Captain Myles Standish, were long narrow panels on which the needlework was set out in horizontal bands. By the late eighteenth century, the form had become square or slightly oblong, with the addition of a border to frame the text. Nearly all samplers are dominated by an alphabet or a pious inscription. Better specimens include embroidered figures, houses, animals, ships, and flowers, as well as the maker's name and date—all often executed in a variety of stitches.

By 1850, the stitching of samplers had mostly been discontinued; there are few interesting examples from a later period. Samplers have been collected for many years, and large numbers of very similar English examples are on the market. Names and dates are of little help in distinguishing them, so the wise buyer looks for specimens that are not merely signed but also incorporate a recognizable American place name.

Women's academies, which were established in large numbers in the late eighteenth and early nineteenth centuries, included "fancy

work"—elegant sewing—as an important part of their curriculums. In addition to samplers, made mostly by the younger girls, needlework pictures were popular—carefully stitched representations of houses, landscapes, ships, flowers, and historical and biblical scenes. The most common form was the mourning picture, a standardized composition containing a large urn-shaped memorial (which often bore the name of a deceased relative), several weeping willow trees, and the figures of mourning survivors.

Like samplers, mourning pictures were also made in England, but most were made in the United States, and their source can often be identified by the names they bear or the localities they illustrate.

Quilts

Few American antiques are more popular, here or abroad, than patchwork quilts, remarkable works of art that are also practical and truly native. Though patchwork quilts were made in England, the craft was developed to its finest form on these shores—by women with little formal education and certainly no artistic training.

Actually, what is popularly known as the quilt should more correctly be called the stitched coverlet, since the term *quilt,* as popularly used, covers several different techniques: patchwork, or piecing, is the sewing together of small, colored patches of cloth so as to form a particular design; quilting is the taking of tiny running stitches to bind together several layers of cloth (normally, two or three layers); appliqué is stitching colored cloth design elements on top of a solid piece of cloth. Later "quilts" often are not quilted at all but are tied—stitched together with a single tufted stitch at regularly separated intervals. Likewise, the earliest American quilts, from the eighteenth century, contain no patchwork; rather, they are made of solid pieces of cloth—cotton or linsey-woolsey— fastened together with quilting that is sometimes remarkably elaborate.

Nineteenth-century quilts—pieced or appliquéd—are quilted too, more often in geometric patterns than in the floral patterns common in the preceding century. In any case, the earlier the quilt, the finer the stitching.

The design elements of appliqué quilts are usually figurative—garlands, flowers, and occasionally birds and animals. Pieced quilts, with much smaller individual pieces, are most often geometric; their designs are remarkably intricate and spectacularly beautiful. They carry equally fascinating names, which either describe an image that the pattern resembles—Crown and Thorns, Flying Geese—or commemorate an event—Lincoln's Platform—or are purely poetic—Delectable Mountains.

Eighteenth-century quilts are hard to find on the market these days. More common are pieced and appliquéd quilts, which first appeared in the late eighteenth century and have continued to be made right up to our own day (though with noticeable changes in design and type of cloth). Pieced and appliquéd quilts are usually made of cotton, occasionally of wool; a notable exception is the Victorian crazy quilt, made of scraps of silk, satin, and velvet seamed together and bound over with elaborate embroidery stitches. At this point the original purpose of the quilt, to provide a bed covering, disappears. Crazy quilts, too fragile for beds, served only as decorative throws for furniture or pianos.

Quilts vary in desirability dependent on several factors. Earlier pieces are sought not only for their age but for the fact that their designs are frequently unique, whereas at a later date many patterns became standardized. Signed quilts are important, particularly the friendship quilts, in which each block was sewed by a different person; the whole was intended as a gift for a new bride or a minister's wife. Dated examples are, of course, also most desirable. Quilt prices are, in general, quite high, even for the common types. Any quilt in good condition will sell for at least fifty dollars, and sought-after variations such as early free-form quilts, Amish, and crib quilts may go for as much as a thousand dollars. It is hardly surprising then that quilts are being made, repaired, and cut down, in the interest of providing for this active market. At a bare minimum, quilt collectors should learn to distinguish between the tight, even flow of the machine stitch (common in quilts made after 1900) and the freer hand stitch. It is helpful to know something of the materials used at different periods and the approximate age of more popular patterns. The presence of seeds in the cotton stuffing is another indicator of age (they may be felt with the fingers or seen if the quilt is held up to the light). Quilts made before 1880 are likely to contain them, since only by that date did the mechanical seed picker become universal.

Coverlets

While every woman was a quilt maker—and some men were too—the highly patterned woven coverlets popular today were produced by a limited number of people. Some housewives had their own looms; others relied on the itinerant weavers, who carried their looms in a wagon. After the middle of the nineteenth century, factories took over the chore entirely.

The American coverlet is based on English and European designs, though it varies sufficiently that there is no danger of its being confused with the foreign product. American coverlets are woven in two or more strips, each about two and a half to three yards long, and seamed together. Colors vary and in earlier examples were produced by use of natural dyes.

The least complex type is the overshot weave, which has a linen or cotton warp and a woolen weft. Its geometric patterns appear in three tones, dark, light, and a half tone. It is the first type of native woven coverlet, and some of the oldest of existing examples are traceable to the eighteenth century.

In New York and Pennsylvania, a variation, the Summer–Winter coverlet, was popular in the early nineteenth century. This is two-toned—traditionally, blue and white; dark on the side where the colored woolen pattern dominates, lighter on the reverse where the linen warp is found. Again, geometric patterns predominate, though they are more complex than in the overshot.

Block, or double-woven, geometrics are more complex, produced by interweaving a natural-colored cotton fabric with a colored woolen one; they are completely reversible.

Latest and most spectacular are the Jacquard, or fancy floral coverlets, which were made in one piece on a larger loom (often in a factory). The pattern is dominated by a central floral medallion surrounded by elaborate borders, often containing flowers, birds (including the eagle), trees, buildings, and human figures. Unlike earlier coverlets, Jacquards were frequently signed and dated by their makers and also may bear the names of their original owners.

Coverlets are extremely attractive and desirable antiques. Prices are generally much more reasonable than for quilts; good specimens sell for seventy-five to one hundred dollars and really top pieces go for no more than three hundred dollars. Names, dates, and inscriptions add greatly to value.

Hooked Rugs

Hooked rugs are the youngest group of American textiles. There are few specimens that can be reliably traced to the first half of the nineteenth century; the first written mention of the craft appears in 1838. This is odd, particularly in light of the fact that rug hooking is not difficult. The materials required—old rags, a hook or bent nail, and, perhaps, a wooden frame—are easily obtainable. The process is hardly complex. A design is drawn in charcoal or crayon on a piece of burlap or other coarsely woven material. The worker then attaches short pieces of rolled cloth to the hook and draws them through the backing, using a variety of colors to produce the pattern.

The most desirable hooked rugs are those that were done from a design created by the worker. These are often spontaneous and truly artistic. After the Civil War, most rug makers copied standardized commercial patterns, which were stamped onto burlap backing. These are considerably less inspired.

Of the three types of hooked rugs—pictorial, geometric, and floral—collectors are at present most interested in pictorials. These are least common but still abundant; the designs depict everything from cats, dogs, and

other animals to houses, human figures, and complete pastoral scenes. Those that commemorate an event such as a wedding or Fourth of July celebration are much sought after.

Geometric rugs are, superficially at least, the simplest of all since the design consists of a repeated basic form, such as a circle or a square. In fact, some makers supposedly laid out their designs using tea cups or bricks, the outlines of which they would trace on the backing. Nevertheless, the color and line variations in geometric hooked rugs can be as subtle as those found in a modern painting. They are particularly suitable for use with modern furniture, and they are very popular today.

There are many different floral rug patterns. Some, such as those made in Canada and the Waldoboro, Maine, area, have raised, or "hove up," portions and are extremely attractive. Most, though, are rather ordinary examples of Victorian excess. Hooked rugs attracted collector attention for the first time in the late 1920s and early 1930s. At this time florals were all the rage, and vast numbers were made. The new interest in these floor coverings, which may be traced to a ground-breaking exhibition at New York's Museum of American Folk Art in 1975, has concentrated more on pictorials and geometrics. Prices remain favorable to the buyer at present. Good rugs can still be found in country shops for ten or fifteen dollars, while standard prices range from thirty to eighty dollars. A truly unique rug may go for a thousand dollars, but those are few and far between.

Mention should also be made of rag, or braided, rugs, which were made throughout the late nineteenth and much of the twentieth centuries. Homemade examples are constructed simply by coiling and binding together strands of rolled rag. The same material was also woven into larger rugs on special looms. Both types are seen frequently at country auctions and house sales, and prices are still very low. These attractive and inexpensive rugs represent an exciting and relatively unexplored area of folk craft.

Sampler by Emma Watkins, Maine, 1838; $185-265.

Sampler, by Elizabeth Johnson, Longtown, N.J. (?), 1829; $400-650. Good needlework and interesting details in a fine early sampler.

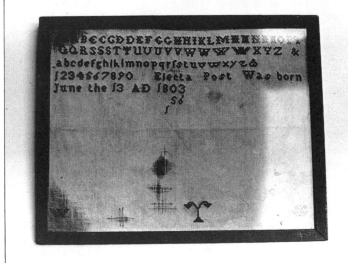

Sampler, probably unfinished; by Electa Post, first quarter 19th century; $90-130.

Sampler; New England, 1841; $400-750. Excellent pictorial detail makes this a very desirable sampler.

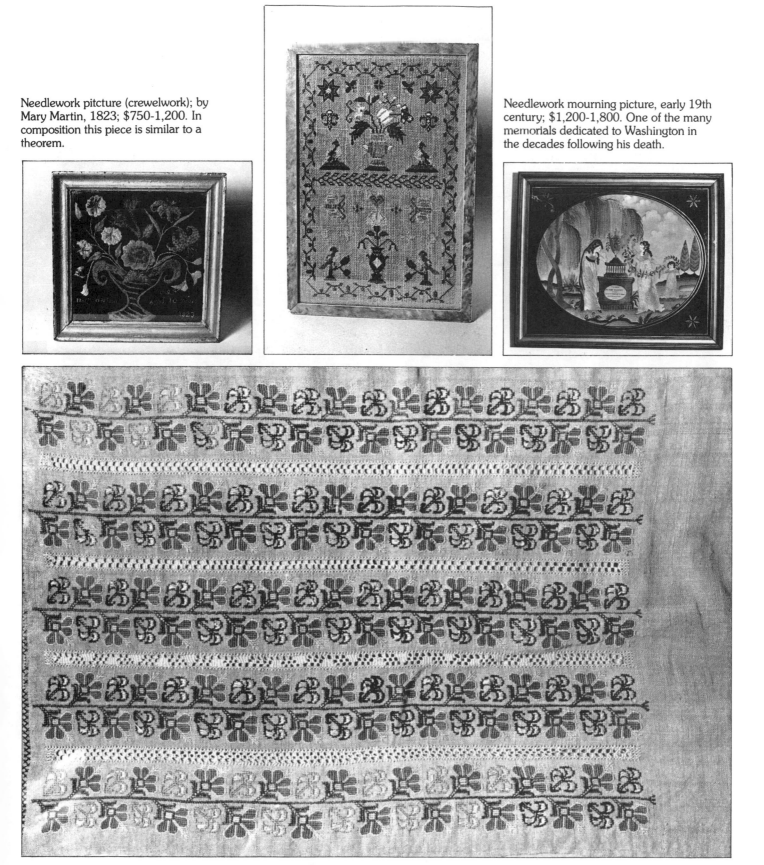

Needlework picture; New York, first quarter 19th century; $300-450.

Needlework pitcture (crewelwork); by Mary Martin, 1823; $750-1,200. In composition this piece is similar to a theorem.

Needlework mourning picture, early 19th century; $1,200-1,800. One of the many memorials dedicated to Washington in the decades following his death.

Section of embroidered cloth; New England, mid-19th century; $90-140.

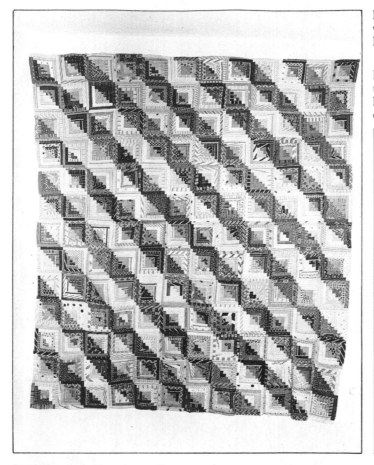

Log cabin quilt, Straight Furrows variation, cotton, predominantly browns, New York, late 19th century; $350-500.

Light and dark Log Cabin quilt in the unusual medium of wool, predominantly lavender and brown; Pennsylvania, 19th century; $450-650.

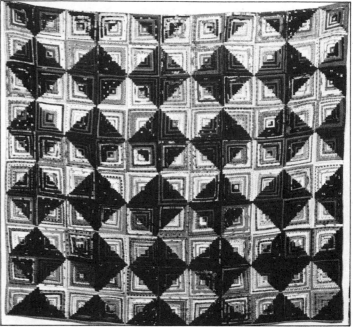

Log cabin quilt, Courthouse Steps variation, cotton, brown and aqua; Pennsylvania, late 19th century; $275-400.

Log cabin quilt, Plowed Furrows variation, cotton, predominantly orange and brown; Massachusetts, ca. 1900; $250-350.

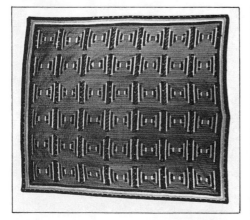

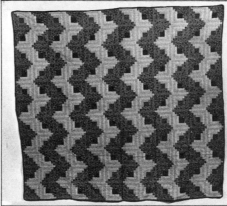

Detail of light and dark Log Cabin quilt as shown above.

Light and dark Log Cabin quilt, cotton, predominantly blue; Indiana, early 20th century; $500-750. This is a single-bed size.

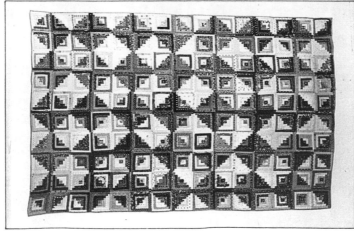

326

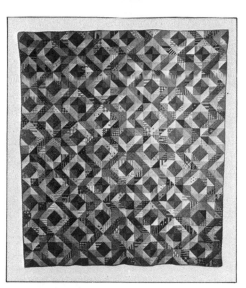

Double-T quilt, cotton, in unusually bold colors, yellow and rust; Pennsylvania, late 19th century; $350-500.

Zigzag quilt, cotton, predominantly browns; New York, late 19th century; $225-350.

Spectacular Star of Bethlehem quilt, cotton, multicolored; Pennsylvania, late 19th century; $700-1,000.

Cross and Crown quilt, cotton, multicolored; Pennsylvania, late 19th century; $200-270.

Geese in Flight quilt, cotton, brown on white; Rhode Island, second half 19th century; $350-500. A well-done and attractive quilt.

Lone Star quilt, cotton, black and gray on white; Pennsylvania, late 19th century; $250-400.

Drunkard's Path quilt, cotton, red and green; Pennsylvania, 19th century; $400-550.

Courthouse Square quilt, cotton, red and white; New York, late 19th century; $250-350.

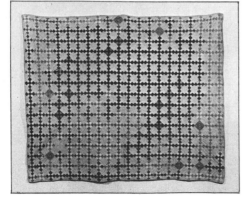

Blazing Star quilt with Oak Leaf applique border, cotton, red and white; New Jersey, 19th century; $550-700. A large and spectacular quilt.

Stars quilt, cotton, multicolored; East, late 19th century; $175-250.

Postage Stamp quilt, cotton, multicolored; New York, early 20th century; $425-550.

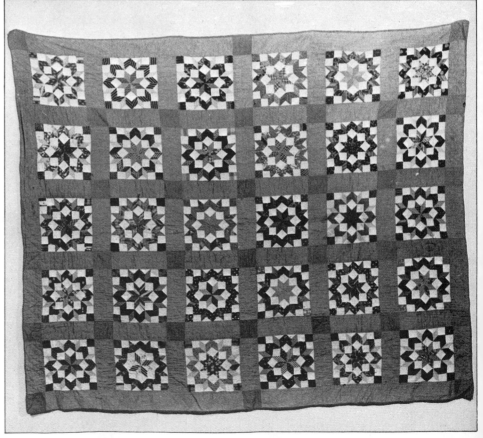

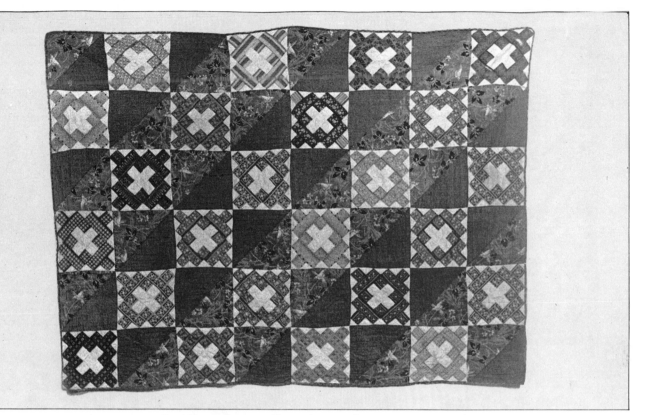

Courthouse Square quilt, predominantly
red and green; New York, early 20th
century; $100-160.

Diamond quilt, cotton, blue, red, black,
and white; New York, 20th century;
$375-450. A good example of the
geometric quilts popular in the early part
of this century.

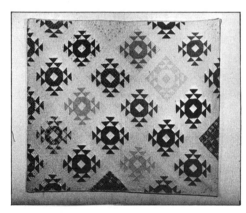

Crown and Thorns quilt, cotton,
multicolored; New York, 20th century;
$150-225.

Lightning quilt, cotton, blue and white;
New York, 20th century; $600-900.

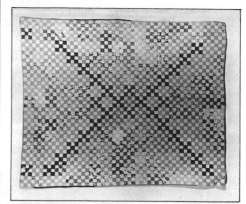

Geometric quilt, cotton, multicolored, tied not quilted; New York, 20th century; $75-130. Tied quilts are less desirable and less expensive than quilted examples.

Postage Stamp crib quilt, multicolored; New Jersey, 20th century; $300-450. Crib quilts are now attracting long overdue attention.

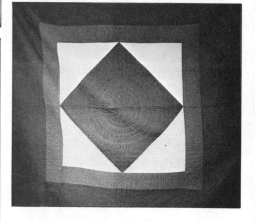

Rare and finely done Amish quilt, wine, green, and dark blue; Pennsylvania, 19th century; $2,500-3,500. Amish quilts are enormously popular with collectors.

Crazy quilt, silk and velvet with a variety of unusual embroidery stitches; New York, late 19th century; $450-750.

High-quality Friendship Crazy quilt, silk with a variety of embroidery stitches; Massachusetts, late 19th century; $550-850. The squares represent many of the states.

Overshot-weave coverlet, wool and cotton, blue and white; Pennsylvania, mid-19th century; $200-225.

Very fine fringed overshot-weave coverlet, cotton and wool, red and white; Pennsylvania, mid-19th century; $250-375.

Overshot-weave coverlet, wool and cotton, red, green, and black; Ohio, 19th century; $225-350.

Overshot-weave coverlet, cotton and wool, blue, light blue, and white; New York, mid-19th century; $250-375.

Summer-Winter coverlet, cotton and wool, blue and white; New Jersey, mid-19th century; $200-325.

Unusual fringed overshot-weave coverlet, cotton and wool, red and white with an interesting pattern; New York, mid-19th century; $250-400.

Jacquard coverelet, cotton and wool, blue and white; by M. Coleman, dated 1825; $900-1,300. Fine eagle and state house border.

Jacquard coverlet, cotton and wool, blue and white; by Archibald Davidson, Ithaca, N.Y., dated 1838; $1,500-2.500. A reversible coverlet with a superb border of running deer, trees, eagle and state house.

Fine fringed overshot-weave coverlet, cotton and wool, blue and white; Pennsylvania, 19th century; $200-325.

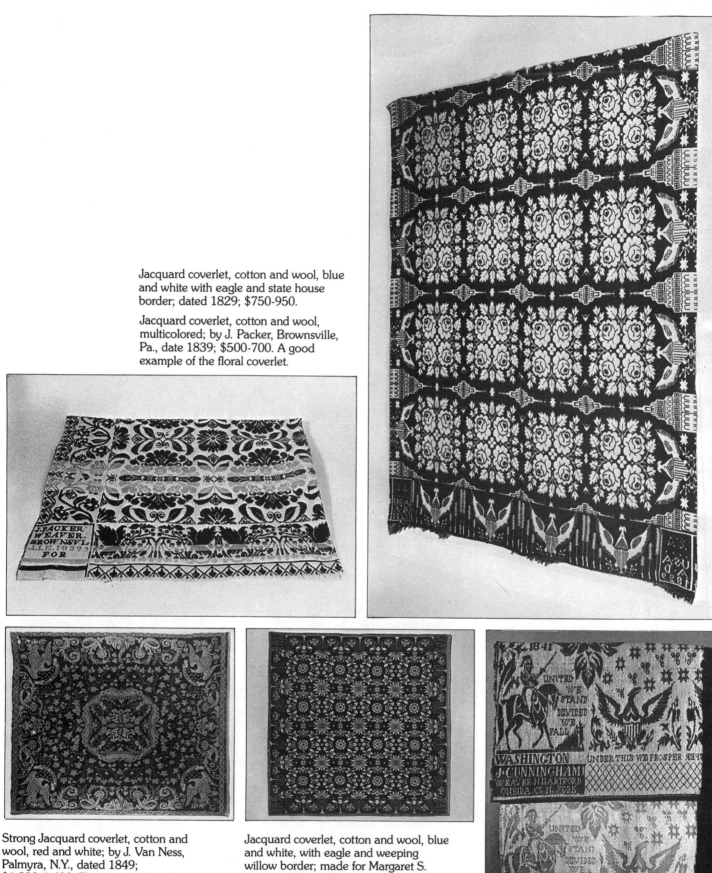

Jacquard coverlet, cotton and wool, blue and white with eagle and state house border; dated 1829; $750-950.

Jacquard coverlet, cotton and wool, multicolored; by J. Packer, Brownsville, Pa., date 1839; $500-700. A good example of the floral coverlet.

Strong Jacquard coverlet, cotton and wool, red and white; by J. Van Ness, Palmyra, N.Y., dated 1849; $1,200-1,600. The large eagles at corners are unusual.

Jacquard coverlet, cotton and wool, blue and white, with eagle and weeping willow border; made for Margaret S. Parker, Orleans County, N.Y., dated 1839; $550-750.

Two woven table covers, with motifs of eagle and mounted George Washington; by J. Cunningham, North Hartford, N.Y. **Top:** Blue on white; dated 1841; $800-1,200. **Bottom:** Red on white; 1841; $650-950.

Geometric hooked rug, rag on burlap; red, black, and gray; Pennsylvania, late 19th century; $90-145.

Remarkable hooked rug, wool on burlap; mid-19th century; $1,750-2,500. A real piece of folk art and an outstanding example of hooked rugs.

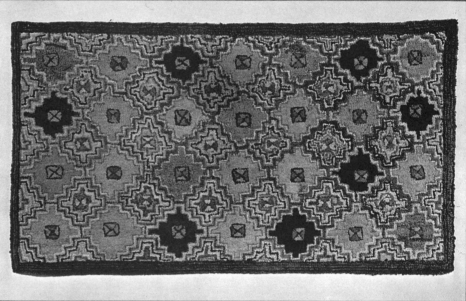

Hooked rug with Maltese cross, wool on burlap, multicolored; New England, late 19th century; $80-130.

Geometric hooked rug, wool and rag on burlap; New England, late 19th century; $135-195. An attractive rug of the sort that goes well with modern furnishings.

Floral hooked rug, rag and wool on burlap; Massachusetts, 20th century; $50-75. Simple pattern-made rugs of this sort are readily available today.

Floral hooked rug, rag on burlap; New York, 20th century; $75-125.

Ric-rac" hooked rug, rag on burlap, multicolored; Connecticut, early 20th ▼ century; $70-120.
An attractive and inexpensive geometric rug.

Floral geometric hooked rug, rag on burlap; New York, late 19th century; $75-135.

Pictorial hooked rug, wool on burlap; Pennsylvania, second half 19th century; $225-285. Stenciled pattern on burlap base of this rug is dated 1867.

Pictorial hooked rug, wool on burlap; New England, 20th century; $350-500. A nautical rug of the sort often made along the coasts of Maine and New Hampshire.

Pictorial hooked rug, rag and wool or burlap; Maine, 20th century; $200-525.

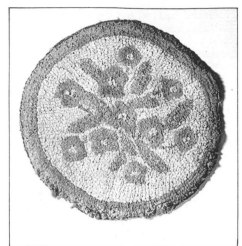

Hooked floral chair cover, rag on burlap; Connecticut, 20th century; $25-40. Small hooked pieces of this sort are low priced and make attractive wall coverings. Pictorial examples will bring $75-125.

Hooked floral seat cover, rag on burlap; New York, 20th century; $65-90.

Pictorial entrance rug, rag on burlap; New York, 20th century; $125-185. A desirable figure, but late date of rug reduces its value.

Hooked entrance rug, wool on burlap, black and gold; Pennsylvania, early 20th century; $225-350. An interesting rug in attractive colors.

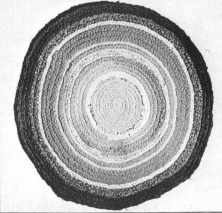

Round braided rug, multicolored; New York, 20th century; $45-75. Rugs of this type were usually made at home from remnants of rags.

Oval braided rug, multicolored; New England, 20th century; $35-85. Good color and low price make these rugs an excellent buy.

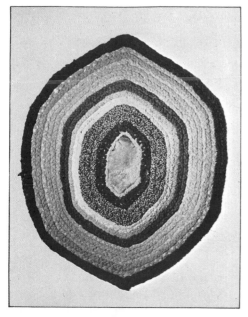

Hexagonal braided rug, rag and leather, multicolored; New York, 20th century; $75-135. Leather center and six-sided shape make this an unusual example.

Woven rag rug, multicolored; Vermont, late 19th century; $45-85. Such rugs were woven on looms in sizes as large as 10″ × x12″.

Woven rug, blue and white; Maine, 20th century; $20-30.

Berlin work picture, wool with beadwork; Maine, ca. 1860; $75-135.

Needlework motto; Maine, early 20th century; $45-75.
Mottoes of this sort were often worked to be hung in homes or churches.

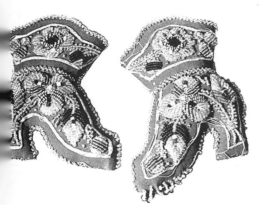

Beadwork pincushions in form of high shoes; New York, late 19th century; $85-125 the pair. Highly detailed beadwork of this sort was often done by Indians on reservations for sale to tourists.

Beadwork pincushions; New York, late 19th-early 20th century. **Left to right:** $65-85; $50-70; $55-75. These pieces are becoming popular.

Woodenware

Particularly for the new collector, or one of modest means, woodenware provides a vast field for exploration and purchase. Since nearly every utilitarian object has at one time or another been made of wood—or treen, as it is often called—the variety of forms available is far greater than in any other field of antiques. Even the most casual lover of antiques is aware that plates, bowls, and spoons were often made of wood instead of the pottery or metal common today. It is less often recognized that other objects common today in many mediums were once manufactured exclusively from treen. Coffee grinders, ink bottles, washing machines, flour sifters, and meat grinders are just a few examples. We know the purpose of these implements; but every day there come to light other, strange wooden utensils to which we can assign neither name nor function. The need for which they were fashioned has long since vanished; and so they exist, like objects from an Egyptian tomb, as mysterious and fascinating artifacts.

Partly because of its abundance, and partly because of a certain snobbish prejudice against such simple, handworked things, old treen has remained at a reasonable price level while other antiques have risen steadily in value. True, unusually attractive or signed or decorated pieces have always been sought after, but average woodenware is still one of the best buys available. For a few dollars, one can often obtain the nucleus of a good collection.

Making Treen

At the time of the colonization of this country, there existed in Europe guilds of coopers, men whose craft concerned the working of wood. Many of them came to this country, including the well-known John Alden of Plymouth Bay. Those whose labors are of greatest interest to us are the "white coopers," or dish turners, the men who made utilitarian housewares. Some of their production—spoons, plates, and shallow bowls; the so-called flatware—was cut out and shaped by hand. A tree would be felled, hewed to an appropriate size, and then roughed out with an ax and a cooper's adz (a curved iron blade with a short handle). When necessary, as in the making of bowls, the interior might be burned out

to facilitate gouging. Such simple methods were similar to those employed by the American Indians, and early colonial treen is often difficult to distinguish from that shaped by the Indians.

Advanced collectors are always on the lookout for hand-finished flatware. They watch for odd shapes that reflect the natural form of the material used; they run their hands along the outsides and insides to detect the rough marks of the maker's tools. It is an exciting game—but an uncertain one. Wooden flatware can be of great age, but it can also be very recent. Settlers moving west made it to replace broken dishes and lost spoons. Poor people in the Ozarks and other isolated areas whittled out useful items throughout the nineteenth and early twentieth centuries. They are, in fact, still doing it! Given some rough wear, stain, and a few years' weathering, such pieces sometimes can scarcely be distinguished from their seventeenth-century cousins. Moreover, in the past decades there has grown up a thriving import business devoted to the sale in this country of European treen, primarily Spanish and Portuguese. These specimens are for the most part quite old, hand carved, and in form not unlike similar objects produced on this continent. It takes experience to distinguish American from foreign woodenware. There are no hard and fast rules. Generally, one should be aware that the imported pieces are of unfamiliar woods rather than our own pine, maple, or ash and are usually more elaborately decorated. If on top of this the form looks slightly unfamiliar, the piece is probably an immigrant.

From the very first, American coopers worked with a lathe as well as freehand. The basic purpose of the lathe is to produce a circular movement so that an object fixed on the machine can be shaped as it rotates by chisellike tools pressed against it. A great variety of hollowware—goblets, deep bowls, tankards, sugar and salt containers—can be made on a lathe. The earliest of these devices, the spring-pole lathe, could cut only half a revolution, so that anything made on it had to be turned and worked in two stages. Specimens cut on such a lathe often can be distinguished by the fact that the tool marks on the two sides are slightly out of line.

By the seventeenth century, the fully turning mandrel lathe had been developed, and it is on some variation of this machine that most old American hollowware has been cut. Early pieces turned on a mandrel lathe can be recognized by the wide, deep concentric lines cut into their outer surfaces. As machine-powered lathes were developed in the nineteenth century, the cooper's hand was replaced by a locking device that held the cutting tools. As a result, later work shows a pattern of tightly drawn and very even concentric circles, a consistency that can be achieved only with mechanization.

Various wooden storage containers, particularly boxes, are of great importance to collectors. At one time, the making of such containers was a highly specialized craft. "Wet," or "tight," coopers made kegs and casks for liquids. "Dry," or "slack," coopers produced barrels for bulk commodities such as flour or sugar. There were even "butt" coopers to make whiskey barrels and hogsheads and "rundlet" coopers to turn out small kegs and water flasks. There were also those artisans who manufactured boxes. Because their technique consisted of several rather simple stages, it was the first area of the craft to be handled in something akin to modern production-line methods. A box top was cut, usually from pine, by use of a pattern, or template. Sides were formed from a single, thin, flexible strip of wood, known today as veneer, butted up against the edges of the top; the ends of the piece were then usually overlapped, cut off straight up and down, and nailed into place. Common round cheeseboxes of the type still manufactured are good examples of this method. Earlier specimens might be joined to top and bottom with tiny wooden pegs, and the side fastenings would also be pegs or copper brads; factory-made boxes of the late nineteenth and early twentieth centuries will be fastened only with tiny wire nails or glue. By 1850, vast numbers of boxes were being made, often by women, in small shops throughout the land. The operators worked by the piece, usually being paid three to seven cents per hundred.

Though made in basically the same way, there is a second type of box that varies from the type just described: instead of being cut off vertically at the veneer joint, one end of the thin panel is cut into triangular "fingers"; these in turn are either inserted into holes previously cut in the veneer or tacked into place. Such containers often are extremely well made and have for many years been spoken of as "Shaker boxes." There is no doubt that Shaker craftsmen did make such boxes, since their labeled specimens are known, and they may well have developed or at least refined the technique. On the other hand, old advertisements make it clear that many non-Shaker coopers were quite capable of producing high-quality fingered boxes. As with "Shaker baskets," it is advisable to buy as Shaker only marked examples or those with a reliable history of origin in a Shaker community.

Age Signs

Since so much woodenware is of relatively recent origin, it is important to be able to judge the age of a given specimen. Fortunately, the characteristics of wood itself assist us in this process. As wood ages, it shrinks across the grain. In bowls this effect is especially noticeable, and old examples will often be oval rather than round. In boxes, the shrinking tops and bottoms draw away from the veneer sides. Barrel staves separate; knots in wood drop out, leaving holes in the surface. Aging wood also grows lighter and with handling takes on a velvet smooth quality hard to duplicate by other means. Look also for wooden pegs and crude wrought or cut nails—all long ago ceased to be employed in the manufacture of woodenware. Repairs can also be important clues to age. Wooden objects were once so important that when damaged they were restored rather than thrown out. The presence of a wrought-iron butterfly hinge to repair a cracked bowl or a piece of copper at the foot of a candleholder goes a long way to assure age and authenticity.

Boxes, barrels, and bowls in particular may bear internal clues to age and former use. Spice boxes still smell of their long-gone contents; grease bowls show a dark oil stain; milk containers are bleached white; butter bowls have a distinct fat line; and any vessel once used for chopping will bear across its interior a network of fine lines, indicating the relentless attack of the iron food chopper. Paint, where present, should be hard and spidery with age and worn away at points of contact, such as handles, bottoms, and lips. Of course, some of these marks of authenticity can be faked, but not all, and the presence of several in the same piece is a strong indication that you have found a fine, old piece of woodenware.

Certain items indicate their antiquity by form alone. Few salts, inkwells, noggins, or tankards were produced in wood after 1850, so for these and other archaic items there exists a certain built-in guarantee of age.

Burl

Certain trees, particularly ash, elm, and maple, produce large protuberances on their trunk and limbs when attacked by insect pests. The grain in such growths, instead of running in straight lines, becomes convoluted. Since fracture in wood occurs along the grain, the twisted interior of a burly piece makes it extremely durable. It also takes a high polish and shows an attractive grain. Both Indians and the early settlers were drawn to such wood. They burned and gouged out the interiors of burl blocks to make massive mixing and eating bowls and laboriously whittled smaller pieces into cups, scoops, and plates. Since burl growth was never common and is, moreover, extremely hard to work, pieces were never abundant and are rare today. This factor coupled with the beauty of highly polished burl has led to great collector enthusiasm. Few good specimens of American burl sell for less than a hundred dollars. There is a problem, however. The Europeans also worked in this wood, and some of their burl is now entering this country. Aside from the characteristics previously mentioned for distinguishing foreign treen, it should be noted that most of the nondomestic ware is of oak, a wood whose burly form was rarely if ever employed here.

Decoration and Marking

As in other areas of antiques, decoration enhances the value of treen. Most wooden objects were left in the natural state or, at most, varnished or shellacked. Mortars, barrels, boxes, and the like were frequently given a solid coat of paint on the exterior. Red, gray, brown, green, and blue are the most common colors. Such examples are considered more desirable; and the addition of decorative motifs—bands or floral patterns of a contrasting color—further enhances the quality of a piece.

Early specimens, particularly those from Pennsylvania and New England, may show carved or incised names and dates and chip-carved ornamental devices, such as stars, hex signs, and rosettes. Generally, such work indicates that the piece was made for presentation; as such it is unique. Names, where present, generally prove to be those of owners rather than makers; for the most part, it was not common for woodenware manufacturers to mark their wares. An exception is the box industry, in which mass producers during the second half of the last century often stenciled their names on their products. This was also frequently true of the makers of patent churns, washing machines, and similar household gadgets.

Decoration can be faked and pieces repainted. Fortunately, most such specimens are crudely done. New paint looks new. It does not show wear at contact points, and it does not have age cracks. Those who repaint also frequently touch up areas that would rarely have been painted originally, such as the interiors of bowls and scoops. Also, the new decoration may be of a type wholly unsuited to the piece or the area from which it comes.

Butter molds.
Left: Maple with leaf pattern; Maine, ca. 1900; $45-75.
Right: Pine and maple, initial; New England, 19th century; $85-135. Butter prints and molds are among the most popular of all woodenware; those with an initial are rare. Piece at right probably bears initial of its owner.

Left: B utter mold, maple, with sheaf of wheat pattern; New Hampshire, early 20th century; $45-65. **Center:** Butter print, pine, with pinecone and leaf pattern; Maine, 19th century; $50-75. **Right:** Butter mold, birch, with sheaf of wheat pattern; Massachusetts, early 20th century; $35-55.

Cake mold, pine, with eagle pattern; Pennsylvania, mid-19th century; $350-500.
A well-designed piece of folk art.

Back row: Two boxed butter molds, pine; Massachusetts, late 19th century.
Left: $45-75. **Right:** $40-60. **Front row:** Butter prints. **Left:** Pine with floral pattern; New York, 20th century; $35-55. **Center:** Maple, with pineapple pattern; Pennsylvania, mid-19th century; $100-175. Piece is highly valuable because of its uncommonly large size.
Right: Pine, with pineapple pattern; Maine, late 19th century; $60-90.

Top: Sugar cutter, wrought iron, and pine; New England, ca. 1850; $60-90. Sugar cutters were common until the introduction of granulated sugar in the years following the Civil War. **Bottom:** Maple-sugar mold, pine; Massachusetts, early 19th century; $40-70.

Juice press, walnut, with wrought iron accessories; Maine, 18th century; $175-265. An extremely early example of a common household item.

Maple-sugar molds.
Left: Hinged, pine, with cow shape; Maine, ca. 1850; $90-120. **Center:** Pine, with heart shape; New Hampshire, ca. 1880; $65-85. **Right:** Pine, with fish shape; Maine, ca. 1850; $110-160. Molds such as the fish and cow are true folk art and should increase in value.

Top: Wash stirrer, pine; $5-10.
Center top: Pair of lard squeezers, pine; $5-15.
Center bottom: Wash paddle, pine; $50-80. All, New England, late 19th century except skimmer, which is late 18-early 19th century.

Cigar mold, pine; Connecticut, early 20th century; $25-40. A common and popular collector's object.

Sailor's wooden accessories. **Top left:** Weighted mallet, maple; $40-50. **Top right:** Needle box, pine and bamboo; $40-75. **Bottom left:** Fid, mahogany; $65-110. **Bottom right:** Box, turned pine, with scratch-carved decoration; $90-145. All, mid-19th century. Scratch decoration considerably enhances the value of any woodenware.

Left: Scraper, maple; New York, ca. 1920; $5-10. **Center:** Maul, pine and oak; New York, ca. 1910; $10-15. **Right:** Pestle, or masher, maple; New York, ca. 1920; $5-10. Good specimens of well-aged but not very old woodenware.

Factory-made sander, turned and line-decorated pine; Maine, ca. 1875; $50-85. Wooden sanders are relatively rare.

Top: Well-coverd wash stirrer, pine; Ohio, late 19th century; $65-100. **Center:** Button-ended rolling pin, maple; Connecticut, 19th century; $35-65. **Bottom:** Hand-carved scoop, pine; New York, early 19th century; $35-50.

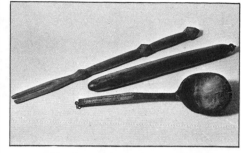

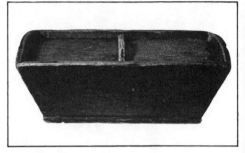

Dough box, pine, with old green paint and original cover; East, mid-19th century; $175-250.

Double lift-top box, pine; Pennsylvania, late 19th century; $70-120. Possibly used as a scouring box or carpenter's line-and-chalk holder. Good carving on handle enhances its value.

Stack of four grain measures, oak and pine; Daniel Cragin, active in Wilton, N.H., in the 1880s. **Top to bottom:** $250-350 the set. Extremely large and small sizes are most valuable Since the maker of grain measures was normally required by law to stamp his name on his products, it is possible to acquire complete marked sets.

Bottom left: Shaker box, pine and maple, salmon paint and black latticework decoration on cover; Ohio, mid-19th century; $500-850. **Top center:** Cheesebox, green paint; Maine, ca. 1910; $60-95.
Top right: Cheesebox, gray paint; Maine, ca. 1890; $55-80. Both of pine and birch. **Bottom right:** Cheesebox, pine and hickory, old red paint; New York, ca. 1870; $125-175. Authenticated Shaker boxes such as the one illustrated command a premium among collectors.

Spice box set, birch veneer with tin bindings; Massachusetts, late 19th century; $85-145. A characteristic example of factory-made boxes.

Left: Scoop, burl ash; New York, ca. 1840; $225-375. **Center:** Bride's box, pine and maple; Midwest, mid-19th century; $185-245. **Right:** Funnel, pine; New York, mid-19th century; $85-135.

Left: Barber's box, pine; Pennsylvania, 19th century; $85-145.
Right: Utility box, pine and horn; mid-19th century; $135-195.
This box evidences extremely fine craftsmanship.

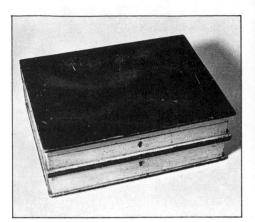

Examples of common boxes readily available today. **Top:** Hinged wall box, old white paint; Maine, early 20th century; $25-55. **Center:** Slide-top candle box, oak; Massachusetts, late 19th century; $50-85.

Bottom: Ballot box, pine in old red paint; Maine, late 19th century; $40-65.

Box in shape of a book, pine, old black and white paint; New York, $300-475. A mid-19th century whimsey, and quite rare.

Box, pine inlaid with white wood, natural finish, brass handle and latch and unusual molding; New York, 1880; $250-450.

Slide-top candle box, pine with smoked decoration in yellow; Maine, 19th century; $285-475. Painted boxes are in great demand today, and the more elaborate the decoration the higher the price.

Box, pine inlaid with birch, old black paint, diamond inlay in gold; Connecticut, ca. 1860; $200-350.

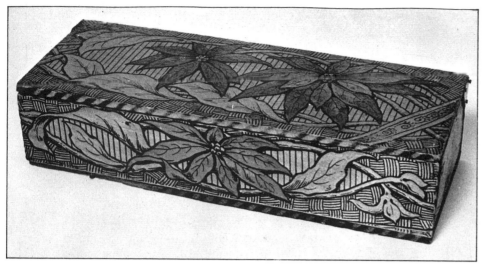

Lift-top box, pine, with burned decoration, New England, 20th century; $20-45. This decorative technique, known as pyrography, was a popular hobby during the period 1890-1920. Specimens are common but increasing in value. A coming area for collectors.

Cranberry rake, pine; Maine, late 19th century; $35-55. Tools of this sort are at present of little interest to most collectors and so may be obtained easily.

Patented beehive, pine, blue paint; Tennessee, ca. 1871; $110-175. A piece of this sort may vary greatly in value. It would have a substantially greater worth in Tennessee or vicinity than in other areas of the country.

Left: Grain shovel, pine; Massachusetts, ca. 1850; $85-145. **Center:** Line winder, pine and maple; Maine, ca. 1850; $60-100. Used by fishermen to dry line. **Right:** Early pestle, pine; Maine, ca. 1830; $35-65. Used in a crude samp mortar in an area where no grain mill was available.

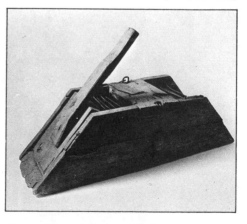

Rattrap, pine and iron; New England, late 19th century; $65-110.

Coffee mill, pine, with brass and iron fittings; New England, late 19th century; $75-135. Dovetails and brass make this a desirable example of a common item.

Bean-sorting rack, pine; Pennsylvania, late 19th-early 20th century; $55-95.

Meat grinder, pine and iron; New York, mid-19th century; $165-235.

346

Folding wash ringer, pine and cast iron; patented by the Larkin Company, New York, late 19th century; $145-215.

Churn, pine bound in iron, old gray paint over blue; Maine, ca. 1860; $240-320. Churns are popular collector's items.

Footed churn, pine; New England, late 19th century; $55-85. A homemade version of a popular factory-made churn.

Churn, pine in yellow paint; New England, late 19th century; $90-130. A good example of a commercially manufactured patented churn.

Cheese press, pine and oak; Pennsylvania, ca. 1850; $175-250. Dovetails and pegs indicate the handmade nature of this early press.

347

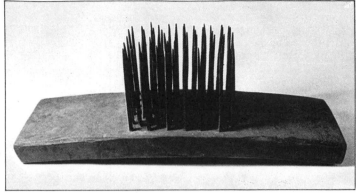

Flax hatchel, oak with wrought iron spikes; Maine, early 19th century; $65-90. An unusual example; good body shape and fragments of flax still caught in the teeth.

Flax wheel, pine and maple; unpainted; Maine, ca. 1850; $200-275. A good example in working order.

Flax hatcher, maple with cut nails; New England, mid-19th century; $40-70. This piece has an unusual cant to the body.

Spinning wheel, pine and maple; New England, late 19th century; $300-400. Graceful lines and good condition in a popular object.

Flax wheel, pine, ash, and birch, blue with red and white trim; Iowa, dated 1863; $350-450.
Signed and dated spinning and flax wheels are the top of the line in this field.

348

Swift, birch, and maple; Maine, late 19th century; $80-140. Few pieces of woodenware can boast of the sculptural quality possessed by the swift, a simple device for holding and measuring yarn. Decorated specimens often sell for several hundred dollars, but a simple piece such as this goes for considerably less.

Yarn winder, oak and pine; New Hampshire, ca. 1830; $60-85. Serving the same purpose as a swift but lacking its adjustability, the yarn winder was a crude but often attractive device.

Clock reel, pine and maple; New York, ca. 1850; $90-160. Another spinner's measuring device of attractive shape. Any decoration would enhance its value.

Amish sewing box, pine, old red and brown paint; mid-19th century; $300-450. A simple Pennsylvania form.

Left: Shaker-made spool rack, birch; $175-275. Holes in rack once contained pegs to hold spools. **Right:** Tiny mirror, turned birch; $100-175. Both, New England, mid-19th century.

Left: Tape loom, pine and oak; Massachusetts, ca. 1830; $90-145. Small hand looms of this sort were used to make suspenders or decorative braid. **Right:** Bucket for carrying water or milk, pine and hickory; 19th century; $75-100.

Left: Canteen, hickory and pine, ca. 1850; $70-135. Canteens are generally early since they were soon replaced by tin or glass containers. **Right:** Flour or sugar storage bucket, pine and maple; ca. 1900; $40-75. Storage buckets of this sort are frequently refinished and used for storing magazines. Both, Maine.

Well bucket, pine bound with iron; New Hampshire, late 19th century; $90-140.

Shaker-made firkin, or cask, in pine, hickory, and birch; Massachusetts, late 19th century; $450-600. A fine example of Shaker craftsmanship.

Storage buckets; New England, late 19th century. **Left:** Old yellow paint; $90-130.
Right: Old red paint; $75-115. Original color adds value to pieces such as these.

Left: Knife box, pine, old blue paint; Massachusetts, ca. 1870; $60-90. **Center:** Water barrel or keg, oak, old green paint; New Hampshire, ca. 1860; $80-120. **Right:** Mortar and pestle, pine; Maine, early 19th century; $35-60.

Grease bucket, staved pine bound in ▶ iron, old blue paint; Vermont, ca. 1850; $235-315.

Storage bucket, pine bound in iron, old blue-green paint; New York, ca. 1860; $125-195.

Shaker knife box, pine and birch, old red paint; Maine, late 19th century; $150-225. Boxes of this sort were made and sold commercially by the Shakers at the end of the 19th century. They are not uncommon, but like all Shaker items, they are costly.

Knife box, pine, dovetailed, with cut-out heart and old yellow paint; Pennsylvania, ca. 1850; $375-625. A top-quality piece.

Turned wooden plate, pine; New England, ca. 1830; $125-185. Treen plates are getting harder and harder to find.

Unusually large pie peel, pine, New England, ca. 1870; $80-110.

Left: Single-handled rolling pin; maple; New York, ca. 1880; $25-40. **Top right:** Bread board, pine; New York, ca. 1900; $15-25.
Bottom right: Mixing bowl, bird's eye maple; early 20th century; $45-75. Attractive wood like bird's eye maple adds to the value of otherwise routine items.

Left: Mortar and pestle, lignum vitae; Maine, ca. 1860; $75-100. **Right:** Unusually large mixing bowl (30"in diameter), pine; Maine, ca. 1880; $95-145.
Large size or odd shape is a plus in bowls.

Unusual oval chopping bowl, pine; New Hampshire, ca.1860; $125-165. Butter paddle, maple; $10-20.

Checkerboard, pine; New York, late 19th-early 20th century; $85-145. An example of playing boards often made by hand.

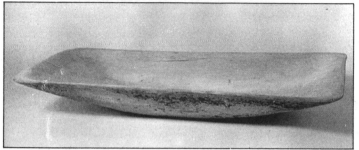

Very large chopping bowl (32″ × 17″), pine, old green paint on exterior; $295-335. A very fine shape.

Two crude bootjacks, pine; New York, late 19th-early 20th century. **Top:** $25-40. **Bottom:** $25-45. Example at top has been carved to take advantage of natural form of root.

Watch box, walnut and pine; New England, ca. 1800; $1,250-1,800. A Federal-style piece dating from the days when the master of the house often owned the only timepiece and it might be used as a clock when not on his person. A very rare specimen.

353

Basketry

It has sometimes mistakenly been assumed that the colonists learned basketmaking from the American Indians, but such is clearly not the case. Basketmakers were common in Europe and the Far East long before Columbus, and old records indicate that they were among the earliest arrivals on these shores. Of course, since both settlers and natives knew the art of basket weaving, there was a certain interchange of technique and style between them. Today, many professional basketmakers in the United States are of Indian descent.

At present, the most common woven basketry form is some variation of the basket itself; but surviving examples indicate that at one time the technique was used to produce a greater variety of forms—such as fish traps, funnels, and cribs.

As recently as five years ago, baskets, except for the very unusual ones, were a glut on the antiques market. Today, all that has changed, and the market continues to rise. However, the field is still open, and good pieces can be found at country auctions, yard sales, and in shops. Prices vary greatly, but it is still possible to spend no more than a few dollars for a good specimen.

The serious collector of baskets must view his avocation in a historical perspective rather different from that of other antiques. Few baskets are really old. Both material and construction make for a fragile container, one that was often put to hard use; consequently, many were long ago left bottomless in field or shed. Moreover, baskets are still being made. Great numbers were produced in Appalachia during the 1920s and 1930s. Baskets are still made there as well as in New Hampshire, Maine, and New Brunswick, where basketmakers, often of Indian extraction, turn out examples indistinguishable in style from those their ancestors made a century ago. Since few baskets are signed or dated, it is extremely difficult to determine just how old they are. But there are certain signs that do indicate age: abrasive wear on the bottom; natural darkening in color; holes, indicating brittle ends or sections that have snapped off over the years; and in baskets decorated with paint or dye, a mellowing or fading of color.

Baskets are basically homely, simple

objects, and the wise collector will look not so much for great age, signatures, or dates, as for originality of style, excellence of technique, and a love of the craft manifested in a beautiful and useful form.

Splint Basketry

More than 50 percent of all old baskets on the market are made, at least in part, of splint—long, flat strips of oak, ash, or hickory. For many years, splint was produced by the laborious process of soaking logs, splitting them, and shaving them to size. Though some modern basketmakers still employ this method, most now use commercial splint, which is machine-cut into extremely thin pieces. The hand-cut variety may be recognized by its relative thickness (at least an eighth of an inch), the lack of uniformity—few strips are of the same width—and its rough texture, since the froe or drawknife used by the craftsman lacks the planing effect of the machine. The presence of hand-cut splint is some indication of age in a basket, since machined material was not widely available until the 1880s. If solid wood parts such as handle, ears, or rim show marks of a knife and handwork, one may assume a nineteenth- or early twentieth-century origin.

Most splint basketry is made in the crosshatch technique, in which the strips of splint are woven across each other at right angles, creating a checkerboard surface. Less common and therefore in a sense more desirable are items made in the hexagonal, or openwork, weave, in which the bands of splint cross each other at a forty-five-degree angle, creating six-sided openings in the surface. The hexagonal weave was used for baskets that required considerable drainage, such as fish, clam, or oyster carriers or cheese-drying baskets. Since there was relatively little need for this type, hexagonal baskets are comparatively rare.

Most splint baskets are unmarked. A few bear a name or signature, which is usually that of the owner rather than the maker—except for those made at the northeastern Shaker settlements in the nineteenth century, which were stamped with ciphers such as "Sabbathday Lake" or "Shaker." Unfortunately, the general interest in all things Shaker has led some people to label as Shaker any well-made basket

that at all resembles known marked examples. A word to the wary here: there were many excellent non-Shaker basketmakers—indeed, hundreds—and their ware is frequently indistinguishable from that made at Shaker shops. Don't pay high prices for a "Shaker" basket unless it has a good mark or an authenticated history linking it to one of the sect's settlements.

By 1880, the invention of splint-cutting machines and wire staples had sparked the development of a thriving commercial basket manufactory. The bulk of the containers produced were for berries or vegetables; they are readily distinguished from handmade specimens by their wide, thin, machined splints and their wire staples, tacks, and handles. The earliest types may bear a stamped trademark.

Decoration of any sort, being relatively uncommon, especially in old pieces, adds interest to all kinds of baskets; it is most frequently seen on splint containers. The earliest decorative technique used was overall painting or staining in a solid color such as red, brown, blue, or green; a good coat of old, well-faded paint should double the price of any basket. Also much sought after is the so-called Indian decoration—colored circles, squares, stars, and the like applied to the natural surface by a stamp. In addition, commercial splint was frequently stained red, green, blue, or gold. Basketmakers might use stained splint in combination with the unstained to create a variety of color patterns.

Willow Basketry

The long slim shoots of the willow tree make an ideal basketry material. They are supple and over time more durable than splint. Willow containers are mentioned in eighteenth-century inventories, so there is no doubt that they have long been popular. Their greatest period of use, though, was in the late years of the last century. In the 1870s and 1880s, farmers in places such as the Finger Lakes region of western New York State began to cultivate purple and Caspian willow for sale to manufacturers, who ran the shoots through machines to produce a standard size and shape. The commercial willow was sold primarily to city basket weavers who used it in a variety of decorative ware, from

354

jardinieres and planters to hanging baskets, sconces, and bottle covers. Though a few unusual types, such as cradles, bonnets, and chicken-nesting boxes exist, willow has always been used chiefly for baskets and trays.

Some variation of the crosshatch weave is most common in willow baskets, but a number of other weaves were also used, and sometimes in the same piece. Current interest in willow basketry is not noticeably great. This is partly because so much of it is not old at all, perhaps thirty years at most. In addition, the forms are limited, and the baskets are difficult to distinguish from the willow or cut-reed baskets (a close relative) that are regularly imported from Asia.

Willow basketry is nevertheless a valid craft that has produced some attractive specimens. Look for the older pieces, which will show bottom wear and cracked strands and may appear in the natural brown wood, now weathered, rather than the dark brown stain and shellac so common in recent work. Heavy field baskets and old covered hampers are the most interesting forms. Occasional examples may be painted in a solid color; but since the material is not flat, they will rarely carry stamped or stenciled decoration. There are, however, some interesting small, handled baskets that bear floral designs carefully painted on by hand. These are of some age and though not uncommon are not yet much appreciated. They may well be the best buy in willow.

Willow, along with reed, splint, and rattan, was employed in the construction of the well-known Nantucket baskets. These are round or oval containers, generally with handles, that have been made on and near Nantucket Island, Massachusetts, since the time of the Civil War. They have several characteristics that appeal strongly to collectors: they are often marked with a maker's name and the date and place of manufacture. They are very well made and of a distinctive type. Their tightly woven willow body rising from a block of wood at the center bottom is unique and assists in the identification of unmarked examples. So does the fact that the handles are set into metal rather than the usual wooden ears.

Nantucket baskets in good condition may sell for hundreds of dollars apiece, even though many of the most attractive ones were made only a few decades ago. Moreover, they are still being made for sale today. The danger of confusing the new with the old, and the serious possibility that the present craze—and inflated prices—for them will not continue much longer, mean that the collector of these baskets should proceed with great caution.

Straw Basketry

Straw—generally rye—was used in basketmaking by the German settlers of Virginia, Pennsylvania, Delaware, New Jersey, and Maryland. It was not woven but rather sewed in long strips and then coiled. Each successive round of straw was bound to the developing vessel by pieces of grass, thread, or string. The technique limited the product to round or oval shapes; and, as a result, the forms of straw baskets are rather restricted. Most common are small bread-raising baskets, covered hampers, and egg baskets. Less often seen are conical beehives known as skeps, grain sower's baskets, and winnowing trays.

Because of the nature of the material, decoration is limited. A few pieces are painted, but most are found in the natural color. Handles, hardware, or fastenings of any sort (other than the twine that binds the vessel together) are uncommon.

Pricing of straw baskets varies greatly. Their production was confined to a small section of the country, and in that area the supply is ample and prices moderate. In other locations where the supply is smaller, the demand for examples may drive prices up well above the average.

Miscellaneous Basket Types

Aside from the three major types of basketry, collectors may hope to encounter vessels made from materials found only in certain areas of the country. From the South come trays and baskets made from the needles of the Florida, or longleaf, pine. They are constructed in much the same manner as rye straw baskets and generally date from the present century. A typical type consists of a glass-covered tray about which the pine needles are woven, the tray itself containing seashells and a salutation such as "Greetings from Ft. Lauderdale."

In the Appalachian Mountains, honeysuckle vines, carefully cut and trimmed, have served in the construction of sturdy sewing and storage hampers. Porcupine quills were also employed in that region to make attractive baskets, which were offered to tourists and have, as a result, been dispersed throughout the country.

Throughout the Northeast and along the Great Lakes, several types of long-leafed swamp grass have been used to make the so-called sweet grass baskets. The grass is braided and coiled, often quite intricately, resulting in an extremely sophisticated basket type. Most such baskets were made by women, and most were small, no more than a couple of inches high. Miniature baskets, which were sometimes made also in willow or splint, are now among the most popular items in the antiques field; a tiny basket will often sell for several times the price of its brother of normal size.

In the Midwest, corn shucks have served as basketmaking material. Loosely woven, they may form a bread plate or fruit-drying tray, or they may be coiled into an airy storage hamper. In Indiana, they were even made into horse collars. Unfortunately, most such items were not highly prized and were discarded as soon as they had to be replaced. As a result, only a limited amount of corn-shuck basketry is to be found today.

Swing handle splint market basket; Massachusetts, ca. 1880; $200-275. A classic example of the well-formed, completely handmade vessel so popular with collectors. Note the hand-carved ears and handle.

Splint market basket; Maine, ca. 1900; $75-130. A completely hand-finished basket in a common form.

Splint market or school basket; New Hampshire, ca. 1910; $110-180. A later basket of machine-cut splint in a form most popular with collectors, many of whom use them for handbags.

Splint field baskets. **Left:** Round; Maine, ca. 1900; $65-90. **Right:** Square, New Hampshire, ca. 1900; $75-100. Baskets of this sort are very common. They served both to carry produce from the field and to transport it to market.

Splint egg basket; New Hampshire, ca. 1900; $70-100. A good basket made from machine-cut splint.

Small kidney-shaped baskets with handles; East, 20th century. **Left:** Splint; $75-115. **Right:** Sweet grass and splint; $50-65.

Splint baskets with handles; late 19th century. **Left:** Nantucket style; New England; $125-175. **Center:** Swing handle, New England; $185-225. **Right:** Kidney shape; Southeast; $75-125.

Splint and iron-wire oyster or clam basket; Pennsylvania, ca, 1880; $130-180. The wire bottom is unusual.

Splint field basket; New Hampshire, ca. 1890; $80-120. A particularly strong example of a common type widely used on eastern farms.

Early splint field basket; New England, ca. 1870; $100-175. An extremely well-formed basket similar to those made in the Shaker shops.

Splint wood basket; Southeast, late 19th
century; $250-325.
Footed baskets of this sort were often
used to dry dyed wool.

Large splint wool-storage basket; New
York, early 20th century; $75-115. The
variation in form from top to bottom is
skillfully done.

Splint drying baskets; Connecticut, ca.
1880. **Top:** 13″ × 22″; $90-135.
Bottom: 4″ × 12″; $70-95. Baskets of
this nature were used to dry sliced apples
and other fruit. They are fragile and
seldom found, particularly in the larger
sizes.

Covered splint goose-feather basket;
Maine, ca. 1920; $135-200. Unusual
form and good size make this a most
desirable item.

Extremely large splint storage basket
with cover, 40″ high; Maine, ca. 1920;
$175-265. Large baskets are always
choice.
The use of red, green, and yellow dyed
splint in this piece enhances its already
substantial value.

Small, rough splint berry basket, 4″ × 4″;
New England, late 19th century; $50-85.
the forerunner of the machine-made
berry basket.

Splint sifter, possibly used in shelling beans or peas; Pennsylvania, late 19th century; $125-185.

Rare splint nose basket used for feeding livestock; New York, late 19th century; $175-285. Among the hardest to find of all basket form.

Splint fish or eel trap; New England, 19th century; $200-300. Another extremely uncommon piece of basketry.

Very early handmade splint creel; East, ca. 1870; $85-150.

Uncommon splint pigeon basket; New Jersey, 19th century; $110-160. Pigeons were released from such baskets at pigeon shooting contests.

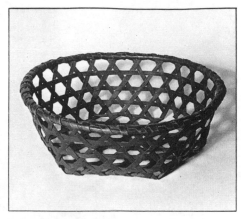

Splint cheese or field basket, hexagonal weave, East, late 19th-early 20th century; $250-375.

Fine splint table baskets, hexagonal weave, Connecticut, 20th century. **Top:** $250-400. **Bottom:** $150-275. Late but interesting and well-woven pieces.

Extremely crude splint clam or fish basket, hexagonal weave, New England, 19th century; $90-130. Hexagonal-weave pieces are far less common than those woven in the crosshatch technique.

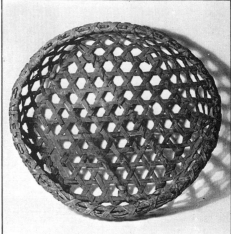

Splint cheese basket, hexagonal weave; New England, late 19th century; $325-450.

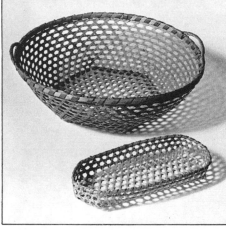

Early factory-made splint field basket; Ohio, late 19th century; $55-85. An interesting version.

Painted splint baskets. **Left:** Loom basket, old white paint; Maine, ca. 1910; $65-85. Loom baskets were used to hold a weaver's thread bobbins. In the 20th century, the form was modified to serve as a brush and comb holder. **Right:** Field basket, orange paint; New York, ca. 1880; $120-185.

Factory-made splint field basket with handle; 20th century; $35-65. A type not yet of much interest to collectors, though it has good form.

Commercially cut splint baskets with red and green banding; New England, early 20th century. **Left:** Table basket; $30-45. **Right:** Market basket, with fine carved handles; $85-125.

Machine-cut splint storage baskets with interwoven red and blue bands; New England, early 20th century. **Left:** $50-75. **Right:** $75-100.

Left: Cut splint work basket with handles and Massachusetts Indian decoration in red; $170-220. Massachusetts Indian decoration, applied with sponge or corncob, adds to value of any basket. **Right:** small splint knickknack basket; $30-45. Both, New England, early 20th century.

Well-made commercially cut splint work basket; early 20th century; $75-115. The sweet grass rim indicates a New England origin.

Factory-cut splint table or work basket with Indian decoration in red; New York, ca. 1910; $75-100,

Left: Elaborate splint sewing basket, red and blue stain; Maine, ca. 1930; $35-55. The twisted splint decoration is typical of Maine Indian work. **Right:** Splint market basket; New Hampshire, ca. 1920; $15-25.

Splint and sweet-grass sewing basket, decorated with red-stained splint; Maine, ca. 1930; $145-195. Interior compartments are unusual in basketry. A choice item.

Splint storage baskets; Maine, ca. 1920. **Left:** With stained splint decoration; $30-50. **Right:** $25-40. Late, factory-made baskets of machine-cut splint; both probably once had lids.

Splint and sweet-grass basketry; Maine, 20th century. **Rear:** Unusual tray, 4″ × 8″; $45-70.
Covered box, 3″ × 4″; $35-60. **Center:** Basket with handle, 2″ diameter with pink stained splint; $20-35. **Right:** Basket with handle, 3″ diameter; $45-65.

Splint and sweet-grass basketry; Maine, 20th century. **Left:** Covered sewing basket, 8″ diameter, 4″ high; $25-40. **Center :** Table basket, 7″ diameter, 8″ high; $15-30. **Right:** Covered pin box, 3″ diameter; $35-50. The combination of braided sweet grass and machine-cut splint is typical of 20th-century Indian baskets from Maine and New Brunswick.

Splint and sweet-grass basketry; Maine, 20th century. **Left:** Miniature urn with handles, 4″ high; $14-17. **Back right:** Urn with handles, 9″ high; $30-50. **Front right:** Basket with handles, 3″ diameter, red and blue stain; $20-35.

Willow and sweet-grass box with cover and feet; New Hampshire, late 19th century; $55-80. An unusual example of a Victorian sewing or whatnot box. .

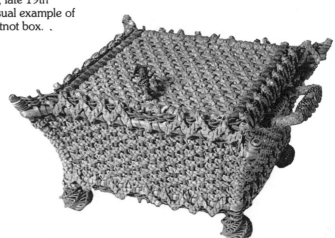

Splint and sweet-grass basketry; Maine, 20th century. **Rear:** Barrel-shaped storage basket, 16″ high; $40-65. **Left:** Covered box; $25-45. **Right front:** Tapered, covered sewing basket; $30-55.

Splint and sweet-grass basketry; Maine, 20th century.
Back left: Covered basket, banded in pink, 4″ high; $45-65. **Front left:** Fancy basket with handle, 1-½″ high; $15-25.
Back right: Covered box, 3″ high; $25-40.
Back right: Urn, red, 3″ high; $20-25. Miniatures are becoming increasingly popular with collectors.
Smaller items such as these are an excellent investment.

Splint and sweet-grass basketry; Maine. **Left:** covered box; $20-35. **Center:** Hat-shaped box with pink splint ribbon; $35-50. **Right:** Basket-shaped pincushion; $15-20. 20th century basketry whimsies are common.

Splint and sweet-grass basketry; Maine, 20th century. **Left:** Handled basket showing unusual skill in weaving of grass; $25-50. **Center:** Large tray with handle, 10″ in height and diameter; $30-45. **Right:** Fan; $20-35.

Willow field basket; New York, 20th century; $20-30. A form still made, of small interest to collectors.

Willow clothes or field basket; Midwest, 20th century; $15-25. A utilitarian piece in a style still seen. Handles are constructed as an integral part of basket.

Willow market basket with cover; New Hampshire, early 20th century; $60-90. A particularly well-shaped example in this medium.

Willow market or field basket with handle; Midwest, late 19th century; $45-75.
Good weaving and old red paint make this a desirable example.

Covered willow sewing basket; New York, late 19th century; $60-90. An example of good willow basketry.

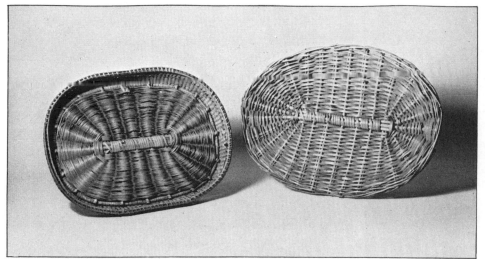

Willow basketry; New York, 20th century. **Left:** Serving tray; $10-20. **Right:** Basket cover; $5-10.

Willow openwork serving or table basket; 20th century; $15-35. The sort of willow basketry practiced in children's camps.

Willow storage basket; Southwest, late 19th-early 20th century; $10-20. An unusual form in crude weave.

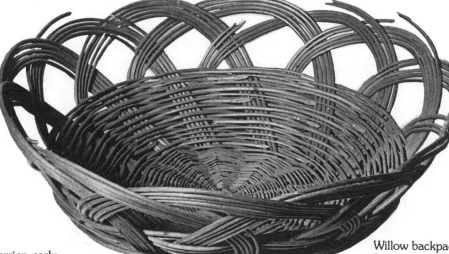

Willow and iron animal carrier; early 20th century; $85-115. The forerunner of the modern cat and dog carriers.

Willow backpack or Indian basket; Pennsylvania, late 19th-early 20th century; $75-115. Such baskets are still often made by hand.

Extremely large willow traveling case, 3' × 3'; New York, late 19th century; $90-140. Very few of these old suitcases have survived.

Painted willow; Pennsylvania, 20th century. **Left:** Silent butler, pink; $5-10. **Right:** Openwork flower basket, red; $30-45.

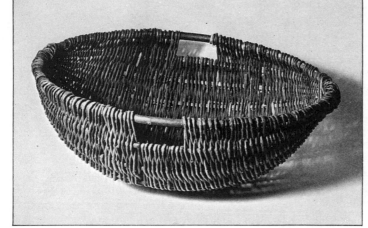

Split willow open-handled field basket; Southeast, late 19th-early 20th century; $115-155.

Split willow sewing or market basket with double-lift top and fine carved wood handles; Southeast, late 19th century; $185-265. In the mountains of Georgia, Kentucky, and other southern states, willow baskets of a distinct style, like this one, are woven.

Split willow market basket, wood handle; Southeast, late 19th-early 20th century; $100-145.

Willow and wood fruit-drying tray; New York, late 19th century; $85-125.

Rye-straw field basket; Pennsylvania, late 19th century; $175-250. Extremely well made and rare.

Rye-straw bread-raising basket; New Jersey, late 19th century; $30-50. Rye-straw basketry was practiced primarily in Pennsylvania, New Jersey, and Virginia.

Large rye-straw beehive or skep; Pennsylvania, 19th century; $125-200.

Rye-straw and wood beehive or skep; Pennsylvania, late 19th century; $95-130.

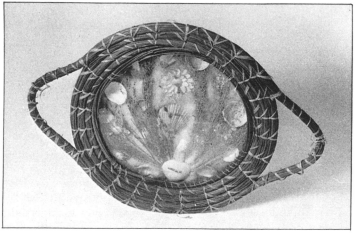

Pine-needle tray decorated with shells and dried vegetation; Florida, 20th century; $20-40. Souvenir pieces like this were made mostly in Florida, though they were often stamped with the names of towns in other states.

Lighting Devices

In frontier settlements, from the earliest days until well into the nineteenth century, firelight was often the only artificial light that was available. Though farm people did most of their work between the hours of dawn and dusk—a practice that continues into our own time—daylight hours seldom allowed enough time to complete the daily chores. Houses were poorly lit by their few small windows, but wood was plentiful, and often a fire was kept burning at all hours—winter and summer—to cook the meals and warm the water for washing, as well as to provide light and heat.

In new settlements in heavily forested areas, firelight was supplemented by the burning of pitch-pine knots, slivers of wood that gave off a bright though brief flame. As early as 1642, the author of *New England's Prospect* noted that

> Out of the pine is gotten the candle wood that is much spoke of, which may serve as a shift among poore folks, but I cannot commend it for singular good because it drippeth a pitchy kind of substance where it stands.

Pine knots—or light wood, as it was called in the southern colonies—were burned on the hearth or in fire pans, wrought-iron basins that were set in a corner of the fireplace. For outdoor work or for fishing, open-work iron baskets called cressets were filled with blazing knots. They made a bright light but a dangerous one and could not be used indoors.

Though pitch pine was used for lighting as late as the mid-eighteenth century, the devices used in firing it were so few and so crude that associated antiques either are uncommon or have gone unnoticed. A few fire pans are in museum collections, but they are seldom seen elsewhere. Much the same may be said of cressets.

The common cattail, or swamp rush, which grows in damp areas, was another crude early device used to provide interior light. It was prepared by stripping part of the outer bark from the rush; the pithy heart thus exposed would then be soaked in tallow or grease and, once dry, burned in a wrought-iron cliplike holder. The rushlight holder was usually mounted on an iron tripod or a wooden block. Because the light generated in this manner was both uncertain and smoky, pine knots were generally preferred in this country, though rushlight was widely used in Europe. Rush holders are frequently seen at antiques shows and museums, but it is likely that most have been brought over from the Continent; none are known to bear the mark of an American smith.

Candleholders

Both knot and rush were regarded by the settlers as little more than temporary expedients to light their homes. Almost from the beginning, the Massachusetts Bay Colony imported English candles, and as soon as enough tallow became available from wild or domestic animals, the domestic manufacture of candles began. In every home and until well into the nineteenth century, fall was the traditional period for candlemaking—as it was for slaughtering of livestock, whose fat provided the necessary tallow. To make the candles, the tallow was mixed with water in great iron pots, boiled, and then skimmed until of a suitable consistency. Candlewicks were prepared by attaching loosely spun hemp, tow, or milkweed cotton (known as silk down) to short sticks. The wicks, hanging downward, were then dipped repeatedly into kettles of hot tallow and after each dipping were allowed to dry, so that layers of fat built up successively until the desired thickness was achieved. The process was not as lengthy as it might sound, and a rapid worker might turn out two hundred candles in a day.

Candle molds were also employed, both by the homemaker and by itinerant candlemakers. These molds, of tin, pewter, or pottery, were set in a frame accommodating any number from a single stick to eight dozen. Wicks were inserted into the individual tubes, and boiling tallow was poured in; when it cooled, the finished candles were removed. There was a commercial candle manufactory in Massachusetts as early as the 1750s, and gradually the chores of candlemaking were taken over by other such factories. The candle sellers who once traveled from farm to farm with their tin molds now carried only the finished product.

Candles were made of substances other than tallow. Beeswax was employed to a limited extent, particularly for church lighting; and in New England the pale green, sweet-smelling bayberry candle was always a favorite. It was a chore to pick the tiny berries, but their wax could be dipped or molded into candles that were harder than tallow and would not melt during the hot summer months; nor did they smoke. Even better candles could be made from spermaceti, a waxy substance obtained from the head of the sperm whale. It was not common, though, and candles so manufactured were too expensive for the average citizen.

Candle-associated antiques are of great interest to collectors. Molds come in a variety of shapes and tube quantities. The most common were made of tin and sell today for about six dollars per tube. Pewter and earthenware molds are much more expensive, especially the marked pottery ones, such as those made by the potter Alvin Wilcox, of Westmoreland, New York. Cylindrical tin candle boxes with lift tops, made to hang on a wall, are popular, particularly if tole-decorated. There are also numbers of wooden slide-top boxes, which were intended for shipment or storage of larger quantities of candles. These vary greatly in price depending upon age and decoration: late factory-made dovetailed examples may be purchased for a few dollars, while a fine old grain-painted piece may go for several hundred.

Tin tinderboxes were essential to the lighting of fires and candles, and these flat, round containers are still occasionally seen. If complete, they will contain flint, steel, and a piece of tinder (usually scorched linen). They are seldom decorated, and their identity often goes unrecognized.

The most popular of all candle antiques is the candlestick or candleholder. It comes in many shapes and may be made of wood, pottery, iron, tin, pewter, brass, silver, or gold. As one might suspect, given the flammable nature of the candle, metal is the preferred material.

The first device made to hold candles was a pointed piece of iron onto which the base of the candle was stuck. It was soon replaced by a hollow tube—the candlestick—and the only significant modification since has been the development of the ejector, a device for elevating the candle as it burns down in order to ensure complete use. Probably the most familiar type of candlestick is the so-called hog scraper, a tin or iron tube holder with a sliding ejector on the side and a wide, round base that was supposedly used for removing the bristles from freshly killed hogs. Hog scrapers have attracted a lot of attention lately. Many are signed by their makers, and these go for thirty-five to forty-five dollars each. The addition of a decorative brass band around the middle of the stick—called a wedding ring—ensures an even higher price.

Tube-type candlesticks vary in height from three to sixteen inches. Some were fitted with floor stands; these metal or wood candlestands, some of which could be adjusted in height, seem to have been quite popular during the eighteenth and early nineteenth centuries. Chandeliers were introduced in the mid-seventeenth century and were made in some number; they were used most often in churches, taverns, and public halls. A good, early wood and tin or iron chandelier with original paint commands a high price in today's market. Unfortunately, though, the demand exceeds the supply, and reproductions are common. Most are advertised as such by their manufacturers, but once a replica has changed hands a few times, its origin may become obscured. This is particularly the case with those pieces that are copied directly from known colonial examples.

Old iron candleholders and stands have also been imported from southern Europe. Though some of them are too ornate to pass for native fabrications, most are simple enough in form to look uncomfortably like something that might have been made in Massachusetts or Pennsylvania. Let the buyer beware.

Lamps

The concept of the oil lamp, a hollow receptacle in which an inflammable fluid is burned, is very old. Though they varied considerably in design, all ancient lamps consisted of a fluid-holder, usually round or oval, and a wick of cloth or tow. One end of the wick was usually supported on a raised shelf on the nose of the vessel to keep it free of the fuel. Both hanging and standing lamps are found, some with elaborate decoration. The most common are the oddly named Betty lamp and its more complex sister, the crusie, a Scottish variation that incorporated a second lamp and wick below the first; unburned oil dripped from the upper into the lower reservoir and was there consumed rather than being wasted.

Both types of lamp were popularized here by German and Swiss settlers, who brought the first ones with them and were soon manufacturing their own, generally of wrought iron or steel. Makers, particularly in Pennsylvania, tended to mark their lamps, and such names as Hurxthal, Derr, and Eby are prized among collectors. Lamps of this sort were also made in red earthenware, though they are far less commonly found in that medium than in metal.

As is true of candleholders, metal Betty and crusie lamps have been imported in quantity. Since the imports closely resemble native examples, unmarked lamps must be regarded with suspicion. Again, a reliable dealer is the best protection.

Though widely used for hundreds of years, the various open lamps shared common defects. They did not give off a strong light, and they wasted fuel. This problem demanded an answer; and in 1787, England's John Miles supplied one with the whale-oil, or agitable, lamp. This consisted of a sealed reservoir with a tightly fitting burner, which had two or more metal tubes to hold the wicks. The new lamp burned whale oil, which was then becoming available in quantity. The lamp was cheap, clean, and attractive. Early specimens were made of tin, brass, or pewter, but with the introduction of mechanical pressing in the 1820s, pressed glass became the favorite material. Such important American manufacturers as the New England Glass Company and the Sandwich Glass Company produced vast quantities of whale-oil lamps in a variety of patterns, all of which are known and avidly collected at present.

Actually, the whale-oil lamp was a derivation of the Argand lamp, patented in 1783 by the Swiss Amie Argand. This controlled-air-draft lamp had a vertical tubular burner containing a single tubular wick that was hollow in the center. The heat of the flame created a draft in the center of the wick, which increased combustion and, consequently, the amount of available light. Argand lamps also used whale oil.

By the middle of the nineteenth century, whales were becoming scarcer and the cost of whale oil was mounting. One Isaiah Jennings had invented a "burning fluid," which consisted of alcohol and turpentine, later modified to eliminate the alcohol; the final product, known as camphene, was widely used in the 1840s and 1850s. The results were sometimes disastrous. Camphene was extremely volatile, and fire and

explosion were visited upon its users. Modifications in the design of camphene lamps decreased the risks somewhat, but the problem was not resolved until the introduction of refined petroleum, or kerosene, in 1854.

The kerosene lamp made obsolete all that had come before. The basic principle, an air draft, was not unlike that of the Argand lamp, but the safety and low cost of fuel (particularly after the opening of the western Pennsylvania oil fields in the late 1850s) made it attractive to everyone. Kerosene lamps are still manufactured today, and in principle they have changed little. They have been made of several metals as well as of glass. Most popular with modern collectors are the "gone-with-the-wind" and Aladdin lamps, both of which have brass or white metal bases; the former boasts one or two large, round, hand-painted ball-shaped shades. These lamps are popular enough to have been reproduced, but many original examples are also available. Gone-with-the-wind lamps may sell for over a hundred dollars apiece, while Aladdin lamps are less expensive. They may be found both in the original nickel finish and in brass from which the nickel has been stripped.

Pressed-glass kerosene lamps are by far the most common. They arrived on the scene after most of the great pressed-glass manufactories had closed their doors, but enough are found in attractive patterns to keep enthusiasts busy. Prices are generally reasonable, averaging eight to twelve dollars for all but the choicest pieces.

Lanterns evolved in basically the same manner as lamps. Early specimens burned candles; then whale oil, camphene, and kerosene had their turn. The first panes were of thin, shaved horn, followed by isinglass and, finally, glass. The so-called Paul Revere lantern, a cone-shaped device of tin with pierced decoration, is popular—and often reproduced—as are the very large early ship's and tower lamps. Among oil lanterns, the most interesting are the many different railroad lanterns manufactured by Dietz and other producers. These are increasing in value, since they are sought by two groups, lighting collectors and railroad buffs.

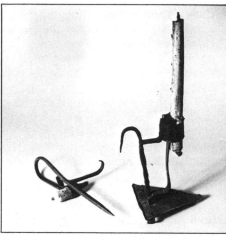

Adjustable candlestand, wood and iron; New York, early 19th century; $600-750.

Left: Pricker-type candlestick, wrough iron; New York, late 18th century; $75-100. **Right:** Standing or hanging candleholder, wrought iron; Pennsylvania, 18th century; $200-275.

Candle and rushlight holder, wrought iron; probably New England, late 18th-early 19th century; $275-380. These pieces are difficult to distinguish from European examples.

Very fine double candleholder with weighted base, tin and iron; New York, ca. 1820; $900-1,500. Pieces of this sort are rare and choice.
Hanging from center: Candle snuffer, pewter, New England, 19th century; $45-85.

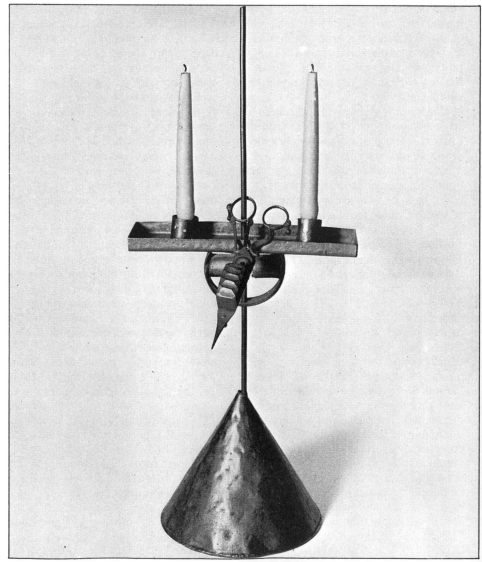

Candelabra, wrought iron; East, 19th century; $250-350.
Pieces similar to this are being made today in southern Europe.

Left: Candleholder, tin; Pennsylvania, mid-19th century; $35-55.
Right: Spiral candleholder, wrought iron; East, 19th century; $85-115.

Pair of candelabra, tin; New England, mid-19th century; $350-500 the pair.

Hog-scraper push-up candlestick, iron; with so-called wedding-ring brass banding; New Jersey, 19th century; $235-315.

Left: Snuffer tray, tin; New England, 19th century; $30-50. Candle snuffer, iron; New England; $35-55. Right: Push-up candlestick, tin; New England; $35-65.

Iron push-up candlesticks; New England, 19th century. **Left:** Wedding ring; $200-275. **Center:** Wrought iron, spiral shaft; $215-285. **Right:** Plain hog scraper; $35-75.

Simple candleholder, tin with glass insert; Midwest, late 19th-early 20th century: $25-45.

Candlestick, pewter, New England, first half 19th century; $100-145. Like most American pewter, this piece is unmarked.

Candle lamp in style of kerosene lamp, tin; New York, 19th century; $85-135.

Left: Candleholder with drip pan, tin; Maine, 19th century; $60-85. **Center:** Kerosene lamp, tin and iron with brass fittings; New Hampshire, 19th century; $25-40. **Right:** Large candleholder, tin, with extinguisher and drip pan; Maine, possibly Shaker, 19th century; $75-125.

Chamber sticks; New England, 19th century. **Left:** Tin; $35-55. **Top center:** Brass; $60-90. **Bottom center:** Pewter; $75-110. **Right:** Brass; $60-85.

Left: Crimp-decorated candleholder with handle, tin; Maine, late 19th century; $55-90. **Right:** Candle sconce, tin, with stamped star decoration; New Hampshire, early 19th century; $275-375. Decorated sconces are not common.

Triple sconce, tin and iron; New York, early 19th century; $400-550.

Left and right: Pair of sconces, crimped tin; Maine, early 19th century; $350-475.
Center: Large sconce, crimped tin; Maine, 19th century; $275-325.

Very fine candle reflector, glass, mahogany and fruitwood inlay; ca. 1800; New England; $1,200-1,600.

Left: Candle lantern, tin and iron with punch decoration; Pennsylvania, early 19th century; $285-345. **Center:** Tin sconce with glass reflector; Massachusetts, first quarter 19th century; $375-465. **Right:** Candleholder, crimped tin; Maine, late 19th century; $45-75.

Twenty-four-candle mold, tin and wood; New York, mid-19th century; $465-625. Molds in frames were generally used by professional candlemakers.

Candle molds, tin; New England, 19th century. **Left to right:** 80-125; $65-105; $75-100.

Back left: Wall-hanging double match safe, tin, old black paint; $15-25, **Front left:** Pocket matchbox, tin; $20-30. **Center:** Pocket matchbox, tin with molded rim; $20-30. **Right:** Wall-hanging match safe, tole-decorated tin; $25-55. All, East, 19th century.

Two painted wall-hanging match safes, cast iron; late 19th century. **Left:** $25-40. **Right:** $ 35-55. Iron match safes were widely made in the Midwest.

Large wall-hanging match safe, tin; New York, 19th century; $20-30.

Wall-hanging candle box, tin; New England, mid-19th century; $275-415.

Tinderbox with candleholder, flint, and steel, tin; New York, early 19th century; $245-315.

Cruise lamp, wrought iron; New York, early 19th century; $165-245.

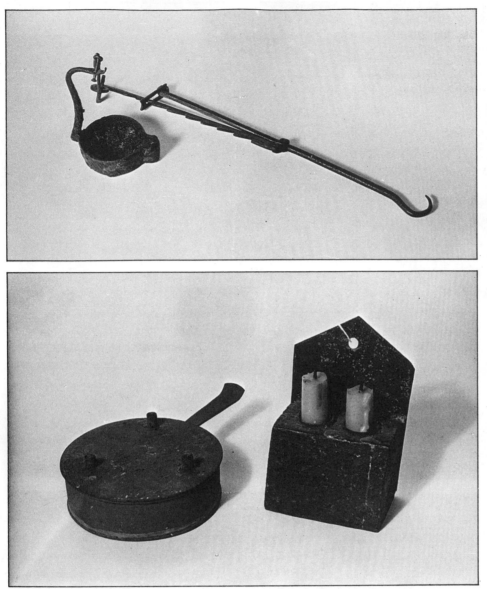

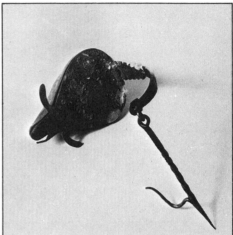

Cruise lamp, wrought iron with fine adjustable iron trammel; New England, late 18th-early 19th century; $400-635.

Betty lamp, wrought iron; Pennsylvania, early 19th century; $145-225.

Left: Triple-burner fat lamp, tin; Pennsylvania, early 19th century; $150-225. **Right:** Double wall candleholder, toleware; East, mid-19th century; $145-215. Both are rare and possibly unique lighting devices.

Unusual hanging fat lamp, tin and brass; Connecticut, first half 19th century; $135-185.

Left: Fat lamp in unusual form, tin; East, early 19th century; $75- 125. **Right:** Candleholder with matchbox attachment, tin; East, late 19th century; $100-145.

376

Left: Small camphene lamp, tin; Pennsylvania, mid 19th century; $45-75.
Right: Fat lamp with handle, tin; East, early 19th century; $75-110.

Unusual fat lamp on stand, tin; New Jersey. early 19th century; $210-285.

Fat or whale-oil lamp on stand, tin; New England, first half 19th century; $190-270.

Tin lighting devices; East, mid-to late 19th century. **Left rear:** Kerosene lamp; $15-25. **Center rear:** Hanging fat lamp with pick; $70-115. **Right rear:** Parade torch; $65-105.
Front left: Candle lamp; $65-105.
Front right: Betty lamp with double reflectors; $95-145.

Two rare lighting devices. **Left:** Triple-burner camphene lamp, tin; New York, mid-19th century; $215-285. **Right:** Double-burner whale-oil lamp in sconce, tin; New England, ca. 1825; $200-275.

Reflector mounted Argand lamp, tin; East, mid-19th century; $175-265. These lamps are uncommon.

Left: Tin candleholder, East, mid-19th century; $55-95. Iron snuffer; Pennsylvania, first half 19th century; $35-55. **Right:** Double-burner whale-oil lamp, tin; Massachusetts, ca. 1830; $90-140.

Double kerosene lamp holder and reflector (lamps not shown), punch-decorated tin; Connecticut, mid-19th century; $300-450.

Very rare punch-decorated sconce with double-burner whale-oil lamp, tin; New England, ca. 1830; $375-525.

Lighting magnifier, cast iron and glass; Midwest, late 19th century; $50-75. This magnifier was filled with water to provide more light in a rural home.

Kerosene lamps with large reservoir, tin; Midwest, late 19th century; $45-75. Possibly used as a stove rather than for light.

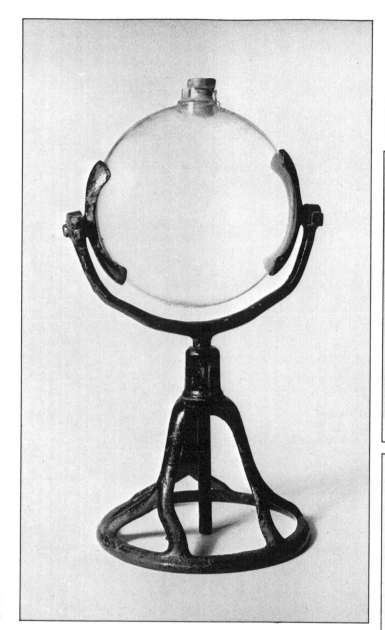

Kerosene lamps, tin and glass; Midwest, late 19th century. **Left:** $20-30. **Right:** $45-70.

Kerosene lamps, tin; Midwest, late 19th century. **Left:** $65-105. A homemade and possibly unique item. **Right:** $45-85.

Attractive kerosene lamp, tin and glass; Maine, ca. 1870; $125-185.

Aladdin lamp, nickel-plated copper; Connecticut, late 19th century; $75-155. Lamps of this sort were very popular in late Victorian times and continue so today. Like this one, they are often electrified.

Pressed-glass kerosene lamps; New England, late 19th century. **Left:** Milk glass; $90-95. **Center:** Plain pressed; $20-45. **Right:** Lincoln drape pattern; $80-110.

Pressed-glass lamps; New England, 19th century. **Left:** Kerosene lamp, pattern glass; $40-65. **Center:** Whale-oil lamp with single burner; $90-155. **Right:** Whale-oil lamp; $80-140 (without burner).

Electric lamp, multicolored slag glass and white metal; East, 20th century; $550-750. Many glass lamps of this sort were made by Tiffany, and the general interest in Tiffany items has caused the prices of all such lamps to reach astronomical heights.

Electric lamp, pewter and slag glass; East, 20th century; $325-525. Another popular new antique.

Electric counter lamp with stained-glass shade, designed as an advertising device for Whitman's Chocolates; 20th century; $425-525.

Early candle lanterns; New England, late 18th-early 19th century. **Left:** Pierce-decorated with isinglass windows; $315-400. **Right:** Tin and glass; $175-235. Isinglass is rare in lanterns.

Candle lantern of the sort commonly known as a Paul Revere lantern, punch-decorated tin; Pennsylvania, first half 19th century; $185-275. These lanterns are being reproduced.

Hurricane lantern, tin and iron; New York, 19th century; $225-350.

382

Left: Dietz railroad kerosene lamp; Midwest, early 20th century; $35-50.
Center: Barn or work lantern, sheet metal and glass; early 20th century; $25-40. **Right:** Candle lantern, punch-decorated tin; ca. 1850; $145-195. Both pieces at right are from New England.

Candle lantern, tin and glass; Vermont, early 19th century; $225-325.

Early candle lantern, vented tin and isinglass with sliding door; New York, first half 19th century; $225-300.

Left: Candle lantern, tin and glass; Maine, ca. 1840; $315-425.
Center: Wall hanging match safe, cut and crimped tin; 19th century; $50-65.
Right: Rare candle lantern, wood and glass; New Hampshire, mid-19th century; $300-385.

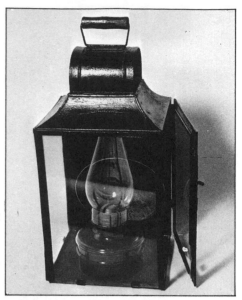

Double candle lantern, tin and glass, old black paint; New York, first quarter 19th century; $400-650. A rare and attractive lantern.

Kerosene barn lamp, tin and glass, black paint; New England, ca. 1880; $165-215.

Tiny house-shaped candle lantern, tole-decorated; New England, mid-19th century; $25-35.

Policeman's "bulls-eye" lantern, glass and sheet iron; Dressel, New York, first half 19th century; $50-75.

Early keresene railroad lantern, glass and sheet iron; Dressel, New York, first half 19th century; $75-125.

Dietz railroad lantern, glass and tin; East or Midwest, early 20th century; $60-90.

Dietz kerosene railroad or construction lantern, sheet metal and glass; East, 20th century; $45-75.

Dietz railroad lantern, tin and colored glass, early 20th century; $55-85.

Kerosene dark lights in two sizes, tin, with original black paint; East, late 19th-early 20th century. **Left:** $35-55. **Right:** $ 60- 85.

Tools

The collecting of tools has often been thought of as a particularly male pastime, probably because most of the objects sought are ones that have long been associated with such traditionally male occupations as carpentry, logging, and smithing. Until rather recently, interest was focused primarily on early hand-formed tools, those made by blacksmiths or in small two- or three-man shops during the period preceding the Civil War. However, it is now becoming fashionable to acquire factory-made objects of the late nineteenth and early twentieth centuries, such as those made by the Stanley Company and other early manufacturers.

There is no doubt that early tools have a charm and beauty exceeding that of later mass-produced wares. They were often made by, as well as for, the ultimate user and have a sense of personality—a decorative quality and a feeling of good workmanship—that is usually lacking in later production. On the other hand, there is some fascination in the complexity of the later pieces; and since they were produced in standardized forms, it is often possible to obtain complete sets of such tools as planes and chisels. The survival of several manufacturers' catalogs makes it possible to identify and date specimens with accuracy.

Tool collecting as a field is very broad. Carpenter's tools alone could occupy the collector for a lifetime. Axes are the choice items here, ranging from the hewing ax used to clear trees to the early and odd-shaped broadax with which the carpenter squared logs for house building. Like many tools, ax heads were hand-forged, and their wooden handles were made from patterns handed down from one generation to another. Several types of ax were used; there were also hatchets for shingling, lathing, and cooper's work.

Hammers are a second major category of carpenter's tools. Among them may be distinguished the ancient claw hammer, whose form can be traced back to Roman times, and the veneer hammer, as well as a variety of wooden mallets. All are relatively easy to find and are reasonably priced. Screwdrivers, braces, and bits are also common.

Perhaps the most popular of all carpenter's tools are planes. They exist in so many varieties that some enthusiasts limit their collections to them alone. Some planes are very small, and some are huge: the cooper's long jointer reaches a length of six feet; and the giant crown molding plane, which can cut a complete door- or window frame, requires two men for its operation. There were long planes called tryers, and jointers to smooth rough surfaces; rabbets to cut notches for the joining of cabinetry, and complex plow planes (most in demand) to cut a simple groove. Planes are for the most part relatively inexpensive.

Other carpenter's tools are less often seen, and their functions are sometimes little understood. The heavy adz, a flat-bladed tool, is used to smooth large surfaces such as floors; it is often mistaken for a hoe. The froe, used with a hammer to split shingles, looks like a crude knife. Scorpers, drawknives, and spokeshaves are all smoothing or finishing tools.

Less complex crafts employed a smaller variety of tools, and many of these items are as fascinating as they are rare. Loggers had felling axes, of course, but they also had the peavey—a device for pushing and pulling logs invented in the 1870s by a blacksmith named John Peavey—and the giant raft auger—five feet long and designed for drilling holes from a standing position. Loggers also employed many different kinds of chisels and the bucksaw.

The heart of the blacksmith's craft was his anvil, an instrument found in many variations. To hold and shape the hot iron, he also used hammers, chisels, tongs, and bits. The bellows to feed his fire might be four feet across; but the very few existing examples are rapidly finding their way into museum collections.

Wheelwrights made wagon and carriage wheels with the help of hammers and saws of various sorts. They also required the traveler, a wheel-shaped measuring device; the sturdy wooden wagon jack; and various awls, augers, and gouges to drill holes.

There were lesser-known crafts whose purpose and memory are today only dimly recalled. Farriers shoed horses and cared for their hooves with the help of chisels, pincers, and the odd-looking butteris, or hoof parer. Curriers owned a variety of knives and slickers with which they cleaned, scraped, and softened hides. Ice working as a craft no longer exists, since refrigeration has put an end to the need for vast amounts of cut and stored ice; but a century ago, thousands of men each winter swarmed upon the lakes and rivers of the north, cutting out ice blocks with special axes, chisels, and saws. The men now are gone; only the tools remain.

Other devices remain in use though somewhat altered in appearance. Bricklayers still use a special hammer and a brick ax, though the S-shaped raker that was used to remove old cement from around bricks is seldom seen. Farmers continue to find a purpose for the sickle and the scythe, but the old-fashioned hand seeder, the giant bull rake, and the odd-looking hay knife—designed for cutting hay out of a stack, not a field—have passed on.

The list could go on and on: shipwrights, machinists, foundrymen, plumbers, and stonecutters, all had tools particular to their craft or trade that are considered desirable by modern-day collectors. Often, an area of specialization is determined by the individual's own present trade or one that was or is pursued by a member of his family.

Fortunately, tools for the most part remain rather inexpensive and quite abundant. True, some, such as those used by whalemen, sailors, and early railroad workers, are rare and expensive. In general, though, the diligent collector in this field has an opportunity to find what he seeks. He may discover to his surprise, however, that he is competing not only with fellow antiques buffs, but also with carpenters and other craftsmen, who are also buying the old tools—for use on the job!

It should also be noted that since many tools, both metal and wood, bear manufacturers' marks, there exists a vast area for study in the identification and dating of thousands of early tools. Some work has been done in the field of planes and edge tools; but for the most part, very little research has been undertaken as yet, so that for each tool collector, there exists the exciting chance to become an authority in his own specialty.

Carpenter's T squares, wood and metal; 20th century. **Left to right:** $5-10; $5-10; $10-20; $20-25. Common examples of a common tool. Brass trim adds value to example at far right.

Iron calipers; 20th century. **Top:** For inside measurement; $45-65. **Bottom left and right:** For outside measurement; $29-40; $45-65.

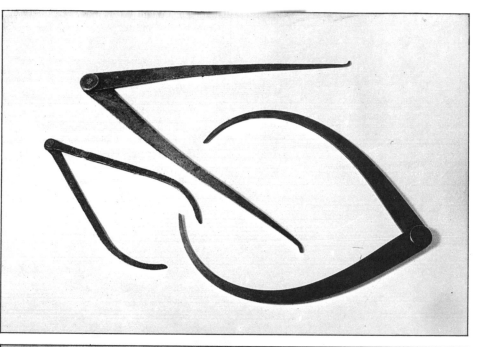

Top left: Cooper's croze, pine and ash; $30-45. **Top right:** Cooper's croze, pine nad maple; $20-35. **Bottom:** Carpenter's marking scribe, pine and birch, $15-25. All, 19th century.

Top left: Two marking gauges, pine and maple; late 19th century; $15-25; $20-30.
Right: Two travelers, iron; late 19th century; $35-65; $50-75. Traveler at center is of wrought iron.

Left: Carpet cutter, maple; 20th century; $15-20. **Right:** Cabinmaker's veneer cutter, maple; late 19th century; $45-80.

Spokeshaves. **Left:** With adjustable screw, pine and iron; $20-30. **Center left:** Birch and iron; $15-25. **Center right:** Pine and iron; $15-20. **Right:** Pine and wrought iron; $30-50. All, 20th century, except piece at far right, which is mid-19th century.

Patent spokeshaves, cast iron; 20th century. **Left to right:** $20-25; $35-50; $20-25; $15-20.

Left: Prunning hook, wrought iron; $20-35. **Center:** Curved pruning hook, wrought iron; $30-50. **Right:** Zake (a rare tile-roofing tool), wrought iron; $40-60. All, 19th century.

Top: Rare currier's knife, pine and wrought iron; $45-65. **Center:** Tanner's unhairing knife, pine and wrought iron; $45-65. **Bottom:** Tanner's slicker, pine and glass; $10-15. All, 19th century.

Drawknives. **Top and bottom:** Cooper's, hardwood and wrought iron; $15-25; $20-30. **Center:** Coach maker's, hickory and wrought iron; $30-45. All, late 19th century.

Top: Froe club, pine; $10-20. **Center and bottom:** Two froes, hickory and iron; late 19th century. **Center:** $25-40. **Bottom:** $30-50.

Early hay knife, maple and wrought iron; $65-90. A less common variant dating from the 1840s.

Scorps. **Top:** Single handle, iron and pine; $20-25. **Bottom left and right:** Open scorps, iron and maple with brass fittings; $30-50; $35-55.

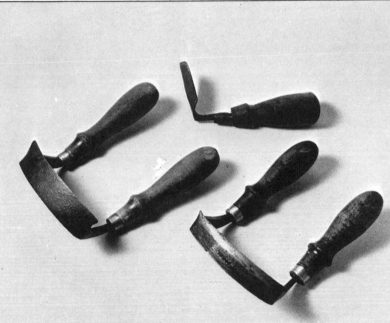

Chamfer knife, a cooper's tool, maple and pine; ca. 1850; $65-105. An uncommon piece with good form.

Hay knife, maple and wrought iron; mid-19th century; $35-55. Another tool with an attractive shape.

Two plow planes, maple; late 19th century; $35-55 each.

Plow planes, maple; late 19th-early 20th century; $30-50 each.
Intended to cut a groove.

Patent scrapers, cast iron and steel; 20th century. **Left:** Veneer scraper; $35-55. **Center:** Cabinetmaker's scraper; $20-35. **Right:** Plane-style veneer scraper; $55-85.

Left: Wooden router, pine and wrought iron; late 19th century; $20-30. **Center:** Patent router, cast iron; 20th century; $35-60. **Right:** Stanley Patent all-purpose plane, cast iron; 20th century; $350-475. **Bottom:** Scraper, pine and cast iron; 20th century; $15-25.

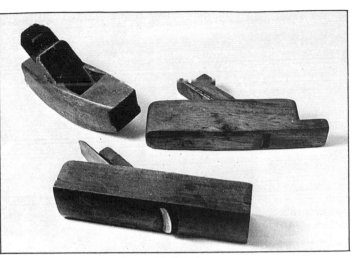

Top left: Adjustable double-molding plane, maple; ca. 1870; $65-100.
Bottom: Double-bladed dado plane, birch; late 19th century; $55-85. **Top right:** Bead plane, maple; early 20th century; $25-35.

Jointer plane, cast iron and steel; Stanley Patent, early 20th century; $145-215.

Group of planes.
Top left: Compass plane, maple; late 19th century; $55-75. **Top right:** Round molding plane, pine; ca. 1850; $40-55.
Bottom: Round molding plane, birch; 20th century; $20-30.

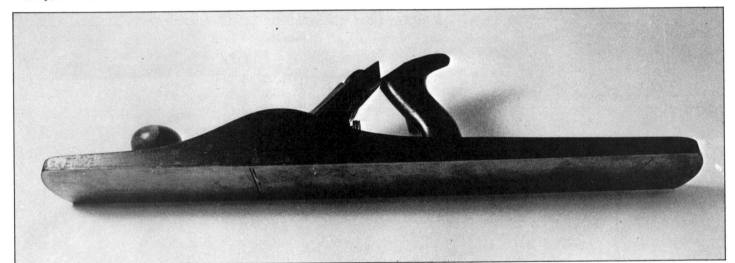

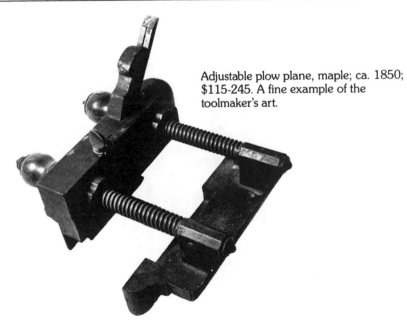

Adjustable plow plane, maple; ca. 1850; $115-245. A fine example of the toolmaker's art.

Two examples of Stanley Patent jack planes, cast iron and steel; 20th century. **Top:** $75-125. **Bottom:** $70-115.

Top: Long jointer or floor plane, pine and maple; 19th century; $55-85. **Bottom:** Trying or trueing plane, pine and maple 19th century; $40-60.

Top: Stanley Patent fore plane, cast iron, steel, and pine; $85-135. **Bottom:** Stanley Patent jack plane, cast iron, steel, and maple; $90-160. Both, early 20th century.

Two carpenter's clamps, maple and pine; 20th century. **Left:** $40-70. **Right:** $20-30. Prices depend on size, with largest and smallest examples most sought after.

Left: Early carpenter's vise, maple; $15-20. **Right:** File vise, pine and maple; $20-35, Both 19th century.

Frame saw, maple with pegged joints and wrought iron blade; first half 19th century; $75-110. Early and a fine form.

Common framed bucksaw of the sort still widely used to cut wood; late 19th-early 20th century; $20-30.

Two miter-box saws, pine and steel; factory-made, 20th century. **Top:** $15-20. **Bottom:** $10-15.

Top: Early crosscut saw, pine and steel; $35-50. **Center:** Ripsaw, pine and steel; $30-40. **Bottom:** Pruning saw, maple and steel; $30-45. All, 19th century.

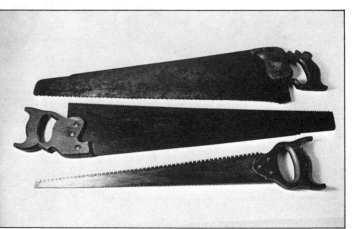

Keyhole saws. **Top to bottom;** Steel and cast iron; $10-15. Steel and pine; $5-10. Steel and pine; $10-15. Early steel and pine with unusual handle; $10-15. All, 20th century, except bottom saw, which is late 19th century.

Broadaxes. **Top:** Maple and steel; ca. 1830; $85-135. **Bottom:** Hickory and steel; ca. 1880; $55-75.

Top left: Mortising hatchet, maple and steel; 19th century; $45-60. **Top right:** Standard factory-made hatchet; 20th century; $10-15. **Bottom:** Broad hatchet; 19th century; $30-50.

Top: Lathing hatchet, hickory and steel; 19th century; $20-35. **Center:** Patent wrecker's hatchet with pry bar, cast iron; $15-25.
Bottom: Cast-iron hatchet; $10-15. Both, 20th century.

Left: Two shipbuilder's adzes, distinguished by spurlike nail punch; $75-110 each. **Right:** Two carpenter's adzes; $40-70; $45-80. All with hardwood handles and iron heads; 19th century.

Left: Hewing ax, maple and steel; $90-135.
Center left: Mortising ax, ash and steel; $80-125.
Center right: Broadax, ash and steel; $120-155.
Right: Mortising ax, maple and steel; $70-120. All, 19th century.

Left: Tinner's hammer; $10-15.
Center: Cooper's hammer; $5-10.
Right: Tinner's hammer; $10-15.

Hammers, iron and hardwood. **Top:** Square-headed bricklayer's hammer; $18-27. **Center:** Cobbler's hammer; $15-25.
Bottom: Blacksmith's hammer; $10-20. All, late 19th century.

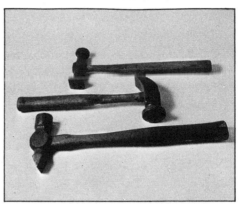

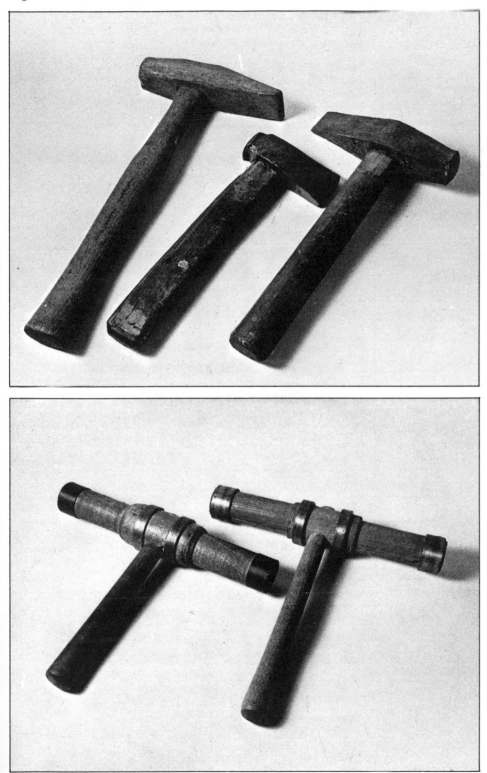

Left: Magnetic tack hammer; $5-10.
Center left: House trimmer's hammer; $15-25. **Center right:** Machinist's hammer; $10-20. **Right:** Early tack hammer; $15-20. All, iron and hardwood; 20th century, except tack hammer, which dates from mid-19th century.

Two shipwright's caulking mallets, hickory with iron heads and brass fittings; both, late 19th century; $30-45 each.

19th-century mallets.
Left: Maple; $5-10. **Center left:** Carpenter's, oak; $5-10. **Center right:** Oak; $5-10. **Right:** Wheelwright's, maple; $20-30.

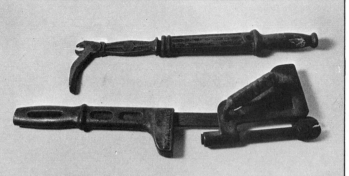

Patent clamp wrenches, cast iron; 20th century; $5-30 each, depending upon size and complexity of operation.

Patent nail pullers, cast iron; factory made, 20th century. **Top:** $25-40. **Bottom:** $35-55.

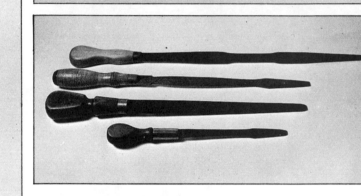

Machinist's screwdrivers, ranging in length from 12″ to 20″, iron with hardwood handles and brass fittings; 20th century. **Top to bottom:** $15-25; $12-18; $20-28; $15-20.

An assortment of iron and hardwood screwdrivers, some with brass fittings; 20th century; $1-10 each, depending on size and quality of workmanship.

Steel chisels with hardwood handles; late 19th-early 20th century. **Top:** Corner chisel; $10-15.
Center top: Corner chisel; $12-22.
Center top: Firmer, or forming chisel; $12-22. **Center bottom:** Rare curved gooseneck chisel; $35-50. **Bottom:** Framing chisel; $30-45.

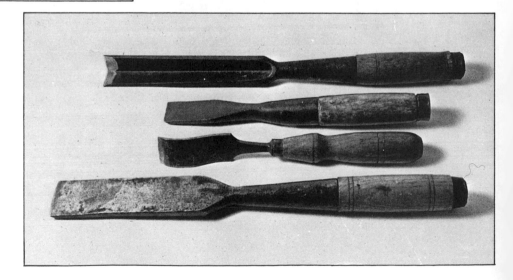

Patent breast drill, over 2′ long; factory made, iron; late 19th-early 20th century; $75-135.

Three steel and hardwood slicks, or giant chisels, ranging in length from 22″ to 34″; late 19th century. **Top to bottom:** $40-65; $50-60; $60-80.

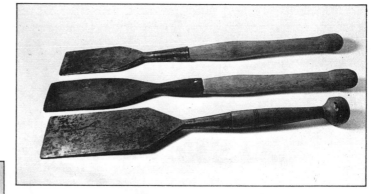

Three steel and hardwood gouges. **Top:** Late 19th century; $10-15. **Center:** With good brass fittings; late 19th century; $40-65. **Bottom:** Early wrought iron; ca. 1850; $25-35.

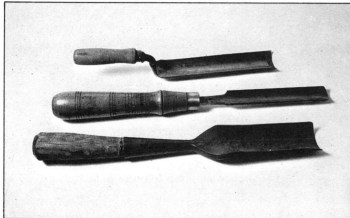

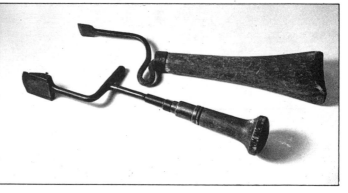

Two examples of the farrier's butteris, or hoof parer. **Top:** Early wrought iron and pine; ca. 1860; $50-65. **Bottom:** Maple and iron; ca. 1890; $40-55.

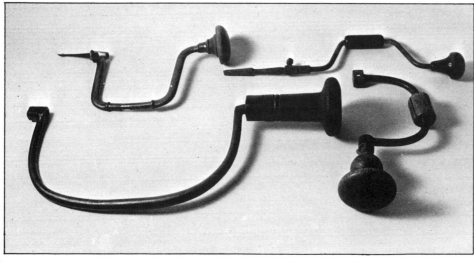

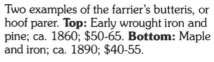

Top left: Brace and bit, brass, iron, and pine; early 20th century; $40-65. **Top right:** Brace and bit, iron and pine; late 19th century; $40-60. **Bottom left:** Large brace, iron and pine, ca. 1850; $100-125. **Bottom right:** Brace, iron and pine; ca. 1870; $55-80.

Reamers, iron and hardwood; late 19th-early 20th century. **Top to bottom:** $15-25; $20-30; $20-30.

Bale, or box, hooks, iron or iron and wood; late 19th-early 20th century; $5-15 each, depending on workmanship. Common implements still in daily use.

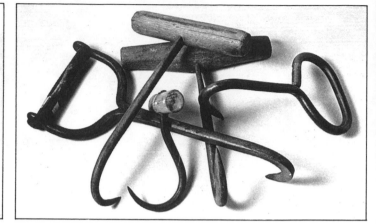

Group of augers, iron and hardwood; late 19th century; $15-30 each, depending upon age, size, and quality of workmanship.

Wrought iron blacksmith's tools; late 19th century. **Top to bottom:** Flat bit; $15-20.
Pincer; $15-25; and hollow bit; $10-20.
Round bit; $14-24. Hammer tongs; $20-35. Long pincers; $10-15.

Iron anvils; 19th century. L4" high; $30-50. **Center:** 14" high; $125-185. **Right:** 8" high; $65-95.

Cobbler's shoe forms, iron; 20th century. **Left:** $15-20. **Center:** $3-5. **Right:** $40-60.

Cobbler's vise, maple, traces of old paint; late 19th century; $85-135.

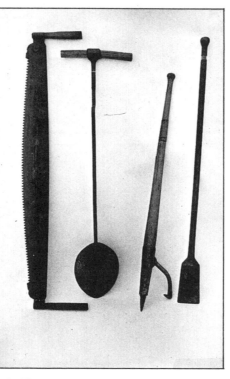

Left: Two-man crosscut saw, steel and maple; $25-40. **Center left:** Rare whale-blubber slick, iron and hickory; $250-350.
Center right: Logger's peavey, iron and hickory; $10-20.
Right: Ice chopper, iron; $20-35. All, mid-19th century.

Left: Potter's clay fork, ash and iron; $25-45. **Center:** Peat fork, ash and iron; $40-60.
Right: Ice-cutting tool, iron and hickory; $35-50.
Uncommon tools of uncommon trades.

Top: Early shingling tool, wrought iron; mid-19th century; $35-60.
Bottom: Knife sharpener; walnut and stone, late 19th century; $30-50.

Carpenter's nail and screw holder, cast iron; factory made, 20th century; $35-55.

Block and tackle, late 19th-early 20th century. **Left:** Iron and maple; $10-15. **Center left:** Cast iron; $5-15. **Center right:** With double tackle, iron and maple; $20-35. **Right:** Iron and pine; $10-15.

Instrument for capping bottles, iron and pine; late 19th-early 20th century; $35-50.

Ice-worker's tongs, wrought iron; early 20th century; $20-35.

400

Wagon jack, hickory; late 19th century; $55-70. Despite its name, a device of this type was often used to move logs and rocks.

Tobacco cutter, iron and pine; late 19th century; $30-55. Less common and more desirable than the cast-iron factory-made examples.

Cobbler's bench, pine; Maine, ca. 1875; $350-600. Typical of the utilitarian pieces now employed as furniture.

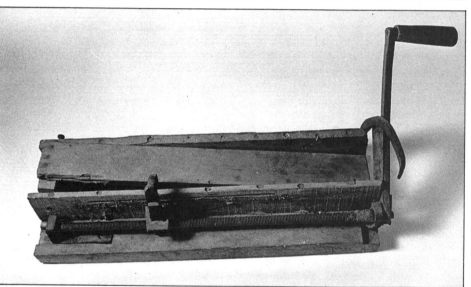

Seeder, pine and maple; early 20th century; $45-75.

Wheelbarrow, pine and iron, traces of old blue paint; $90-145. Other than for use as planters, these tools are of little interest to most collectors.

Toys

Whether they serve as reminders of our lost innocence, or because they call us back to the playfulness and joy we only rarely experience as adults, old toys have become the object of one of our fastest growing national pastimes. The collecting of toys, however, differs in some respects from the collecting of other antiques.

First, few "old" American toys are really old. Until after the Civil War, most children in this country played with either imported or homemade toys, since there were only a small number of domestic toy manufacturers. Toy collectors are seldom troubled by this lack of age; in fact, some of the most eagerly sought specimens were made in the 1930s or even the 1940s. Furthermore, most collectors are not very interested in the older handmade toys; those they leave largely to the folk-art collector. The toy specialist usually confines himself to standard factory-made items. And as with other factory-made "antiques," one of the toy collector's objectives, besides the good condition and esthetic appeal of his examples, is to obtain complete sets or "runs" of a given type of toy, be it train, bank, or boat. In this respect, toy collecting, like tool collecting, resembles the collecting of stamps or coins.

The growing enthusiasm of collectors has created some problems in the field. To begin with, since there are simply not enough examples available to satisfy the demand, most old toys are now extremely expensive. Mass-produced, factory-made objects that sold originally for a few pennies now regularly change hands for hundreds of dollars. As often happens, the excess demand has given rise to reproductions and forgeries. There is no other area of American antiques where the inexperienced collector is so likely to make a poor buy.

The earliest toys made in this country were of wood or pottery. Dolls, boats, houses, and numerous toy animals were often made at home from material readily available in any woodlot, while the local potter turned out everything from marbles to banks to whistles. Many old homemade wood toys survive, but the pottery ones are relatively rare.

Little is known of the nonindustrial makers of wooden toys except for a few names. Wilhelm Schimmel and his pupil Aaron Mountz of Pennsylvania were itinerant carvers who wandered the nineteenth-century countryside whittling pull toys, bird figures, and Noah's arks for the families of their numerous hosts. Since their ware is highly individualistic, most of it has been bought by museums and is not accessible to the average collector. Factory-made wooden playthings are something else again. Push-and-pull toys such as those manufactured in the 1890s by the Gibbs Manufacturing Company of Canton, Ohio, are considered highly desirable, as are sleds, sleighs, and other toys of wood.

Much greater interest is focused on metal playthings, particularly those of a mechanical nature. The earliest are of tin and date to the 1830s. By 1848, the Philadelphia Tin Toy Manufactory was producing an extensive line of horse-drawn buses, trains, and wagons, which were either painted freehand or stenciled, in contrast to late nineteenth- and early twentieth-century tin, which was decorated by lithography. Another early maker was George W. Brown of Forestville, Connecticut. Existing sketchbooks used by this company indicate that a fascinating variety of tin pull toys was available to the child of the 1850s and 1860s.

Through the use of a clockwork mechanism, first employed in the 1870s by the Ives Company of Bridgeport, Connecticut, it became possible to produce tin toys that moved automatically. Some of them involve two or more separate figures and are remarkably complex—dancing figures, locomotives, and a rowboat that worked on water or land! They are among the most desirable of all early toys.

As a general rule, in tin toys, the larger sizes are the best, in both workmanship and detail. Many types, such as boats and wagons, were made in a range of sizes, with the largest always being the most complex—and most expensive, then and now.

Toys of cast iron were developed later than those of tin, with no significant production prior to the 1880s. In that decade the Hubley Manufacturing Company of Lancaster, Pennsylvania, came to the fore with a wide variety of mechanical and nonmechanical iron playthings. Other makers, such as the Kenton Hardware Company of Ohio, soon joined the field, and in the next sixty years thousands of different cast-iron toys appeared on the market.

Some of them, such as the horse-drawn fire engines, circus wagons, and sleighs, have proved to be so popular that they have been widely reproduced. Intentionally or otherwise, such reproductions are often offered for sale as originals. Since few of the new toys are marked (and marks, where existent, are readily removed), collectors of cast-iron toys must exercise considerable caution. Where possible, always buy from reputable sources that guarantee their goods. Moreover, while only long experience in the field will ensure complete safety in purchase, collectors can often learn to detect fakes. Try to locate original pieces in museums and private collections, and study them; avoid buying examples whose originals you have not seen. In examining a prospective purchase, observe its surface. Reproductions are often sand-cast from parts of original pieces, and individual units of the new models will show a rougher surface than the old. They will also be slightly smaller and will show a loss of clarity or sharpness in detail. Also, paint that looks "too good" for an old toy is probably just that—too good to be true. Nor is a rusty surface any assurance of age. Bright, flaky, red orange rust often indicates rapidly induced oxidation. Old rust is black and shiny, with a patina that can be acquired only through age and exposure.

These precautionary words, which apply primarily to cast-iron mechanical toys, also apply to toy banks, whether mechanical or not. The first children's banks were made of tin and were "still"; they had no moving parts. Examples from the last half of the nineteenth century are common, for manufacturers such as Stevens and Brown of Cromwell, Connecticut, turned out vast numbers of tin banks in the 1860s and 1870s. Several shapes were made, the most popular being the house; one example even had a porch complete with Victorian gingerbread trim. Decoration was applied by stencil and later by lithography.

Cast-iron still banks were also made in great quantity. The Hubley Company sold some in the 1890s in the shapes of mailboxes and cash registers; at a later date, the Williams Company of Ravenna, Ohio, specialized in banks representing cartoon characters, such as Mutt and Jeff or Little Orphan Annie.

Tin and iron still banks, while popular enough, are not in such great demand as to encourage fakery, and they can still be bought at reasonable prices.

Mechanical cast-iron banks are quite a different matter. In the 1870s, Stevens and other companies brought out banks incorporating figures that would spring into action when a coin was deposited—an Indian that would shoot a bear, for instance, or a prizefighter that would strike his opponent. The many figures and actions depicted are delightfully inventive, with the result that these banks are in great demand; mechanicals such as Jonah and the Whale or William Tell are valued in the hundreds of dollars. As a secondary result, large numbers of them have been issued in modern reproduction, and the prospective collector would do well to observe all the precautions previously discussed in regard to buying iron toys.

Trains, both tin and cast, are a highly specialized branch of toy collecting. The earliest successful mass producer was the Ives Company, and that firm's products are most often sought. Other desirable makers are W. B. Carpenter, Hubley, and the Wilkins Toy Manufacturing Company of Medford, Massachusetts, all of which manufactured cast-iron pull trains or tin and iron windup trains. Electric trains came later, and they also are in great demand. There has as yet been little intentional production of forgeries in this field, but prices are extremely high, particularly for the earlier models.

Various steam-driven toys were also popular at the turn of the century. The Weeden Manufacturing Company of New Bedford, Massachusetts, produced several steam engines as well as belt-driven mechanical toys, such as organ-grinders, knife sharpeners, and wood sawyers, that could be set in motion by attaching them to the engines. Weeden steam engines were given away as premiums by *Youth's Companion* magazine in the 1880s. They are well made and attractive and for the most part reasonably priced at present.

Toy weapons and military miniatures appeal to a special, and large, group of collectors. The army of toy soldier enthusiasts alone numbers in the thousands. While there are some early paper, wood, and metal soldiers of American manufacture, most interest today is centered on the lead and cast-iron examples made in the period

between the two world wars. These are abundant, attractive, and fairly priced. Cannons, a related item, were made in many sizes, from tiny companion pieces for the soldiers to large outdoor guns for holiday celebrations. The larger pieces have attracted the most attention.

Cap pistols have been made in the United States since Civil War times, and many variations are encountered, though most collectors have taken little interest in them. An exception is the animated cap pistol, a device incorporating one or more figures that are activated when the pistol hammer is struck. There are not many of these toys, and they are eagerly sought.

For the quiet hours, Victorian children (and their parents) had many different board games, which were made of cardboard and wood and packaged in chromolithographed boxes. In addition to providing amusement, they were often intended to educate the young in the strict moral values of the day. It would have been difficult, indeed, to take the wrong side in a game titled "Pope and Pagan, or the Missionary Campaign; or the Siege of the Stronghold of Satan by the Christian Army." That tongue twister was issued in 1844 by W. and B. Ives of Salem, Massachusetts, one of the most prolific games producers. Board games haven't yet caught on with collectors—in part, perhaps, because they are seldom found intact or in good condition—so they represent a relatively inexpensive area of toy collecting.

Dolls and their accessories have always held a strong fascination for American collectors. While many of the dolls cherished now—as then—were imported from Europe, there was a strong tradition of American manufacture. The first dolls produced here were undoubtedly made at home of carved wood and rags, generally unbleached cotton or linen stuffed with sawdust. Their features were hand painted, and their hairstyles are often a clue to their age.

Ludwig Greiner of Philadelphia was among the first of many factory-based dollmakers. In 1858, he took out the initial patent for a papier-mâché doll head. Such heads were sold through shopkeepers to individual customers, who then added bodies of their own making, usually of wood or kidskin.

Born of England's "penny woodens"—simple, unpainted wooden dolls—the wooden doll tradition

continued long in this country. The earliest examples were rigid until a Vermonter, Joel Ellis, patented a jointed wooden doll in 1873; an improved version was marketed by a neighbor, F. D. Martin, in 1879. The Schoenhut Company of Philadelphia later put out a similar doll with ball-and-socket joints.

Dolls were made of other materials as well, including wax-headed figures, popular during the 1870s and 1880s, and rubber dolls, which made their first appearance in the same period. Ceramic and celluloid figures were also popular.

By the middle of the nineteenth century, many dolls were beginning to assume a distinct form and image. Previously, doll faces had impersonal features, but now attempts were made to give them individual traits—in some cases those of real people, such as Jenny Lind or President Lincoln. In the twentieth century, this custom has continued. Betty Boop, Little Orphan Annie, Alice and a whole cast of characters from Wonderland, and Charlie Chaplin are just a few of the many so-called celebrity dolls manufactured in the last seventy years. Indeed, some of the later creations are among the most popular and expensive of all.

American children have always taken great delight in dollhouses and doll furniture, and for many grown-ups the charm continues to exert its hold. Most of the early examples have disappeared, but dollhouses from the Victorian era are plentiful, and furniture may be found in every style from the Queen Anne period on. Miniature furniture of any age is today extremely expensive, but child-size pieces (eighteen to thirty inches high) are surprisingly cheap, though not especially common.

Much like the larger furniture are such working miniatures of adult household objects as musical instruments, some of which were extremely well made. Schoenhut made children's pianos of fine tone in the 1870s, and there were whole orchestras of toy musical instruments.

For as long as children have existed, there have been many other toys of every description. Indoor and outdoor activities of all sorts had special equipment, just as they do today. Sleds, skates, tops, marbles, hoops, balls, bats, and numerous others may be found to satisfy the desires of every grown-up lover of toys.

Fire engine drawn by three horses, cast iron; ca. 1880; $450-650. Addition of tin and wood parts mark this as a rare and early piece.

Horse-drawn hook and ladder, cast iron; by Kenton, ca. 1922; $375-550. Very large with excellent design.

Horse-drawn sleigh with female occupant, cast iron; by Hubley, ca. 1920; $350-450.

Rear: Express Wagon drawn by goat, cast iron; $110-160. **Front:** Horse and sulky, cast iron; $75-125. Both, ca. 1920.

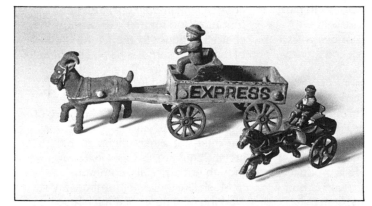

Cast iron automobiles; ca. 1920. **Rear:** Ford touring car; $175-235. **Front:** Couple with rumble seat; $110-170.

Horse-drawn Overland Circus, cast iron; Kenton, 1940s; $225-295.

Left: Rare dirigible, cast iron, silver paint; $90-130. **Right:** Airplane marked "Lindy," cast iron; $115-145. Mark on plane is a reference to Charles A. Lindburgh, who made his historic flight in 1927. Both, 1920s.

Fordson tracter, cast iron; 1924; $110-145.

Oil truck, marked "Champion Case & Motor Oil," cast iron; ca. 1920; $145-205.

Motorcycle and rider marked "Harley-Davidson," cast iron; ca. 1925; $200-265.

Hubley Popeye on motorcycle, cast iron, rubber tires, ca. 1930; $275-375. Figure has movable arms. A large and most attractive piece.

Locomotive and cars, cast iron with silver finish; ca. 1920; $120-165.

Mechanical bank, Indian shooting bear, cast iron; ca. 1910; $500-650. Like many mechanical banks, this one has been issued in modern reproduction.

Early locomotive and cars, cast iron; by Ives, ca. 1880; $350-475.

Electric trains, tin and iron; by Ives, ca. 1880; $275-450. An early example of the electrically powered train.

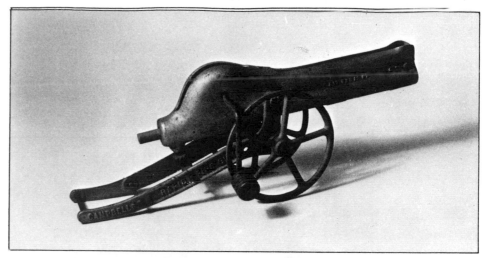

Toy cannon, marked "Campbells Rapid Fire Gun," patented 1907; $65-100. A mechanical toy that can shoot pellets.

Selection of cast-iron soldiers painted olive drab, ca. 1930; $10-30 each, depending on type.

Left: Toy cannon, brass and iron; ca. 1900; $50-75. **Right:** Group of toy soldiers, cast iron, unpainted; ca. 1920; $2-5 each.

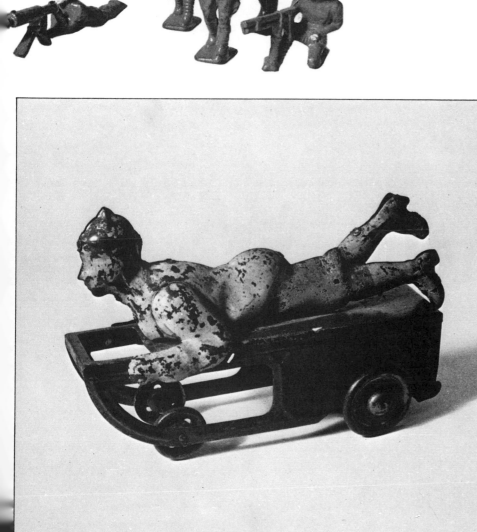

Pull toy with three bells, tin, steel, and iron; ca. 1900; $65-85.

Boy on sled, painted tin and cast iron; ca. 1910; $135-185.

Very large friction-powered toy
locomotive, tin and iron; ca. 1935;
$125-185.

Unusual friction toy, Hansom cab, tin
and iron; ca. 1897; $200-250.

Left: Toonerville Trolley, cast lead;
1923; $65-85. **Right:** Wind-up
Toonerville Trolley, tin and iron;
Fontaine-Fox, ca. 1922; $275-375.

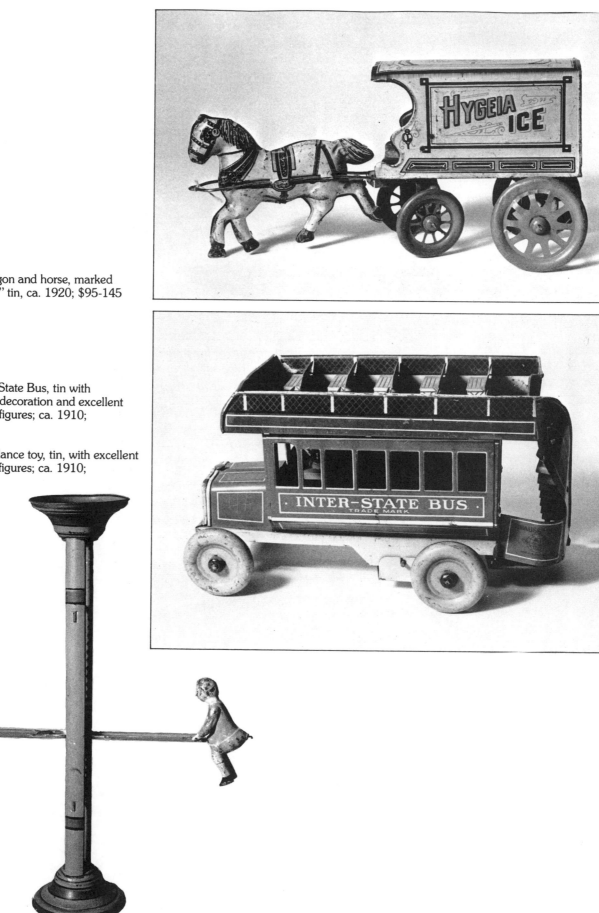

Delivery wagon and horse, marked "Hygeia Ice," tin, ca. 1920; $95-145

Strauss Inter-State Bus, tin with lithographed decoration and excellent detail on the figures; ca. 1910; $300-425.

Fine early balance toy, tin, with excellent detail on the figures; ca. 1910; $175-245.

Wind-up toy, Fresh-Air Taxicab, tin, ca. 1930; $475-675. One of the many toys inspired by once-popular radio programs.

Wind-up toy, Blondie's Jalopy, tin; ca. 1935; $300-400. Occupants' heads nod when toy is set in motion.

Tin and sheet-metal spaceships; late 1930s. **Front left:** Pull toy with rubber tires; $35-55. **Rear:** Wind-up Rocket Fighter, by Marx; $175-275. **Right:** Wind-up Buck Rogers; $110-170.

Mechanical Chalie McCarthy car, tin; by Marx, late 1930s; $310-390.

Mechanical Dogpatch Band, tin; by Unique Art, ca. 1945; $350-400.

Horizontal steam engine, iron and brass; by Weeden, ca. 1903; $85-135. A working model.

Mechanical knife sharpener at work, tin; ca. 1930; $95-135. Much more sophisticated than the average mechanical toy of the period.

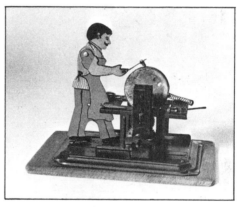

Mechanical Popeye figures, tin; 1930s.
Left: With punching bag; $175-245.
Right: With pet parrot; $160-230.
These are among the most popular of the comic-inspired toys.

Doepke mechanical sand conveyor, tin and steel; ca. 1935; $130-180. An example of the many working models of earth-moving machines produced by Buddy-L and other manufacturers.

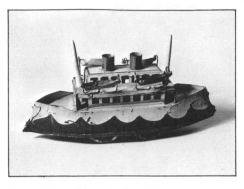

Steamship pull toy, steel and tin; ca. 1900; $220-290.

Mechanical submarine, steel and tin; by Wolverine, ca. 1940; $85-135.

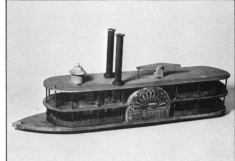

Early wood side-wheeler, the *Columbia*; ca. 1890; $425-600.

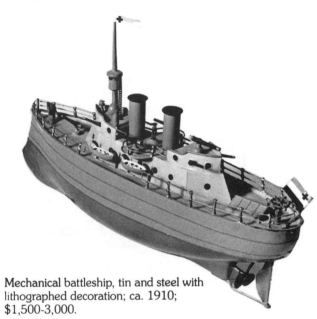

Mechanical battleship, tin and steel with lithographed decoration; ca. 1910; $1,500-3,000.

Barney Google and Spark Plug, jointed wood and cloth; ca. 1930; $300-425 the set.

Gypsy wagon, wood, with two stamped-wood horses; Sears-Roebuck, 1912; $140-190.

Unusual and extremely well-done nodding doll, plaster and wood; ca. 1910; $75-115. Items of this sort are rarely duplicated.

Chinese acrobat, celluloid and wood balance toy; ca. 1930; $65-105.

Ferdinand the Bull, compostion wood, jointed; late 1930s; $50-80.

Wooden tops; early 20th century. **Left:** $15-25. **Right:** $10-15.

District Messenger Boy, board game; by McLaughlin Brothers, New York, patented 1886; $80-120. An example of Victorian children's games intended to promote hard work and adherence to traditional values.

Excelsior Paint Box, wood with an excellent lithographed cover, ca. 1900; $30- 60.

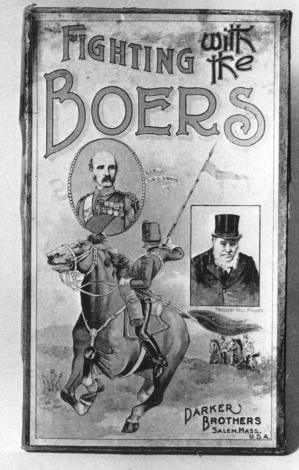

Magnetic Fish Pond; by McLaughlin Brothers, New York, patented 1891; $100-175.

Board game, Fighting with the Boers; by Parker Brothers, Salem, Mass., ca. 1900; $120-180. Board game prices have not kept pace with the general sharp increase in toy prices; they offer a good area for purchase.

Philadelphia Baby doll, rag body; J.B. Shepherd and Co., ca. 1860; $550-800.

Two jointed dolls, wood with pewter hands and feet. **Left:** By Mason Taylor, ca. 1878; $450-600. **Right:** By Joel Ellis, Springfield, Vt., ca. 1873; $400-575.

Greiner doll, papier-mache head, kid body; patented 1893; $600-900. A popular early American doll type.

Unusual black doll, gutta-percha; Kentucky, ca. 1865; $375-525.

Jointed figurine, a "Lay" stick figure, wood; mid-19th century; $350-550. These were often used as artist's models.

Baby doll in sailor suit, known as "Tootsie Wootsie"; by Schoenhut, Philadelphia, early 20th century; $500-700.

Two wood dolls, by Schoenhut, Philadelphia, ca. 1911. **Left:** Rare baby doll; $900-1,500.
Right: Standing doll; $550-675.

Large jointed doll; by Fulper, New Jersey, ca, 1917; $350-475. A fine-quality doll produced in response to the cutoff of European imports during the First World War.

Bylo dolls; ca. 1923. **Left:** Laughing Bylo; $600-850. **Right:** With composition body; $475-575.

416

Rare set of Alice-in-Wonderland figures; by Martha Chase, ca. 1905; $3,000-4,000 the set. Only six complete sets are known.

Peterkins; by Fulper, New Jersey, ca. 1919; $350-450. A small porcelain bisque figure designed by the well-known Helen Trowbridge

Betty Boop doll; by Kallus, ca. 1932; $250-375. Inspired by the cartoon figure, this doll once sold for $1.

Amos Andria, black rubber character doll; Sun Rubber Co., ca. 1940; $60-90.

Empire-style toy chest of drawers with mirror, pine, 16″ high; ca. 1860; $80-120.

Early Teddy Bear, stuffed with straw; $245-310. Countless variations of this toy were inspired by the story of President Theodore Roosevelt in which he spared a small bear while on a hunting trip.

Empire-style chest of drawers, pine; New Jersey, ca. 1870; $70-95. A child's toy, some 12″ high.

Victorian toy chest of drawers with mirror, pine, 18″ high; Midwest, ca. 1900; $75-125.

Toy kitchen cabinet, pine; by Cass, ca. 1940; $35-65. A factory-made piece.

Victorian spool-turned toy bed, maple, with quilt and coverlet; Maine, ca. 1880; $75-125.

Country Sheraton toy rope bed, pine and maple; New Hampshire, ca. 1840; $175-275. A fine early piece.

Excelsior washing set, pine; East, ca. 1920; $50-75 the set.

Schoenhut toy piano and stool, walnut; ca. 1910; $250-350. A working model with excellent detail.

Empire-style child's music box in form of a piano, walnut and iron; East, ca. 1860; $275-375.

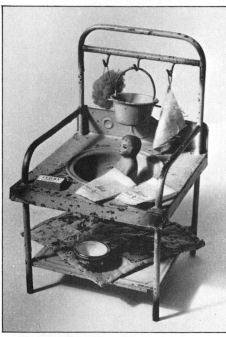

Doll's bathing set, ceramic, tin, and iron; ca. 1910; $165-235.

Toy stove and accessories, cast iron; by Royal, ca. 1935; $145-215. Stoves of this sort could actually hold a small fire.

Little Orphan Annie electric stove; ca. 1940; $45-70. A working model.

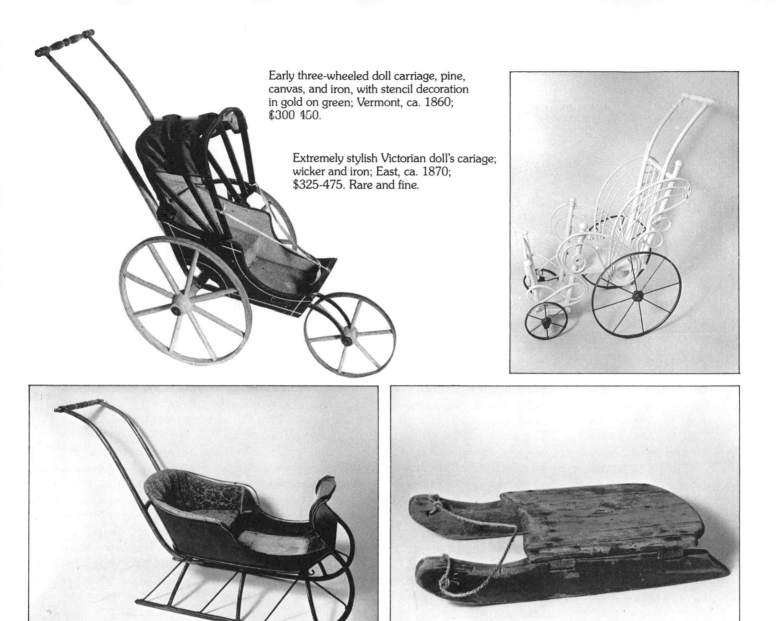

Early three-wheeled doll carriage, pine, canvas, and iron, with stencil decoration in gold on green; Vermont, ca. 1860; $300 450.

Extremely stylish Victorian doll's cariage; wicker and iron; East, ca. 1870; $325-475. Rare and fine.

Child's sleigh, pine and iron, with overstuffed upholstered interior; Vermont, ca. 1880; $200-275.

Toy sled, pine, only 1' long, dovetailed, with traces of old red paint; Maine, ca. 1860; $20-40.

Child's ice skates, pine and iron, leather straps; Maine, ca. 1870; $65-90.

Games

Toys and dolls have been widely collected in the United States for decades. Prices for most items are high, and competition among collectors is fierce. However, one related area has been left relatively untouched: games.

As long as people have had leisure, they have had games with which to pass the time. Backgammon, a current craze, was known in the seventeenth century, and dice and playing cards go back to the Middle Ages. The era with which we are concerned, however, saw the culmination of the parlor game. With the increased free time that the prosperity of the late nineteenth century brought to an expanding middle class and the invention of electric lighting—which made it possible for the first time to comfortably perform activities at night—the public clamored for amusements.

One of the most popular of these amusements was checkers, and the number of paintings and lithographs depicting checker players sitting on the porch or around the old potbellied stove is mute evidence of the popularity of this pastime among our ancestors. Many commercial manufacturers produced checkerboards, but the boards most interesting to today's collectors are the handmade versions of light and dark wood inlaid in a contrasting pattern or painted in bright hues. The most interesting of these boards can be viewed as a form of folk art, and many today are collected as such. Much the same can be said of backgammon and Parcheesi boards, some of which were made of glass with the board design painted in reverse on the back of the glass.

There are also the counters with which the games were played. Checkers, being only plain circles of wood, are of little interest, but chessmen have been made of everything from wood to precious metals, and they are collected with great enthusiasm.

The greatest variety of games is found among those played upon a board, and these are, appropriately, known to collectors as board games.

Most board games are similar in concept, involving a race to the finish line between two or more players who move their pieces, or counters, along a printed track at a rate determined by the fall of dice, the turn of a numbered spinner, or the selection of cards.

The earliest known board game, Goose, was played in Italy in the sixteenth century, but it was not until the 1800s that such recreational devices existed in any quantity. Yet from about 1870 to the 1960s, when television began to affect their popularity, thousands of such games were put on the market. Some never caught the public fancy and were soon discontinued, while others enjoyed phenomenal success. The Mansion of Happiness, a game with a religious theme, was first marketed in 1843 and was still being reissued as late as the 1880s. That is nothing compared to everyone's favorite, Monopoly. Though a relative latecomer (it was invented in 1935) compared to such games as Lotto, Old Maid, and even bingo, Monopoly has already sold over 80 million sets! The story is that its creator, Charles Darrow, was broke and out of work when he came up with this bright idea, and he made enough money from it to indulge his own interests in real estate speculation as well as to become a world traveler and orchid grower.

Games collectors are always interested in the themes of their acquisitions and how they are played, but the main reason that most people collect is that they are attracted by the lovely graphics with which the boards and particularly the box covers are adorned. Early examples were lithographed in black on white and then carefully hand tinted, but by the 1880s, chromolithography had made possible multicolored designs. Some of these are faithful reproductions of Victorian dress and customs, and others are strikingly abstract. In either case the cover is the object of greatest importance. If it is lost or damaged, few collectors are interested in the game. The absence of markers, cards, or spinners is not critical, though it detracts from the value of the set. The ideal acquisition, of course, is a game that is complete and in good condition.

Given the large number of games that have been produced, one would expect that the game collector would have little trouble acquiring specimens. However, since most games were made of cardboard and paper, time has taken its toll. All too many games have been either lost or damaged beyond repair. Fortunately, the field is relatively new, and serious collectors are few enough that good examples can still be obtained at reasonable prices. Knowledgeable dealers will charge thirty or forty dollars for a full-size game (about eighteen inches across), but similar games can be found at flea markets or even yard sales at a fraction of that price.

The observant collector soon realizes that the majority of games from the period from 1880 to 1950 were made by one of three companies. One of the earliest of these companies was the W. & S.B. Ives Company of Salem, Massachusetts. Ives developed the game with the longest name, Pope and Pagan, or The Missionary Compaign; or the Siege of the Stronghold of Satan by the Christian Army. Like many other late-nineteenth-century games, Pope and Pagan had a religious message to convey—other board games of the period were designed to teach geography or simple bookkeeping or to inculcate social values such as honesty and respect for hard work.

The other major board-game producers were McLoughlin Brothers of New York City, active from 1850 until its absorption in 1920 by the Milton Bradley Company of Springfield, Massachusetts; and Parker Brothers, of Salem, Massachusetts, manufacturer of Monopoly.

Puzzles are also collectible. Wood or cardboard puzzles have been popular a long time—during the 1860s Milton Bradley made a puzzle called The Smashed Up Locomotive. Puzzles with unusual shapes or themes (such as animals or national maps) are considered the most desirable.

Building blocks—from the early ones that were made of wooden blocks to which lithographed paper was pasted to the modern plastic version—are considered highly collectible. Because age is very important with these, twentieth-century examples remain underpriced. As with board games and puzzles, original boxes in good condition are critical.

Game of Mail, Express or
Accommodation; by Milton Bradley
Co.; ca. 1923; $150-220. The fine
lines and dynamic coloring of this
board game's box top typify what
collectors look for in this area.

Doodle-Bug Race; by Selchow and
Righter; 1925-35; $120-170.
So-called Mexican jumping beans
are the counters in this unusual
game.

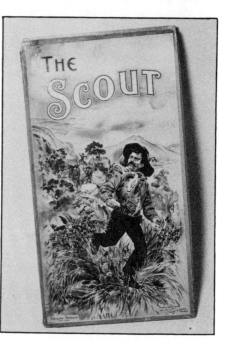

Barney Google and Spark Plug
Game; by Milton Bradley Co.; ca.
1923; $90-165. Many games are
based on comic strip figures.

The Scout; by Edgar O. Clark;
1900-05; $130-185. Though based on
an American theme, this game was
manufactured in England.

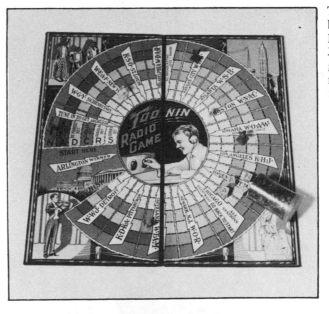

Board games; by Milton Bradley Co.;
1930-35; $75-95 each. **Top** Fox and
Geese. **Bottom.** Bang.

Toonin Radio Game;
by Aldermann,
Fairchild Co.; 1930-
35; $65-90. This
game reflects
manufacturers'
interest in the
booming
communications
industry.

Telegraph Game; by Milton Bradley
Co.; 1920-25; $185-235. Good
lithography and no missing pieces
make this a most desirable game.

Game of the Spider's Web; by Milton
Bradley Co.; 1920-25; $45-75.

425

The Gypsy Fortune Telling Game; by
Milton Bradley Co.; 1930-40; $55-85.

Conjuring Tricks; by Spears;
1930-35; $55-80. Amateur magician
sets have been popular for a long
time with both children and adults.

The Hand of Fate Fortune Telling
Game; by McLoughlin Brothers; ca.
1901; $130-180.

Peg Baseball; by Parker Brothers;
1915-20; $115-165.

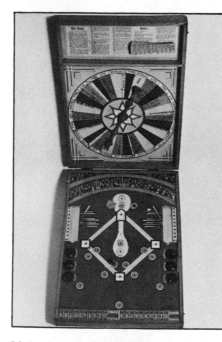

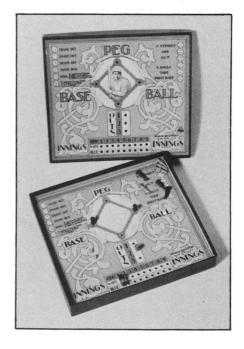

Major League Baseball Game; ca.
1912; $215-300. This early game is
highlighted by the presence of Babe
Ruth-on the Boston Braves!

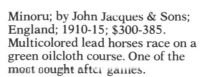

Minoru; by John Jacques & Sons; England; 1910-15; $300-385. Multicolored lead horses race on a green oilcloth course. One of the most sought after games.

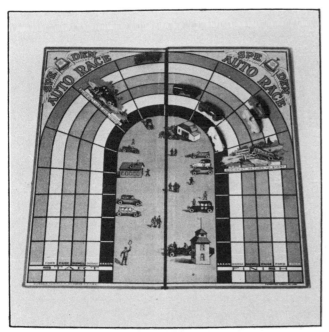

Speedem Auto Race; by Aldermann, Fairchild Co.; ca. 1922; $220-275. Unusual metal cars add much to this game.

Board games with religious themes; by Goodenough & Woglom; 1930-40; $15-25 each. **Top:** Bible Lotto. **Bottom:** Bible Quotto. Such games have little interest for most collectors.

Glass and metal puzzles that involve rolling balls; 1925-35. **Left:** Baseball; $25-40. **Center:** Spider; $15-25. **Right:** Cootie Game; $20-35.

Handmade wooden checkerboard in pine with green and gray paint; 1890-1900; $130-175. Many checker-and chessboards were homemade.

Left: Checkers set and black and red checkerboard; by Embossing Co.; 1940-45; $15-25. **Right:** Parcheesi set; 1930-40; $20-30.

Checkers and backgammon board and box in the form of books; by McLoughlin Brothers; 1925-35; $30-45.

Board game; 1920-30; $75-95.

Dominoes in domino-shaped wooden box; 1930-35; $60-85. An unusual and well-designed set.

Chinese Marble Checkers; by Whitman Publishing Co.; ca. 1939; $20-35.

Ark Dominoes; by Wilder
Manufacturing Co.; 1940-50; $15-25

Card Games; 1925-35. Left: Snap; by
Milton Bradley Co.; $15-20. Right:
Touring; by Parker Brothers; $20-30.
Bottom: Dr. Busby; by Milton
Bradley Co.; $15-20.

Lost Heir; by Milton Bradley
Co.; ca. 1908; $35-50.

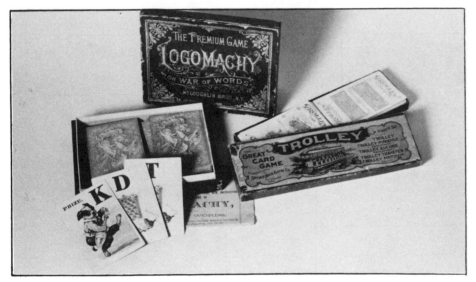

Left: LogoMachy; by McLoughlin
Brothers; ca. 1889; $30-45. Right:
Trolley by Snyder Brothers Co.;
1910-20; $20-30.

Left: Have U It?; by Selchow and
Righter; 1930-35; $25-35. Right top:
Lindy; by Parker Brothers; 1925-30;
$30-45. Right bottom: Stock
Exchange; by W.W. Gavitt Co.; ca.
1903; $15-25

Top: Tiddledy Winks and Tiddledy Tots; by Transogram; 1935-45; $30-45. **Bottom:** Tiddledy Winks; by Parker Brothers; 1900-10; $20-30.

Left: Magnetic Jack Straws; by Milton Bradley Co.; 1920-25; $15-25. **Right:** Jack Straws by Milton Bradley Co.; 1930-35; $20-30.

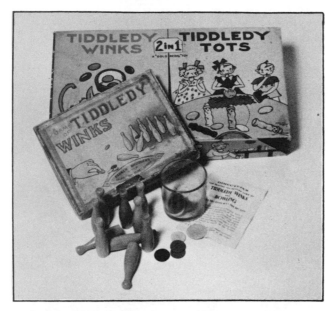

Magnetic Fish Pond; 1935-40; $135-175. The brightly colored fish are particularly well done.

Alabama Coon; by J.W. Spear and Sons; 1915-25; $255-345. Although this game is a sad reminder of racism, its graphics make it valuable to collectors.

Table Croquet; 1910-15; $65-85.

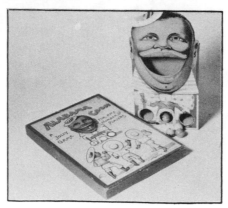

Pitch Em The Game of Indoor Horseshoes; by Walbert Manufacturing Co.; 1925-30; $45-75.

Jumpy Tinker; by Toy Tinkers Inc.; 1930-35; $65-95. "The sport that keeps us young."

Tinkle Target; by Milton Bradley Co.; 1890-1900; $175-245. When a thrown ball hits the cat's head, a bell rings.

Educational games that promote wise spending; by Parker Brothers. **Left:** My Mother Sent Me to the Grocery Store; 1910-20; $35-45. **Right** Corner Grocery; ca. 1887; $45-60.

North Atlantic Squadron Picture Puzzle; 1910-20; $250-325. A rare picture puzzle with great graphics.

The Horse Scorll Puzzle; by McLoughlin Brothers; ca. 1898; $90-130.

Favorite Picture Puzzles; by Madmar Quality Co.; 1920-30; $60-90. Puzzles too are very popular today.

Storming of Weissenburg puzzle blocks; Germany; ca. 1872; $285-335. Extremely rare.

Building blocks; by Richter & Co.; 1900-10; $150-200. Sets of these unusual blocks are rarely found intact.

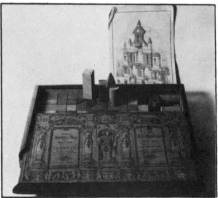

Block puzzle; 1910-20; $135-185. Because portions of a different puzzle are glued to each side of the wooden blocks, this set can produce six completely different puzzles.

Block puzzle; 1890-1900; $115-140.

Carboard puzzle blocks; 1915-25; $75-125.

Wooden building blocks in unpainted pine; 1900-10; $55-75.

Put a Hat on Uncle Wiggly pinup game; by Milton Bradley Co,; ca. 1919; $40-65.

Pat and His Pipe pinup game; 1930-35; $55-75.

Goof Race and Ten Pins; by Russell Manufacturing Co.; 1930-40; $45-65.

Soldiers on Parade, including fifty cardboard soldiers; by McLoughlin Brothers; ca. 1898; $200-285. Soldiers of all kinds are in great demand.

Sports Memorabilia

Sports collectibles, a field of great interest and variety, comprise a rapidly growing sector of interest—particularly for the male collector.

Perhaps the oldest and certainly the most popular area today is hunting memorabilia. Sporting firearms, rifles and shotguns, have been collected for a long time, and few antiquarians are unaware of such fine items as Kentucky rifles and carved powder horns. But these things are both scarce and expensive, so the contemporary collector must look elsewhere. Many fine examples of sporting arms were made between 1880 and 1940 by such prestigious manufacturers as Stevens and Remington. Interesting items such as octagonal-barreled .22 caliber rifles and double-barreled shotguns may be purchased quite reasonably. Of course, as with military arms, one should bear in mind that functioning weapons are subject to state licensing laws.

Associated gunning paraphernalia, such as powder horns, bullet molds, loading tools, and game bags, are also collectible, as are trophies, which range from the usual set of deer antlers to gigantic, stuffed and mounted moose heads. As to the latter, however, keep in mind that under Federal law it is unlawful to own certain bird trophies (such as hawks and eagles) even though they were mounted long ago.

Decoys are very popular with sports enthusiasts today. These full-size replicas of ducks, shorebirds, crows, and even owls, were usually carved from wood, though examples in tin, papier-mâché, and even plastic can be found. Originally intended to deceive waterfowl, they are now perceived as folk art or, in the words of an early collector, Joel Barber, as "utilitarian, floating sculpture."

Duck decoys are the most common type, with some thirty-four different species having been duplicated. The most commonly seen types are the black duck, canvasback, redhead, and Canada goose. Less available are tiny shorebirds, such as curlews and plovers. Unlike duck decoys, which were designed to float on the water, these shorebird decoys were mounted on a stick that could be stuck in the ground. Since shorebird hunting was largely outlawed over fifty years ago, these decoys are hard to come by, and the enthusiast should be wary of recent reproductions and outright fakes.

Pigeon, owl, and crow decoys are less often seen but are regarded as quite desirable by some collectors. Many of these decoys were produced in factories (as were some duck and shorebird decoys), and they are usually inexpensive.

Until recently, fishing collectibles were for the most part ignored by collectors. Now, however, the craftsmanship of the old-time reel and rod makers has come to be appreciated by a growing number of enthusiasts. Fly rods, those long, slim bamboo wands, which can delicately drop a tiny fly on the water dozens of feet from the caster, were made one by one by men such as Hiram Lewis Leonard and Edward Payne. These makers have come to be recognized as true artists in their field. Their products were not cheap when new, and at present may sell for hundreds of dollars apiece. For the more modest collector there are the production-line rods turned out in the 1920s and 1930s by such well-known fishing-tackle factories as James Heddon & Sons and the South Bend Bait Company.

The reels that held the fishing line are also of interest, particularly the pre-1900 handcrafted models by makers such as Julius Vom Hofe and Yawman & Erbe. Though collectors are seeking nearly all pre-1940 reels, they particularly desire the giant salmon reels and the tiny (less than two inches in diameter) "midge" trout reels.

Nets, fly boxes, and even trout flies are also considered fair game for collectors. As in the area of hunting memorabilia, paintings or sculpture of fish or fishing scenes are considered to be of great interest. The field of fishing memorabilia is growing fast, but there is still a good chance for the new collector to get in on the ground floor.

For many people, horse racing is the number-one American sport, and when one adds to the millions who follow the "sport of kings" the many thousands who ride for pleasure, it becomes evident that a vast number of people have some interest in horse-related memorabilia. For many this involves no more than collecting some of the many prints or paintings that depict horses or horse-racing scenes. For others, however, such memorabilia is supplemented by actual riding gear, such as crops, riding caps, jockey silks, bits, bridles, spurs, and—naturally—the ubiquitous horseshoe. Though such items as Spanish silver spurs and early Western saddles can be fabulously expensive, most racing and riding collectibles can be purchased rather inexpensively. This is particularly true of associated items such as bookends, ashtrays, and the like, depicting or made in the form of horses or horse heads. These pieces alone can provide the nucleus of a good collection.

A much newer area is that of hobby or amateur sailing. For many years collectors have been interested in mementoes of the great days of sailing ships—scrimshaw, whaling gear, clipper ship models and paintings, and naval weapons—but only recently have collectors become aware of the interesting relics associated with small-boat sailing.

The most obviously appealing collectibles here are models of famous racers such as the *America*, first winner of the cup that bears its name. These can be either fully rigged or of the flat-backed type known as "half models." Equally popular are paintings or lithographs of racing scenes.

A fortunate few can afford to collect the boats themselves, but for most collectors the equipment used aboard the boats will have to do. This includes such items as compasses, wheels, porthole covers, sextants, and even the binoculars used by the men or women on watch. Since many of these items are made wholly or in part of brass, they make attractive additions to the den or living room.

In a nation as sports minded as this one, the vast field of sporting memorabilia must inevitably continue to expand. Everything from hockey sticks to mountain-climbing gear will eventually become collectible, and the wise collector or dealer will purchase these things now while many can still be found at relatively low prices—a situation that can't last forever.

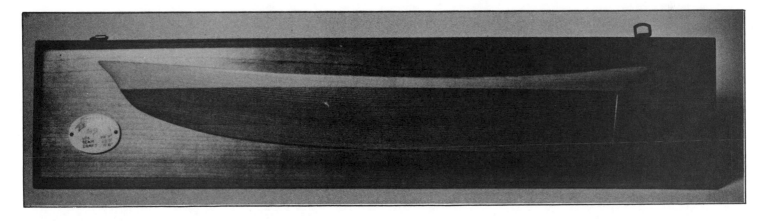

Wooden half model of the racing vessel **America,** winner of the first America's Cup; 1960-65; $225-285.

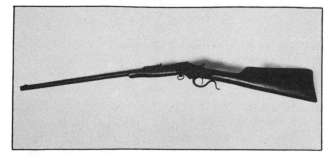

Single-shot .22 caliber sporting rifle; by Winchester; 1890-1910; $95-140. The .22 was the traditional "boys' rifle" during the Victorian era just as it is today.

Double-barreled fowling piece or shotgun with silver and brass inlay; 1860-85; $315-385.

Single-barreled 12 gauge shotgun; by Union Arms Co.; Toledo, Ohio; 1905-15; $75-105

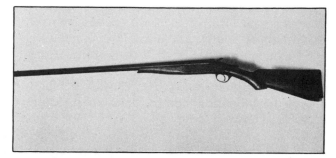

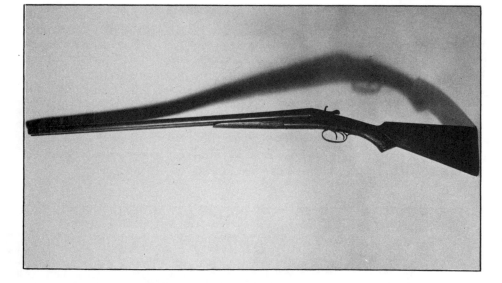

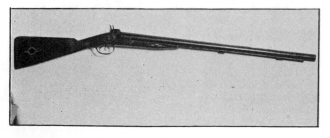

Double-barreled 16 gauge shotgun; by Gordon Gun Co.; 1920-30; $110-170.

Buckshot mold, iron and wood; 1880-1900; $65-85.

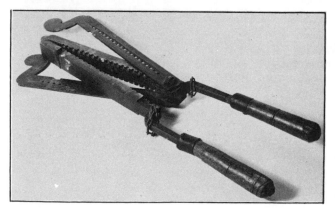

Bronze sporting sculpture, "Hunter with Stag"; by H. Malle; 1875-90; $750- 1,100.

Bronze sporting sculpture, "Hunter with Dog"; by M. Malle; 1875-90; $800-1,200.

Duck decoys in black and white. Left: Bufflehead drake; 1925-30; $80-120. Right: Old-Squaw; 1930-40; $100-150.

Mallard drake decoy in black, blue, brown, and white; 1920-30; $145-165.

Red-breasted merganser decoy; 1900-10; $250-325. Well-carved decoys in old paint, such as this one, are highly prized by collectors.

Fly rod probably made of ash; by
William Mitchell; 1885-90; $600-800.
Early nonbamboo fly rods are rare.

Fly rod of bamboo; by James Heddon
& Sons; 1930-35; $250-350.

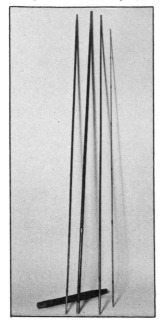

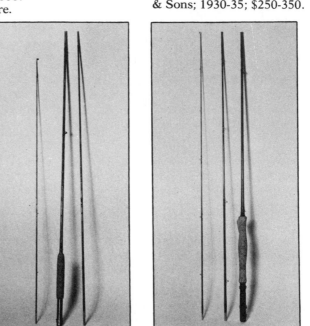

Fly rod of bamboo; by Edward
Payne; 1910-20; $700-950. Payne is
one of the most highly regarded of
early rod makers.

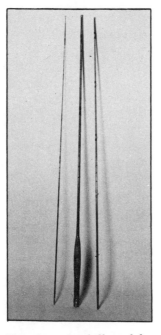

Left: Fishing net of wood; by
Thomas; 1930-35; $55-75. Right:
Collapsible fishing net in metal and
wood; 1925-30; $40-60.

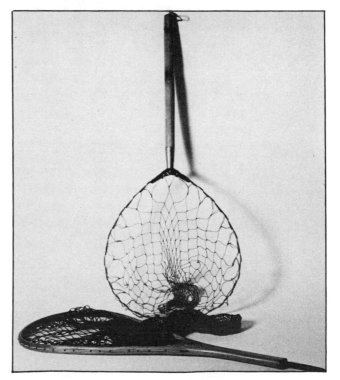

Fly rod of bamboo, Catskill model;
by Hiram Lewis Leonard; 1915-20;
$650-850. The Catskill line is a
forerunner of the modern fly rod.

Storage box for trout flies in oak and brass, by Hardy Brothers; 1920-30; $300-450.

Model of a brown trout, carved and painted wood; 1910-20; $350-475.

Genre painting of jumping brook trout; Maine; 1890-1910; $375-500. Folk paintings of fishing and hunting scenes are in great demand.

Riding cap in black wool felt; 1940-50; $35-55. Riding crop in leather, deer horn, and silver; 1900-10; $85-135.

Horse bits of cast and wrought iron; 1900-15; $5-15 each.

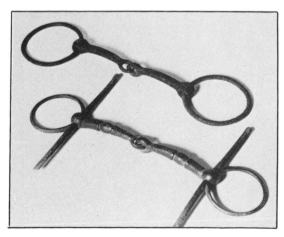

Bookend in pot metal and wood;
1930-40; $35-55 the pair.

Bookend in painted pot metal;
1910-20; $55-85 the pair.

Miniature figure of a horse and
jockey in cast metal; by Britains;
1925-35; $20-35.

Miniature figure of a horse and
jockey in painted pot metal; 1935-40;
$15-25.

Hand-tinted lithograph of a racing
scene; 1880-1900; $225-300.

Half model in wood of the racing
yacht **Columbia;** 1960-65; $175-255.

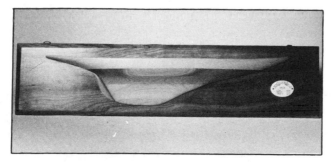

Ship's sextant in brass; 1900-10;
$275-400.

Compass in brass housed in a brass
binnacle with attached oil lamp for
night use; 1880-90; $350-450.

Reprint of 19th-century Currier &
Ives lithograph of the cutter yacht
Maria; 1930-40; $45-65. Currier &
Ives marine prints are so popular
that even reprints have some value.

Binoculars in brass and steel;
1900-20. **Left:** $65-85. **Right:**
$85-115.

Antique Decoys

It was many years ago—a thousand at least—that men learned how to lure flying wild fowl to their doom through the use of decoys. That this method works is because of the gregariousness of certain species. Ducks, geese, and various small shorebirds tend to seek out their own and to rest or feed where they see others of their species. The American Indian knew of this characteristic and used grass, wood, rushes, bird feathers, and even mud to shape forms that from a distance might be taken for resting wild fowl. Such decoys were in no sense true replicas of the birds they were intended to lure but were more in the nature of symbols—they resembled the species sufficiently to be able to deceive.

At first, the colonial settlers copied Indian decoys. There was no European tradition in this area, and the settlers had to learn from experience. By the 1800s, there were so many hunters working the inland and coastal waterways that the birds were becoming shy, and it became necessary to devise more efficient decoys. At this time, two distinct types emerged. The first, and probably the oldest, was the stickup, a birdlike figure mounted on a rod or rodlike legs so that it could be stuck into mud or a sandbank. Examples of stickup decoys in the guise of ducks and geese are known, but the form proved more suitable to the smaller shorebirds that habitually roamed the tidal flats seeking food—mostly because the greater weight required for a model of the large birds caused the stickup to sink into the mud, giving the decoy an unnatural posture.

To lure the larger wild fowl—which tended to land, feed, and rest on the water—hunters created floating decoys in a vast array of shapes and sizes. Unlike the symbolic decoys employed by the Indians, both the floaters and the stickups were meant to be replicas, imitating more or less exactly the shape and plumage of a particular bird.

For most collectors, floaters are the only type of decoy. Shorebird stickups were never widely made beyond the Atlantic coastal area, and in 1918 a Federal law forbade shooting of the diminutive shorebirds, bringing to an end any need for new stickup decoys. Floating decoys, on the other hand, are still made and used today.

There are many species of duck, and for each species decoys have been created. The so-called sea ducks are those that feed and rest almost exclusively on salt water: bays, estuaries, and even the open ocean. They include the whistler, canvasback, bluebill, bufflehead, scoter, coot, redhead, eider, ruddy duck, and old squaw. Decoys for these birds tend to be large and sturdily built so that they might be seen from a distance and could withstand rough weather.

Marsh ducks, such as the mallard, black, pintail, widgeon, and teal, frequent the calmer waters of inland ponds and rivers. For them the decoy need not be so large nor so sturdy.

Other and even larger birds are or have been lured with decoys. The great Canada goose is eagerly sought, and many variations of the goose decoy may be found, with the rarest being the feeding and sleeping versions. Before the taking of plumage for hats and garments was outlawed, hunters sought the swan, the crane, the loon, the heron, the gull, and the egret, and lifelike models of these species are also available. It was also known that the sight of wily birds like the swan and the gull gave flying ducks a feeling of security when they were looking for a place to land, so that even after swans and gulls could not be taken for their feathers, they were copied and used as "confidence" decoys. Nevertheless, in numbers, decoys of the plumage birds cannot be compared with ducks, and the former generally sell for a good deal more money.

At least 90 percent of all decoys are made of wood, chiefly pine, though cedar, basswood, cottonwood, cork, and balsa have also been employed. The making of such a lure generally takes the following course. A log or wooden block is split in two to provide material for two bodies. Each of the resulting pieces is pointed at one end for a tail and rounded at the other to simulate the breast. The head is carved from a separate piece of wood and then inserted into a hole drilled into the body. Most decoys are then painted and, as a final step, rigged with ballast (so that they will float properly), a mooring line, and an anchor. Today's decoy collectors are not necessarily hunters (indeed, they often oppose the sport), and they often overlook the fact that until the advent in recent years of the "art," or model, decoy, all decoys were intended to be used; thus, their ability to float properly was a far more critical factor than good paint or an artfully carved head.

The decoy maker employs few tools: an ax, a drawknife, a gouge, a jackknife for whittling heads, and a piece or two of sandpaper. He may have cardboard patterns from which to model heads, but more often than not, these are done freehand. Most available decoys were made by unknown workers who produced a few each year for their own use or for sale to fellow sportsmen. A certain number of craftsmen in each area of the country did become full-time professional carvers, producing hundreds of birds to sell to gunning clubs or to commercial hunters, who, before the outlawing of their trade, would use a hundred or more decoys in a single rig for hunting sea ducks. Most professional carvers marked their birds, but decoys can also be identified by style. The work of these makers is now extremely valuable and may sell for thousands of dollars apiece; examples by such men as Elmer Crowell of East Harwich, Massachusetts, Albert Laing and Charles "Shang" Wheeler of Stratford, Connecticut, and Nathan Cobb of Chincoteague, Virginia, are highly prized. The collector should bear in mind, though, that most decoys carry no maker's mark, and that a well-made example may be a splendid piece of folk art even though it remains anonymous. It may also be a lot easier on the purse.

The great demand for decoys during the last years of the nineteenth and first decades of the twentieth centuries led to the development of decoy factories. Here the bodies were formed on duplicating lathes, but the painting and finishing was done by hand—thus the pieces may still be thought of as handmade. Perhaps the best-known commercial decoy manufacturer was the Mason Decoy Company of Detroit, Michigan. Mason produced four grades of birds, all of which were of high quality and are avidly collected today: Premier, Challenge, Detroit, and Fourth. Another well-known producer of commercial decoys was the Wildfowler Company of Saybrook, Connecticut.

The great majority of wood-bodied decoys are made with solid bodies, but hollow types may be found. These were harder to make but were preferred by sportsmen because of their light weight. The same rationale explains the existence of cork and balsa examples. Also, where dealing with very large forms such as the goose or swan, the craftsman might resort to a frame body covered with canvas. At a later period, the slat frame was replaced by one of heavy wire. The same need to reduce weight explains, in part, the existence of the extremely simple decoys known as shadows. These are simply flat boards cut in the general shape of a duck and given a coat of paint. At a distance they do appear birdlike, and they are a lot easier to carry long distances over mud flats. At the opposite end of the spectrum are those gunners who used decoys made from cement or even cast iron. These were generally employed in floating shooting boxes called batteries; and the individual decoys often might weigh as much as forty pounds. Such birds are rarely found today.

Stickup decoys for shorebirds and other species can present a sticky problem for the collector. Since no legal working models have been made for nearly sixty years and since so many were destroyed when the prohibitory laws went into effect, good-quality authentic examples are not common. The gap has, unfortunately, been filled with many fakes and reproductions, some of which are difficult to spot.

There are several types of small birds that frequent marshy coastal areas, including the plover, yellowlegs, curlew, sandpiper, ruddy turnstone, willet,

dowitcher, and knot. Decoys have been made for all. Since the birds are small, seldom more than six inches long, the decoys are tiny and often carefully painted, with a hole in the bottom into which a standing rod may be placed. Both size and quality of decoration make these "peeps," as they are called, extremely suitable for table or shelf display. They have, accordingly, been collected for some years not only by decoy enthusiasts but also by general collectors of folk art. As a result, prices are high. Shorebirds by Elmer Crowell may go for as much as seven thousand dollars, while ordinary unmarked examples often bring several hundred dollars apiece.

Not all stickups were made of wood. One frequently encounters lithographed tin examples that were produced in factories at the end of the nineteenth century. These are often very attractive, and specimens retaining a good coat of paint are not cheap. Papier-mâché was also used to make peeps, as was balsa. Both are light, and their fragility did not present as great a problem as it would have for floating decoys. Stickups were also used in hunting inland species, such as crows, pigeons, and doves. Few of these decoys were modeled; with the maker contenting himself with a flat, painted shadow. Tin was also used to make these decoys, as was rubber, particularly as the twentieth century advanced. Rubber decoys seem singularly mass-produced and unattractive, being more a matter for

curiosity than anything else. They are said, however, to draw crows well.

In collecting decoys one should look for two things: good form and old paint. Form is the more important factor. A well-shaped lure is a piece of sculpture and should be revered as such; no amount of paint will hide an ugly and ill-proportioned body. Also, good original paint is rare on working decoys. Wind, rain, and water soon put an end to even the hardest finish, and many wild fowlers habitually repainted their decoys each year. Since it was not often that the owner was as competent a craftsman as the maker, subsequent coats of paint are usually indifferent work at best. A good early coat of paint is a blessing to be treasured.

Marks are, of course, very important. Some can greatly increase the value of a decoy. However, as noted, most decoys (including some of the most artistic) are not marked, or they bear names that cannot be found in books on decoy makers. Often, this just means that the bird was stamped by its previous owner. It could, however, mean that the piece is by a previously unknown craftsman. A lot of men made and sold decoys, and new makers are coming to light all the time. It is always possible to find a specimen by someone who in time will be regarded as another "Shang" Wheeler or Elmer Crowell. If possible, the collector should track down the unidentified names that appear on his pieces. It's fun, and it could be profitable.

Broadhill hen decoy; New York, early 20th century; $135-180.

443

Rare stickup duck decoy, probably a brant; Maine, late 19th century; $300-425.

Shorebird stickup decoy, probably a yellowlegs; New England, late 19th century; $350-600.

Sanderling stickup decoy; New York, early 20th century; $175-325.

Crudely made shorebird stickup decoy; New York, late 19th-early 20th century; $150-275.

Pair of very well-made snipe stickup decoy; Long Island, N.Y., late 19th century; $2,500-4,000 the pair.

Yellowlegs stickup decoy; New England, late 19th century; $800-1,000.

444

Sanderling stickup decoy; cork body; early 20th century; $95-125.

Crow stickup decoy, with wire legs; Connecticut, late 19th century; $185-245.

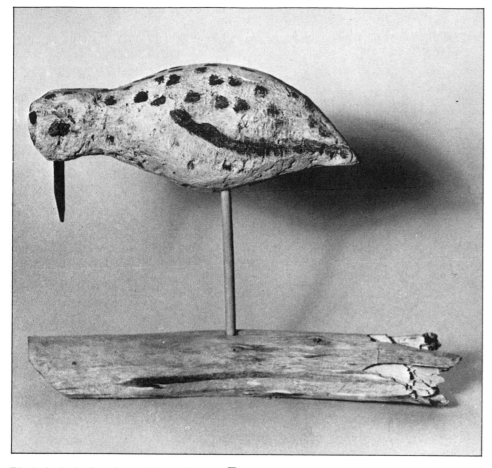

Black duck shadow decoy; Pennsylvania, ▼ 20th century; $65-85.

Uncommon factory-made pigeon stickup decoy, East, early 20th century; $90-140.

Interesting crow shadow decoy; New York, 20th century; $75-95.

Extremely well-made eider decoy; Pennsylvania, late 19th-early 20th century; $750-1,350.

Redhead drake decoy, pine; New Jersey, early 20th century; $200-350.

Teal decoy, pine; New York, 20th century; $135-195.

Broadtail decoy, hollow carved pine; Midwest, 20th century; $250-400.

Bluebill drake decoy; East, 20th century; $185-265.

Widgeon decoy, pine; Ontario River region of New York, 20th century; $135-185.

Primitive decoy, probably a black duck; late 19th-early 20th century; $50-70.

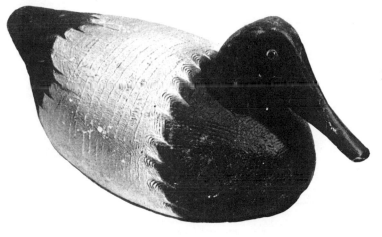

Well-done canvasback decoy, with good
original paint; East, early 20th century;
$240-310.

Merganser decoy, pine; New York, late
19th century; $55-80.

Scoter decoy; Stevens Factory, early
20th century; $350-550.

Bluebill hen decoy, pine; East, 20th
century; $90-145.

Canvasback decoy, pine; Illinois, early
20th century; $310-390.

Black duck decoy; New England, late
19th century; $400-655.

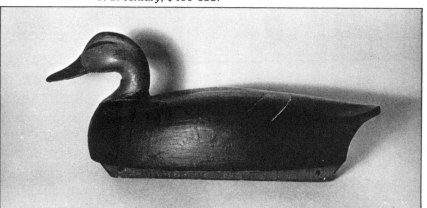

Broadtail drake decoy, with original paint; Upper New York State, ca. 1920; $140-210.

Black duck decoy; Wildfowler Decoy Company, Connecticut, 20th century; $185-315.

Whistler hen decoy; East, early 20th century; $50-65. Recent painting such as this, always decreases the value of a decoy.

Fine brant decoy; East, late 19th century; $1,350-1,850. This decoy was in the well-known Mackey collection, and such a history always boosts the price.

Primitive redhead decoys, male and female, pine; New England, late 19th century; $150-220 the pair.

Oversize canvasback decoy; Virginia, late 19th-early 20th century; $200-275.

Crude goldeneye decoy, pine; East, late 19th century; $45-65.

Black duck decoy; Mason Decoy Company, Detroit, Mich., early 20th century; $385-535.

Well-painted Canada goose decoy; New York, late 19th-early 20th century; $275-400. Goose and swan decoys are generally high-priced.

Broadbill hen decoy; East, 20th century; $85-125.

Extremely rare and very large (3 1-2') Canada goose decoy in the feeding postion, made and marked by William Holzman, Long Island, N.Y., 20th century; $350-650.

White winged scoter decoy, cork body; East, late 19th century; $60-85.

Bluebill hen decoy, so called Victor type; Mississippi, 20th century; $95-135.

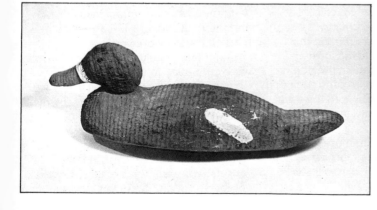

Weathervanes and Whirligigs

Weathervanes

Weathervanes and whirligigs today are regarded as interesting and valuable examples of American folk art. Not too long ago, they served an important function, too, as adjuncts to every person's own weather service. In the days before radio and its daily or even hourly weather forecast, nearly everyone was a weatherman. Sailors and farmers were the people most critically affected by sudden changes in weather, and they strove always to predict the weather and thereby keep ahead of it. It has long been known that changes in wind direction presage weather changes, both the long-term seasonal type and, more immediately, those short-range shifts that mean rain or storm.

At its simplest—a flat board mounted on a swivel rod—the weathervane could record those changes. It is, therefore, hardly surprising that vanes are known to have existed even in the days of the ancient Greeks and that they are among the earliest of American antiques. Some have survived from the seventeenth century, including a wooden fish studded with copper nails that once topped the roof of a Massachusetts copper shop. The first known vanemaker in America, Shem Drowne of Boston, created several vanes in the 1740s that still stand in that city. Best known of these is the copper grasshopper that graces old Faneuil Hall; it has survived several disasters, including earthquake, fire, and assorted hurricanes.

The earliest weathervanes were made of wood, and that medium is still employed by some makers. It is relatively simple to saw or chisel a vane from a board, and the silhouette thus produced stands out well against the sky. More sophisticated workers, who wanted to achieve an illusion of depth, carved vanes in the round, creating a full-bodied animal or other form. Wood used for this purpose has a serious defect, however: with daily exposure, even the stoutest piece is vulnerable to the elements. It is therefore understandable that artisans soon turned to other mediums. Iron, either wrought or cut from a solid sheet, has often been employed in the construction of weathervanes, and some of the most interesting examples are found in this medium. Iron will eventually rust, however; more important, it is heavy, which makes it an impractical material for the very large weathervanes that were often mounted atop public buildings. By the middle of the nineteenth century, copper had been found to serve the purpose best. The bulk of the weathervanes collected today were made of copper by professional manufacturers during the period from 1870 to 1920.

In order to make a copper vane, the craftsman first carves a wooden form and from this casts an iron mold. The mold is cut into workable sections, which are hinged together to facilitate removal of the completed vane. Next, the worker fills the mold with molten lead, which contracts when cool, leaving a space between it and the wall of the iron mold. A sheet of copper is sandwiched into this area, and by pounding on the lead, the craftsman causes the copper to conform to the shape of the mold. The individual sections of the vane are then soldered together to produce a full-bodied hollow form. Even today, weathervanes are made in essentially this manner; and though produced in a factory, they may be said to be handcrafted.

Copper is light and extremely weather resistant. By the second half of the nineteenth century, nearly all major weathervane manufacturers were using it almost exclusively for their products. The variety of forms they produced was truly astonishing, particularly in the light of the fact that for hundreds of years there had been only two: the cock and the banneret. The figure of the crowing rooster appeared early and became traditional when, in the ninth century, a papal decree required that all churches employ this form of weathervane in order to remind the faithful of Peter's denial of Christ and the penalty for abandoning the dogma. So universal was the use of the cock that in England and New England the term *weathercock* was synonymous with *weathervane*.

The banneret is a flat, more or less rectangular metal piece that customarily terminates in an arrow. It may be as much as four feet long, with names or initials cut into the body so that they may be seen against the sky. The form may be traced to the heraldic banners flown from medieval castles.

Even in Shem Drowne's time, vanemakers had gone well beyond these basic forms, and by the 1880s, manufacturers' imaginations were running rampant. Animals were always most popular, reflecting, no doubt, the fact that the farmer and stock man was always the vanemaker's best customer. Horses appear in many forms, including "portrait" examples of such great racing horses as the trotters Hambletonian and Nancy Hanks and the flat racer Dexter. Inspiration for most of the horse, horse-and-buggy, and horse-and-rider weathervanes appears to have been provided by popular lithographs, such as those printed by Currier and Ives. Today, the horse is by far the most desirable antique weathervane, although the deer and the eagle are also in great demand. Of farm stock, one can list cows, bulls, hogs, sheep, chickens, and rabbits. The fox may be found as well as the pigeon, the bear, and the swan. There are also many exotics not likely to be found on most farms—elephants, dragons, boars, lions, buffalo, peacocks, ostriches, and tigers. Not to be forgotten is man's best friend, the dog, as well as his constant prey, the squirrel. Many of these forms are exceedingly scarce and when offered for sale may bring thousands of dollars.

The number of vanes in existence whose forms are associated with a particular craft makes it evident that workmen and shopkeepers found the weathervane a handy advertising device. To the farmer's (or plowmaker's) plow, one may add the blacksmith's anvil, the shoemaker's shoe, the cigar and tobacco leaf of the local cigar store, and the carpenter's saw. Also found are wheels for wagonmakers, the writing master's pen, and the malt shovel and barrel that marked the local brewery.

Other less readily identifiable symbols were employed in weathervanes. Arrows, the sunflower, the bicycle, Indian chiefs and maidens, fish (chiefly the cod and the mackerel), and even the butterfly appear. Some of these may have had social or fraternal significance. Certainly, the Liberty Cap and the various representations of the Goddess of Liberty and the Statue of Liberty were patriotic in intent.

As new modes of transportation appeared in the late nineteenth and early twentieth centuries, they too were immortalized in copper. The sailing ship vanes, always popular in coastal towns, gave way to steamships and ferryboats. The horsecar was succeeded by the trolley. Locomotives of various types were available, as were many different examples of firefighting apparatus. These, along with the fireman's hat and trumpet, were frequently seen atop turn-of-the-century firehouses. Cannons and the soldier's cap and gun were placed above the local armory, and by 1920 a new airport might boast its own weathervane in the form of the current model of flying machine.

These are but a portion of the various vane types one may expect to encounter about the country. In addition, new specimens are still appearing, for not all the old weathervane manufacturers went out of business. Two of the most famous nineteenth-century companies, J. W. Fisk and E. G. Washington of Danvers, Massachusetts, are still making vanes in the same old way. As one might suspect, this presents problems for the collector. The makers offer their vanes as new, but they often employ the old molds and the same materials as those found in vanes a hundred years old. With a little "weathering," a new vane can look pretty old. That such faking can take place is understandable in light of the fact that weathervanes are one of the most popular items on the current antiques market. Even the little eight-inch cows and horses once given away by feed and milk companies sell for a hundred dollars or so, and any full-size vane will bring anywhere from several hundred to several thousand dollars, depending on type and size.

One of the saddest side effects of the weathervane craze is the gradual disappearance of these noble symbols from the American skyline. Either lured by the value they possess to sell them or driven to hide them away by fear of thieves (who in recent years have resorted to helicopters to seek out their prey), owners are taking down the old vanes. It is a sad commentary on the state of our society that such beautiful and useful objects are not even safe on rooftops.

Whirligigs

Whirligigs are, in essence, wind toys, although those that are mounted on a free-moving shaft can serve also as weathervanes. The basic and earliest form is that of a figure with paddlelike arms, which are set on and revolve about a shaft running through the shoulders. When the wind blows, the arms turn like propellers. Traditionally, the first American examples were models of Hessian soldiers and were supposedly made by Pennsylvania settlers of German origin in mockery of the German mercenaries employed by the British during the Revolutionary War. There is little support for this story, but there is no doubt that the whirligig was known and made in Europe long before the settlement of this continent.

Few whirligigs are made of any substance other than wood, though they may often have various metal accessories. This is especially true of the late nineteenth- and twentieth-century examples, which are far more complex than the traditional models. These more recent wind toys often have several moving parts, so that when motivated, they can perform various functions. A sawyer may saw a log, a blacksmith may strike his anvil, or a whole group of people may perform a jerky dance. Such compositions are aptly termed "twentieth-century folk art" by collectors, for few of the devices date prior to 1900. They are eagerly sought today despite their rather recent vintage, and the collector will be well advised to watch for them at country yard sales and auctions. Unlike weathervanes, whirligigs can often be purchased for next to nothing.

The very simplicity and crudeness of the average whirligig make it fair game for the faker. With a little paint, some old wood, and a few bits of iron, someone with ingenuity can put together a representative example. New examples do appear regularly, but so far they seem to lack the sophistication of reproductions in other fields. The paint is generally too new, and there is little sign of the weathering that should be present on an object that has been outdoors for a few years. If prices go up in the field, no doubt more skilled operators will enter the arena.

Pig weathervane, painted pine; New York, 20th century; $350-500.
Good form and color in a late adaptation of an old favorite.

Sea serpent weathervane, pine and wrought iron; New England, first quarter 19th century; $8,000-13,000. Early wooden vanes are rare, particularly those with such an unusual motif.

Mare and foal weathervane, painted pine; Rhode Island, mid-19th century; $800-1,000. A simple saw-cut vane of a type still made today.

Crude fish weathervane, pine; New England, late 19th century; $250-400.

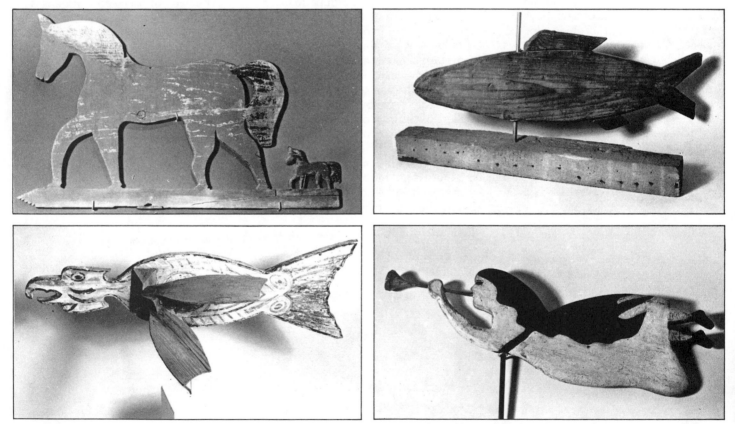

Eagle or buzzard weathervane, painted pine; East, late 19th century; $700-1,000. The head on this piece is particularly well done and sets it apart from most sawed wood eagles.

Full-bodied Angel Gabriel weathervane, molded and rounded polychromed pine; New York, mid-19th century; $7,500-10,000. A fine example of the carver's art.

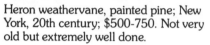

Heron weathervane, painted pine; New York, 20th century; $500-750. Not very old but extremely well done.

Horse and rider weathervane, painted sheet iron; New York, mid-19th century; $1,000-1,500. Though much of the original painting has been worn away, enough remains to indicate that it was of unusually high quality.

Horse weathervane, painted sheet iron; East, late 19th century; $450-650.

Horse and rider weathervane, tin with traces of original paint; Rhode Island, ca. 1840; $2,250-3,000. An example of an early full-bodied vane.

453

Carved wood form for weathervane, East, late 19th century; $15,000-25,000. Used to prepare the molds from which copper vanes were made; few of these forms survive.

Rooster weathervane, cast iron with tail of sheet iron; Massachusetts,, last quarter 19th century; $4,500-6,500.

Rooster weathervane, copper, late 19th-early 20th century. New England, $3,000-4,500. An example of a common full-bodied form.

Rooster on arrow weathervane, strongly molded copper; East, last quarter 19th century; $1,500-3,000.

Prancing horse weathervane, copper and iron; East, 19th century; $1,500-2,500. A spirited steed; the disheveled mane is rather unusual for an American-made piece.

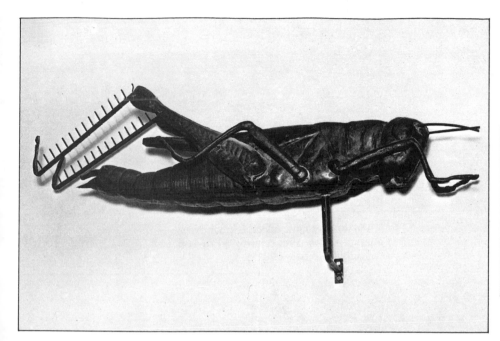

Grasshopper weathervane, copper; New England, last quarter 19th century; $25,000-35,000. An old and prized type.

Eagle on orb weathervane, copper; New England, late 19th century; $3,000-5,000.

Sailing ship weathervane, tin and wood; Maine, 20th century; $2,500-3,500. A fine specimen of a 20th-century craftsman's work.

Goddess of Liberty weathervane, copper with traces of gilding; New England, 1858; $25,000-40,000. This is a small version of a popular vane.

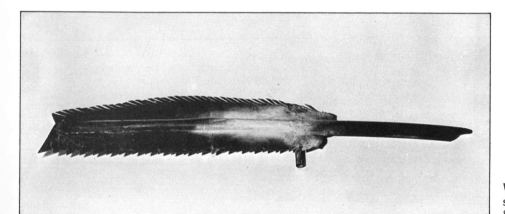

Writing quill weathervane, copper and sheet iron; New York, late 19th century; $2,800-4,000.

Cow weathervane, gilded tin, approximately 8″ long; East, early 20th century; $150-300. Small vanes of this sort were given away as premiums by companies that sold grain or purchased raw milk.

Horse weathervane, gilded tin; New England, 20th century; $150-300. Another small vane used as a premium.

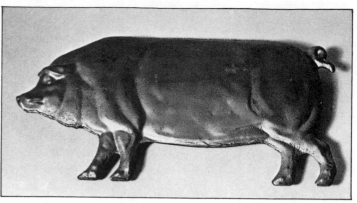

Pig weathervane, gilded copper; New England, late 19th century; $125-165. This vane is only 6″ long.

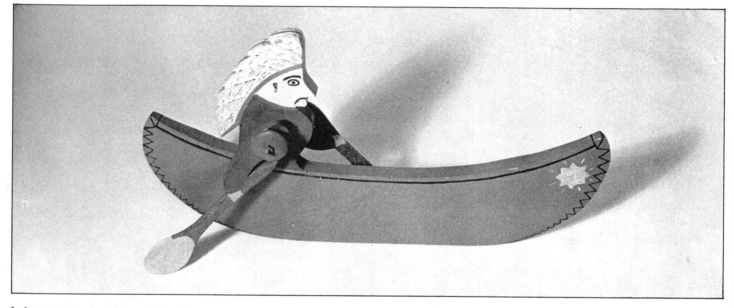

Indian in canoe whirligig, painted pine, New York, late 19th-early 20th century; $115-185. A very well-done piece.

Man and propeller whirligig, painted pine; East; early 20th century; $350-575. A very well-done piece.

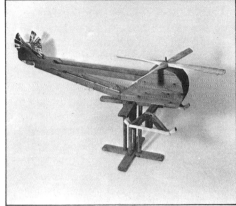

Airplane whirligig, painted pine; 20th century; $350-550. A large interesting piece, though not very old.

Helicopter whirligig, pine and tin; New York, 20th century; $220-310.

Sulky and trotter whirligig, painted pine and iron; New England, late 19th-early 20th century; $550-750. Complex movable whirligigs of this sort are attracting increasing collector attention.

Windmill whirligig, painted tin; East, late 19th-early 20th century; $150-220.

Tramp Art

Few areas of American folk art have slumbered unnoticed for as long as tramp art. A wide variety of objects was made in this distinctive style for well over a half century, but it was not until very recently that more than a few astute dealers and collectors began to appreciate the form.

The term *tramp art* refers to objects made by a specific technique that produces a unique style. Construction is characterized by gluing or nailing together layers of thin board, usually obtained by dismantling old cigar boxes or fruit crates. By gradating the size and shape of the layers, it is possible to create depth and varying perspective, which could otherwise be achieved only by very sophisticated deep carving. Combined with layering is the ancient art of chip, or notch, carving, the cutting of V- or Z-shaped notches into the surface of the wooden components. Changing the number and placement of the notches greatly alters the appearance of the object. Layering and chipping can be combined in an infinite number of ways to create objects with highly decorative surfaces and considerable individuality. No two pieces of tramp art are exactly alike.

The origin of the craft is unclear. Its name reflects a general supposition that the objects were made by itinerant carvers—hoboes, perhaps—who made pieces to sell or to barter for food and shelter as they wandered from town to town. Certainly, some work may well have been done in this manner. Many of the pieces are small enough to have been made on the move, and their materials were readily obtainable. A knife for carving was a standard item carried by itinerants, and the wood—mahogany or cedar from cigar boxes, pine from packing cases—could be picked up along the way, in public dumps or at stores where discards were stacked high in the alleys. But such an origin could account for only a portion of the output. Hoboes were hardly likely to have made large items such as beds and bureaus. Moreover, many pieces show the mark of cutting tools other than the knife—fretsaws, gouges, and chisels, unlikely possessions for a drifter.

Recent research has indicated a much more complex development for this craft than was originally supposed. Chip carving itself is characteristic of early American decorative woodworking as well as German and Scandinavian art from the seventeenth century on. The earliest dated tramp art in America is from the 1860s, which coincides with the period of great immigration from these areas. This and the fact that tramp work has been found in Germany strongly indicates that the style was brought to the United States by immigrants, probably itinerant craftsmen or apprentices who carved as they traveled and spread the technique by example. Unfortunately, there is little reliable oral tradition associated with the work, and no written references exist prior to the 1920s, a time when it was already on the wane, driven out by new uses for leisure time and a declining interest in cigar smoking, which reduced the availability of material.

At its zenith, tramp art must have been extremely popular. It was made in jails (though apparently only as a time killer, not for public sale), in lumber camps, by members of the military, and at public schools, where it appears to have been at one time part of shop courses. Pieces that can be attributed to a definite source are few, however; the great bulk of the ware remains unidentifiable.

This anonymity is particularly surprising in light of the fact that known specimens cover such a wide range of forms and styles. Yet there was much, much more. In a very real way, tramp art mirrors the changes in popular taste. The earlier work is strongly Victorian with a lavish busyness that is almost a parody of its inspirational source. As the twentieth century progressed, Deco influences crept in. Always, while remaining individualistic, the work is responsive to current styles.

The variety of forms in the medium is very great, and new types keep appearing. Picture frames, boxes, and mirrors are the most common items. Large pieces of case furniture, though hardly common, are found often enough to lead one to suspect that many others have been consigned to the woodshed. Full-size chests of drawers, cupboards, sideboards, sofas, and desks are known. There is even at least one floor-model radio cabinet! Many smaller household objects were made as well: coatracks, hanging wall pockets, plant stands, and tables; birdcages, ashtray holders, comb cases, pincushions, and barometer boxes; and a variety of clock cases ranging from a stately grandfather to wall and shelf models. Toys were also made in this style, and more than one child thrilled to the sight of a tramp-work miniature chest of drawers, cradle, rocker, or table. Hardest to come by are the whimsies, one-time projects that are unique and cannot be duplicated. Among the known examples are a model of the Brooklyn Bridge, a church, and a boxed wooden turtle.

Besides layering and chip carving, these pieces frequently display other decoration. Certain symbols occur repeatedly as decorative motifs: stars, hearts, flowers, birds, fish, deer, and various geometric forms. In addition, glass fragments, brass tacks, porcelain knobs, bits of colored stone or paper, and even complete lithographed pictures may be pasted onto the composition. While most tramp ware was left in the natural state or shellacked, some specimens were painted. Where present, the color is often highly fanciful. Bright reds, blues, greens, and yellows were applied indiscriminately, producing an effect that once must have been garish in the extreme. Fortunately, the natural fading with the passage of time has often transformed these to more subtle hues, which appeal to the modern eye.

Tramp art is rarely signed or otherwise specifically identifiable. Some pieces may be dated approximately, by determining the dates of operation of the cigar company or fruit packer from whose wood the ware was made. However, since by its nature the art was anonymous, it is not especially important to know the date or maker—to know the work is enough.

Prices in the field have risen steadily over the past five years. Smaller and more common examples such as frames seem a bit high at present, but one can hardly quarrel with the sums asked for the larger, rarer specimens. These are, in large part, unique or nearly so, and to own one is a rare privilege.

Left: Pincushion; $50-75. **Center:** Penny bank; $70-90. **Right:** Lift-top box; $40-65. All, 20th century.

Left: Small pedestal box with star motif; $90-125. **Right:** Mirrored lift top box; $90-125. Good examples of inexpensive

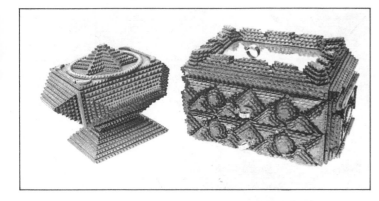

Left: Unusual layered bank; $115-185. ▶
Right: Lift-top box with heart motif and red satin interior; $65-115. Both, early 20th century.

Box with two drawers concealed behind hinged panel; late 19th century; $125-175.

Octagonal storage box in shape of a minaret; late 19th century; $375-475.

Extremely well-done double-pedestal storage box with handle; late 19th century; $350-450. Only a few tramp art boxes have more than one pedestal.

Left: Large, well-done pedestal box; $185-285. **Right:** Humidor; $150-200. Both, late 19th-early 20th century.

Gold-painted box with mirrored top and sides, containing man's shaving set, late 19th century; $250-375.

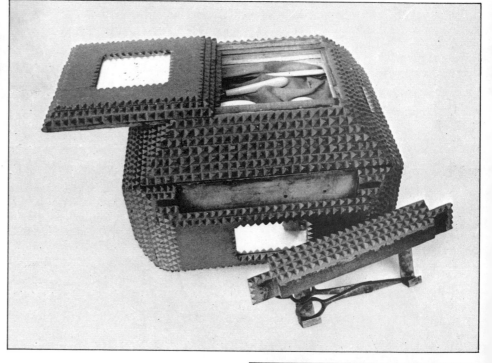

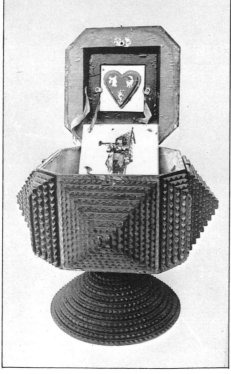

Pedestal box with multicolor decorated interior, early 20th century; $275-385. A very unusual piece.

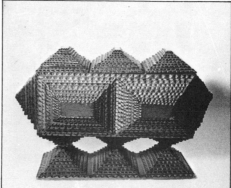

Triple-pedestal storage box; late 19th century; $400-525.

Simple lift-top storage box; 20th century; $35-50. This box is typical of the simple and inexpensive items in this line.

Interesting lift-top boxes. **Left:** With clasped hands and lover's message; $175-250. **Right:** With painted blue interior; $60-95. Both, late 19th-early 20th century.

Well-decorated hanging cupboard or spice chest; late 19th-early 20th century; $235-295.

Sewing box in old red paint; 20th century; $200-275. Note use of cheeseboxes as drawers.

461

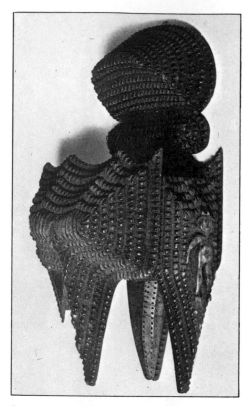

Complexly cut wall pouch with rare cutout figure of a man; late 19th century; $550-750.

Wall box and mirror with motif, dated 1912; $275-365. In this area, as in others, dated pieces are prized.

Wall pockets. **Left:** With incised representation of flag; 20th century; $90-155. **Right:** Late 19th century; $45-75.

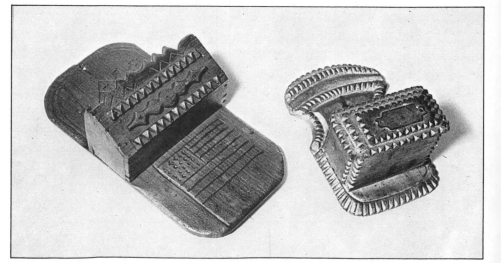

Mirrored wall pocket, red and gold paint;
late 19th-early 20th century; $325-475.
The heart is a popular tramp art motif.

Elaborate mirrored wall pocket with
acorn, leaf, and heart devices, gold trim;
possibly Canadian, 20th century;
$300-380.

Mirrored wall box with elaborate carving
and layering; late 19th-early 20th
century; $250-325.

Presentation wall box, black and gold paint; dated 1919; $350-500. Photos and initals of donor and receiver may be seen on this choice piece.

Wall pocket with shield device and porcelain button trim, early 20th century; $185-245.

Gothic-style multicolored wall mirror, late 19th century; $225-350.

Small wall mirror in shape of a star; late 19th century; $200-295.

Round wall mirror with hearts-and-flowers motifs; late 19th century; $350-475. A rare and beautiful piece.

Small, nicely carved wall mirror, late 19th century; $125-185.

Wall mirror with representations of eagle and eaglets, silver paint; early 20th century; $350-500.

Full-size grandfather's clock elaborately decorated with numerous tramp art motifs, late 19th century; $2,000-2,750. An extremely rare example.

Two small wall mirrors nicely painted in red, green, and gold; 20th century; $75-135 each.

Standing clock case with lower shelf, drawer, and mirror, early 20th century; $400-575.

Nicely carved clock case; 20th century; $250-350.

Cross on pedestal; 20th century; $75-125. Tramp art crosses are common, particularly in Canada.

Left: Cross in shrine; $70-90. **Right:** Cross on pedestal; $75-100. Both, late 19th-early 20th century.

Cross-decorated picture frame with cut-paper representation of the Garden of Eden, late 19th-early 20th century; $200-300.

Lady's vanity mirror with interesting chip carving; late 19th century; $300-425.

466

Picture frame in form of a heart; late ▶
19th century; $150-185.

Bureau-top mirror, late 19th century;
$150-175.

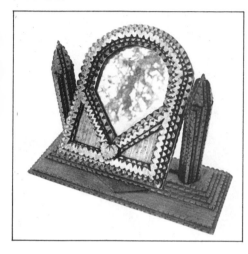

Hanging frame for family record in form ▶
of tramp art house; two silhouettes and
six daguerreotypes included;
$1,500-2,100. A possibly unique
example from the 19th century.

Picture frame, pine; Midwest, late
19th-early 20th century; $120-170. An
unusual four-frame form.

Large flower pot, gold paint, 20th
century; $225-300.

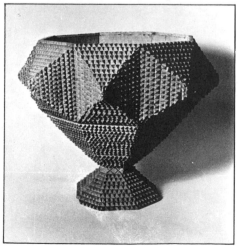

Plaque with depictions of first twenty-five
presidents and facsimile of Declaration of
Independence; ca. 1900; $1,500-2,100.
Almost certainly a unique
commemorative piece.

Carved pedestal for lamp or vase; late 19th-early 20th century; $265-345.

Elaborately decorated plant stand, multicolored; early 20th century; $900-1,400. An outstanding example.

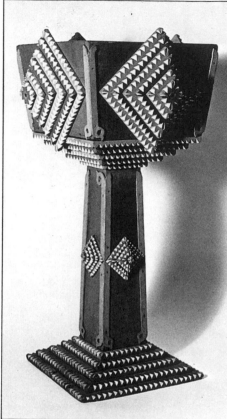

Carved plant stand; 20th century; $400-550.

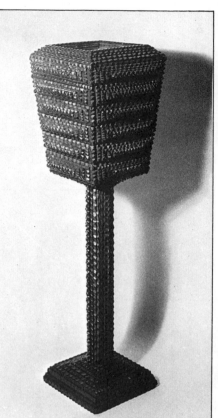

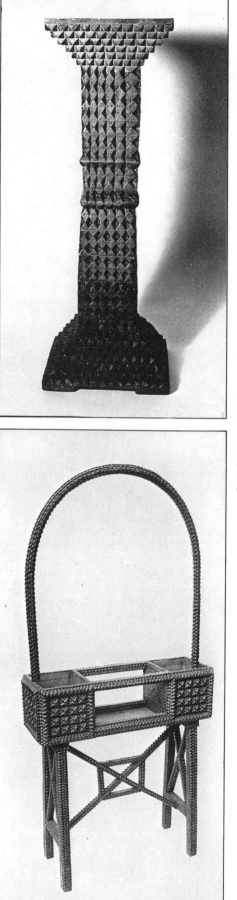

Unusual double-pocket plant stand on elaborate base; early 20th century; $750-1,100. Tramp art's answer to the wicker craze.

Very large multilevel candle lamp, purple and gold paint; 20th century; $450-650.

Rare chaise lounge composed entirely of
cigar-box mahogany; late 19th century;
$1,700-2,500. Probably a unique item.

Dome-top trunk decorated with tramp
art motifs; early 20th century; $350-500.

Unusual lamp, 20th century;
$900-1,300.

Miniature billiards table; late 19th-early
20th century; $800-1,200.

Radio cabinet in elaborate tramp art style creating the impression of a church; 20th century; $1,500-2,000.

Ashtray on pedestal; 20th century; $190-260. A rare piece.

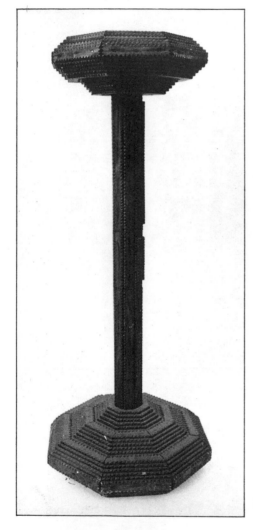

Foot stool, white paint; late 19th-early 20th century; $65-100.

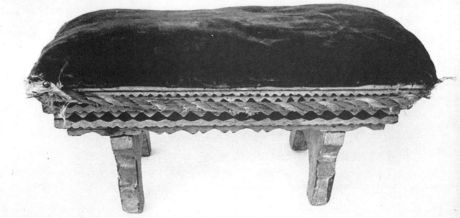

Two-shelf stand, white paint; 20th century; $165-275.

Elaborately decorated Victorian bureau, gold paint; late 19th-early 20th century; $1,750-2,250.

Child's chest of drawers with porcelain knobs, early 20th century; $275-375.

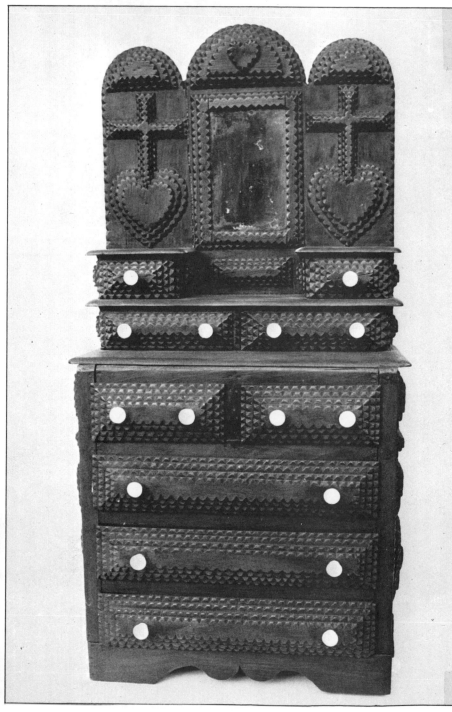

Panel from large tramp art cupboard with extraordinary design and workmanship; late 19th century; $1,500-2,500.

471

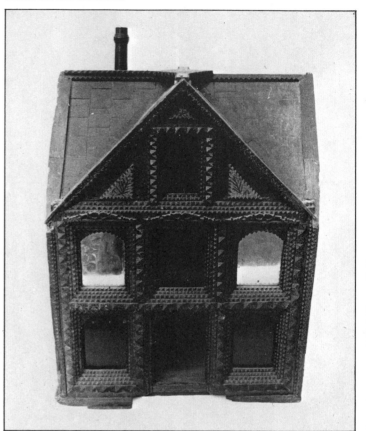

Child's chest of drawers with elaborate decoration, ceramic tile inlay, and bureau-top boxes; late 19th-early 20th century; $450-550. A little bit of everything.

Dollhouse, 20th century; $500-640. These are not common.

Child's toy cupboard, early 20th century; $300-375.

Set of doll furniture; 20th century; $175-245 the set.

Victorian-style overstuffed doll furniture; late 19th-early 20th century; $300-425 the set.

Victorian carved whimsey, late 19th century; $200-275.

Glass box for ship model in tramp art technique known as Crown of Thorns; early 20th century; $350-485.

Elaborate birdcage; late 19th-early 20th century; $600-850.

Unusual representation of a bridge, believed to be a model of the Brooklyn Bridge; late 19th century; $1,500-2,200. Unique.

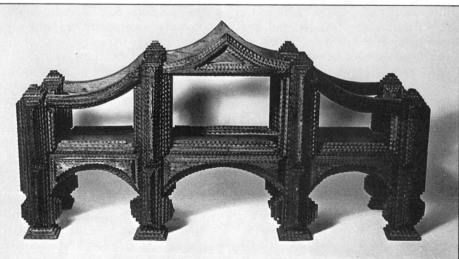

Scrimshaw

To a lover of the sea or to someone fascinated by the life of the early sailor, no antique art form better expresses this aspect of American folk history than scrimshaw. But good scrimshaw is rare and expensive, and reproductions and outright fakes abound.

Knowing something about the background of the craft will help the collector distinguish the good from the bad. Most simply stated, scrimshaw is bone—usually that of a whale—that has been carved or on which a design has been scratched or engraved. This work appears to have been done exclusively by sailors, who could easily obtain the preferred material and whose long sailing trips gave them ample leisure to perform this very detailed and time-consuming work; however, decorative carving of bone was not unique to American sailors, nor to sailors in general. It was known in prehistoric times; and in the modern era it was common in Africa and among the Eskimos and the natives of the South Pacific. Since American sailors had contact with these cultures, it is reasonable to assume that their work was influenced by earlier efforts.

The making of American scrimshaw took place over a relatively brief period, one that coincided with the most prosperous years of the whaling trade. Colonial sailors were seeking the whale throughout the eighteenth century, but there are few dated examples of scrimshaw from that era. A whalebone tooth, marked 1790, with an engraving of Boston harbor seems to be the earliest piece that is clearly native. The great bulk of existing specimens are from the period 1820 to 1890. By the later date, whaling had declined, and with it the whaler's art.

The relationship between whaling and scrimshaw is clear. Bone such as ivory that was available for carving and decoration in other cultures was not readily available to the sailor. He soon learned, however, that the teeth and jawbone of the sperm whale, as well as the pan bone (the hinged end of the jaw) of other whales, could be employed with equal effectiveness. Not all sailors, of course, sailed aboard whalers; but it was not difficult for those who didn't to buy or swap for the necessary material at a seaport. As long as the supply of bone remained constant, scrimshaw was made.

The creation of a piece of scrimshaw began with killing the whale. Once the usable portions of bone were removed from the carcass, they were divided among the crew. Each sailor scraped his bone clean with a sharp knife and then ground it smooth with sandpaper or sharkskin. It was then buffed to a high polish with ashes from the ship's fire. As final preparation, each was soaked to an appropriate softness for cutting.

Scrimshaw work itself included both carving and engraving. Many items, such as the tiny jagging or crimping wheels used to crimp the edges of pies, required shaping and fitting. After a piece was assembled, it might or might not be decorated. The lack of decoration on a piece of whalebone does not disqualify it as scrimshaw. Decoration was a long and tedious process feasible only because the crew on sailing ships had large blocks of free time in their work schedules.

The decoration found on scrimshaw is of two types. The earliest, and some of the best, was done freehand. The sailor simply scratched out a picture or various decorative devices on the bone surface and then gradually deepened the scratches. Pieces done in this manner may be crude, but they also often have the power and vitality of true folk art. More common is pattern-based decoration. This technique called for the sailor to paste to the bone surface an oiled pattern, usually made from a picture cut from a popular periodical; he would then carefully prick out with a steel pin those portions of the pattern he wished to incorporate into his design. The pinpricks would be joined and deepened by scratching, and a recognizable picture would emerge.

For this work the mariner would employ a surprisingly large array of tools. The jackknife was the basic tool, but iron needles of various sorts, awls, files, gimlets, and various polishing devices were also employed.

Once the line work was completed, the design would be darkened by rubbing grease, lampblack, or India ink into the scratches. Infrequently, other colors were used, most commonly red, green, and blue. Finer pieces or those designed as gifts might be further embellished by silver or wooden fittings or inlay in mother-of-pearl.

The subject matter found on decorated whalebone varies, but certain motifs predominate.

Many different scrimshaw items are available. Decorated teeth are in greatest demand, and these present the most problems for the collector. Throughout the twentieth century, various engravers have tried their hands at scrimshaw. Much of this work is intended to look old and is deliberately aged or is done on old blank teeth. Differences in style, methods of cutting, and lack of wear may help to distinguish the late from the early; but the best guide is an honest dealer.

Large pan-bone wall engravings, often of naval actions, are found, but they are rare and expensive. More readily and reasonably obtained are small worked objects, such as jagging wheels (of which there are a great number), corset busks, rulers, rolling pins, napkin rings, cane heads, whistles, needle cases, clothespins, sewing bodkins, and cribbage, chess, and checkers sets. Prices for these items will vary depending on the amount and quality of decoration. Rarer or more complex items such as bootjacks, swifts, and elaborate work or sewing boxes will be more expensive. Sailors' work items such as fids or marlinespikes, planes, sail seam rubbers, and measuring devices are not especially common and are much sought after by collectors of nautical antiques. Most of these items have not been reproduced, but the abundance of fakes in the scrimshaw field dictates that an enthusiast should proceed with caution. There are, fortunately, a number of good public scrimshaw collections, notably at the Kendall Whaling Museum in Sharon, Massachusetts; the New Bedford Whaling Museum in New Bedford, Massachusetts; and the Mystic Seaport Marine Historical Association in Mystic, Connecticut. Examination of examples in these collections will enable the collector to familiarize himself with the types and decorative techniques involved in scrimshaw and thus avoid making unwise purchases.

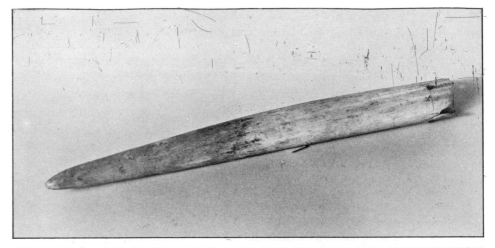

Old, uncarved walrus tusk; $120-180.
Bone of this sort is eagerly sought for
reproducing carving.

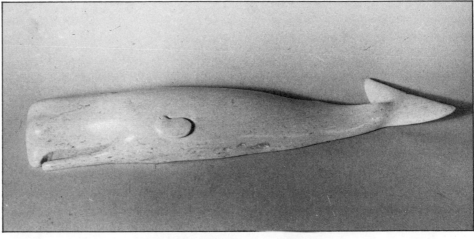

Extremely fine carved whale nearly 10"
long, whalebone; New England, 19th
century; $150-850. Possibly used as a
paperweight.

Pie crimper, or jagging wheel, in shape of
a whale, whalebone; late 19th century;
$250-375. Jagging wheels are among
the most common of scrimshaw; this is a
crude but strongly shaped piece.

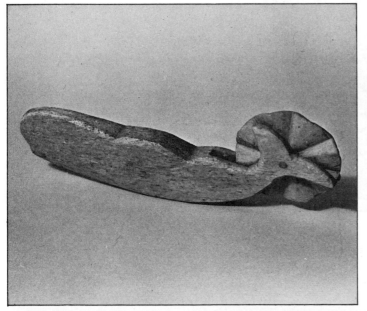

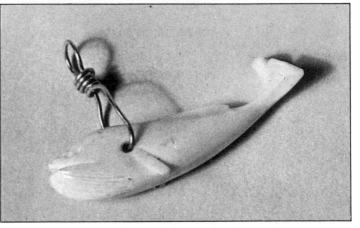

Watch fob or charm, whalebone or tooth
with gold-wire clasp; New England, late
19th century; $165-235.

Harpoon, whalebone, 6" long; late
19th-early 20th century; $365-435.

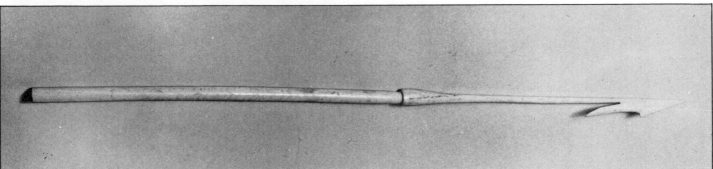

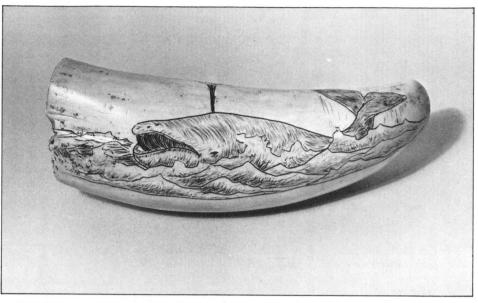

Needle box, whalebone; New England, or New York, late 19th century; $75-125.

Spouting whale, engraved on sperm-whale tooth; New England, mid-19th century; $900-1,300.

Whalebone stamp used to indicate lost whales in ship's log; New England, mid-19th century; $300-425. A very unusual piece.

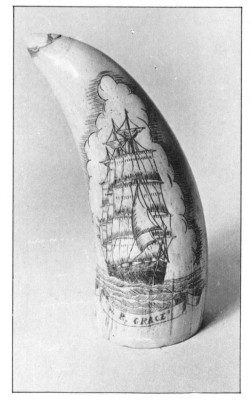

Whaling ship and whales, engraved on whale tooth and mounted on mahogany stand; New England, 19th century; $750-1,000.

Well-worked representation of the sailing ship **W.R. Grace,** engraved on whale tooth; East, 19th century; $1,500-2,200.

Battle between the **Essex** and the **Alert**, engraved on a whale tooth; New England, early 19th century; $1,750-2,350.

Representation of the Civil War battle between the U.S.S **Cumberland** and the Confederate States ram **Virginia**, engraved on whale tooth; East, 1860s; $1,500-2,000. This piece is more highly decorated than usual.

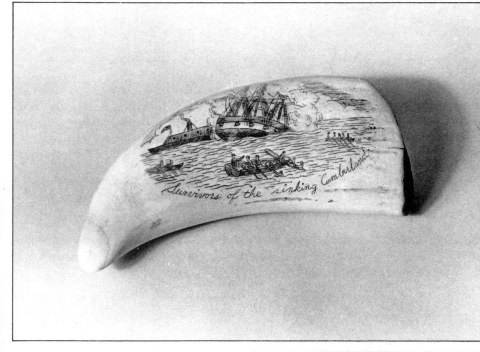

Depiction of the sinking of the **Cumberland** following its batle with the **Virginia**, engraved on sperm-whale tooth; East, 1860s; $1,100-1,600.

Portrait of Captain Maffitt of the Confederate Navy, commander of the warship **Florida**, engraved on whale tooth; Southeast, 1860s; $850-1,250.

Portrait of Admiral Farragut, Civil War naval hero, engraved on whale tooth; New England, 1860s; $900-1,400.

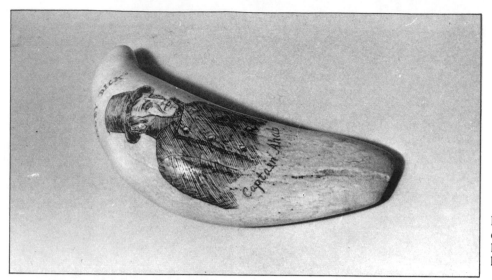

Representation of Captain Ahab, famous character in Herman Melville's **Moby Dick,** engraved on whale tooth; East, late 19th century; $175-245.

Seated Liberty or Columbia, engraved on whale tooth; New England, 19th century; $750-950.

Early, crudely engraved eagle and shield, on whale tooth; East, first half 19th century; $600-800.

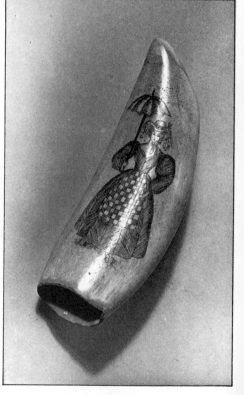

Representation of a Victorian lady, engraved on sperm-whale tooth; East, second half 19th century; $700-800.

Carved whistles, whalebone engraved with sailing ships; New England, 19th century; $275-400 each.

478

Unusual storage container of the type commonly called a ditty box, carved and engraved baleen and whalebone; New England, mid-19th century; $1,800-3,000. Baleen, a coarse, flexible membrane found in the whale's throat, was used in the construction of boxes and corset stays.

Well-carved cane head in the form of a fist, whalebone, with engraving; New England, mid-19th century; $650-950.

Watch fob engraved with a dolphin, whalebone or tooth mounted in silver; New England, 19th century; $200-325.

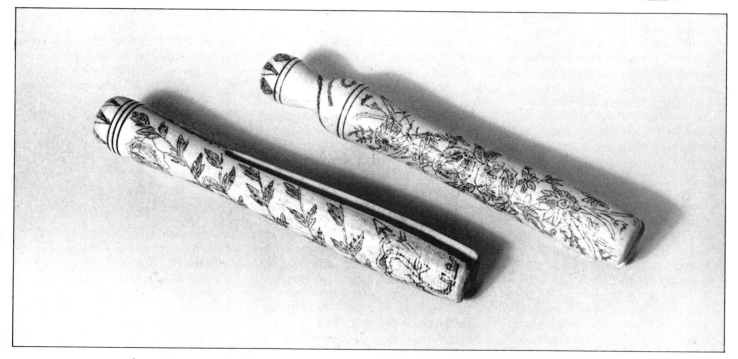

Intricately engraved clothespins, whalebone; East, 19th century; **Top:** $225-300. **Bottom:** $175-250.

Cane head or umbrella handle, whalebone with carved knot work and engraved representations of whales; New England, mid-19th century; $400-575.

Advertising Memorabilia

Although most advertising antiques date from the very late nineteenth and the twentieth centuries, the concept of advertising is much older. On this continent, the manufacturers of patent medicines were advertising their wares n local papers during the 1700s, and by 1810 they were marketing their concoctions in bottles embossed with company names.

Trade cards—small pieces of stiff paper printed with the name, address, and product of a craftsman—are the most abundant of the early advertising devices. Specimens from before 1850 are relatively uncommon, but by the end of the Civil War, the widespread use of lithography led to a proliferation of trade cards. Hand-colored lithographed trade cards exist in great numbers. Everything from whiskey to sewing machines was promoted in this manner, with the cards being handed out at stores or given away on the streets by boys. Prices are moderate, with only the earliest or rarest types selling for more than ten dollars apiece, and many cards are available for no more than a dollar.

Paper was utilized for other advertising devices. The boxes and other containers in which products were sold were printed with eye-catching designs. The labels on fruit and vegetable crates are particularly appealing to collectors. Cardboard fans, given out at country fairs and in hotels prior to the days of air conditioning, were used to promote anything from funeral parlors to ice-cream parlors. Manufacturers provided their distributors with large lithographed paper and cardboard posters extolling the virtues of their wares. Other paper memorabilia include beer coasters, seed packs, and a vast number of other decorated containers. Cigarette and cigar packs are a particularly popular and interesting area. Everything from beautiful ladies to war planes appears, and the collector's cards given away in some packs provide an added bonus.

It didn't take long for advertisers to figure out that if an attractive design and catchy slogan would draw business, a useful gadget would do even better. Such items were distributed at two levels. First, manufacturers sold, leased, or gave to their distributors such things as lamps, shop signs, and cigar lighters or cutters. These served a purpose, and

they also carried the painted or embossed slogan of the manufacturer. In addition, any number of household aids were given away to consumers or offered as premiums. The list is endless, including wooden cutting boards, tin scoops, bottle openers, buttonhooks, pokers, ice picks, pie plates, graters, goblets, and knickknack containers. All carried somewhere on their surface the advertiser's message, and all are today of great interest to collectors.

Tin advertising trays were widely distributed during the period 1890 to 1940. Beer, whiskey, soft drink, and mineral water makers provided them for their clients, and they came in several sizes. Large sixteen-inch wall plaques can be found as well as the more common twelve- to fourteen-inch serving trays and the tiny round or-oval tip trays. All bear lithographed designs or pictures and, of course, the name of the distributor. Perhaps the best known are Coke trays, which today may fetch several hundred dollars for certain hard-to-find examples.

The most outstanding example of the advertising antique—and perhaps the most familiar—is the cigar-store Indian. Trade figures of various sorts were quite common in the nineteenth century: purveyors of nautical goods might have a statue of a sailor outside the shop; a bakery might feature a jolly representation of the man in the white cap and apron. But by far the most popular were the hand-carved figures of Indian chiefs and maidens that were associated with tobacco shops. These were produced in large numbers during the period 1850 to 1890. The Indians, which were nearly life-size, were traditionally placed outside the shop, where they might attract the attention of passersby but where they were also exposed to wind and weather. Over the years, most have fallen prey to fire, theft, or general deterioration. The few hundred remaining examples are in great demand. The whereabouts of most are known, and when one changes hands, the sale price is usually around five thousand dollars.

One must be extremely wary of modern reproductions. High demand has led to sophisticated faking in this area, with expert carvers copying known genuine pieces and employing old wood and techniques. Cigar-store Indians should be purchased only from

reputable dealers who can provide an authenticated history and a money-back guarantee.

There were other figures, many of them Indians, that stood inside shops on a table or counter. These are usually two or three feet high and may be of plaster of Paris, iron, or wood. These are more common and less expensive than their big brothers.

If the seller of tobacco or liquor directed his advertising primarily to men, the lady of the house was certainly not ignored by other merchants. Perfume, cologne, and toiletries distributors regaled her with a variety of eye-catching enticements. Small mirrors for pocket or purse were popular. These were round, oval, or square and usually incorporated a lithograph of a beautiful and obviously wealthy woman.

As the twentieth century advanced and women added smoking cigarettes and wearing makeup to their life-styles, advertisers adjusted the pitch. Attractive lighters and cigarette cases carried the commercial message as did a variety of cosmetic cases. For those of more conservative taste, there were still the traditional give-aways. Maxwell House coffee offered cups and saucers emblazoned with the firm name. Egg beaters extolled the virtues of, naturally, an egg company.

Many of these small articles are inexpensive and offer an appealing area for collectors. Good mirrors can be found for less than twenty dollars, and advertising paperweights, at five to ten dollars apiece, seem somewhat underpriced considering their quality and the fact that many date from the nineteenth century. Compacts and lighters are somewhat higher but also seem to be a good buy at present.

If one is interested in an area that allows for an infinitely expanding collection, the previously mentioned trade cards are available. There are also tin tobacco tags. These were introduced in the 1880s by the Lorillard Company and were provided with prongs with which they were clamped into plugs of chewing tobacco. Originally, these tiny pieces of tin were intended by the manufacturers to be redeemed for various premiums. They were, however, interesting in their own right, often being cut in the shape of hatchets, stars, guns, crosses, and the like. Accordingly, they were frequently accumulated rather than redeemed, and large collections are often found.

Another major collector interest in this field is "tins," various lithographed tin containers not unlike the ones seen in stores today. The earlier examples are much more elaborately decorated, though, and contained such things as gunpowder, rat poison, and stove polish, none of which would be packaged in this way today. Shapes and sizes vary greatly, ranging from large round or bin-shaped coffee and tea dispensers to tiny rectangular cigarette boxes. The qualities that determine price are the degree of rarity and attractiveness. For most collectors, the latter is of major importance. Good lithographed design is a plus, and the quainter the better. Rarity can lead to very high prices, but only among a small group of very sophisticated collectors. For most, the decoration is the thing. Decorated tin containers of this sort have been on a spectacular price rise for the past five to ten years. Even certain recent tins, such as those of Sir Walter Raleigh pipe tobacco and du Maurier cigarettes, are worth a few dollars, and earlier examples frequently sell in the tens of dollars. A great deal of material is available here, though, and it is possible to amass a representative grouping without spending a great deal, particularly if one frequents yard sales and country fairs where tins often are sold for just a few cents.

Advertising antiques is one of the largest fields of antiques collecting, and the definition of the category is constantly being expanded. For example, attention is now for the first time being directed to lithographed box tops. Though fragile, these are a good buy. Old newspapers are filled with advertisements, many of them illustrated with woodcuts; and these are a virtually untouched area.

Lift-top tobacco box, lithographed tin; Illinois, late 19th century; $150-250.

Storage and dispensing box, lithographed tin; Midwest, late 19th century; $225-300. One of the best of its type, this is one of a series depicting the ships of America's famed "White Squadron." Shown here is the U.S.S. **Chicago.**

Cut-plug box with bail handle, lithographed tin; East, 20th century; $25-40.

Packing case, lithographed tin; New Jersey, late 19th century; $75-150.

Tobacco packing box, lithographed tin; Michigan, early 20th century; $75-110.

Tea canisters, lithographed tin; 20th century. **Left:** Wells Tea; New York; $25-40. **Center:** Tetley Tea; East, $5-15. **Right:** Family Tea; Midwest; $20-35.

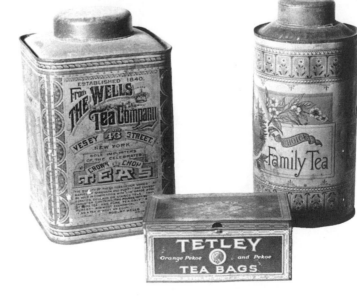

Peanut roaster, tin and sheet iron; East, early 20th century; $275-400.

Hinged coffee bin, lithographed tin, paper label, East, early 20th century; $45-65.

Storage canister, wood, lithographed paper label; New Jersey, late 19th century; $80-125.

Storage canister, wood, lithographed paper label; New York, late 19th century; $55-85.

483

Wall-hanging ruler, tin, reverse has 6″
rule; Valentine and Co., Varnish
Manufacturers, Delaware, late 19th
century; $25-55.

Cottolene shortening pie plate,
graniteware, white with blue trim; East,
early 20th century; $5-15.

Serving tray, lithographed tin; Midwest,
20th century; $65-90.

Glass paperweight with lithographed
advertisement of Babcock Manufacturing
Co., Connecticut, late 19th century;
$25-45.
Paperweights of this sort come in a wide
variety and are a good investment in the
advertiques area.

Advertising pin, lithographed tin; East, early 20th century; $30-55.

Serving tray, lithographed tin; New York, 20th century; $85-140.

Advertising pin, lithographed tin; New England, early 20th century; $40-65.

Pill boxes, lithographed cardboard; East, late 19th century. **Left:** Ma-Le-Na Liver Pills; $5-10. **Center:** Fellow's Liver Pills; $3-5. **Right:** Dr. White's Liver Pills; $10-15.

Handkerchief box, lithographed cardboard, ca. 1870; $10-20.

Tobacco packages, lithographed paper; late 19th-early 20th century. **Left:** Veteran; $10-20. **Center:** Lucky Curve; $40-65. **Right:** Luxury; $15-25.

Underwear packing box, lithographed cardboard; New England, ca. 1920; $20-35.

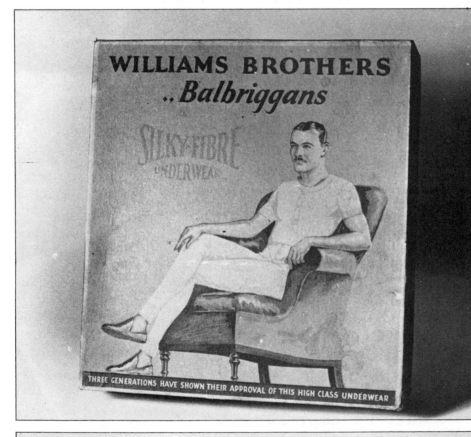

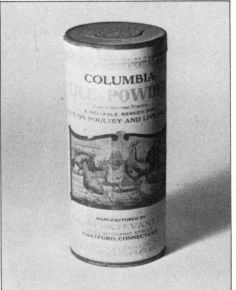

Columbia Flea Powder, lithographed paper, cardboard, and tin; Connecticut, early 20th century; $10-20.

Three examples of seed packages, lithographed paper; Midwest, 20th century; $10-15 each.

Packing boxes, wood, lithographed paper labels, Elate 19th century. **Above:** Defiance Mustard; $30-50. **Below:** Welcome Soap; $65-100. The more decorative the detail, the higher the price.

Packing box, wood, multicolored lithographed labels; New York, late 19th century; $85-145.

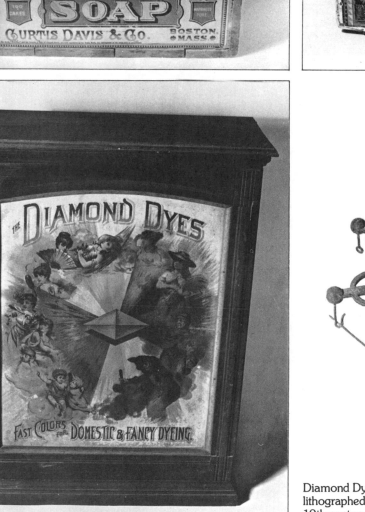

Revolving store rack, lithographed tin; New England, late 19th century; $200-325.

Diamond Dyes display case, lithographed tin and wood; East, late 19th century; $325-450. One of the most desirable advertiques.

Penny match dispenser, cast iron; New England, late 19th century; $275-400. Advertiser's name appears on side.

Rare cast-iron Jaxon Soap pot, gold paint; Midwest, late 19th century; $150-250.

Combination cigar cutter and lighter, cast iron and brass; New York, 19th century; $260-330. Another advertising store fixture.

Planter's Peanuts counter jar, East, 20th century; $125-250.

Store coffee grinder, cast-iron and lithographed tin; "Hunters' Cabinet Coffee Mill, Patent 1888," Midwest; $65-90.

Trade card, lithographed cardboard; Pennsylvania, late 19th century; $15-30. An example of inexpensive and very popular advetising items.

Trade cards, lithographed carboard; East, late 19th century. **Left:** Ammens Cough Syrup; $10-15. **Right:** Pinkham's medicines; $10-15.

Lithographed carboard trade cards in the form of sailing ships, issued by the Honest Cut Plug chewing tobacco company; New York, 19th century. **Left:** $20-30. **Right:** $25-35. These cards came with the tobacco and were intended to be collected in a series.

Ayer's trade card, lithographed cardboard; Lowell, Mass., late 19th century; $20-30. For obvious reasons, one of the most popular cards.

Trade cards, lithographed cardboard; late 19th century. **Left:** Brown's Bitter; $10-15. **Right:** Melvin's Nerve Liniment; $5-10.

Trade cards, lithographed cardboard; late 19th century. **Left:** Pond's Extract; $5-10. **Right:** Morse Dock Root Syrup; $10-15. Bottle collectors often collect proprietary medicine trade cards such as these as "go withs."

Trade cards, lithographed cardboard; New England, late 19th century. **Left:** Hire's Cough Care; $10-15. **Center:** Florida Water; $5-10. **Right:** Tarrant's Aperient; $5-10.

Trade card, lithographed cardboard; New York, late 19th century; $10-20. Merchants as well as manufacturers issued trade cards.

490

Vinegar jug, stoneware; New Jersey, late 19th century; $100-150.

Stamford Hotel spittoon, stoneware; Stamford, N.Y., ca. 1870; $200-275.

Maccoboy Snuff jar, stoneware with applied lithographed label; New Jersey, 19th century; $75-135.

Covered cheese crock, stoneware; Wisconsin, 20th century; $5-10.

Advertising picture for Weyman's Snuff, lithographed paper on board; Pennsylvania, 19th century; $300-450. One of the best of its type.

Sample bean pot, redware; Massachusetts, late 19th-early 20th century; $20-35. Advertising pottery in redware is uncommon.

Advertising picture, lithographed paper on board, Midwest, 19th century; $250-325.

Advertising picture, paper on board; Midwest, late 19th century; $400-650.

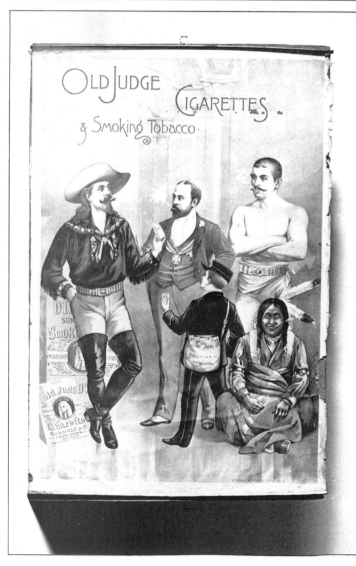

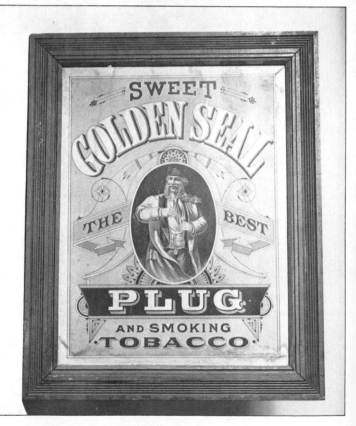

Advertising picture, paper on board; East, late 19th century; $200-285.

Illustration from lithographed paper advertising calendar, New York, late 19th century; $450-700. Figures include Buffalo Bill, Prince Albert, John L. Sullivan, and an unknown Indian.

Advertising picture, lithographed paper on wood; New York, ca. 1891; $275-375.

Advertising picture, lithographed paper on wood; East, late 19th century;

Advertising picture, lithographed paper on wood; Massachusetts, 1884; $325-450.

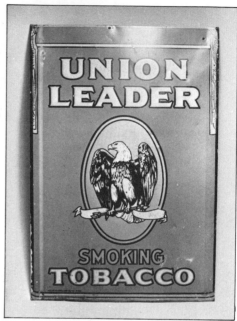

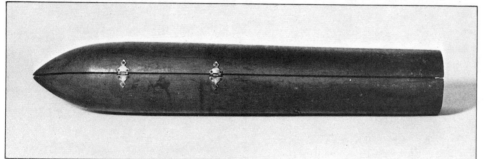

Trade sign, sheet iron with traces of old paint; East, 1825; $1,000-1,700. Figure on horse is believed to be Andrew Jackson.

Barber pole, polychromed wood; New York State, ca. 1880; $550-900.

Counter-top-size cigar-store Indian, plaster of Paris; East, early 20th century; $275-450.

Hand-carved life-size cigar-store Indian, polychrome paint; New England, ca. 1880; $9,000-14,000. These figures are rare and in demand.

Lithographed paper advertising poster for the Boston Rubber Shoe Co.; ca. 1900; $165-195.

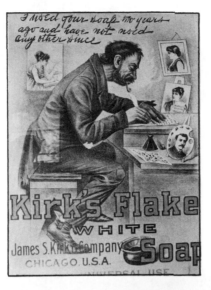

Lithographed paper advertising sign for Kirk's Flake Soap; 1880-90; $500-650. This sign is an extremely rare example of an early advertising poster.

Lithographed paper advertising poster for Knox Gelatine; ca. 1920; $95-145. This poster was intended for display in a trolley car.

Lithographed cardboard advertising poster; 1890-1900; $375-500. This rare poster was intended to promote the mill at Wahoo, Nebraska.

Lithographed carboard advertising sign for Arbuckles' Ariosa Coffee; ca. 1893; $450-550.

Right: Top to bottom: Reverse-glass painting of Statue of Liberty; Massachusetts, ca. 1890; $150-250. Grain sieve; New York, early 20th century; $35-50. Decorated candlebox, pine, New York, late 19th century; $150-250. Small chest, pine, old red paint; Vermont, late 19th century; $75-110. Lap desk, pine, old red and black paint; Connecticut, late 19th century; $70-95. Country side chair, hickory, old blue paint; New Hampshire, late 19th century; $75-150.

Opposite top: Harvest table, pine; Pennsylvania, ca. 1830; $2,000-3,500. Four of a set of eight matching fancy chairs, painted pine and hickory; Pennsylvania, ca. 1860; $2,500-4,000 the set. **Opposite bottom:** Library steps, oak; early 20th century; $175-250. Victorian double-drawer library desk, oak; late 19th century; $300-500. **On wall:** A group of tin and paper advertising signs; late 19th-early 20th century; $100-250. LEFT: Pewter cupboard, pine, old gray-green paint; late 18th-early 19th century; $1,300-1,700. A simple but good New England example.

499

Above right: Country Sheraton sofa; New England, early 18th century; $850-1,100. Fine pictorial hooked rug, wool on burlap; New York, late 19th century; $700-950. **Right:** Cupboard, pine and maple, old grain paint; Pennsylvania, mid-19th century; $3,500-5,500. A nicely made example of a common piece. OPPOSITE: Open-top hutch, pine, old blue paint; New Jersey, mid-19th century; $900-1,300. Cricket stool, pine; New England, mid-19th century; $60-90.

Right: Middle shelves: Glass canning jars; mid-19th century; $10-75. **Bottom shelf:** Redware and stoneware crockery; mid-19th century; $50-250. **Left, on wall:** Yellow tole salt holder; early 20th century; $50-75. All East. **Below right: Left to right:** Cupboard, pine, old black grain paint on red; East, mid-19th century; $550-750. Country bannister-back chair, pine and ash; New York, late 19th century; $50-80. Pie safe, pine, old red paint; East, mid-19th century; $650-850. **Opposite:** Pine harvest table; Pennsylvania, 1840-55; $1,200-1,500. Well-turned ladder-back side chairs, old paint; New England, 1830-50; $800-1200 the set; PAGE 264: Victorian country mirror, painted pine; East, late 19th century; $90-125. Manganese-spotted redware bowl; New England, ca. 1850; $150-200. Lamp, brass and glass; early 20th century; $60-85.

Country Empire desk, pine and maple; Pennsylvania, ca. 1840; $450-650. Ladder-back chair, pine and maple traces of old red paint, New England, ca. 1830; $650-850.

502

Lithographed cardboard advertising poster for J.M. Doud and Co.; 1900-10; $375-475. One of the many posters to utilize children as attention getters.

Lithographed paper advertising poster and duplicate trade card for Eagle Brand Condensed Milk; c. 1899. Poster; $275-350. Trade Card; $5-10.

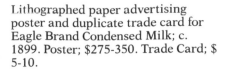

Lithographed paper advertising sign for the Northwestern Yeast Co.; 1920-25; $125-175.

Lithographed tin advertising sign for Lipton's Cocoa; 1920-30; $95-155. This sign shows evidence of modern advertising techniques.

Lithographed paper advertising poster; 1910-15; $85-135. Posters such as this were made with blank spaces for advertisers' names. They would then be printed to order.

Lithographed carboard trade cards; ca. 1890; $5-10 each. **Left:** Glenn's Sulpher Soap. **Center:** Radway's Ready Relief (a pain killer). **Right:** Hoyt's German Cologne.

Lithographed tin advertising poster for Royal Baking Powder; ca. 1920; $155-235. Incorporates adjustable butter and egg prices.

Lithographed paper advertising poster for the Metropolitan Life Insurance Co.; 1898; $100-115. Incorporates a calendar. Calendars were among the most popular advertising giveaways.

Lithographed cardboard advertising poster for the Stillman Bottling Co; 1915; $25-45. Includes a calendar and cutouts. A smaller and less expensive calendar of the sort often available to collectors.

Lithographed paper advertising calendar, one of a set of four produced to promote Buster Brown Shoes; 1906; $300-375 the set.

Lithographed tin advertising sign for Whistle soda pop; 1920-30; $150-200.

Lithographed tin advertising sign for Old Fashion Root Beer; 1930-35; $85-135.

Lithographed tin advertising sign for Batey's Lemonade; 1930-40; $55-75. Tin signs of this sort were usually hung outside a shop. Damage substantially reduces value.

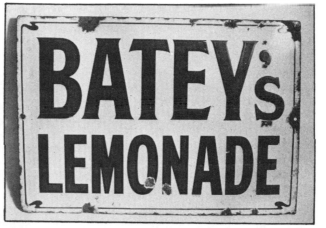

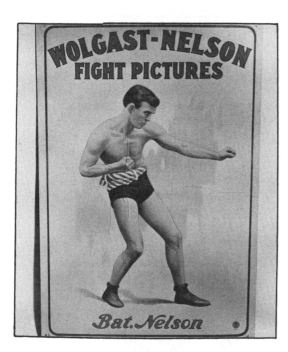

Advertising sign in gold leaf on red glass background; ca. 1940; $85-145. This sign directed people to the hosiery department in the nationwide chain of Woolworth stores.

Lithographed paper poster indicating registration of a store under the National Recovery Act; 1934; $50-75. These posters were common throughout the United States during the 1930s.

Lithographed paper poster advertising motion pictures of a championship boxing match; 1920-30; $175-215. Posters promoting sporting events are popular with contemporary collectors.

507

Reverse-glass advertising sign for
Buster Brown Shoes; 1920-30;
$275-350. This sign is in far better
condition than most glass signs.

Reverse-glass advertising sign for
Beech-Nut Fruit Drops; 1930-35;
$135-185.

Lithographed tin advertising cutout
for D.S. Brown & Co.; 1880-90;
$3,500-5,000. The Jolly
Washerwoman-the only example
known. This counter-top
promotional device is the top of the
line in advertiques.

Lithographed tin string dispenser
advertising Swift's Pride Soap; ca.
1908; $1,800-2,400. Another
one-of-a-kind advertique, this
example is in excellent condition.

Lithographed tin match safe
advertising Buster Brown Bread;
1900-05; $265-325.

Lithographed paper advertising fans;
1920-30. **Left to right:** $20-30;
$15-25; $; $10-15. Because of their
fragile nature, advertising fans are
relatively uncommon, but they
remain inexpensive and a good buy.

Photograph-on-glass advertising thermometer; 1930-40; $20-40.

Thermometer advertising Wool Soap; 1925-35; $50-75. Thermometers are of little interest to many collectors because they are usually not very colorful.

Lithographed tin tip tray for Coca-Cola; 1910-20; $110-160. Coca-Cola collectibles are particularly popular.

Lithographed tin tip trays; 1900-20. **Top:** Baker's Cocoa; $65-95. **Center:** Dorne's Carnation Chewing Gum; $35-45 **Bottom:** Fairy Soap; $60-85.

Lithographed carboard washing-powder boxes; 1920-35. **Left:** Grandma's; $20-35. **Center:** Fun-to-Wash; $45-75. **Right:** Gold Dust; $40-65. Watch for reproductions of Gold Dust box!

Lithographed tin and cardboard cleanser and starch containers. **Left:** Chic; ca. 1925; $15-25. **Center left:** Polly Prim; 1920-30; $15-20. **Center right:** Wyandotte; 1930-35; $35-55. **Right:** Electric Starch; ca. 1883; $25-35.

Lithographed tin talcum powder tins; 1900-10. **Left:** Perfumed Violet; $55-65. **Center:** Pompeia; $45-60. **Right:** Yankee; $145-180. The Yankee container is the only known example.

Glass bottles in the Art Deco style with lithographed paper labels; 1925-35. **Left:** Brilliantine; $5-10. **Center:** Carminade; $15-25. **Right:** Lily of the Valley; $15-20.

Lithographed tin coffee containers; 1910-20. **Left:** Bunker Hill; $50-75. **Center top:** Kamargo; $70-120. **Center bottom:** Gillies; $75-95. **Right:** Rose Bud; $25-40. Rose Bud has a paper label.

Lithographed tin storage bin for pepper; 1900-10; $175-245.

Wooden storage and shipping box with lithographed paper labels for Austin & Graves Biscuit; ca. 1900; $95-135

Wooden shipping barrel with lithographed paper label for Keystone Mince Meat; 1920-25; $45-65. Barrels of this sort are seldom found intact.

Beauty aid containers; 1925-35. **Left:** Lithographed carboard box for Three Flowers Vanishing Cream; $10-15. **Center:** Lithographed tin for Three Flowers Face Powder; $20-30. **Right:** cardboard box for Hair Youth; $10-20.

Lithographed tin cookie box with a portrait of the actress Gloria Swanson as an Indian maiden; 1930-35; $65-95. This cover was designed by famous illustrator Henry Clive.

Pressed-glass storage jar for National Biscuit Co.; 1915-20; $90-120. An attractive and well-formed collectible.

Glass and enameled-steel penny peanut machine; by Northwestern Co.; Morris, Ill.; 1925-35; $135-165.

Oak and cast-iron Baby Grand penny boubble-gum machine; 1930-40; $175-235. Candy and gum machines are fast becoming prime collectibles.

Lithographed metal penny chewing gum machine; 1935-40; $95-135.

Lithographed tin and steel dispenser for Sweet Chocolate; by National Automatic Vending machine Co.; Philadelphia, Pa.; 1930-40; $80-120.

Glass, oak, and lithographed tin storage container for Mansfield's Pepsin Gum; 1885-90; $200-275.

Uneeda Biscuit Boy advertising doll,
bisque head in yellow coat with
black compostion boots; 1915-20;
$350-475. Lithographed paper poster
for N.B.C. (National Biscuit Co.)
products; 1920-30; $100-150.
Advertising dolls are rare and in
demand.

ZU ZU Ginger Snaps advertising
dolls; ca. 1915; $165-245 each. ZU
ZU lithographed paper advertising
poster; 1920-30; $115-155.

ithographed steel toy delivery truck
dvertising Tag Soap; 1915-25;
15-305. This was probably
tended as a giveaway.
thographed Tag soap wrapper;
ith original bar of soap; 1915-25;
-8.

Lithographed tin candy containers;
dated 1914; $35-65 each.

Posters, Postcards, and Other Printed Material

The amount of antique paper material of interest to collectors is so extensive that most people specialize in one particular type, be it posters, postcards, or magazines. As might be expected from its fragile nature, most collectible paper is of rather recent vintage (post-1900), though a surprisingly large number of earlier examples do exist.

The earliest widely collected form is the broadside, a single sheet of rag-based paper crudely printed in black and often decorated with primitive wood-block designs—a coach and horse team, for example, on a sheet advertising a stage line. Like the modern poster, broadsides were intended to convey quickly a brief message; they were passed out on the street or pasted up on walls, and few survived for any length of time. As a consequence, they are not common today and, when offered on the market, can command a good price. The form generally disappeared with the widespread use of lithography, and most specimens found today date from before 1850.

Lithography was invented in 1796 by Alois Senefelder. Despite its advantages over the earlier art of engraving, as a quicker and cheaper means of reproduction, it spread slowly, and it was not used to any extent in the United States until after 1825. The earliest lithographs were simple monochromatic line drawings, usually in black, but it soon became customary to add color. This was done by hand on a production line, where women and older children, seated at a long table, would each tint certain areas of a lithograph before passing it on to the next person to tint certain other areas. It is rare in early pieces to find more than four colors: gold, black, blue, and green.

The first known American lithographers were Barnet and Doolittle of New York City, active from 1821 to 1822. They were followed by a host of imitators. By far the best known of them is the firm of Currier and Ives, which was established in 1833 by Nathaniel Currier, joined by James Ives as partner in 1857, and flourished in New York City until 1906.

The secret of Currier and Ives's success was two-fold: they employed the best artists available, and they had an uncanny knack for spotting what the public would like. In the days before radio, television, and journalistic photography, they illustrated for America the major events of the period: the Civil War, the opening of the Indian Territories, the glories of the great American West, and the triumphs of leading sports figures from boxers to horses. They also published religious lithographs and nostalgic scenes, such as the beloved *Home for Thanksgiving*. Today, some Currier and Ives lithographs are worth hundreds or even thousands of dollars—not bad for a mass-produced item.

In collecting Currier and Ives prints, one should keep in mind that the popular (and valuable) prints have been reproduced many times, so that it is not always easy to distinguish the originals from the later prints. Furthermore, the name alone, even on an original print, is not enough to ensure a profitable investment. Certain Currier and Ives lithographs, primarily the religious scenes, don't sell. They can be had at auction for ten or twelve dollars and are worth little more retail.

As popular and long-lived as they were, Currier and Ives were just one of many nineteenth-century lithograph publishers. Peter Mavrick, H. R. Robinson, Imbert and Company of New York; Moors Lithography Company of Boston; and Edward Webber of Baltimore, to name but a few, also produced many high-quality lithographs, which are often available at a fraction of the cost of a Currier and Ives. A form particularly in demand, but still inexpensive, is the fashion illustration found in such early magazines as *Godey's Lady's Book*. Hand-tinted lithographs, they accurately portray women's and children's styles for several decades of the nineteenth century, and they are of great interest to students of design. At a later date, when the invention of chromolithography made it possible to print a full-color illustration rather than coloring by hand, lithographers such as Louis Prang of Boston turned out a whole array of multicolored lithographed items, from framed mottoes for the home to postcards. All are highly collectible today.

The development of chromolithography also gave rise to the advertising poster of the twentieth century, a form that came into its own during World War I. At that time, posters ranging in size from the standard single sheet (twenty-eight inches by forty inches) to twenty-four-sheet billboard fillers were widely used in publicizing the four great Liberty Loan campaigns. Such well-known artists of the era as Charles Gibson and James Montgomery Flagg collaborated in the creation of some two thousand different designs from which, it is estimated, over 20 million posters were printed. A similar effort during the Second World War produced another imposing array of political posters. While the later examples are not as yet widely collected, World War I posters are in great demand. Some rare or particularly well-done pieces go for several hundred dollars, and even ordinary ones bring from twenty-five to seventy-five dollars if in good condition.

In no area did chromolithography have greater effect than in that of postcard art. Prior to the twentieth century, postcards, while important as a means of communication, were severely limited in their use by postal regulations. When the Post Office Department in 1907 amended its rules to allow writing a message on the back of the penny postcard (where previously only an address was permissible), the door was opened to rapid expansion of the postcard industry. During the years from 1907 to 1918, the height of the craze, thousands of different colored postcards were produced, many by German lithographers for sale in this country.

Collectors have been actively seeking these cards for some years, and now postcards may be said to be one of the more popular collecting categories. Most enthusiasts favor a single type of card—patriotics, for example, which were commonly exchanged on the Fourth of July, Lincoln's or Washington's Birthday, and Memorial Day. At present, no less than five hundred different patriotic designs are known. Disaster cards offer another interesting area. They were reproduced primarily from photographs and offer views of such assorted unpleasantnesses as the Johnstown Flood, the San Francisco Earthquake, and a variety of fires and train wrecks. On a more peaceful and bucolic note, there are scenes from the national forests or depictions of famous buildings and historic sites. The categories may be limited, but the number of postcards seems limitless, with new finds being made constantly in every area. Best of all, most cards can still be obtained for a dollar or two, or even less, except for those with rare views or those done and signed by such well-known postcard artists as Bernhardt Wall and Frances Brundage.

For many people the most interesting type of paper memorabilia is the greeting card, foremost among which is the valentine. The tradition of giving valentines to loved ones on Valentine's Day is very old. At least as early as 1750, Americans were exchanging handmade cards exhibiting fine scissor-cut decoration and elaborate watercolors. Valentines from this period are, of course, rare; but commercially manufactured cards, which first appeared in the 1840s, are generally available. Though some valentines made before 1900 were engraved, the great majority were lithographed and then carefully tinted by hand. They were never inexpensive, even when new. T. W. Strong of New York, a major producer in the 1840s, advertised in 1848 that he had cards "to suit all tastes and customs, prices ranging from six cents to ten dollars." This was at a time when a working man might make no more than a dollar for a day's labor!

As the nineteenth century advanced and handwork gave way to mechanical construction, valentines became increasingly more elaborate. In the 1850s, tiny daguerreotypes or tintype photographs were sometimes added to the cards. Silk pillow centers and textile netting appeared in the 1860s; and later Victorian examples, from about 1870 to 1890, might feature stand-up figures, mechanical devices, feathers, and mother-of-pearl inlay. The less common

and more elaborate of these valentines are far from inexpensive. Fortunately, though, it is possible for the collector to acquire attractive lacy valentines with interesting features for prices seldom in excess of twenty dollars. Earlier examples and those made by hand will, of course, go for much more.

On a somewhat more prosaic level are paper materials printed for commercial purposes, such as almanacs and trade catalogs. Almanacs contain a calendar along with a variety of useful information about the weather, care for illnesses, cooking, and any number of other concerns. Since they were nearly all advertising gimmicks issued by patent medicine firms, they contain a plethora of testimonials from satisfied users of whatever concoction might have sponsored the publication. As such, they are historical documents that provide interesting insight into the customs and attitudes of earlier generations, and they are worth preserving. Prices at present are extremely reasonable, particularly since some of the cover illustrations are superb.

Trade catalogs are an even more important piece of Americana. It was not until late in the eighteenth century that American businesses were wealthy enough to produce catalogs, and only after 1850 did these publications appear in any abundance. Even then, they were usually jobbers' or distributors' catalogs, since few manufacturers had an extensive enough inventory to justify printing a catalog for the public. Catalogs are significant both as research tools and for their often high-quality engravings or lithographs. Their appeal to the general public is evident from the spectacular sales of the reproductions of early Sears-Roebuck catalogs. In general, the most valuable catalogs are first editions: the first ice-box catalog, the first color-illustrated catalog, the first catalog by a prominent firm such as Montgomery-Ward. There is much interest in this field at present, and prices are climbing steadily. On the other

hand, many catalogs undoubtedly lie yet undiscovered, and it is possible to pick up good examples at country shops or in box lots to be found at auctions.

Cookbooks were also given away in large quantities as an advertising device. They contained recipes as well as household hints and cures and often were illustrated by such well-known commercial artists as Maxfield Parrish and Grace Drayton, whose Campbell Kids worked for Campbell Soup. Since Jell-O alone produced a quarter million recipe books during the period 1900 to 1925, most types cannot be said to be rare. Nevertheless, the high quality of their illustrations and the historical or social insights they provide make them a valuable addition to any paper collection.

Illustrations are also the key to the increasing interest in old magazines. Such publications as *The Country Gentleman* and *The Delineator*, which could hardly be given away a few years ago, are valued today for their fine illustrations and sell for three dollars or more apiece. If the cover happens to be by an artist such as Norman Rockwell, the magazine may go for fifteen dollars. Cover art is, in fact, becoming so important that desirable covers are being framed and sold like prints.

Beyond the realm of literature but within the realm of paper is the bandbox, a storage box popular during the period 1800 to 1850. Usually oval, bandboxes were used to hold such articles as hats, sashes, and collars. They were made of wood or cardboard and were covered with lithographed or block-printed paper much like wallpaper (and frequently made by wallpaper manufacturers, though to a different size). The current interest in American bandboxes and the resulting high prices are explained both by their extremely attractive colors and by the fact that they often portray early American scenes—particularly those illustrating various modes of transportation—current at the time the boxes were made.

Hand-tinted lithograph of the wreck of the steamboat **Swallow;** New York, ca. 1845; $475-650.

Printed broadside; New York, 1841; $275-350. Though abundant in their day, these broadsides are now uncommon.

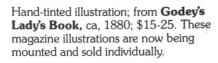

Hand-tinted illustration; from **Godey's Lady's Book,** ca, 1880; $15-25. These magazine illustrations are now being mounted and sold individually.

Chromolithograph; by Prang, New York, late 19th century; $50-80.

Hand-tinted lithograph; by Kellogg and Thayer, New York, ca. 1860; $35-55. Though of the same genre as Currier and Ives prints, these sentimental lithographs have attracted less attention.

Chromolithograph of the centennial of the British evacuation of New York City; by J. Koehler, New York, ca. 1883; $250-400.

Chromolithograph motto; East, late 19th century; $20-35. Framed mottoes of this sort are attracting collector interest.

"Spirit of America," by Howard Chandler Christy, 20"x30"; 1919; $150-225. An extremely well-done poster of the World War I era by a famous artist.

"Keep Him Free," by Charles L. Bull, 20"x30", ca. 1919; $175-235.
One of the most famous of all American posters from the World War I era.

"Weapons for Liberty," by J.C. Leyendecker, 20"x30"; World War I era; $140-235.

"Boys and Girls!" by James Montgomery Flagg, 20"x30"; World War II poster, ca. 1943; $115-155.

"This Is the Enemy," 20"x30"; World War II poster, ca. 1943; $70-95.

World War II poster; early 1940s; $50-75. War-time posters are increasing in value.

"Years of Dust," by Ben Shahn, 25"x38"; ca. 1936; $2,500-3,200. One of the finest posters created in the 20th century, by the well-known artist.

Advertising poster for **Harper's** magazine, by Edward Penfield; 12"x18"; 1895; $145-215.

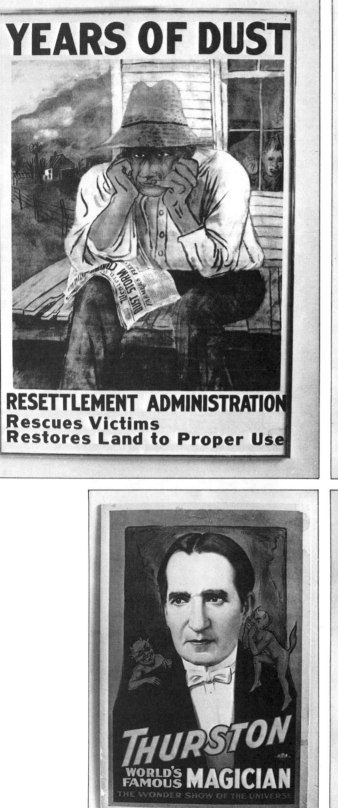

"Thurston, World's Famous Magician," 27"x41"; $200-275. A show business poster typical of the late 19th-early 20th centuries.

Advertising poster for the book **Miss Traumerei,** by Ethel Reed, one of the early female illustrators, 14"x22"; ca. 1895; $225-275.

Advertising poster for Chesterfield cigaretts, by C.E. Chambers, 14"x30"; ca. 1929; $85-115,

Three late-19th century postcards of a sort now sought by collectors. **Left to right:** $3-5; $2-4; $1-3.

Well-done Art Nouveau greeting postcard; ca. 1900; $3-6.

Three good examples of the greeting postcards popular in the 19th and early 20th century. **Left and center:** $1-2 each. **Right:** by Francis Brundage; $4-8.

Scenic postcards; late 19th-early 20th century; $1-3.

Seasonal and novelty postcards; late 19th-early 20th century; $1-4.

Seasonal greeting postcards, early 20th century; $1-3 each except lower right, by Frances Brundage; $4-8.

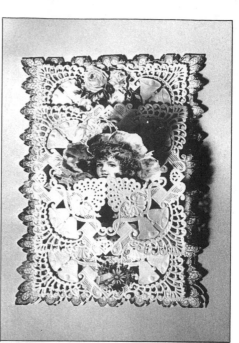

Punched gilt valentine paper; late 19th century; $15-40.

Lacy valentine with chromolithographed insert; 1880; $30-50.

Excellent lacy valentine with chromolithographed inserts; 1870-80; $40-65.

Lacy valentine with chromolithographed inserts, ca. 1870-80; $35-60.

Lacy valentine with chromolithographed inserts; 1870; $35-60.

Lacy valentine designed to hold sachet; 1860-70; $35-55.

Embossed lace and mesh valentine with gilt inserts; 1850; $55-85.

Lacy valentine with Chromolithographed inserts; 1880-90; $20-35.

Embossed lacy valentine; 1880-90; $30-45.

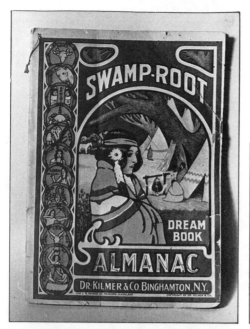

Almanac; by Dr. Kilmer's Swamp-Root patent medicine; New York, early 20th century; $10-20.

Recipe book, by Crisco, the sort given away as an advertising device; early 20th century; $5-10.

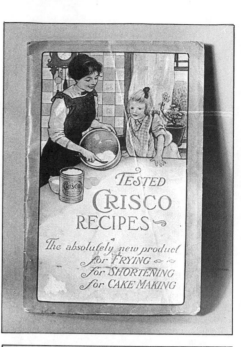

Joke book given away as an advertising device by the Alka Seltzer Company; ca. 1924; $5-10.

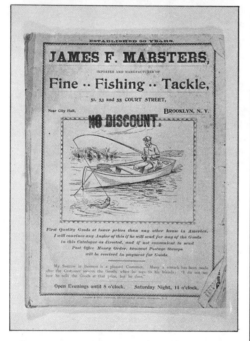

Trade catalog from a fishing tackle manufacturer; New York, late 19th century; $65-85.

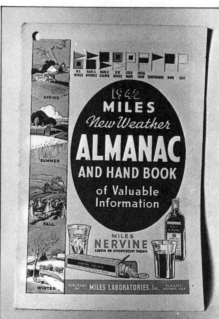

Almanac; by Miles Nervine patent medicine; Indiana, 1942; $5-10.

Trade catalog; from E.T. Barnum Iron and Wire Works, Michigan, ca. 1923; $25-35.

Cosmopolitan: 1913; $4-7.

Women's Home Companion; 1922; $5-12. Their elaborate covers and interesting illustrations have made early 20th century magazines a paper collector's favorite.

Leslie's Illustrated Weekly, Newspaper; 1914; $6-10.

Interior illustration from **Leslie's;** 1914; $6-10.

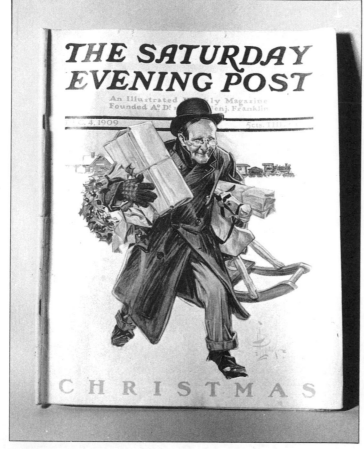

The Saturday Evening Post; 1909; $3-7.

McCall's Magazine; $4-8.

The Country Gentleman; 1921; $8-12.

The Country Gentleman, with cover by Norman Rockwell; 1921; $15-20. A Rockwell cover boosts the price of any magazine.

The Delineator; 1911; $5-9.   **Collier's;** 1904; $3-7.   **Good Housekeeping;** 1926; $4-7.

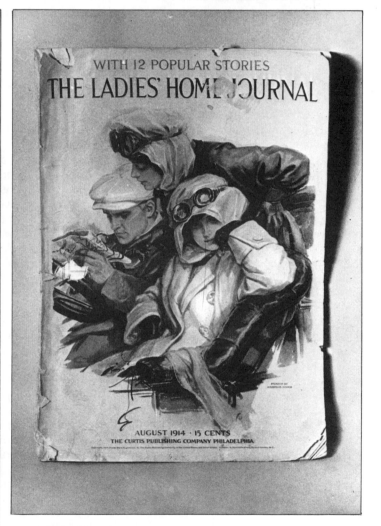

The Ladies' Home Journal; 1914;
$5-8. This magazine frequently carried
Kewpie-doll cutouts, and their presence
brings the price per copy to $40-65.

Harper's Bazar; 1910; $9-10.

527

Photographic Memorabilia

The collecting of photographic memorabilia—photographs, cameras, and auxiliary equipment—is a rather recent American interest. There were few large collections prior to 1900, and the majority of the important collections have been assembled since the 1930s.

Photography itself can hardly be called new. Daguerreotypes, the most popular form of photograph collected today, were developed in 1839 by the Frenchman Louis Daguerre. Though few daguerreotypes were made before 1841, the art was well developed by 1853, when it was estimated that 3 million such images were produced annually in the United States alone.

The daguerreotype is a photograph taken by exposing a silver-coated copper plate in the camera. This plate is a positive image, not a negative; since no duplicate prints can be made of it, each daguerreotype is unique. Moreover, like a mirror image, the daguerreotype image is the reverse of what the camera sees, a characteristic shared by the later ambrotypes and tintypes. Techniques for coloring or tinting the images were introduced as early as 1842, and many show such features as pink cheeks and lips, but the color is often poor. Daguerreotypes are fragile, and vast numbers have been destroyed, either through carelessness or in an effort simply to obtain the minute amount of copper in each plate. They must be handled with care and cannot be cleaned or polished.

Daguerreotypes were housed in small hinged cases usually made of wood covered with embossed paper or, at a later date, a plasticlike substance mistakenly referred to as gutta-percha. Case sizes were varied to fit the images, which ranged from one and one-half by one and three-quarter inches, the ninth plate, to eight and one-half by thirteen inches, the double whole plate. In general, the larger the image, the more valuable is the daguerreotype, since the great majority was quite small.

Ambrotypes, which were invented by F. Scott Archer of England in 1852, differ from the earlier daguerreotypes only in that the image is taken, or "secured," on glass rather than on a copper plate. To most people the two products look much alike. They can be distinguished, however, by holding an example of each up to a bright light and turning it slowly to the side. The daguerreotype will reflect the light, while the ambrotype will not. Like its predecessor, the ambrotype is a unique positive image, not a negative, and cannot be duplicated. In order to be seen, the image must be backed with varnish or black paint.

Ambrotypes were somewhat cheaper to produce than daguerreotypes, and they were extremely popular during the period 1854 to 1865. Among the vast quantity made were the photographs in the first "rogues gallery" established by the New York City Police Department in the 1860s.

The prices of daguerreotypes and ambrotypes depend on several factors. As previously mentioned, larger examples are hard to come by and command a higher price. Subject matter is also very important. Images of famous persons can be very valuable—in 1973, a half-plate daguerreotype of Edgar Allan Poe sold for nine thousand dollars. Most images, though, are of ordinary men and women. But something may take them out of the ordinary and thus elevate the price; this could be the clothing the subject is wearing, some props, or anything else that might reveal information about the person. Photographs of cowboys, Indians, workmen with tools, gold miners, soldiers or other men with weapons, and nudes, for example, are all eagerly sought. A few people even share the Victorians' morbid preoccupation with death and collect images of the dead.

Far less common than likenesses of individuals are cased daguerreotype or ambrotype views of buildings or localities. Such views of Washington, D.C, were first discovered in the 1970s, but so far none of New York City has been found, though it is known that several series on the city were prepared. In perhaps no other area of antiques does such a distinct possibility exist of finding something truly rare and valuable.

Other elements may affect price to a lesser extent than those so far discussed. The work of certain photographers who have obtained posthumous fame commands a premium. Mathew Brady, for instance, the great Civil War photographer, placed his name on thousands of images, which are now of substantial value; some even remain to be discovered. The photographer's name generally appears on the front matting or the case of an ambrotype or daguerreotype, and new acquisitions should always be examined with this factor in mind. The quality of the image is also a consideration, although a lesser one, in price. Good, sharp reproductions, which are the exceptions in both techniques, will bring more than the standard images.

The cases in which these images were housed are also collected. The first mass-produced containers, which appeared in the 1840s, were made of wood with an embossed paper covering. Between five and six hundred different patterns appear on the embossings, mostly falling in one of three categories: birds, flowers, or fruit. The cases are in general rather ordinary and are of minor interest to most collectors. However, certain unusual types, produced mostly during the 1850s, are exceptions to the rule. The Mascher-type case, which incorporated a lens to enable one to view the image stereoscopically, is rare and choice, as are those papier-mâché specimens that were inlaid with mother-of-pearl.

The bulk of collector interest focuses on the so-called Union cases, which were made of a mixture of sawdust and colored shellac and compressed in a powerful mold to produce a fairly hard finished product. There are over eight hundred different case-cover designs in the Union category, mostly related to nature, religion, history, or patriotic events. Among the most popular are those that portray Washington crossing the Delaware to attack Trenton and Columbus landing in the Americas. Neither is rare, but both sell for well over a hundred dollars. Other designs are less common, and all are eagerly sought by collectors.

The introduction of the tintype in 1856 revolutionized photography, making available, for the first time, a cheap and relatively rapid method for the production of multiple images. The tintype is made by exposing in the camera a varnished iron plate. Its invention coincided with development of the multiple-lens camera; by employing a tintype plate in this new camera, it was possible to expose as many as four 2½- by 3½-inch images on a single plate, which after being developed could be cut apart.

Tintype "galleries" sprang up all over

the country during the 1860s, offering photographic portraits—though rather inferior ones—for as little as twenty-five cents per shot. Because they were so cheap, they were seldom enclosed in cases, and most are found loose today.

On the whole, tintypes are neither as popular as daguerreotypes or ambrotypes, nor as expensive. Images of famous persons are seldom found, since they preferred the traditional forms of photography. Some of the popular tintype subjects are Indians, soldiers, and artisans. In addition, a number of outdoor scenes and interesting interiors are found; they are the most expensive tintypes. Prices in this area, in general, are moderate, and it offers a good field for the new collector.

Another mass photographic device was the carte de visite, or visiting card, which received a French patent in 1854 and quickly gained international popularity. The visiting card is a piece of photographic paper showing a bust or full-length portrait of an individual on photographic paper, mounted on cardboard; the average size is 2¼ to 3¾ inches. It was produced in a multiple-lens camera by exposing a glass negative, from which a contact print with from four to eight photos was made. These were then cut apart to make individual photographs.

During the period of their greatest popularity, 1860 to 1885, millions of visiting cards were manufactured. Over a hundred thousand copies of a single photograph of Abraham Lincoln were made for the election of 1860 alone. Yet that card, like others of celebrities, is hard to find today. A card with the bust of Alfred Lord Tennyson sold recently for three hundred dollars, and other comparable portraits are equally expensive. As in earlier photographic mediums, the unusual sells best. The common, anonymous family portrait is of little value, but outdoor scenes, animals, Indians, machinery, and other unusual images command substantial sums.

Similar to visiting cards were cabinet cards. They were made in essentially the same way but in a larger size, the average being 3¾ by 5½ inches. The peak of their popularity was from 1867 until just after 1900, during which time large quantities appeared on the market. More sophisticated lighting, methods of posing, and background materials were employed in an effort to make each cabinet card a work of art. Today, the best portraits of famous individuals may sell for several hundred dollars apiece.

Stereographs, or stereo views, were a popular form of nineteenth-century entertainment. First developed in 1851, they consist of paired views of the same subject, which, when viewed through a stereoscopic viewer, show a single three-dimensional image. The first stereo views were taken by two cameras mounted side by side, but photographers soon adopted the dual-lens, or binocular, camera for this purpose. Daguerreotype and ambrotype stereographs were made in large numbers, primarily in Europe, while American manufacturers turned first to glass views and then to card stereographs, which were produced here in vast numbers from the 1850s on. By 1862, one stereo view manufacturer, Edward Anthony of New York, could boast of an output numbering in the hundreds of thousands. Many other companies joined the business, including mail-order houses such as Montgomery Ward and Sears Roebuck.

Lithoprints, or multicolored stereographs, were developed at the close of the nineteenth century, and they quickly gained public acceptance. Lithos were made from photographs or artist's renderings and often had as their subject humorous or sentimental themes.

Stereographs today are quite reasonably priced. Those that are among the oldest or that depict famous events, locales, disasters, or famous people are expensive enough, ranging upward from a hundred dollars. But most stereographs do not fall within these categories, and it is still possible to purchase interesting views or genre scenes for a few dollars or even less.

What we think of today as photographs—that is, images secured on paper, with film negatives—are the end product of extensive experimentation with various techniques. The first of these involved the calotype, invented in England in 1841. There followed in rapid order salt prints (so called for the salt solution in which the photographic paper was dipped before printing), albumen prints (where the print paper was coated with albumen, or egg white), and emulsion prints. The use of gelatine bromide emulsion on photographic paper enabled photographers to greatly increase the rapidity with which prints could be made from a negative and heralded the introduction of modern photographic methods.

The result of these advances was a vast number of paper-backed photographs, most of which until recently have been of little interest to collectors of photographic memorabilia. In the 1970s, though, as the supply of inexpensive daguerreotypes, ambrotypes, and other early forms has dwindled, photograph enthusiasts have turned their attention to the later images. The choice is so great that, at present, most collectors are seeking either prints by famous photographers or photographs with unusual subjects—famous personages, events, or localities. Prices vary greatly. Interesting photos may be purchased for less than a dollar, while those bearing the mark of renowned photographers such as Alfred Steiglitz may sell for hundreds of dollars. Only the collector's inclination and his pocketbook will determine what he will collect.

Photographic equipment, cameras, and the like have their devoted enthusiasts, though in number they hardly compare to those who collect images. There are several reasons for this. Early cameras, particularly those used prior to 1900, are scarce and expensive. Many are found in damaged condition, and restoration is expensive. Camera equipment is more difficult to store and to display than photographs, because equipment requires more space.

Despite these problems, the number of collectors interested in cameras appears to be growing. Early Kodaks and other mass-produced and relatively common cameras may be obtained for well under a hundred dollars; and a group of them can form the nucleus for an expanding collection.

Sixth-plate daguereotype of a woman, with tinted features; 1850s; $20-30.

Quarter-plate daguereotype of two children; 1850s; $45-70.

Rare ninth-plate daguerreotype of a primitive painting of a woman; papier mache case; 1850s. The daguereotype is worth $150-200; the painting if found, perhaps a hundred times that!

Sixth-plate daguereotype of a nun; 1850s; $65-110.

Ninth-plate daguereotype of a child in unusual Mascher magnifying viewer case; 1850s; $150-225.

Set of nine daguerreotypes in a walnut ogee frame; late 19th century; $300-475.

Half-plate ambrotype in wood and paper case; mid 19th century, $500-750. Unusual view of western gold miners and rare gold tint applied to rocks give the plate its high price.

Quarter-plate ambrotype of four children; 1850s; $35-55.

Quarter-plate ambrotype of little boy, wood and paper case, dress tinted yellow; 1850s; $50-85.

Half-plate ambrotype of New England building, Union case; mid-19th century; $250-325. The larger the plate size, the more valuable the ambrotype.

Quarter-plate ambrotype of Civil War soldier in wood and paper case; early 1860s; $85-135. A pink tint has been applied to man's cheeks.

Cartes de visite from the 1860s. **Left:** General Banks, by Mathew Brady; $40-65. **Right:** Civil War soldier; $25-35. Photographic material by a leading photographer like Brady is always at a premium.

Carte de visite of Niagara Falls; last quarter 19th century; $30-50. Scenic views are relatively uncommon in this medium.

Sixth-plate ambrotype of boy in school uniform, cheeks tinted pink; 1850s; $20-30. An example of the inexpensive ambrotype.

Rare two-sided ambrotype of a woman by Matthew Brady, mid-19th century; $150-275.

Carte de visite of the famous midgets Commodore Nutt and Minnie Warren; 1860; $65-100. Midgets were popular material for cartes de visite.

Carte de visite of a woman; 1860s; $5-10. Inexpensive pieces like this one are a good buy at present.

Tintype of a crippled young man in the standard 2"x3" size; second half 19th century; $25-45. The unusual subject matter makes for a higher price.

Tintype of a man in standard 2"x3" size; second half 19th century; $5-10. Tintypes in standard size are moderately priced; the larger sizes are rare and more costly.

Stereoscopic view of the ruins of the Great Chicago Fire; ca. 1871; $15-20.

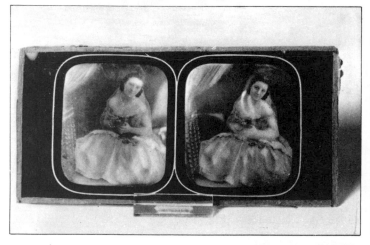

Extremely rare stereoscopic daguereotype; 1850s; $450-650.

Stereoscopic view of buildings in Buffallo, N.Y., second half 19th century; $5-10. Collecting stereo cards is becoming a major American hobby.

Stereoscopic view of destruction caused by the Johnstown, Pa. flood in 1889; $15-20. Stereoscopic views of disasters were very popular. The "dead" body in foreground is probably posed.

Top: Stereoscopic view of risqué ladies; 18902; $20-45. **Below:** Stereoscopic view of Indian woman; Nevada, late 19th century; $75-150.

Two examples of the less expensive Keystone-type stereoscopic views; 1890s. **Top:** View of Missouri zinc mine; $5-10. **Below:** Steamboat; $20-35.

"Love Reigns Supreme," colored or tinted stereoscopic view of the sort popular at the turn of the century; $5-10.

Stereoscopic viewers; late 19th century; $55-90 each.

Pressed sawdust daguerreotype case, "Capture of Major Andre"; mid-19th century; $75-120.

Photograph on card of train wreck, 8"x12"; ca. 1900; $75-115.
With the increase in prices for daguerreotypes and ambrotyps, more collectors are turning to the abundant supply of early photographs.

Pressed sawdust daguerreotype case, seated Liberty; mid-19th century; $65-95. Many people make a collection solely of these attractive cases.

Pressed sawdust daguerreotype case, mother and child; mid-19th century; $75-125. Holds four images.

Cabinet photograph of Prairie Flower, Indian show woman and sharpshooter; late 19th century; $75-135. Disaster and personality photographs like this one, rate high with collectors of old photos.

Photograph of early American hotel, 10″x12″; late 19th century; $65-95.

Photograph of the warship **Columbia,** 6″x8″; late 19th century; $30-45.

Photograph of a wagon shop, 6″x8″, late 19th century; $30-50.

Photograph of a group of World War I soldiers, 4″x6″; ca. 1917; $20-35.

Photograph of two women on horseback, 8″x10″; early 20th century; $15-25.

Photograph of a large summer hotel, 8″x10″; early 20th century; $25-45.

The Quad camera, a mechanical plate camera; ca. 1896; $65-115.

Photograph stand, ebony inlaid with mother-of-pearl; late 19th century; $35-55.

Victorian photograph album of the type once owned by every family; late 19th century; $20-50. The albums are attractive with or without pictures.

Pocket Kodak folding camera with wooden interior; early 20th century; $20-40.

Folding Pony Premo A, plate camera; early 20th century; $75-110.

537

Cameras

Although cameras have been around since 1839, there were no real collectors or collections of photographic materials before the 1900s. In fact, before Eastman Kodak's purchase of the Parisian Gabriel Cromer's collection in 1939, there was no major photographic collection in the United States. The Cromer collection became the nucleus of the famous International Museum of Photography at Rochester, New York, and its acquisition greatly stimulated American interest in photographic collectibles. Today, there are thousands of collectors of photographic "hardware" (cameras and projectors) and ephemera (advertisements, manuals, and books), and there are more than twenty collector clubs.

Today's collectors have a wide field from which to choose. Thousands of cameras were made between 1839—the year in which Louis Daguerre marketed the first daguerreotype—and the present time. Some types, of course, are rare and hard to obtain at any price, but most are abundant and inexpensive.

While some collectors specialize with a given type of camera or concentrate on a single manufacturer, such as Eastman Kodak or Leica, most seek a broad range of products. The bulk of the acquisitions of such collectors fall within one of three categories: box, folding, or 35mm. In each of these divisions the majority of the machines found are either studio models, used by professionals, or the more common hobby or general purpose devices sold to the general public. There are, however, a limited number of other cameras that served unusual purposes, such as detective cameras, often designed to look like books or handbags; miniature cameras, such as the famous Minox; panoramic cameras for photographing landscapes or large crowds; and the stereo cameras used to produce the stereoscopic cards that were so popular in the period from 1880 to 1910.

The first photographic devices were plate cameras: the image was taken on a metal or glass plate and was one of a kind. There was no negative. Between 1839 and the middle of the nineteenth century several kinds of plate cameras were developed. However, by the beginning of the period in which we are interested (1880 to 1950) only one type continued in use—the tintype camera, which was commonly used, even in the 1930s, by itinerant or street photographers. These cameras were wood framed, with leather bellowslike bodies that could be moved back and forth on a track to focus the picture. Although many of these cameras are a century old, they are usually inexpensive because of the large number still available.

Most collectors concentrate on paper-film cameras, the first of which was made in 1887 by George Eastman. Eastman's invention revolutionized photography and enabled him to found a photographic empire. Before Eastman, photography—because of the complex processes required to shoot pictures and, particularly, to develop the film—was primarily a field for professionals. Eastman changed all that by designing a simple, inexpensive (by 1901 his Kodak Brownie was selling for twenty-five cents!) instrument and doing the developing himself. His slogan, "You press the button, we do the rest," told it all. The novice photographer bought the film and camera, loaded up, took his pictures, and sent the exposed film to the Kodak factory. It came back fully developed. To us this seems ordinary, but at the time it was revolutionary.

Eastman Kodak dominated the camera field for generations and produced dozens of different photographic devices. Most clearly associated with his name, though, is the box camera, a square or rectangular camera made of wood, metal, leather, or, after 1930, plastic. Eastman box cameras are usually one of the novice collector's first acquisitions, and among the most popular of these are the Brownie and the Senior and Junior Pocket Kodaks.

The success of the box camera did not keep Eastman from looking to the future, and in 1890 he marketed a folding Kodak. Folding cameras had been around for some time—they were developed in response to the need for a compact, easily transported photographic device—but Eastman's was the first efficient and inexpensive model. Among the many Eastman folding cameras, two are in great demand with modern collectors. These are the Autographics, which produced postcard-sized shots at a time when postcards were extremely popular, and the Art Deco-style Bantam of the 1930s.

Such American models notwithstanding, many collectors also seek out the many fine European cameras. Among these, Leicas are the favorites. The development of the 35mm camera is associated with this firm. Following the organization of the movie industry in the early 1900s, large quantities of 35mm movie film became available. It was not long before still-camera manufacturers decided to take advantage of this situation. Oaskar Barnade, who was employed at the Leitz Optical Works in Wetzler, Germany, designed a metal-cased 35mm camera in 1912, and by 1925 it was being sold commercially. Though four other 35mm cameras were patented between 1912 and 1915 (including the American-made Simplex and Tourist models), Leica dominated the field. Indeed, one measure of Leica's importance is the large number of pirated Leica reproductions (including Russian and Japanese models).

There are many attractive American 35mm cameras, including types produced both in the 1930s and after the conclusion of the Second World War. Among the more attractive of these collector's items are the Memo, made by the Ansco Company of Binghamton, New York, and the Agfa Speedex, which dates to the 1940s.

Movie cameras are considered highly collectible, though the variety available is considerably less than the variety of still cameras. Eastman Kodak was a pioneer in this field, too, and its 16 mm Cine Kodak was long a popular home-movie camera. Other names to look for are Keystone, Briskin, and Pathé.

Various Polaroid-type cameras are also collectible. These developed from the "street" cameras of the early 1900s which were used by penny photographers and incorporated a developing tank attached to the camera tripod. Though primarily a postwar phenomenon, modern Polaroids are already attracting collector attention.

There are few areas of collectibles in which the range of appealing objects is as great or the opportunity for assembling a collection at modest prices as good as in the field of cameras. Some acquisitions can also be used—another advantage.

Bellows-type wooden camera, the Eastman View Finder; Eastman Kodak; 1881-85; $175-225. Good condition and famous name enhance the value of this camera.

Bellows-type wooden folding camera; by American Optical Co.; 1880-90; $65-95. Lack of the lens devalues an otherwise interesting camera.

Bellows-type wooden folding camera; by Eastman Kodak; 1885-90; $55-80.

Bellows-type wooden folding camera; 1900-10; $45-60.

Bellows-type wooden folding camera; by G. Desse; Namur, France; 1875-85; $140-170.

Box camera; the Midge; 1910-20;
$75-100

Box camera in metal case, the Dollar
Camera; by Ansco; 1920-30; $30-45.

Box camera; the Brownie No. 2, in
original box; by Eastman Kodak;
1900-10; $65-85. The original box
increases the value of this common
camera by 100 percent.

Box camera; by Eastman Kodak;
1910-15; $20-30.

Box camera; the Pocket Kodak; by
Eastman Kodak; ca. 1895; $70-85.
This small box camera is a great
favorite with collectors.

Box cameras; by Eastman Kodak. **Left:** Bulls Eye; 1896-1900; $45-60. **Right:** Brownie Box No. 2; 1900-10; $20-35.

Box camera, the Kewpie; by Conley Camera Co., 1900-10; $20-35.

Box cameras; by Eastman Kodak. **Left:** Junior Premo No. 1; 1903-06; $40-65. **Right:** Brownie No. 0; 1898-1905; $20-30.

Box cameras, by Eastman Kodak.
Left: Junior No. 1; 1900-06; $60-85.
Right: Brownie No. 2; 1925-35; $25-35.

542

Box camera; by Eastman Kodak; 1885-90; $30-40.

Box camera; the Bullet Speed; by Eastman Kodak; 1897-1900; $50-65.

Box camera; unmarked but patented; 1903; $65-85. A very well built camera.

Box camera; the B2 Shur Shot, with original box; by Agfa; 1930-40; $20-30.

Box camera; the Shur Shot Special; by Agfa; 1935-45; $15-20.

Box camera, the Brownie Model C; by Eastman Kodak; with carrying case; 1940-50; $15-25.

Box cameras made of plastic and metal; 1950-60. **Left:** Brownie Fiesta; by Eastman Kodak; $5-10. **Right:** Imperial; $5-15.

Left: Art Deco Bantam; by Eastman Kodak; 1935-40; $30-50. Modern case design increases value of this camera. **Right:** Special World's Fair Edition; by Eastman Kodak; 1964-65; $20-25.

Box camera, the Roy Rogers Snap Shot; by Herbert George Co.; 1945-55; $25-35 Association with a popular film star increases the value of an otherwise ordinary camera.

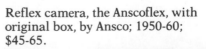

Reflex camera, the Ciro Flex; Delaware, Ohio; 1935-45; $50-65.

Reflex camera, the Anscoflex, with original box, by Ansco; 1950-60; $45-65.

Reflex camera, Coronet; England;
1940-50; $45-65.

Folding camera with wood and
leather bellows, the Wizard; by
Manhattan Optical Co.; 1890-1900;
$50-70. Missing lens.

Folding camera; 1890-1900; $25-40.
Missing lens.

Folding camera, the Premo, by
Eastman Kodak; 1903-08; $35-50.

Folding camera; the Autographic
Brownie; by Eastman Kodak;
1920-30; $20-35.

Folding cameras; by Eastman Kodak.
Left: Autographic; 1902-05; $20-30.
Right: Autographic; 1909-12; $15-25.

Folding camera, the Brownie Hawk
Eye Autographic; by Eastman
Kodak; 1925-35; $20-35.

Folding camera, the Cronos; by
Ernemann; 1925-35; $60-80.

Folding camera, the Anastigmat
Spector; by Lumiere; France;
1910-20; $85-125.

Folding camera, the Anastigmat
Special; Eastman Kodak; 1930-35;
$40-55.

Folding camera, the Vigilant Junior; by Eastman Kodak; 1925-35; $35-45. With Kodet lens.

Folding camera, the Autographic Model C; by Eastman Kodak; 1920-30; $20-30.

Folding camera, the Anastigmat, with Art Deco black and silver metal case; by Eastman Kodak; 1930-40; $55-75.

Folding camera, the Clipper, with original box and advertising material; by Ansco; 1950-55; $35-45.

35mm camera; by Leica; 1920-30; $225-350.

35mm camera; the Minolta 35; by Minolta; 1950-60; $120-180. A Japanese version of the Leica.

35mm camera; U.S.S.R.; 1945-55; $70-100. A Russian version of the Leica.

35mm camera; the Anastigmat; by Argus; 1930-40; $20-35.

35mm camera; the Bantam Special; by Eastman Kodak; 1936-40; $85-145. The sleek Art Deco lines of this aluminum-bodied camera make it a great favorite with collectors.

Left: 35mm camera; the Speedex, in plastic case; by Afga; 1950-55; $25-40. **Right:** Fed Flash; 1945-55; $10-15.

16mm movie camera, the Cine Kodak; by Eastman Kodak; 1925-35; $75-95. There are few movie camera collectors.

Folding camera; by Polaroid Co.; 1950-55; $150-200. An early Polaroid.

Left: 16mm movie camera; by Briskin; 1930-40; $60-80. **Right:** 16mm movie camera; by Keystone; 1945-55; $40-60.

9.5mm movie camera; by Pathe; 1925-35; $40-60. The 9.5mm movie camera never attained much popularity, and few models are available.

35mm stereoscopic camera, the Stereohit; Japan; 1950-60; $55-75. Today they're only a novelty, but stereoscopic slides were once an important additon to almost every home.

Left: Miniature camera, the Pixie; by Whitaker Manufacturing Co.; 1930-40; $20-25. **Right:** Miniature camera, the Midget, in walnut-size plastic case; by Coronet; 1936-40; $30-40.

Miniature camera, the Toyoca 16; Japan; 1950-60; $20-30.

Miniature camera, the Mycro;
1948-55; $15-25.

Miniature camera, the Diplomat;
Japan; 1950-60; $15-25.

Miniature camera, the Emson;
Japan; 1945-55; $10-20.

All-metal box camera, the Self
Worker; by France & Etranger;
France; 1905-15; $135-175. Made for
the English and American markets.

Jigsaw puzzle in the shape of a
camera packed in a camera-shaped
box; 1935-45; $20-30. A popular
novelty item.

Plastic child's toy camera; 1950-60;
$1-3.

Political Memorabilia

For several reasons, political memorabilia comprise a rather young and small group of collector's items. For one thing, electoral campaigning as we know it today—with its buttons and banners and its widespread attempts to influence the votes of millions—did not exist before the second quarter of the nineteenth century. Before that time, voting in the United States—whether for national or local candidates—was mostly the privilege of the wealthy few. But by the mid-1830s, the right to vote had been extended to all white adult males, more than tripling the size of the voting population of the preceding decade; and more and more candidates of national importance were being elected directly by these voters, instead of being chosen in limited party caucuses. The result was an intense rivalry between the political parties to stimulate and sway voter opinion. Then, as now, one of the methods they used to promote their cause was the distribution of various articles bearing the name or likeness of their candidate and perhaps a slogan reflecting the currently contested issue.

However, few political artifacts survive from before the middle of the nineteenth century. This is not so surprising, for such items are transitory by their very nature. Not only are they fragile—being made of paper or other nondurable material—but also, unlike almost all other antiques, they were intended to serve only the shortest-lived of purposes—the few months required to conduct a political campaign. Most political mementos were cheaply produced, because although intended for a mass audience, they were not meant to last; they were often destroyed in use, were discarded immediately, or perished from neglect once their purpose had been served.

Fortunate exceptions are the parade lanterns and torches that were used in traditional nighttime parades prior to the advent of electricity. In the mid-nineteenth century, it was customary for marching clubs to be formed among the politically like-minded in militia battalions or volunteer fire departments for the purpose of conducting ceremonial parades, especially in support of their candidates at election time. To heighten the drama of the occasion, and thus create a greater impression on their fellow citizens, the members would carry large numbers of tin and glass lanterns and torches, which they carefully preserved, to be used again from year to year. As a result, large numbers of such parade lights have come down to us, and many may be found in public and private collections.

Another exception is political whiskey flasks, which, judging by the large numbers that survive, seem to have been prized as much by their original owners as they are today. Until the 1870s, it was the custom to pass out free liquor at political rallies and parades. Wise candidates saw to it that their gifts were bottled in pint or half-pint flasks embossed with their own portrait—often linked with that of an earlier patriot such as Washington, to heighten their own prestige. Today, these flasks are in great demand, and their prices are quite high. (Samples of them are illustrated in Chapter 4.)

The largest collector interest in political memorabilia centers on political buttons and ribbons, items that were far from common prior to the last years of the nineteenth century. One of the oldest political mementos to come on the market in recent years is a brass button cast for Washington's inauguration in 1789. It was dug up in Virginia and sold at auction for four hundred dollars. Such buttons appear to have been quite popular in the early 1800s. So were brass or bronze medallions, which were cast with the likeness of the candidate and had a small hole through which a ribbon might be strung, to be worn around the neck or arm.

Just before the Civil War, lapel and breast pins appeared. They consisted of a circular brass frame within which was mounted a tintype or ambrotype picture of the candidate. Some were pierced for stringing, but others bore the first spring-wire pins. Also popular in the 1850s and 1860s were cartes de visite, or photographs on cardboard, of candidates.

The button collector did not truly come into his own until the election of 1896. At that time, celluloid—which had been invented in 1869—was first combined with a patented pin-back attachment to create the celluloid pin-back button. The manufacturing process was quite simple. A picture or slogan printed on paper was covered with a piece of hard, clear celluloid; then both were wrapped about a round tin shell and fixed in place with a stamped metal collar to which the spring-wire pin was attached. The technique revolutionized political button manufacture. It was quick and relatively inexpensive, and enabled anything that could be printed to be placed on a button. Whitehead and Hoag of New Jersey was the most active early producer of these buttons, but by 1900 dozens of companies were in the business. During the two McKinley-Bryan campaigns alone (1896 and 1900), it is estimated that nearly two thousand different campaign buttons were turned out.

During their period of most active use, 1896 to 1920, thousands of celluloid political buttons appeared. Most were made in vast quantities and are, even today, relatively easy to obtain. But for one reason or another, some were produced in a limited edition and are, accordingly, both rare and expensive. As a general rule, these include odd sizes, both large and small; third-party buttons; and those issued in support of a cause (such as the Women's Vote) rather than a candidate. Jugate buttons, which picture the presidential and vice-presidential candidates side by side, are a special favorite with collectors and may often sell for more than less-common non-presidential items. At present, the rarest jugate and the most valuable of all celluloid pin backs is the Cox–Roosevelt button issued by the Democrats during the 1920 campaign.

In 1920, lithographed tin political buttons made their first appearance and quickly replaced celluloid pin backs, which today are made only in special editions. The tin pin is easier to produce and much cheaper than its predecessor. It is manufactured with a die press, which can shape and stamp a large sheet of tin in one operation, to produce multiple images of the same design. As is the case with so much modern technology, though, something is lost in the process. Tin pins are easily scratched, so that few undamaged examples are found. Moreover, economic practicalities limit the number of colors that may be used, a factor of no consideration in celluloid buttons since printing was done separately on the paper insert. As a whole, the quality of political buttons has declined since 1920; though with the renewed interest in all slogan buttons during the 1960s, some interesting designs have begun to appear.

Though most buttons were used alone, they were sometimes combined with ribbons of various size. In fact, ribbons bearing the printed names of candidates were widely used in the nineteenth century. Tintype picture buttons and ribbons were combined during the Lincoln campaign of 1864, and both ribbons and sashes dating back to the 1820s may be found. The practice has continued in the twentieth century with interesting additions, such as the felt sunflower backing used for Alf Landon's buttons in 1936. (Landon, the Republican candidate in that year, was a native of Kansas, the sunflower state.)

Over the years a variety of other political mementos has been produced, in nearly every medium imaginable. In the 1870s and 1880s, comic statuary was popular, and more than one politician was unhappy to find himself the subject of a comic jug or mug turned out at a pottery such as the one at Anna, Illinois. Tin and other metals were effectively employed not only for buttons and medallions but also for such useful objects as match safes. An extremely desirable political item is the pewter match safe shaped as a bust of General Grant, the Republican candidate in 1868. Tin whistles and horns used at rallies and parades are also in demand, particularly if they incorporate interesting slogans or pictures. In the days when men used pocket watches, they often carried a decorative watch fob with the likeness of their favorite candidate; these may be obtained in silver, pewter, or bronze.

Pressed-glass beer mugs, cups, and saucers were also embellished with the features or names of political figures, both active and deceased. In the twentieth century, the art of decalcomania is utilized to produce these pieces, while in the nineteenth century, such items were made primarily of pattern glass.

Perhaps the most common material employed in political advertising has been paper, since it is so inexpensive. Paper banners and streamers have traditionally decorated the halls where rallies are held; the partisans wear paper hats or beanies; and great posters of the candidates look down on the faithful assembled at their feet. Unfortunately, paper is fragile and very expendable. Vast quantities have been thrown away after every election, so that today, paper political memorabilia in good condition that predates 1900 is extremely hard to come by. Some things, of course, are harder to find than others. Life-size posters and large banners are rare, but sheet music, such as the ''rousing'' ''Keep Cool with Coolidge,'' is relatively plentiful, and the same may be said of printed speeches and general propaganda. Of course, given the politician's fondness for talk, one may safely conclude that the existence of so many speeches, like the tip of an iceberg, gives only an inkling of what once must have existed.

Various slogan buttons related to the Franklin D. Roosevelt campaign of 1940; $10-20 each.

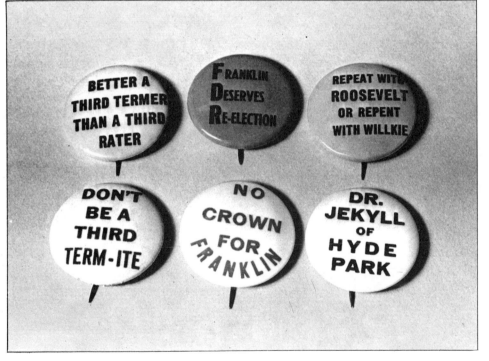

Pocket card, Cleveland-Stevenson; 1885; $35-55.

Delegate's badge, Cleveland-Stevenson Democratic Convention; 1892; $50-85.

Brass-bound ambrotypes of Lincoln; 1860. Both $175-265. Example at right shows early pin back.

Lincoln ambrotype button with multicolored ribbons; 1864; $400-500.

Bronze medallion, William Henry Harrison; 1841; $65-95.
Medallions of this sort were forerunners of the modern political button.

Early ambrotype of Jefferson Davis, President of the Confederacy; ca. 1862; $375-500. Among the earliest of all political buttons.

McKinley and Bryan buttons, with
attached ribbons; 1896; $250-400 the
pair.

Pair of Garfield-Hancock pin-back
eagle-crested lapel pins, ca. 1881;
$485-675 the pair. These are rare and
choice items.

Reverse of the Honest Dollar badge,
showing slogan and platform.

Left: Tillman ("Pitchfork Ben") spear;
$60-85. **Center:** McKinley gold bug;
$175-265. **Right:** Parker and Davis
watch fob; $50-70. All, early 1900s.

Extra large gold-colored metal badge
stamped "McKinley"; 1896; $115-165.
The so-called Honest Dolllar badge.

Teddy Roosevelt rabbit's-foot badge
issued at the time he was campaigning
for Governor of New York; 1898;
$95-145.

Two Nixon miniatures, 1972. **Left:** $10-20. **Right:** $15-25.

Top: Rare Eugene McCarthy bandana; 1968; $25-45. **Bottom:** Barry Goldwater bumper sticker; 1964; $10-20.

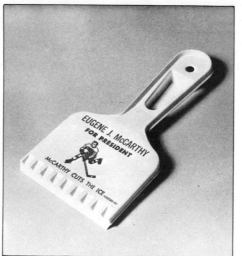

John Kennedy paper hat; 1960; $20-35.

Eugene McCarthy plastic ice scraper; 1968; $10-15.

556

Socialist Labor Party buttons; 1924.
Left to right: $5-10; $15-25; $30-40.

Communist Party buttons; 1936. **Left:**
Browder-Ford; $75-110. **Right:** $25-40.

Left: Truman button; $15-20. **Center:**
Henry A. Wallace; $7-12.
Right: Dewey-Warren jugate; $10-15.
All, ca. 1948.

Rare George McGovern button with
pictures of rock superstars; 1972;
$85-115.

Slogan buttons. **Left:** Anti-Nixon; 1964;
$10-15. **Right:** Anti-Goldwater; 1964;
$17-25.

Ford buttons. **Left:** Presidential; 1976;
$4-8. **Right:** Vice-presidential; 1964;
$45-70.

Clocks and Watches

Unless he or she chooses to collect nonfunctioning timepieces, the clock and watch enthusiast is faced with a problem seldom encountered in other fields of collectibles: making his or her acquisitions work. Nonworking clocks and watches are often quite inexpensive, but having them repaired frequently poses an economic impossibility. Another challenge to the collector is size, particularly if his or her interest is in earlier clocks. Until late in the nineteenth century, most clocks were large, and only a small number of pre-1880 wall and shelf clocks can be accommodated in the average modern home.

The problem of size can be eliminated to a great extent by choosing to collect clocks of the period from 1880 to 1950. By the end of the nineteenth century clockmaking, which as early as 1807 had become a factory business in the United States, was so refined that functional clockworks could be housed within very small cases. As a result, there is an abundance of moderate-size, interesting wall and shelf clocks from the period.

Some of these timepieces can be found in wooden cases, such as the walnut-veneered ogee-frame rectangular clocks that were produced from the 1840s until the mid-1850s. There are also the round or square oak wall clocks that were common in schools and factories from 1910 until the Second World War. Many other materials were used in clock cases. Metal—whether tin, pot metal, cast iron, brass, or stainless steel—is common, as are glass, marble, and the various plastics intended to imitate either marble or tortoiseshell.

Clock shapes are also diverse. The plain round case can be found on clocks dating from 1880 to 1950, but many other styles have had their day of glory. Among these are the large, figurine-mounted mantel clocks made by Ansonia, which offered the buyer an opportunity to purchase both a clock and a figure of anyone from Attila the Hun to Rubens.

Animated clocks were popular during both the late 1800s and the 1930s. In these rare and highly collectible timepieces the movement of the clockwork causes figures to move. As an example, soon after the end of Prohibition, American clockmakers produced a clock incorporating a figure that drank beer as the time passed.

Late-nineteenth-century forms include jigsaw-cut frames in the Eastlake style as well as rectilinear examples in the Mission style popular around 1900. As these examples indicate, clockcases frequently mirror changes in furniture design, and clock styles range from the flowing, natural forms of the Art Nouveau era to the severely geometric plastic and chrome forms of Art Deco. The latter period, which encompasses the introduction of sophisticated electric clocks, is a particularly attractive one for collectors. Both American and European timepieces are available in large numbers, and many styles can be found at moderate prices. Moreover, a higher percentage of the available clocks are functional than is the case with earlier examples.

Although many interesting clocks by minor manufacturers can be found—and should certainly not be passed up if the price is right—most collectors seek out the products of the major American factories such as Ansonia, Seth Thomas, New Haven, and Waterbury.

The oldest of these companies, the Seth Thomas Clock Company, was founded in 1813 by the pioneer clockmaker Seth Thomas. Incorporated in 1853, the company is still in business as a branch of Talley Industries. For some years, however, it has employed foreign-made parts in its clocks. Seth Thomas timepieces are well made and the most popular of collectible American clocks.

Another well-known manufacturer was the Ansonia Clock Company, which was established in Derby, Connecticut, in 1850 and moved to Brooklyn, New York, in 1879. From 1879 until 1929, Ansonia produced a vast quantity of novelty and figural clocks as well as many marble mantle clocks.

Two other giants of the industry are the New Haven Clock Company (manufacturer of the largest variety of late-nineteenth-century clocks), which was active from 1853 until 1960, and the Waterbury Clock Company (active from 1857 to 1944), which made fine calendar clocks as well as various alarm, schoolhouse, and ship's timepieces.

Because of the smaller size involved, watches present greater production problems than do clocks. For many years the United States imported watches, and before the creation of the Boston Watch Company (1853 to 1856), there were no factory-made American watches. Moreover, even after more successful competitors, such as the still existent Waltham Watch Company, entered the field, their products were for many years too expensive for most potential users. Jeweled and cased in silver and gold, throughout most of the Victorian period watches remained the prized possessions of a few. As a result, collectible watches from the pre-1880 period are generally expensive.

In 1880, the Waterbury Clock Company produced a nonjeweled watch that could be sold for only $3.75, and by 1893 Robert H. Ingersoll was selling pocket watches (at first made for him by Waterbury) for only one dollar each. Ingersoll's slogan, "The watch that made the dollar famous," heralded a new day in watch manufacture. His company and others, such as Ingraham and the company that is now Westclox, turned out thousands of inexpensive watches, all of which are now collector's items.

There was no letup, of course, in the manufacture of better, more expensive watches, and jeweled timepieces by such makers as Seth Thomas, Waltham, Elgin, and Hamilton can be found. The variety of these timepieces, particularly those made after 1900, is very great. They offer a fertile field for the collector.

The novice collector may be surprised at his inability to locate early wristwatches. The answer is simple: there were none. Other than a few late-nineteenth-century pendant watches intended for use by women, pocket watches were the sole personal timepiece until after the First World War. Collectible wristwatches, accordingly, date to the 1920s and 1930s.

Also—and this is due primarily to the limitations imposed by their small size—watches show little of the variety of design evidenced in clocks. Though they may be cased in precious metals or encrusted with gems, most watches look pretty much the same from the 1880s right through the 1940s. There are, of course, subtle changes, and one can perceive influences such as Art Nouveau and Art Deco. The important differences among such timepieces are usually found in the backplate engraving. Many watches were given as gifts and were suitably engraved. Others were engraved in commemoration of historic events, from the St. Louis World's Fair of 1904 to the New York World's Fair of 1939. Commemorative watchcases alone could form a sizable and interesting collection.

Unusually large thirty-day windup, oak cased wall clock; by Seth Thomas; 1910-20; $275-350.

Victorian shelf clock in walnut case, Model No. 1; by New Haven Clock Co.; 1880-90; $275-350. Victorian clocks are usually large and ornate.

Neoclassical shelf clock in walnut case; 1890-1900; $200-285. Clocks in the shape of temples, towers and even log cabins were very popular at the turn of the century.

Shelf clock in walnut case; by E. Ingraham; 1910-20; $85-145

Shelf clock in silver gilt pot-metal case; 1905-15; $75-125.

Alarm clock in gold-washed
pot-metal case; 1890-1910; $45-65.
Pot metal was often employed in
inexpensive late-Victorian clocks.

Art Nouveau shelf clock in silvered pot-metal
case; 1900-10; $100-125.   An attractive clock
decorated with glass bead inserts.

Eight-day clock in bronze and
enamel case; by Schild & Co.;
1920-30; $185-255. A sophisticated
clock in the early Art Deco style.

Clock and table lamp combination in
bronzed pot metal; 1935-45; $75-125.
Clock and lamp combinations are
rare and generally of recent vintage.

Dresser clock in imitation
tortoiseshell case; 1930-40; $45-65.
Clocks such as this were often part of
a dresser set.

Cymric pattern mantel clock in sterling silver case; by Liberty Manufacturing Co.; 1900-10; $1,700-2,500. In the Arts and Crafts mode, cymric clocks are rare and expensive.

Art Nouveau mantel clock in bronzed pot-metal and marbleized pottery case; by Seth Thomas; 1920-30; $125-175.

Mantel clock in brass and pink marble case; by Charpentier; 1920-30; $255-365.

Shelf clock in stamped brass and marble case; 1930-40; $75-115.

Coach clock in brass and glass case with original carrying case; 1885-1900; $250-375. A popular collector clock.

Art Deco electric clock in chrome
and blue glass case; by Charlton;
1930-40; $95-145. Deco clocks are
among the most popular of
timepieces.

Mantel clock in glass and chrome
case; by Waltham Clock Co.; 1935-45;
$85-135. An extremely stylish clock
in the late Art Deco style.

Shelf clock in metal and plastic
bamboo-motif case; 1930-40;
$75-100

Shelf clock in glass and metal case;
by Telechron; 1925-35; $275-400.
Designed by Paul Frankl.

Eight-day desk clock in gold metal
and glass case; 1935-45; $60-85.

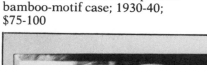

Desk clock in blue plastic case with
white hands; 1945; $60-90.

Alarm clock in pewter case, the Mammoth; by Parker Clock Co.; 1900-10; $45-55.

Calendar clock in metal and Bakelite case; by Hammond; 1935-50; $65-95.

Left: Miniature alarm clock; by Ansonia Clock Co.; 1878-85; $55-70. **Right:** Alarm clock, the Dot Alarm; by Waterbury Clock Co.; 1925-30; $30-45.

Alarm clock, the Royal; by Waterbury Clock Co; 1930-40; $25-40. Like most alarm clocks, this one has a body of sheet tin.

Sylvia pattern dresser clock; by Seth Thomas; 1910-15; $35-45. Made of Bakelite and brass, this clock is a forerunner of the modern bedside clock.

Art Deco cigarette lighter and clock combination in chrome and plastic; by Ronson; 1920-30; $60-85.

Alarm clock in red and yellow plastic case; by New Haven Clock Co.; 1925-35; $45-65. Bold design and color highlight an otherwise ordinary clock.

Wall clock in oak case; 1900-10; $100-175. Until replaced by electric clocks in the 1930s, spring-driven wall clocks were customary in every office and public building.

Hanging wall clock in oak and brass case; by Seth Thomas; 1915-25; $80-110.

Wall clock in oak case; 1920-30; $95-145.

Ships's clock in brass case; by Waterbury Clock Co.; 1900-20; $285-365.

Pocket watch in silver case; by Waltham Watch Co.; 1920-30; $125-185.

Pocket watches in gold-filled cases; 1925-35. **Left:** By Waltham Watch Co.; $155-195. **Center:** by Oscar Fresard; Lucerne, Switzerland; $300-400. **Right:** by Hamilton; $275-350.

Left: Pocket watch in gold-filled case; by Elgin; 1930-40; $100-150. **Right:** Miniature pocket watch in gold-filled case; 1900-10; $200-300.

Pocket watch in gold and silver case; by Waltham Watch Co.; 1930-40; $175-250.

Woman's watch in the form of a pendant; Switzerland; 1920-30; $125-175. Before the development of the wristwatch, women wore watches on chains or pinned to their clothing.

Fine pocket watches in gold-filled cases; 1920-35. **Left:** By Elgin; $375-475. **Right: from** Switzerland; $400-500.

Woman's watch in silver case in the form of a ring; 1910-20; $110-125.

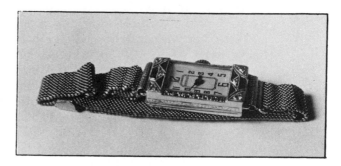

Women's wristwatch in gold-filled case, by Benrus; 1930-40; $325-450.

Indian Crafts

Interest in Indian crafts dates back to the late nineteenth century, but it has only been within the past decade or so that demand has reached the present fever pitch. Today, any well-made example, be it rug, basket, or bowl, commands a good price even if it was made only a few years ago. In part, this heightened interest is traceable to increased curiosity about all things Indian; in part, it reflects the current national craze for craft objects in general.

There are five major areas of Indian collectibles—pottery, basketry, rugs, beadwork, and wood carving—and all five are marked by certain characteristics that make them special in today's world: the items are all one of a kind, handmade, and constructed of natural materials. In our plastic, production-line society, these elements alone are enough to set Indian crafts apart.

Some American pottery can be dated back over two thousand years, but the bulk of collectible pieces were made between 1900 and 1970. Moreover, although archaeological excavations have shown that fine pottery was once made throughout the country, most examples now come from the pueblos of the Southwest.

The Indians of New Mexico and Arizona traditionally have formed their ware from coiled clay and baked it in open fires fed with goat dung. Decoration consists of abstract, geometric designs painted on the surface before firing or of similar patterns cut or scratched into a solid colored background.

Perhaps the best known of this pottery is the black-on-black ware made at the San Ildefonso pueblo near Santa Fe, New Mexico, by the Martinez family. In the early 1930s, Julian Martinez rediscovered the ancient method of smothering the baking fire to produce a rich matte black surface. From then until his death in 1943, Julian and Maria Martinez worked together (unusual in itself because most Indian potters are female), making their distinctive and usually signed pieces.

Today, with other members of the family, Maria carries on.

Black glaze pottery is not typical of the Southwest. Most ware from that area is glazed in several colors—red, yellow, black, and white are the most common—and is burned in an oxygen-rich fire to produce light colors. Typical of the area are the fine examples made at the pueblos of Santa Clara, Santo Domingo, and Acoma in New Mexico and among the Hopi Indians of Arizona.

Light and durable, basketry items are important to any primitive society, and Indians throughout North America have always made them in large quantities. In the extreme Northeast, the Passamaquoddy and Micmac tribes of northern New England still manufacture a great variety of splint and sweet-grass baskets, as do the Iroquois of central New York. Among the tribes of the Southeast, pine needles and sugarcane have served as materials. In most cases, basketry is produced both for personal use and as something to be sold to tourists.

Without doubt, the finest Indian baskets and the ones most sought by collectors are those of the Southwest. The tightly coiled baskets, bowls, trays, and jars of the California Pomo, Yurok, and Washo tribes are made of a variety of materials, including cedar bark, grass, leaves, and even roots all woven together with a remarkable facility. The fine construction and powerful, abstract decoration of these containers have a strong appeal to collectors—so strong, in fact, that certain more desirable examples have sold for over a thousand dollars apiece. Other well-known baskets of the Southwest are produced by the Apache, Navajo, Paiute, and Hopi.

Because of the nature of the materials from which they are constructed, baskets have a short life, and the great majority of them on the market today date to the 1920s or even later. What the collector should focus on here is not age but quality of design and construction.

The strong patterns and vivid colors of Western Indian blankets and rugs have had a great attraction for collectors for a long time. Although the Zuni and Hopi have made some appealing examples, most enthusiasts seek out Navajo textiles. The Navajo weavers work on an upright loom of their own invention and employ natural dyes and wool from their own sheep. Before the turn of the century they made blankets both for their own use and as trade goods. These were usually rectangular and vertically striped, although certain more elaborate pieces, called chief's blankets, were squarish in shape.

As the nineteenth century waned, however, an influx of factory-made blankets made blanket weaving unnecessary. Fortunately, it was at this time that whites began to buy the textiles as wall hangings. From this it was a natural step to producing thicker pieces as floor coverings. Since 1900 the Navajo have made a wide variety of rugs, some pictorial, some geometric, but all highly collectible. Indian rugs and blankets are today treated as art forms to be hung alongside the finest modern paintings.

Though perhaps less well known than the other Indian crafts, beadwork is important not only for its artistic merit but also because it is unique to the American Indian. When the first whites arrived in this country they found Indians decorating clothing and making small containers from porcupine quills. Dyed and flattened, these quills were sewn to background material in a variety of different patterns. When trade beads became available, the native craftsmen quickly began to employ these in their complex, essentially geometric designs.

Eastern Indian beadwork is characterized by rounded, floral designs while that of the Western tribes (such as the Shoshone, Comanche, and Sioux) leans more to geometric forms. Earlier examples, made for tribal use, include beaded pipe and gun bags, moccasins, and gauntlets. Later pieces, made during the period from 1910 to 1950, were often intended for sale to tourists and range from pincushions to watch fobs and souvenir pieces such as those still made by the Indians residing in the vicinity of Niagara Falls.

Indian crafts also include wood carving. The tribes of the Northwestern coast of North America, particularly the Haida and the Kwakiutl, are among the finest wood sculptors of all time. Masks, totems, chests, and carved eating utensils from this area have long been sought by museums and private collectors. Today, most pre-1940 examples are unavailable, but later pieces still come on the market. The only comparable work found in the Northeast are the false faces or medicine-man masks made by the Iroquois of New York. These too are well carved and would be a valuable addition to any collection.

Another form of wood carving is the kachinas of the Southwestern pueblos. Shaped from cottonwood and ranging in size from a few inches to several feet, kachinas are either masks or fully developed figures. In either case they represent figures from the Indian spirit world. Since there are over five hundred such deities, there are a great many pieces to be found, some dating back as far as 1880. However, the collector should be on guard against wood and even plastic or clay reproductions manufactured in Asia and sold at tourist shops throughout the West.

Other collectible Indian craft objects include hand-hammered silver, often mounted with turquoise or coral; elaborately decorated leather clothing; and wooden objects, such as rattles, drums, and weapons. All represent important areas of the collectibles field.

Pottery bowl in red, black, and
white; Acoma Pueblo; ca. 1920;
$130-170. A relatively common but
attractive example.

Pottery bowl in black and white
lightning pattern; Miembres culture;
Southwestern United States; 13th
century; $450-650. Bowls like this
were the forerunners of modern
American Indian pottery.

Alphabet bowl in polished black
clay; Cherokee; 1910-15; $315-425.
Signed Bigmeat.

Left: Pottery bowl in red and
gray; Santa Clara Pueblo;
1930-40; $65-95. **Right:**
Pottery bowl in tan and black;
Hopi; 1925-35; $200-275.

Sculptured clay bowl polished black;
Santa Clara Pueblo; 1920-30;
$175-245 if undamaged.

Pottery bowl with elaborate
geometric pattern in black and
orange on white; Zuni; 1935-45;
$300-485.

Pottery figure of a rain god in red,
black, and white; Tesuque Pueblo;
1940-45; $30-50.

Woven-grass basket stained in red;
Tulare; 1880-90; $750-1,100. A very
early and finely made example of
California basketry.

Woven basket, black on tan; Pima;
1870-80; $650-875.

Woven-grass hats; Hupa; 1880-90;
$170-285 each.

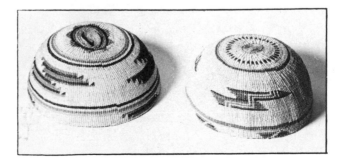

Covered woven-grass basket;
Northwest Coast; 1920-30; $185-245.

Large basketry olla, or jar; Apache;
1900-05; $2,500-4,000. Examples of
this size and artistic merit are hard
to obtain today.

Woven-grass bowl,
brown on tan;
Papago; 1940-50;
$125-175.

Woven basketry bowls, brown and
tan; Papago; 1935-45. **Left:** $90-130.
Right: $235-295. Pictorial designs
enhance the value of the piece at
right.

Wide, flat basket decorated with
abstract human figure; Pima;
1890-1900; $400-550.

Covered basketry water jar; Papago;
1910-20; $250-350. This piece is so
tightly woven it will hold water.

Interior of splint sewing basket; Micmac; 1930-35; $135-185. These pieces are sometimes mistaken for Shaker baskets.

Minature sweet-grass and splint baskets; Penobscot; 1940-55. **Left:** $20-35. Center:$30-45 **Right:** $35-50. The Maine Indians have long specialized in finely woven miniature baskets, many of which are less than three inches in diameter.

Covered sweet-grass basket in unusual octagonal design; Penobscot; 1945-55; $35-55. Bands of stained grass in pink and green highlight this basket.

Woven-grass basket; Micmac; 1945-55; $55-75.

False face society mask of wood, painted black and red with applied black horsehair; Iroquois; 1900-10; $2,200-2,800.

Fasle face society mask of wood, carved and painted white with applied horsehair; Iroquois; ca 1900; $1,750-2,750. These rare masks were carved for members of the tribe's medicine-man group.

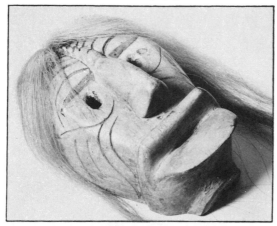

Wooden mask, carved and painted red, black, green, and white; Kwakiutl; 1890-1900; $6,000-9,000. The Indians of the Northwest Coast are among the world's finest sculptors.

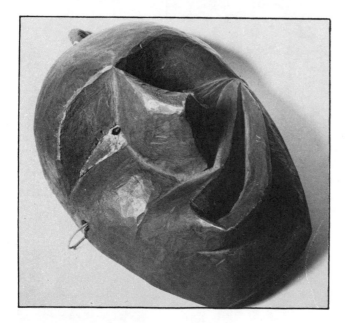

False face society mask of wood, carved and painted red; Oneida; 1890-1900; $2,700-3,200.

Canvas and wood tableta, or ceremonial headdress, in red, yellow, blue, and white; Southwest; 1920-25; $800-950.

Ceremonial bowl; carved wood painted red and black; Northwest Coast; 1890-1900; $2,500-4,000.

Totem figure, or "house key" pine carved and painted black; Shimshim; 1890-1900; $1,400-1,800.

Carved wooden figure; Haida; 1880-90; $2,000-2,500. Small figures such as these were given as gifts at ceremonial feasts, or potlaches.

Ceremonial bowl, unpainted pine inlaid with cowrie shell; 1870-80; $8,000-11,000. Pieces of this quality are rare and expensive.

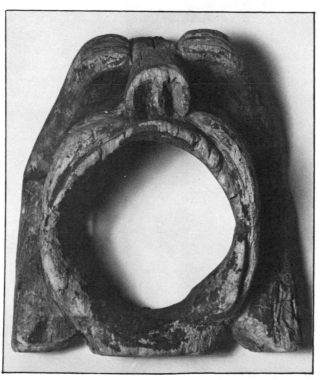

anoe thwart carved in the form of a uman face with traces of red and lue paint; Northwest Coast; 19th entury; $2,500-2,900.

Totem pole with red, white, blue, and black paint; Tlingit; 1890-1900; $3,200-3,800.

Fin from ceremonial carving of killer whale, pine with traces of red and green paint; Northwest Coast; 19th century; $1,900-2,400.

Miniature mat or weaving in Germantown pattern, red, orange, black, and green; Navajo; 1890-1900; $250-325. The Navajo made miniatures such as this for sale to tourists.

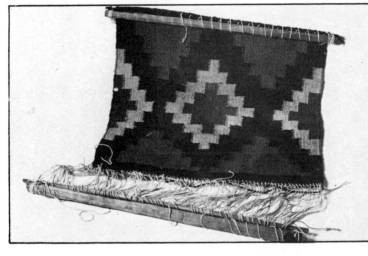

Rug in "eye dazzler" Germantown pattern, red, black, white, and yellow; Navajo; 1895-1900; $2,300-2,800. From the so-called classical period.

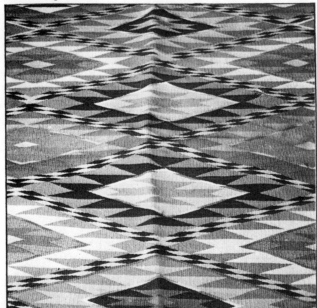

Wool rug dyed red, tan, black, and white; Navajo; 1920-25; $650-800. The Navajos have produced the finest Indian textiles.

Rug in zigzag pattern, gray, yellow, white, and black; Navajo; 1905-15; $800-1,300.

TicNosPas rug dyed red, black, white, orange, blue, and gray; Navajo; 1910-20; $900-1,500.

Germantown pattern double saddle blanket, red, yellow, blue, and green. Navajo; 1880-90; $800-1,100.

Beaded panels for a small carrying bag; Eastern Woodlands; 19th century; $375-475 the pair. The skillful blending of red, pink, blue, and white beads in this work is typical of high-quality Indian beadwork.

Beaded bag in red, white, and green beads on green dyed leather; Kiowa; 1890-1900; $325-415.

Beaded moccasin in red, white, blue, and yellow; Sioux; 1880-90; $245-350 the pair.

Beaded martingale for horse; Nez Perce; 1880-90; $1,200-1,600. This remarkably elaborate example combines tiny brass bells, mother-of-pearl, and seashells, with red, white, blue, pink, and black beads.

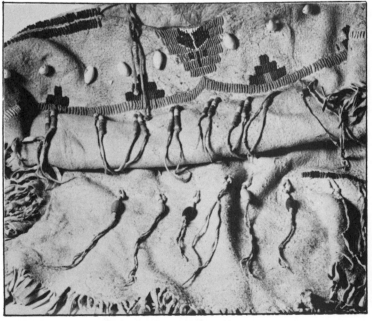

Beaded shirt decorated with cowrie shells and red, orange, blue, yellow, and pink beads; Plateau; 1920-25; $375-545.

Beaded pipe bag; Cheyenne; 1880-85; $550-750. This bag is decorated with dyed porcupine quills and red,

yellow, and blue beads.

Pincushion embellished with red, white, and blue beads; Iroquois; dated 1919; $35-55. For many years the Indians of western New York have made beadwork pieces such as this for sale to tourists.

Beadwork wall pocket, white beads on tan cloth; Iroquois; 1935-45; $30-45.

Beadwork wall pocket in tan, white, and green; Navajo; 1920-35; $50-75.

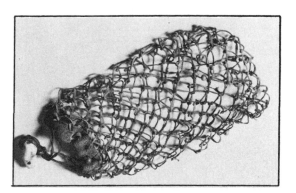

Woven leather bait bag decorated with red and blue beads and bone toggle; American Eskimo; 1880-90; $325-375.

Silver concha belt set with turquoise; Navajo; 1940–Navajo; 1940-45; $800-1,000.

Turquoise and silver bracelet; Navajo; 1890-1900; $1,000-1,600. Old silver like this is often called pawn, because it was frequently pawned by the Indians during the periods between crops.

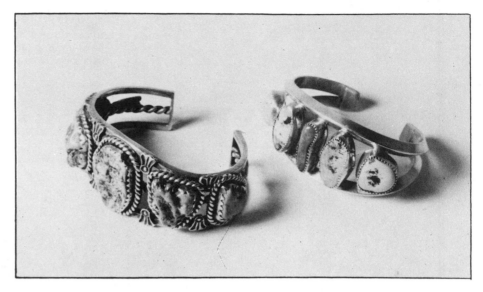

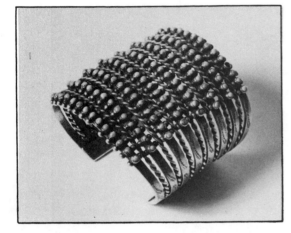

Pawn silver bracelets; Navajo. **Left:** Set with turquoise; 1900-10; $450-625. **Right:** Set with turquoise and coral; 1910-20; $315-385.

Miniature canoe of birch bark and qill work; Micmac; 1880-1900; $100-150.

Silver bracelet set with turquoise; Navajo; 1920-25; $325-425.

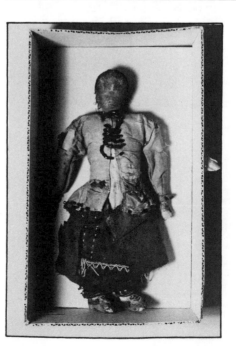

Doll with leather dress decorated in pink, green, yellow, and blue beads; Cree; 1880-90; $900-1,200. Pre-1900 Indian dolls are extremely rare.

Pipe bowls made of catlinite, a form of red soapstone; Plains; 1880-1910.
Left: $60-85. **Right:** $95-135.

Wrought-iron trade axe and pipe combination; 18th century; $1,300-1,900.

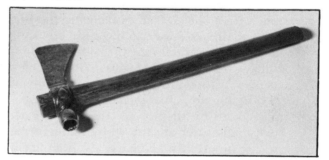

Knife and case; Kwakiutl; 1870-80; $2,100-2,600. The blade has been cut down from a Russian saber, and the head is carved in the form of a totem bear.

Fetish made from an animal vertebrae painted red, blue, and green; Southwest; 1920-25; $120-170. Intended to be worn around the neck.

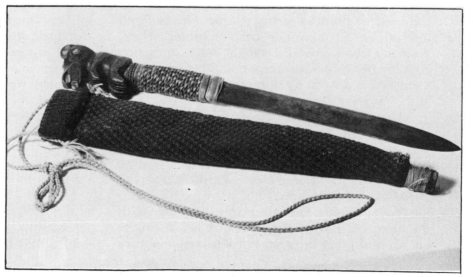

Vintage Clothing

Clothing is a unique collectible because it is usually collected not simply to be admired, but also to be worn. There are, of course, collectors who maintain large costume or period clothing collections, but far more frequently the purchaser of old clothing intends to put his or her acquisition to use. Moreover, most collectors and dealers in clothing are young and live in large cities or in college communities where the wearing of period costume is acceptable and popular. Rural antiques dealers who stock early clothing usually do so in order to sell it wholesale to city merchants.

For the most part, clothing is collected by period, with some collectors favoring the Victorian look and others drawn to the slim, boyish lines of the 1920s or the flamboyant, Hollywood-inspired styles of the 1930s and 1940s. Within each era exists a multitude of interesting collectible objects.

Among women's garments, dresses and evening gowns of all periods are in great demand. Also sought after are the white undergarments of the late nineteenth and early twentieth centuries, which now are being worn, in some cases, as dresses. Hats appropriate to the costumes are also popular, especially the straw hats worn during the 1920 to 1940 era. Shoes, too, are collectible, particularly the high-button version favored during the early years of this century. Handbags and small purses may be found in numerous materials, from fur to precious metals, and these are collected or used by many people who have no interest at all in other early clothing items. Women's coats are also sought after, and such popular 1920s furs as raccoon and beaver are refurbished and worn by numerous young devotees of the "roaring twenties."

There are clothing collectibles for men as well. The trim lines and tailored look of the late Victorian period appeal to some people, though suits from this era are not easy to come by. More available are traditional blue gabardines from the 1930s and the notorious "zoot suits" popular during the late 1940s. The latter are all the rage with the disco set. Early formal wear, when it can be found, is of great interest, but few contemporary men can fit into the smaller sizes that accommodated their forefathers—a problem, incidentally, that is also often encountered by the ladies as well.

Men's hats and shoes are widely available. Among the former, bowlers and top hats are well thought of, and the disco crowd is always seeking 1930s-type snap-brim stetsons—like the gangster hats associated with the Cagney-Bogart movie era. Likewise, the brightly colored felt hats, both porkpies and the wide-brimmed feathered versions favored by zoot-suiters, are once more in style. There is some interest in the pre-1920 high-top shoes, but most buyers want either 1930s wing tips or the saddle shoes and white buckskins associated with Andy Hardy and the bucolic college movies of the period from 1940 to 1950. Neckties, too, are in vogue, particularly the garish hand-painted or silk-screened types so common shortly after the Second World War.

Though influenced on its periphery by "outsider" styles such as the jazz look of the 1930s and the zoot-suiter fad, men's clothing has remained amazingly constant in style over the past century. Such has not been the case with women's wear, and most knowledgeable collectors can date women's clothing to within a few years, going by style alone.

The earliest garments with which we are concerned—those worn at the turn of the century—reflect a life-style in which women were expected to do little other than look pretty. Beauty was conceived in terms of the classical hourglass figure, and women were expected to pad themselves or wear constricting corsets in order to achieve this norm. However, soon after 1900, designers introduced flowing garments that demanded a much slimmer figure and also could not be worn over the previously popular petticoats. Bulky undergarments were out and diet was in, a pattern that has been maintained to the present day.

By the 1920s, high waists had been replaced by styles that hugged the hips, hair was cut short beneath the close-fitting cloche hats, and dress lengths rose to heights never dreamed of during the nineteenth century. Then, in the 1930s, draping and pleating reappeared along with huge hats, a natural waist, and padded shoulders. By the late 1940s, skirts were inching up again, and padding was gone, to be replaced once more by the "natural look," which heralded the coming of dungarees and the casual clothes of the 1960s. Each stylistic variation during these periods has its devotees among clothing collectors.

Because it is used (that is, worn), clothing has problems unique in the collectibles field. To be salable, it must be in good condition or repairable. This means that most dealers and many collectors in the field are, by necessity, amateur tailors. And because it is worn, old clothing wears out. As a result, substantial numbers of early garments are destroyed every year, something that is bound to have an eventual effect on a field in which prices are already rising steadily. On the other hand, clothing is a relatively new collectible, and large quantities of desirable garments can still be found in both urban and rural areas. The collector with the patience to explore thrift shops, house sales, and church benefits will often come up with treasures that can be purchased for next to nothing. Such prizes are undoubtedly out there—it is just a matter of having the patience to seek them out.

Men's high-top shoes. **Rear:** Black leather; 1915-25; $40-60. **Front:** Brown leather; 1920-30; $45-65.

Flocked velvet dress and jacket in royal blue; 1885-1905; $255-375. The hourglass silhouette characteristic of late 19th-century fashions is clearly evident in this attractive costume.

Afternoon dress in lace-trimmed natural silk; 1910-20; $250-325.

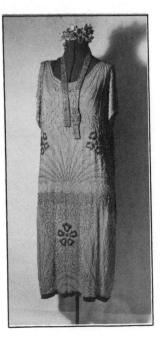

Evening gown in gold embroidered white silk; 1920-30; $225-335.

Tea gown in accordian-pleated silk chiffon with blue velvet trim; 1920-25; $375-550. The short skirt of this lovely blue and gold garment is typical of the 1920s.

Evening dress in black silk and gauze; 1925-30; $125-165.

Tea gown in black satin and silk chiffon decorated with cut crystal and seed beads; 1920-30; $450-575. The handwork on this garment is outstanding.

Tea dress in pink silk chiffon; 1920-30; $125-145. An example of the so-called sweet-sixteen dress.

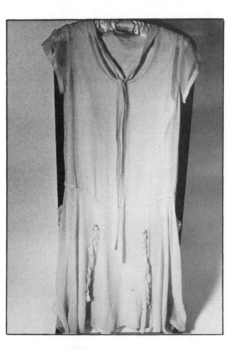

Beauclea dress in wine-colored silk; 1935-40; $150-175.

Evening gown in gauze over black-and-white pattern satin; 1950-55; $115-155.

Art Deco dress in red, black, green, and orange crepe; 1930-35; $275-375. An uncommonly sophisticated print.

Evening gown in pink silk taffeta;
1930-40; $85-115.

Cotton housedress in red, black,
green, and yellow print; 1930-40;
$30-45. Sold by mail order for as
little as ninety-nine cents each, these
"Depression prints" are now popular
with a more affluent clientele.

Evening gown in teal blue satin;
1950-55; $110-150.

"Mini dress" of nylon decorated with
silver plastic bangles; 1960-65;
$90-120.

Three piece evening suit with pink
sequins; 1950-55; $250-375.
Sequined scarf; 1950-55; $15-20.

Suit in navy blue gabardine;
1935-45; $60-75.

Wool suit in black and white stripes;
1940-45; $165-215

Victorian maternity slip in white
silk; 1890-1900; $210-325. This slip
is cut and pleated to provide for the
growth of the baby.

Dressing gown in purple silk;
1920-25; $75-125.

Evening suit in dark blue rayon;
1930-35; $75-115.

587

Dressing gown in rust silk organza;
1950-55; $90-120.

Victorian bodice in silk decorated
with jet beads; 1880-90; $225-325.

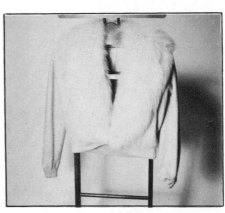

Peignoir in pink lace and slipper
satin; 1940-50; $125-155. Scarf in
peach satin; 1940-50; $10-15

Evening sweater in natural cashmere
trimmed with white fox; 1950-55;
$115-145.

Victorian capelet in black silk with
jetbead trim; 1890-1900; $125-155.

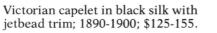

Coat in green wool trimmed with
Persian lamb; 1900-10; $400-575.

Cape in black monkey fur; 1940-45; $1,500-2,500. With the animals now protected by law, there are few monkey-fur capes available.

Coat in maroon wool with white fox trim; 1940-45; $270-340. Blue sequined scarf; 1940-45; $15-25.

Boa of silver fox; 1940-45; $300-400. Tailored jacket in tan and cream gabardine; 1940-45; $45-70.

Left: Hat in tan felt with orange and white artificial flowers; 1930-40; $35-50. **Right:** Hat in lavender straw; 1920-30; $65-85.

Cloche hat in red felt; 1920-30; $45-65.

Women's straw hats; 1930-45. **Left:** Natural with artificial flowers; $30-40. Center: Red with blue satin ribbon; $40-50. **Right:** Natural with veil and brown ribbon; $25-35.

Turban hat in black silk chiffon; 1930-40; $35-50. A hat made famous by Marlene Dietrich.

Woman's high-laced shoe in brown leather; 1915-20; $60-80.

Left: Evening pump in black satin; 1920-25; $40-55. **Right:** Brown suede shoe; 1910-15; $70-95.

Left: Evening shoe with pink sequins; 1950-55; $50-75. **Right:** Shoe in tan and cream leather; 1920-30; $45-65. **Top** Open-toed strap in violet material; 1930-35; $30-45.

Left: Woman's overshoe in fox, velvet, and rubber; 1940-45; $35-45. **Right:** Sling-back pump in blue suede and alligator dyed red; 1940-45; $45-65. These shoes are in the so-called Betty Grable style.

Compact case in pot metal and velvet with silk tassel; 1890-1910; $55-75.

Compact case in red plastic decorated with floral motif in cream, blue, and green; 1920-30; $35-50.

Chain purses. **Left:** Black silk with ivory handle; 1915-20; $55-70. **Center:** Black velvet with sterling silver handle; 1930-35; $60-90. **Right:** Black silk with gold sequins; 1930-40; $45-65.

Chain purses. **Left:** Jet and black sequins; 1950-55; $25-35. **Center:** Needlepoint and beadwork; 1950-55 $35-45. **Right:** Steel point tapestry with marcasite clasp; 1930-40; $60-75.

591

Muff and purse combination in civet; 1940-45; $35-60.

Clutch purses; 1940-50. **Left:** Black sequins; $35-50. **Center:** Red goatskin; $40-55. **Right:** Red and white coiled plastic; $20-30.

Man's overcoat of wool cashmere; 1950-55; $110-160.

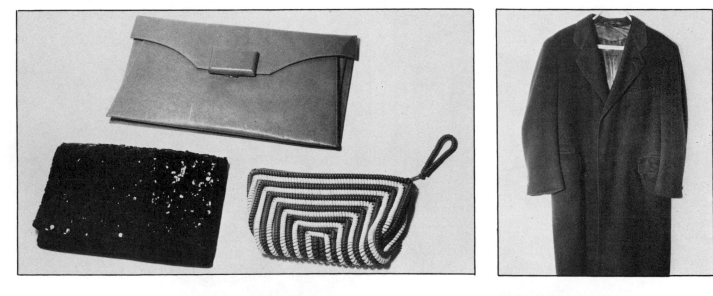

Stormcoat in tan gabardine with artificial wool collar; 1950-55; $40-50.

Raincoat in tan gabardine; 1945-55; $60-75.

Menswear; 1950-55. Jacket in white rayon; $44-65. Shirt in red cotton; $20-35. Red and black striped tie; $5-10.

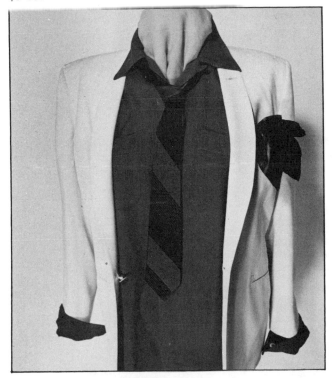

Sportcoat in hand-woven yellow silk; 1950-55; $100-135.

Cutaway coat in black wool; by J. Press; 1915-20; $135-175.

Jacket in black rayon; 1945-55; $55-70.

Sportcoat in cotton with red paisley pattern and brass buttons; 1955-60; $40-55.

Leisure coat in gray rayon tweed and blue gabardine; 1945-50; $30-40.

593

Lounge jacket in wool and nylon in gray and white; 1940-45; $25-35.

Hawaiian-style shirt in red, brown, and white pattern; 1955-60; $35-45.

Menswear; 1930-35. Vest in yellow wool; $30-45. Shirt in cotton in blue pattern; $15-20. Blue and black bow tie; $5-10.

Pullover or Shirt-Jac in green gabardine; 1940-50; $20-30.

Top hats in felt; 1920-30; $65-95 each. The example at left is shown collapsed for storage.

Left: Fedora in brown felt; 1935-40;
$55-70. **Center:** Black bowler;
1920-30; $60-75. **Right:** Straw
boater; 1920-30; $35-55. The fedora
is the "gangster" hat of the 1930s.

Silk-screened neckties; 1940-50;
$10-20 each.

Left: Black and white wing tip;
1930-35; $55-65. **Center:** Brown and
white shoe; 1940-50; $45-60. **Right:**
Brown and white saddle shoe;
1950-60; $45-55. All popular with the
"hip" college crowd.

Left: Brown leather shoe; 1940-50;
$40-50. **Right:** White buckskin;
1945-55; $35-45.

Jewelry

Jewelry is a particularly appealing collectible for several reasons: if set in gold or silver or with precious gems, it has intrinsic value; it can be used; and—of prime importance to many collectors—it is so small that a substantial collection can be housed in the smallest apartment.

The collector interested in American jewelry of the period 1880 to 1950 will find a multitude of treasures from which to choose. There is an abundance of late Victorian pieces. Indeed, the last decades of the nineteenth century were a period of great show and opulence, and jewelry was very popular. There were two general types of jewelry: primary jewelry, made of gem-encrusted precious metals and intended for use only on great occasions; and secondary jewelry, which consisted of semiprecious stones set in silver or plate for everyday use.

Both types of jewelry are of importance to the modern collector; the Victorian flair for detail, excellence of workmanship, and ability to create charming small things is evident in nearly every piece regardless of its original value. The variety available is, in part, a result of the fact that among the moneyed classes women had little to do other than display their wealth. It is also attributable to the general custom, among all classes, of giving jewelry as gifts at both joyous occasions and tragic ones.

Victorian jewelry varies greatly in style and is, in fact, a mirror of the many styles—Gothic, Rococo, Renaissance, and so on—popular during the period. Egyptian Revival, for example, appears not only in scarab rings but also in the far more common snake-form rings and bracelets. The curling serpents, often with glaring eyes of ruby or opal, seem to have had a fascination for women of the time. Even Queen Victoria owned a snake bracelet.

There are also, of course, Art Nouveau pieces, some of them made by famous craftsmen like Tiffany and Lalique. These include bracelets, rings, and especially brooches. The motifs are appropriate to the period: long, flowing floral and animal forms done in everything from gold to natural wood.

For the wealthy, gems were de rigueur, and as the century came to an end, diamonds assumed a place of first importance. In the 1880s they were set in heavy flamboyant mountings, but by the 1890s social usage dictated settings of wisps of gold or platinum from which the great gems hung like drops of dew on a blade of grass.

In polite society diamonds were reserved for the married woman; girls and young ladies were limited to such baubles as rubies, pearls, and emeralds. In the 1880s these were usually set in bracelets and brooches because the long hair and high necklines of the period limited use of other jewelry. But at the turn of the century, short hair and low-cut gowns returned, and with them came a plethora of necklaces and earrings. At the same time, silver, which had been somewhat in eclipse, was returned to favor, particularly in the form of heavy carved bracelets in the Indian taste. The Eastern influence is also seen in the dragon motif common to many pieces.

Much of the finer jewelry made after 1900 was made in suites of several matching pieces (pins, bracelets, tiaras) intended to be worn together. Unfortunately, many of these suites have been broken up over the years, making it difficult to obtain a complete set. It is possible, however, to obtain suites in semiprecious stones from the period from 1900 to 1920. It was during this period also that paste or artificial glass became generally available, and, combined with silver-plated settings, it offered an inexpensive alternative for the frugal. Marcasites, tiny gemlike pieces of cut and polished steel, served a similar purpose.

Though relatively unimportant in comparison with the large quantity of Victorian and post-Victorian jewelry, jewelry produced by craftsmen of the Arts and Crafts movement is available. From 1890 until well into the 1920s these studio jewelers created unusual forms employing semiprecious stones, such as garnet and topaz, and massive settings of silver or even copper. Today, such pieces are rather hard to come by.

Following the First World War the so-called modern movement came to the fore, and jewelry design changed greatly in response to the influence of the arts (particularly cubism), the effects of mass production, and the introduction of new materials, such as plastics and chrome. The forms of jewelry, which had traditionally been based on natural sources, became angular and geometric. During the 1920s this hard line was softened by an almost playful experimentation, but with the coming of the Great Depression, a severity of form set in, a formalism that was in sharp contrast to the pastels that dominated the color scheme.

The trademark of this period was the string of beads, and amazingly long ropes of cut-glass or rock beads adorned the flappers of the 1920s and early 1930s. Other materials used in jewelry production included amber (or its plastic substitute); ivory; black onyx; jade (in large, flat, relief-carved ring stones); tortoiseshell (for belt buckles and hatpins); a whole variety of attractive stones, ranging from granite to rose quartz; and even colored sealing wax. There was also a great deal of enameled jewelry during the Art Deco period. There had been enameled jewelry during the Victorian period, of course, but enamelware became an art form during the 1930s.

Still, Art Deco jewelry does not compare in either quantity or quality with that of the late Victorian era. During the 1920s and 1930s, women, the major wearers of jewelry, were too active to use the great quantities allocated to women of the Victorian age. Moreover, the economic decline of the 1930s made the wearing of lavish adornment both prohibitively expensive and almost immoral (to all but the most insensitive). As a consequence, jewelry of the 1920s and 1930s is for the most part confined to rings, pins, and necklaces. The elaborate pieces so popular during the earlier era are gone.

During the 1940s and 1950s the boom in costume jewelry, which had been developed just before the Second World War, continued, and great quantities of rather grotesque jewelry made of pot metal, plastic, and painted wood flooded the market. Some of these items are now considered collectible, though their value is more nostalgic than aesthetic.

One should not overlook men's jewelry. Rings have been with us for a long time, and in former times there were also lavish buttons and hair buckles. Contemporary men's jewelry is more mundane. Watch fobs, usually made of silver or gold, abound. There are also such oddments as cigar cutters, bill and coin holders, and fraternal jewelry. Pocketknives can form a whole collection, as can cuff links. Although some of these items were adorned with gemstones, men's jewelry was for the most part severe in line and decoration.

Since there is so much of it to choose from, collecting jewelry can be confusing. It is very much a matter of taste and pocketbook. Buy what you like, but look for good workmanship, pleasing design, and soundness of materials. If these qualities are present, the absence of gold or gems will matter little—without these qualities, precious materials are of little help.

Sterling Silver Art Nouveau belt; 1900-10; $1,200-1,700. Elaborately crafted silver belts are rare and expensive.

Sterling silver Art Nouveau belt buckle; 1880-90; $65-80.

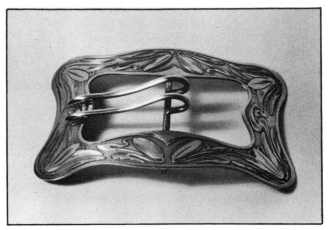

Left: Enamel and silver Art Deco belt buckle; 1925-35; $75-125. **Right:** Silver Art Nouveau belt buckle; by Shiebler; 1890-1900; $125-155.

Electroplated silver belt buckle with Indian-head motif; 1900-10; $25-35.

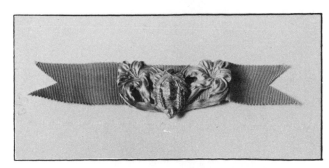

Art Deco belt buckle of artificial diamonds and rubies set in a pot-metal mounting; 1930-40; $15-25.

Sterling silver coin bracelet;
1880-1900 ; $150-175.

Sterling silver bracelet; by Shiebler
Silver Company; 1890-1900;
$125-175. Shows Eastern influence.

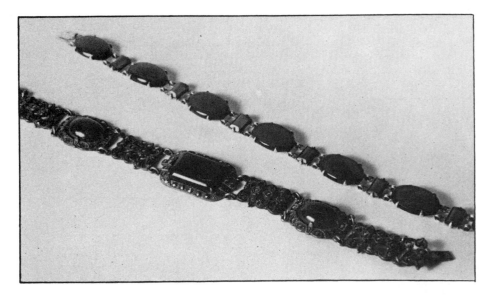

Art Deco bracelets; 1925-35. **Left:**
Silver with marcasites and onyx;
$150-185. **Right:** Silver and onyx;
$95-135.

Sterling silver bracelet set with
diamonds; 1920-30; $1,500-1,800.

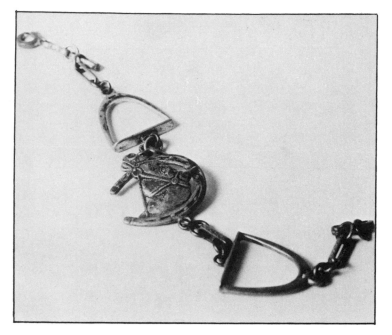

Sterling silver bracelet; 1910-20;
$75-125. Horseback-riding motif.

Sterling silver and enamel snake
bracelet with seed pearls; 1890-1900;
$150-200.

Bakelite bracelet; 1930-40; $25-40.
Bakelite was a popular material for
inexpensive jewelry during the
1930s.

Gold snake rings; 1880-1900. **Left:**
With diamond; $350-500. **Right:**
With ruby; $200-260.

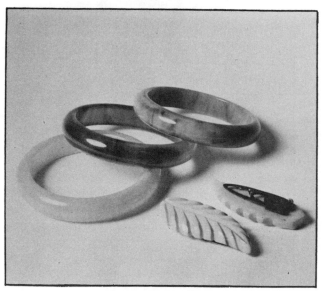

Left: Bakelite bracelets; 1930-40;
$25-50. **Right:** Pair of Bakelite hair
clips; 1930-40; $15-25. The "bloom is
off the rose" with most Bakelite
jewelry.

Left: Gold ring with small rubies; 1930-40; $200-275. **Right:** Silver ring with diamond chips; $125-175.

Silver and marcasite ring; 1930-40; $75-100.

Gold Art Nouveau ring; 1890-1900; $350-500. The excellent work and detail make this an outstanding ring.

Gold rings; 1910-20. **Left:** With garnet and opals; $150-225. **Right:** With garnet and sapphires; $175-275.

Necklace of carved rose quartz; 1920-30; $155-225.

Gold and cut stone ring; 1915-25; $115-165.

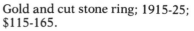

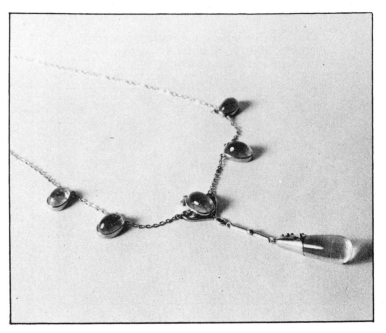

Necklace of sterling silver and enamel with mother-of-pearl drop; 1900-10; $335-395. The naturalistic forms of the Art Nouveau period lend themselves to necklace and pendant construction.

Gold and pink tourmaline necklace; 1900-10; $185-265.

Left: Sterling silver pendant with enamel center; 1900-10; $60-90.
Right: Sterling silver, enamel, and colored glass necklace with glass drop; 1910-20; $310-390.

Carved ivory pendant; 1920-30; $185-255.

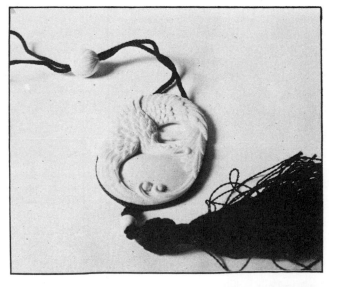

Pendant in black onyx with gold-washed sterling silver mounting; 1930-40; $160-210.

Art Nouveau figural pendants; 1890-1900. **Left:** Gold-washed sterling silver; signed Bryk; $165-205. **Right:** Sterling silver; $135-185.

Left: Sterling silver and enamel pendant; by Charles Horner; 1900-10; $275-365. **Right:** Sterling silver brooch with turquoise; 1925-35; $65-85.

Sterling silver and enamel necklace; 1920-30; $175-245. Art Deco necklaces and pendants are as popular today as they were in the 1920s and 1930s.

Left: Sterling silver and enamel pin; 1910-20; $125-155. **Center:** Sterling silver and enamel pandant; by Charles Horner; 1900-10; $350-400. **Right:** Sterling silver and enamel pin; by Charles Horner; 1900-20; $140-180.

603

Sterling silver and enamel Art Deco pendants; 1930-40. **Top:** $55-75. **Center:** $75-115. **Bottom:** $85-130.

Sterling silver and enamel Art Deco pendants; 1930-40. **Left:** $70-95. **Center:** $85-110. **Right:** $60-75.

Sterling silver and enamel Art Deco necklace; 1930-40; $135-195.

Sterling silver and enamel necklace; 1935-45; $95-155.

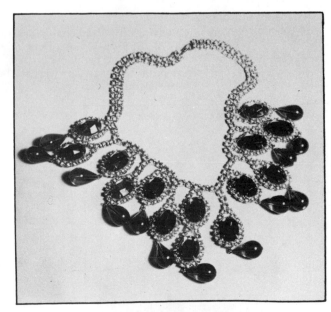

Necklace of gem cut glass mounted on pot metal; 1940-50; $40-60.

604

Brooch of carved pink coral;
1880-1900; $75-115. In the Italian
manner.

Brooches; by Georg Jensen; 1930-45.
Center left: Floral $150-185. **Center
right:** Bird; $175-225. **Top:** Floral
with onyx; $190-245. **Bottom:**
Openwork; $115-145.

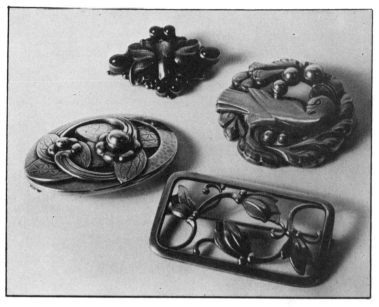

Silver and gold Arts and Crafts
brooch; 1890-1900; $175-275.

Gold and enamel Arts and Crafts
pin; 1900-10; $225-275.

Sterling silver Art Nouveau brooches;
1885-95. **Left:** $40-60. **Right:** $50-80.

605

Sterling silver Art Nouveau brooch;
1880-1900; $55-85.

Left: Sterling silver Egyptian
Revival pin in gold wash; 1930-40;
$30-45. **Center:** Sterling silver
dragonflies with turquoise; 1900-10;
$95-135. **Right:** Sterling silver and
enamel beetle; by Charles Horner;
1900-10; $85-125.

Satsuma porcelain enamel brooch;
Japan; 1920-30; $125-175.

Sterling silver and translucent
enamel pin; 1920-30; $115-165.

Sterling silver dog pins; 1890-193
$45-95 each. Dog related items ar
always popular.

Brooch of pot metal, rhinestones,
and enamel; 1930-40; $25-35.

Brooch and matching earrings of pot
metal and rhinestones; 1940-50;
$25-40 the set.

Bakelite pin in the form of a dog;
1945-55; $ 5-10.

Plastic Mickey Mouse pins;
1950-60; $15-25 each.

Pair of sterling silver turtle earrings;
1920-30; $30-45.

Sterling silver and enamel brooch
and matching earrings; 1930-40;
$75-95.

Plastic earrings; 1940-50; $10-15 the pair.

Earrings of painted wood; 1940-50; $5-10 the pair.

Pair of cuff links in jet; 1920-30; $20-35.

Cuff links of the snap-apart variety in silver metal and plastic; 1930-40; $15-20 the pair.

Left: Rosary of carved wood; 1900-15; $85-125. **Right:** Pencil in the form of a cross; 1900-15; $55-75. Both pieces are novelties of the type called Stanhopes. They have a small viewing hole through which a tiny picture can be seen.

Sterling silver men's jewlery;
1910-30. **Left bottom:** Cigar cutter;
$45-65. **Left top:** Pair of cuff links;
$30-45. **Center:** Enameled stickpin;
$25-35. **Right:** Money clip; $35-45.

Sterling silver charms given away at
fraternal meetings; 1930-40; $35-55
each.

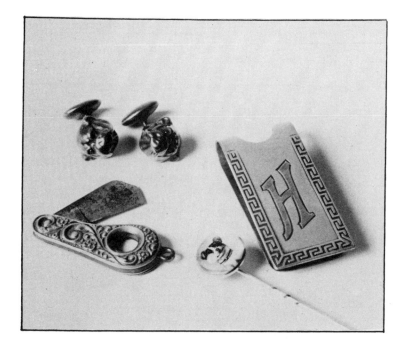

Gold stickpins; 1900-10. **Left:** $55-75.
Right: $60-80. Racing motifs raise
value of these pieces.

Brass pendant in the form of a small
book filled with tiny pictures; dated
1929; $45-65.

Gold Art Nouveau watch pin;
1900-10; $65-85. In the days before
wrist watches, women pinned their
watches to their blouses or coats
with pins like this.

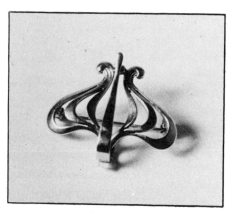

Sterling silver Art Nouveau watch
pin; 1890-1900; $125-175.

Watch fob in the form of a miniature
flask in red and white gold;
1880-1900; $200-285.

Sterling silver perfume flask;
1910-20; $35-55.

Sterling silver Art Nouveau woman's
purse; Germany; 1890-1910;
$95-135.

Compact case of brass, Bakelite, and
glass; 1925-35; $45-65.

Compact case of brass, Bakelite, and
glass; 1930-40; $35-55.

Pair of sterling silver and enamel
shoe buckles; 1920-25; $40-60.

Sterling silver key ring in the form of
a belt; 1920-30; $35-50.

Pair of shoe buckles in cut steel and
glass beads; 1920-30; $25-30.

Radios, Phonographs, and Jukeboxes

Phonographs, jukeboxes, and radios pose both opportunities and problems for the collector. Radios, particularly those from the 1930s and 1940s, are relatively easy to obtain and can often be purchased for very little money. Phonographs, too, are not difficult to come by, but jukeboxes, because of both their size and cost, do not lend themselves to extensive collecting. Moreover, all these devices are frequently found in disrepair, and neither the supplies nor the expertise needed to fix them are generally available.

Although a phonographlike device was patented in 1863 by one F. B. Fenby, the first true talking machine was invented by Thomas A. Edison in 1878. The inventor applied a steel needle to a rotating tin cylinder so that the needle point cut grooves in the metal according to the intensity of the received sound. After these grooves had been cut, the original sound could be duplicated by running a needle through the grooves again.

Alexander Graham Bell, of telephone fame, refined Edison's procedure by substituting wax cylinders, which produced a higher quality sound. Wax cylinders are two to four inches long and were made in great quantities until well into the 1900s. They are collector's items in their own right, with rarer examples such as those made by the Bettini firm selling for several hundred dollars apiece.

However, when Emile Berliner, in 1887, developed the prototype for the modern, flat phonographic disc, he opened the way for the common 78, 45, and 33 rpm phonograph records of this century. Today, many of these are desirable collectibles.

Early phonographs were hand powered and depended on a spring-driven motor that was wound with a long crank handle. Before 1913, they also had large speaker horns of nickel-plated steel or tin that were attached to the outside of the talking machine. The replacement of these "morning glory" (so called for their shape) horns by interior speakers greatly changed the appearance of the phonograph.

Edison phonographs are the most sought after by collectors, and the facsimile signature of the inventor on a 1911 model Home phonograph or a 1909 Maroon Gem is highly prized. But talking machines by other manufacturers are also collectible. The 1898 Columbia Graphaphone, the Zon-O-Phone of the early 1900s, and the many Victor models are all worth looking for. Nor should one overlook the various collectible phonographic accessories. Advertisements, such as those featuring the Victor ("His master's voice") dog and the Columbia Sphinx, are in great demand, as are catalogs, brochures, and record jackets.

The jukebox is the natural culmination of the phonograph. These large, complex machines became popular in the 1930s and can accommodate numerous records, which can be played one at a time or in series. Too large and too expensive for most homes, the "jukes" were intended for use in places of public entertainment, and their styling—featuring colored neon tubing and Art Deco plastic and metal cases—was clearly designed to catch the eye of the paying public. Today, it is this very styling that catches the collector's eye.

Collectible radios are for the most part much more recent than phonographs. Although the groundwork for radio transmission was laid in the nineteenth century and although early wireless and crystal sets were in use soon after 1900, the modern radio did not appear until after the First World War.

Some collectors are interested in the wireless and crystal sets, but because these look more like scientific instruments than what most people think of as radios, they are not generally popular. It was only with the coming of commercial radio stations (Pittsburgh's KDKA was the first) in 1920 that the public at large had a reason to own a set. Once this happened there was a substantial demand for reasonably attractive radios that would fit into the living room as well as the workshop.

Manufacturers such as Atwater-Kent, Magnavox, Zenith, RCA, and Radiola responded with a variety of receivers. In the early 1920s these were battery powered and equipped with earphones or large wooden or hard-rubber speakers similar to those on vintage victrolas. But the consumers were not happy with battery-operated radios. The battery acid was corrosive, and the batteries had to be recharged.

By 1927 manufacturers had solved the problem with the introduction of tube sets, which could be plugged into an AC electric socket. At first these were table models, but by 1929 many companies were making console radios that were built into furniture cases so that they could blend easily with the living room furniture. Well-constructed consoles were the centerpieces of many homes until they were replaced, after the Second World War, by the hi-fi set and the television.

Although consoles are popular with many collectors, their size usually limits the number that can be owned. Table models, on the other hand, come in various collectible sizes. Among the most popular are the smaller cabinet radios in the cathedral style, which were called midgets or depression models, the latter name because of their appearance during the hard times of the 1930s. Other interesting types are the Art Deco plastic table models, also from the 1930s, the early "portables" (some of which weighed forty pounds!), and automobile radios. As with phonographs, accessories and advertising materials associated with radios offer a fertile field for the collector.

The Gramaphone, Eagle model; by Columbia Phonograph Co.; patented 1897; $375-475. This is an early tin-horn phonograph.

Edison Standard phonograph; ca. 1905; $450-500. This early phonograph utilized two-and four-inch wax cylinders.

The Gramaphone, model Q; by Columbia Phonograph Co.; patented 1898; $235-300. Note the wax cylinder in place on this phonograph.

Victrola, model V-VII; by Victor Talking Machine; 1915-20; $225-285.

Early phonograph horns. **Above** Brown papier-mache megaphone type; 1890-1900; $75-100. **Below:** Tin "morning glory" in blue, pink, and gold; 1880-90; $135-165.

Arionola; by Arion Manufacturing Co.; ca. 1923; $300-350.

Edison Tin Triumph phonograph horn; 1900-05; $155-195. An eleven-panel horn with collapsible stand.

Victor Talking Machine; model VV-VI; by Victor Talking Machine; 1918-22; $150- 200.

Victrola, standard model A, with red metal horn; by Columbia Phonograph Co.; ca. 1901; $550-750. An uncommon early disc victrola in excellent condition.

Edison floor model victrola in oak cabinet; 1915-25; $275-325.

Edison Diamond Disc floor model phonograph in mahogany veneer case; 1920-30; $400-550.

Philco combination radio-phonograph in wood and plastic; ca. 1946; $125-175.

Edison wax phonograph cylinders; 1898-1910. **Left:** Gold Moulded; $10-15. **Center:** Amberol; $5-10. **Right:** Blue Amberol; $9-12.

Early 78 rpm phonograph records. **Left:** Edison Re-Creation; 1905-10; $7-12. **Right:** Little Wonder; patented 1909; $9-16. The Edison record is a "fat" record, over a quarter-inch thick.

Record jacket and 78 rpm records by jazz musician "Fats" Waller; 1935-40; $65-95. Records by popular artists always bring good prices.

33 rpm Picture Records; by Sav-Way Industries; ca. 1947; $75-125 for the album. Rare and hard to locate.

Wurlitzer jukebox, No. 1015, in plastic, chrome, and glass with oak veneer case; ca. 1946; $3,500-5,500.

Wurlitzer jukebox, No. 1080A, in plastic, chrome, and glass with oak veneer case; ca. 1947; $4,000-6,000.

Left: Willemin crystal set in metal and wood; 1923-25; $65-95. **Center** and **right:** Philmore crystal set in brown Bakelite with original box; 1935-40; $45-65.

Left: Portable Opera crystal set; by Superior Products; ca. 1925; $110-135. **Right:** All metal crystal set; ca. 1928; $125-155.

Reflect Type D-10 radio receiver with aerial; by De Forest; 1923-24; $600-800. This battery-powered radio is by one of the earliest radio manufacturers.

Ozarka radio receiver with pot-metal speaker, by Algonquin; ca. 1926; $250-325.

Interior view of a Montroset AM radio receiver, showing early tubes; ca. 1925; $125-145.

AM radio reciever; by Freed-Eisemann; ca. 1924; $160-185.

RCA Radiola receiver and speaker in mahogany case; ca. 1928; $175-235. This is one of the first radios that could be plugged into a wall outlet.

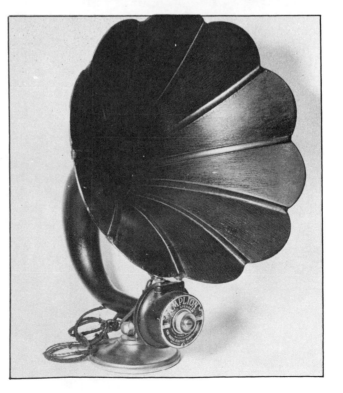

Amplon radio speaker in metal and wood; by Signal Electric; 1922-26; $160-185.

Pathe cone-type radio speaker in bronzed pot metal; ca. 1924; $125-155.

Cathedral-style table radio; by General Electric; ca. 1933; $165-235. The wooden cathedral-or Gothic-style radio was popular throughout the 1930s.

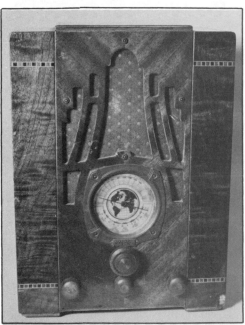

Monarch table radio in walnut veneer; ca. 1936; $150-185.

Philco Junior cathedral-style radio in light and dark wood; ca. 1932; $125-155. A typical "poor man's" radio of the early 1930s.

Art Deco table radio in oak veneer; by Sparton; 1933-35; $120-160. Nearly all wooden table radios were finished in shades of brown.

Philco Baby Grand cathedral-style radio; ca. 1931; $185-225.

Crosly Playtime radio in case of brown molded composition material; ca. 1930; $175-215. This early table radio is in the Art Nouveau mode.

Philco table radio in light and dark wood veneer; ca. 1934; $120-165.

Art Deco five-band radio; by Zenith; ca. 1935; $200-260.

Philco Art Deco table model radio in brown wood finish; ca. 1937; $110-155.

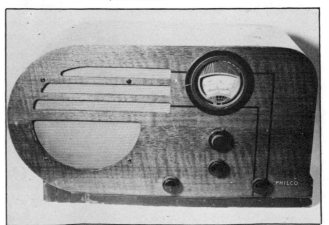

Emerson table radio in brown Bakelite; 1935-40; $135-185. Art Deco styled plastic radios are now in great demand.

RCA Victor table radio in cream-colored Bakelite; 1940-45; $200-275. Brighter colors, such as red or blue, would greatly increase the value of this piece.

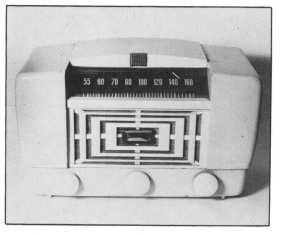

Art Deco table radio in blue glass and chrome; by Sparton; 1935-40; $325-475. A relatively uncommon and very stylish type.

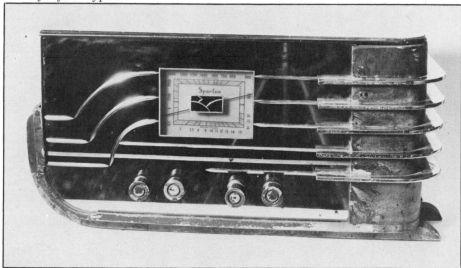

RCA Victor radio in red Catalin; ca. 1940; $350-550. Catalin was a forerunner of modern plastic.

Small table radio in black and yellow Bakelite; by Emerson; 1940-45; $250-400.

RCA Victor table radio in orange
and purple Catalin; 1940-45;
$75-100.

Unusual Art Deco chairside model
radio; 1940-45; $220-285.

Radiobar, combination
floor model radio and
bar; by Philco; ca. 1933;
$450-550. An unusual and
choice example.

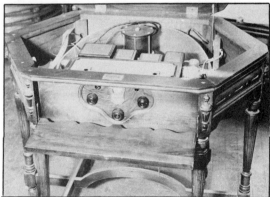

Radio built into Tudor-style
occasional table; by Atwater Kent;
ca. 1929; $275-375.

Refrigerator-top radio in gold and
cream; by Westinghouse; 1935-40;
$125-175. These radios were made in
colors to match various
Westinghouse refrigerators.

Radio built into black-rubber miniature of a General Tire; 1945-50; $150-200. Probably an advertising item.

Radio built into jewelry case; by Emerson; ca. 1946; $65-90. This is one of many novelty radios produced during the 1930s and 1940s.

The Country Belle, radio built into oak wall telephone case; 1940-50; $225-300.

Radio designed to resemble a book; by Sentinel; 1940-50; $75-125.

Radio in the form of a radio
broadcasting mike; ca. 1935;
$135-165.

Salesman's sample of console-type
floor standing radio; 1933-35;
$130-180. Though not a true radio,
the piece could accommodate a
speaker attached to a radio.

Radio broadcasting mike in the form
of a telephone speaker; 1920-25;
$110-140.

Radio related accessories. **Left:**
Radio receiver's log housed in
miniature tin box in the form of a
radio; ca. 1930; $45-65. **Center:**
Radio Tube Trick puzzle; 1935-40;
$20-30. **Right:** Lilliputian Wireless
toy; 1925-30; $25-35.

Magazines devoted to radio. **Left:**
Radio News; April, 1929; $6-9.
Center: QST, Amateur Radio; 1924;
$10-14. **Right:** Radio Guide; October,
1937; $7-10.

Black pot-metal ashtray produced for RCA World Wide Wireless; 1920-25; $30-45.

Set of metal chimes awarded by NBC to every salesman selling over $1 million in advertising; 1930-40; $200-275.

Coca-Cola advertising sign promoting Edgar Bergen and Charlie McCarthy; 1940-45; $135-185.

Papier-mache figure of Nipper, the RCA Victor advertising dog; 1940-45; $750- 950.

Enamel on tin advertising sign for Radiola Dealer; 1930-35; $175-210.

Militaria

Considering the horrors of war, it may seem surprising that there is any interest in the objects associated with it, but militaria has been collected for centuries. Moreover, the abundance of material left over from the First and Second World Wars has led to a greatly increased number of collectors.

Collectible military objects range from such obvious choices as guns and edged weapons to uniforms, medals, and even paper memorabilia such as recruiting posters and handwritten officer's commissions. Much of this material is American, but much is not, and most collectors are interested in foreign items. Those collectors who concentrate on the world wars seek equipment used by all the participants, with German and Japanese items being particularly favored.

Weapons are, of course, one of the most popular areas of militaria. However, they present certain problems for the collector. All cartridge-firing (as opposed to flint- or matchlock) rifles and handguns—which means essentially all post-1880 examples—are subject to state or local licensing. They are regarded as dangerous weapons, and they cannot be owned legally without being registered. As a consequence, many enthusiasts restrict their collecting to earlier or clearly inoperable types of firearms. Edged weapons, such as swords and daggers, while not usually subject to such regulations, can also pose a problem. Not only are they dangerous, but they are also salable; security for a collection of edged weapons is very important.

Though the United States was relatively late developing an efficient military rifle, weapons made by such firms as Springfield and Remington were issued in vast numbers between 1880 and 1940 and are still relatively common. Particularly desirable are the short-barreled carbines used by cavalrymen. It was, however, in the area of handguns that American manufacturers excelled, pioneering development of multiple-shot revolvers such as the Remington .44 and the single-action Colt as well as the famous Colt .45 automatic, which was adopted by the U.S. Army in 1911.

Edged weapons are also of interest to collectors. By the 1880s, the only American military men carrying swords were officers and some cavalrymen, but quite a few of their curved sabers can still be obtained. Bayonets, which have been used since the seventeenth century, are even more common. They range in length from seven to thirty inches, with the earlier, triangular examples considered most desirable. Other cutting tools include machetes of various sorts and the short knives used by rangers and other special forces.

Uniforms are another important area of militaria. The collector can concentrate on the colorful dress uniforms worn by state militia units and by the regular armed forces during the nineteenth century, or the collector can seek out the more available, if less attractive, standard issue garb of the post-1900 era. Dress uniforms were elaborately cut, brightly colored, and festooned with gold braid. They reflect an era when a uniform was often a matter of personal preference and camouflage was yet unknown. The more practical khaki or olive-drab breeches and tunic or jacket became standard issue for the U.S. Army in 1902 and, along with air force and navy uniforms from the two world wars, are readily available.

Military caps, hats, and helmets are both extremely interesting and easy to store. They are found in great variety, reflecting the many changes in military fashions over the past century. For years after the Civil War most American troops wore the kepi, a soft-sided, low-crowned cap. Some units wore the European shako, a spectacular-looking hat in the form of a tall leather cylinder surmounted by a colorful plume. Though abandoned by the regular military soon after 1900, the shako continued to be favored by state militias, particularly as parade garb. The beret, which is widely worn today, was not introduced until 1916, when it was issued for the convenience of tank crews. For many years most American soldiers wore the high-crowned, wide-brimmed hat now associated with the Boy Scouts.

Steel helmets are of no great antiquity. Body armor was abandoned shortly after the introduction of firearms, and it was not until the First World War that helmets once more appeared on the battlefield. Most helmets were roughly pot-shaped, such as the British helmet that was used by the U.S. Army until 1942. Of more interest are unusual types such as the German Stahlhelm and the crested helmet of the French soldiers. Helmets are relatively inexpensive and easy to find.

For the collector who wants something a bit smaller than helmets, there are medals. Medals can be divided into two general categories: campaign medals issued to troops who served in a certain battle or area of operations, and awards for valor, such as the American Distinguished Service Cross, first issued in 1918. Most campaign medals of the post-1900 period were issued in great quantity and are quite inexpensive. Certain awards of valor, on the other hand, are quite rare and command a high price. This has led, unfortunately, to reproductions. There are, for example, more fake Medals of Honor circulating today than there are legitimately issued medals. Since medals are so available and so widely collected, they are graded as to quality much like old coins. Gradations run from excellent (FDC) through very fine (VF) and fine (F) to fair and worn.

There are a great many other military collectibles. Objects available range all the way from the popular brass belt buckles and uniform buttons to such mundane things as trench shovels, canteens, and various bullets and projectiles. Militaria is a wide field, with many specialized areas.

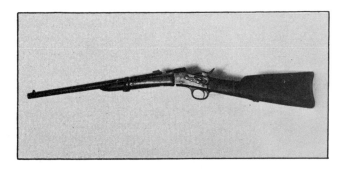

U.S. Army Remington "rolling block" system cavalry carbine, .44 caliber; 1890-95; $175-250.

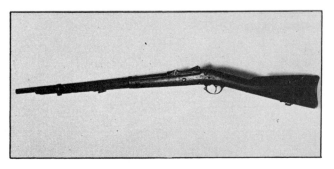

Pair of revolvers; by Remington Arms Co. **Top:** Percussion type; 1870-80; $135-185. **Bottom:** Percussion type modified to rim fire; 1880-90; $165-235.

U.S. Army model 1873 Springfield training rifle; dated 1881; $75-125.

U.S. Army Remington percussion-type revolver, .44 caliber; 1865-80; $200-260.

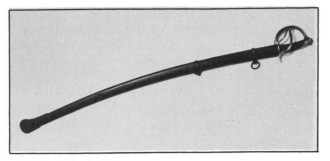

U.S. Army model 1860 cavalry saber,
brass and steel; 1880-90; $135-185.

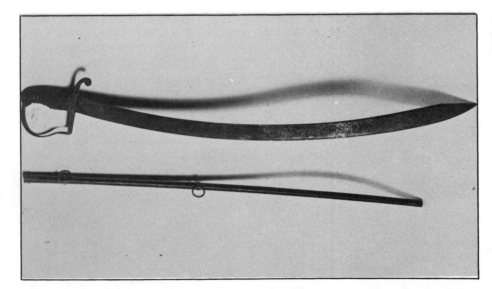

U.S. Army cavalry saber, iron and
steel; by W. Rose Co.; Philadelphia,
Pa.; 1870-80; $270-350.

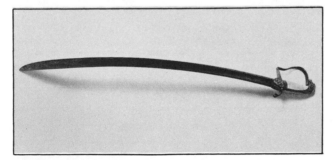

American officer's dress sword, ivory,
iron, and steel; 1910-20; $185-265.

Japanese officer's samurai sword,
iron, steel, and brass; 1935-45;
$245-370.

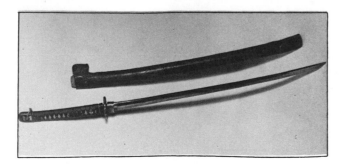

Japanese officer's samurai sword,
iron and steel; 1935-45; $195-285.
Swords such as this were popular
G.I. souvenirs.

U.S. Army bayonets, iron and steel;
by Remington Arms Co.; 1915-20;
$25-40 each.

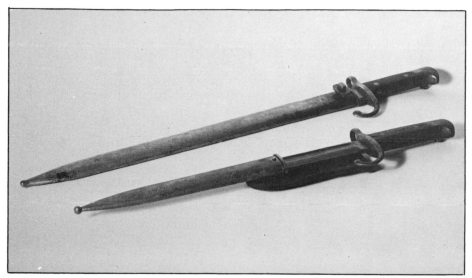

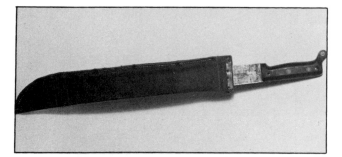

U.S. Army machete, steel and horn;
by Ontario Knife Co.; dated 1943;
$20-30.

Complete dress or parade uniform,
Seventh Regiment, New York
National Guard; 1870-80; $400-500.

American hospital corpsman's knife,
steel and wood; 1905-10; $100-150.
Knives of this sort were issued for
use during the Phiippine
insurrection. A very rare piece.

Dress blue jacket, Vermont Militia;
1880-90; $115-145.

629

U.S. Army uniform jacket in khaki
wool; 1914-18; $25-40.

U.S. Army officer's jacket in khaki
wool; 1914-18; $40-60.

U.S. Air Force uniform coat and shirt
in blue wool; 1942-46; $30-40.

U.S. Army uniform jacket in khaki
wool; 1942-46; $15-25. Note that the
buttons have been replaced.

U.S. Army fatigue caps. **Left:** Kepi in blue wool; 1880-90; $125-165. **Right:** Standard undress cap, Twenty fifth Infantry; 1890-95; $65-95.

New York State Militia shako, black felt, leather, and gold braid; 1880-1910; $165-235.

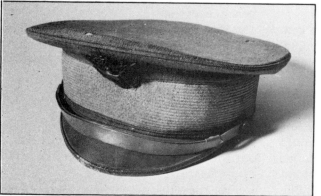

U.S. Army officer's cap in khaki; 1914-18; $40-55.

West Point Military Academy shako, brass and black leather; 1890-1900; $130-175.

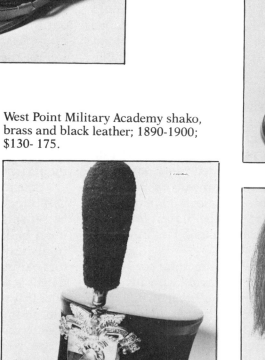

French Army kepi in black leather and red felt; 1914-18; $300-425.

Gambling Devices

Americans are probably the world's greatest gamblers, with fully 70 percent of our population gambling on something at one time or another each year. For many people it is horse racing or the World Series or a big college football game, but for others only the lure of organized gambling will suffice. A great variety of devices, from the roulette wheel and slot machine to the bingo card, has been devised to satisfy this urge, and all the items are collectible.

The greatest range of collector interest centers on the arcade (from penny arcade, of course) games that first appeared in the late nineteenth century. Many of these were not truly gambling games at all, though they were designed to take the customer's money. Devices such as weight lifters, grip testers, and automatic fortune tellers offered a service, albeit a dubious one: They could "predict" the future or help a boy to convince his girl that he was a strongman. But they couldn't double your money, and that was what the public really wanted.

It wasn't long before that desire was satisfied. Soon after 1900, Herbert S. Mills, a Chicago arcade owner, developed the Mills Dewey, a metal box with a color-coded interior wheel activated by a hand crank. The player put his nickel into one of six similarly color-coded slots, spun the handle, and if the color that came up on the wheel matched that of his slot, he collected a handful of coins. Even if he didn't win, the player got to listen to a tune played on the music box built into the machine.

The Mills creation was soon improved upon by Charles Fey of San Francisco, who invented the first true slot machine, the Liberty Bell. The Bell differed from the Dewey by having three independently revolving wheels that had to line up in a predetermined sequence in order to produce a winning combination. Though Fey's device used playing card suits rather than the now familiar plums, oranges, and lemons, it was the prototype of the modern "one-arm bandit."

Mills marketed a pirated version of the unpatented Fey slot machine in 1907, and in 1925 he added the jackpot device to further stimulate play. By that time, slot machines had swept the country and could be found in penny arcades, country stores, and even post offices. But with the coming of the Great Depression, the powers that be decided the people should put what little money they had to some better use. By the end of the 1930s, slot machines had been outlawed in nearly every state.

But the interest never died, and throughout the country there are collectors seeking the machines. Among the brands in greatest demand are Rock-Ola, Evans, Pace, and Jennings. Some of these products are floor standing, but the majority are designed to sit atop a stand or table. As a general rule, the earlier the slot machine, the more desirable it is, though some collectors seek out the most complex or most visually attractive examples.

As the pressure against gambling mounted, many manufacturers came out with machines that paid off in candy, cigarettes, or even golf balls—anything that wasn't money but would still offer an inducement to put the nickel in the slot. These later machines are collectible, and in some cases they are less .common than their money-spitting brethren.

The roulette wheel is another very collectible gambling tool. This enameled metal wheel may be set spinning manually or automatically, causing a ball to roll around suspensefully and eventually settle in one of several numbered slots. Bettors gamble on where the ball will end up. Though hardly a complex game, roulette is a very popular one. It was played in Europe and America during the mid-nineteenth century and continues to attract crowds wherever gambling is tolerated. The larger wheels were built into tables specially designed for use in casinos, and these machines are usually difficult to obtain. More readily available are the miniature versions intended for home use. Collectors are also interested in the colorful "layouts," in wood or cloth, which were used with roulette or various card and dice games. Layouts were the temporary surfaces on which the game was played, and many early examples were hand painted.

For the many gamblers who couldn't afford roulette, there was always bingo, a slightly more complicated version of the Italian parlor game lotto, which was popular in New Orleans as early as 1840. Bingo has long been legal in many states, and is a major source of funding for many church groups. Bingo collectibles include scorecards, markers, numbered wooden or plastic balls, and the large wire cages in which the balls were stirred up and from which they were drawn.

Similar in principle to roulette are the many different "side games" popular at casinos, amusement parks, and carnivals. These usually are based on a revolving wheel, with players betting on which number the wheel will stop at when spun by the operator. Like most "carny" games, money wheels are usually fixed in favor of the house.

Gamblers seeking entertainment involving more skill and less luck could pitch pennies (the collectibles here are the brightly painted boards on which the coins fell) or play one of several versions of the knockdown game. The latter involved either throwing a ball through a small hole in a screen or using it to try to knock over milk-bottle-shaped figures. The painted canvas screens are collectible, and the weighted figures, often colored to look like clowns, are also desirable.

For the gambler's more quiet hours there were the punchboards that once graced nearly every saloon and corner grocery. Punchboards, which were outlawed in the late 1940s, are very simple in concept. Tiny slips of paper imprinted with numbers or names are inserted in holes drilled in a large piece of cardboard. The player pays a nickel or so for a chance to poke out one of the slips. The name or number on the slip is then checked against a master list to see if the player wins a prize—usually a piece of merchandise, though sometimes money was offered.

Punchboards were designed to attract customers, particularly men, and many featured brightly colored versions of latter-day Gibson girls as well as exaggerated descriptions of prizes to be won. Today, unused punchboards and associated advertising materials are hard to come by and can bring high prices.

Punchboards, of course, were often rigged in favor of the seller, just as most gambling devices were rigged in favor of the casino or the professional gambler. In fact, some of the most interesting gambling accessories are the instruments used to cheat. There are machines to shave the edges of cards; "hold outs," which pop the right card into the gambler's hand at the right moment; and many different sorts of rigged dice and card dispensers. All are highly collectible, but none are easy to acquire. Some, no doubt, are still in use!

Other collectible gambling devices include playing cards (an entire field in themselves), lottery tickets, admission stubs to horse races and other sporting events, and bone or plastic dice.

HiTop 7-7-7 quarter-play slot
machine; by Mills; 1930-40;
$750-850. Although outlawed in
many states, slot machines are
among the most favored gambling
collectibles.

"Dandy Vender" gumball slot
machine; 1930-35; $450-600.
Machines like this replaced coin slot
machines as the latter were made
illegal.

Tavern gumball slot machine;
1930-40; $450-550.

Win a Beer tavern gambling game;
1940-50; $250-350. A penny in the
slot causes the dice to roll, and
participants bet on their fall.

Casino-size (thirty inches in
diameter) roulette wheel, inlaid and
veneered in mahogany; 1890-1900;
$3,200-4,300.

Traveling roulette wheel in black Bakelite with a green baize layout; 1930-40; $75-125. These sets were used in private homes as well as by professional gamblers.

Lithographed tin serving tray in the form of a roulette wheel; 1935-40; $70-90.

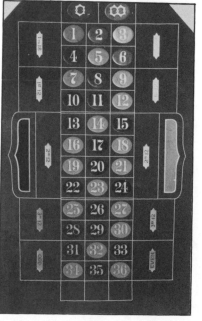

Small (fourteen inches in diameter) roulette wheel of ebonized wood and chrome; 1900-10; $300-375. For home use or use by professional gamblers.

Left: Ivory roulette chips in red, green, tan, and white; 1900-10; $7-10 each. Right: Bakelite faro chips in purple, tan, and red; 1920-25; $4-7.

Roulette layout in red and black on gray felt; 1890-1900; $450-575. Layouts were the surface on which bets were placed in roulette and various dice or card games. Because of their fragile material, few have survived.

Casino-type dice cage of nickel-plated brass; ca. 1920; $275-325.

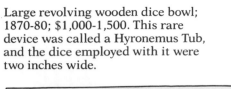

One foot-high home dice cage; 1930-40; $80-110. Though intended to prevent cheating, dice cages could be fixed, usually through magnetic devices.

Large revolving wooden dice bowl; 1870-80; $1,000-1,500. This rare device was called a Hyronemus Tub, and the dice employed with it were two inches wide.

Bubble dice shaker with dice; 1920-30; $200-285. Next to the bubble is a magnet with which the gambler could control the fall of the dice.

Left: Wooden dice drop; 1870-80; $255-285. **Center:** Glass and wood dice drop; 1920-25; $175-245. **Right** Wooden dice drop; 1880-90; $240-280.

Rear: Stamped-leather dice cup; 1900-10; $50-75. **Front:** Poker dice; 1900-05; $30-40.

Automatic draw poker dice box; patented 1890; $500-625. Pushing the rod at the end of the box makes the dice spin. The player can "hold" by pushing in one or more of the five rods in the side of the box.

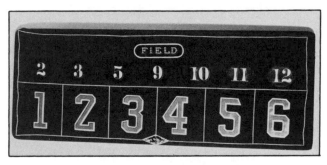

Typical dice game layout in green and orange; by Field; ca. 1900; $450-550.

Poker chip holder of laminated wood; 1930-40; $35-50.

Casino card press used to keep playing cards in good condition; 1880-90; $325-375.

Left: Deck of faro cards; 1880-90; $125-170. **Right:** Dealer's box of German silver; 1885-95; $145-195. Dealer's boxes were intended to prevent unfair deals, but many, such as this one, were rigged in the dealer's favor.

Gaming kit of wood covered in mottled paper; 1870-80; $275-350. Used in playing whist, these boxes came equipped with whist cards and wood or bone markers.

Wooden case used to keep track of cards played in a game of faro; by George Williams; New York, N.Y.; ca. 1870; $1,000-1,500. This box may be one of a kind.

Whist gaming kit in walnut and brass; 1860-70; $285-365.

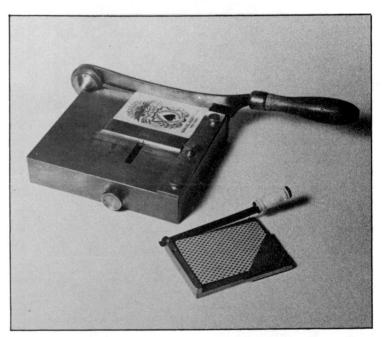

Brass card trimmers; 1850-90. **Left:** Casino size; $1,700-2,300. **Right:** Tiny ivory-handled traveling card sharp's trimmer; $1,500-1,900. These devices were used to shave certain playing cards, making them distinguishable from the others in the deck.

Shears-type card trimmer of brass and steel; 1880-90; $1,600-2,200. Card trimmers are uncommon and expensive.

Corner trimmer of brass and iron; 1870-80; $1,900-2,500. Used to reshape the corners of playing cards after they had been trimmed.

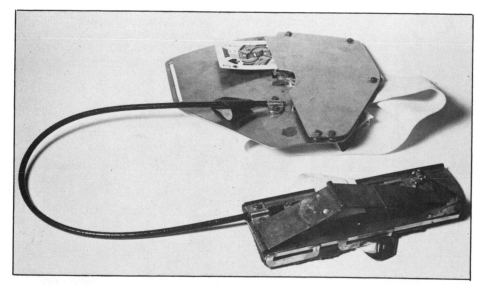

Vest-mounted gambler's "holdout"; 1900-10; $2,000-2,700. Operated by pressure on the spring device concealed behind the knee, the holdout would slip a wanted card into the gambler's hand.

Layout for high-low in red, black, and white on green baize; 1890-1900; $550-650.

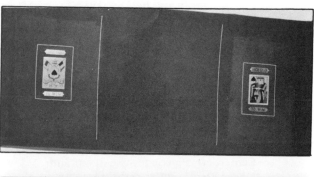

"Cold deck" machine of metal; ca. 1920; $1,800-2,300. Concealed on the card sharp's person, this handy device was used to produce a complete set of new cards in the course of a game.

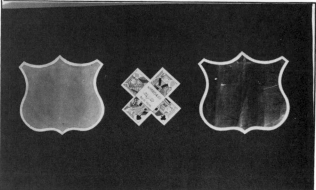

Layout in red and black on green for the game of red and black; by Harris & Co.; New York, N.Y.; $850-950.

Layout for chuck-a-luck in green and white on a black background; by H.C. Evans; Chicago, Ill.; 1880-1900; $550-675.

Layout for the game of diana in wood and baize; by William Suydam; New York, N.Y.; 1870-80; $5,500-6,500. This is one of two known existing examples.

Bingo cage of metal and wood with Bakelite posts and handle; 1930-35; $75-115.

Gambling tops; 1880-1920. **Left:** Plastic for use in high-low; $20-30. **Center left:** Plastic for use in put and take; $15-25. **Center right:** Brass for use in horse race; $35-50. **Right:** Brass dice; $40-55.

Keno scorecards; by H.C. Evans; Chicago, Ill.; 1920-30; $7-9 each. Keno was an early form of bingo.